Facets of Vedic Studies

Editor
Bidyut Lata Ray

2000

Kaveri Books
New Delhi - 110002

First Published in 2000
ISBN-81-7479-037-3

Published by : **Rakesh Goel**
Kaveri Books
4697/5-21A, Ansari Road
New Delhi-110 002 (India).
Tel : 328 8140 Fax : 011–7198902
e-mail : kaveribook@vsnl.com

Laser Typeset by : Delite Printers, Delhi-110 035.

PRINTED IN INDIA

Dedicated

to

Lord Jagannātha

Acknowledgements

At the outset, I acknowledge the inestimable help and co-operation rendered by our contributors who are actually the designers of this volume. I owe my indebtedness to all of them.

I am thankful to my friends and well-wishers who have given me constant inspirations and encouragements.

It is inadequate to express my sincere thanks to my husband and children who have cheerfully and gracefully helped me during the period of my work. My husband Dr. Sadasiva Biswal, Reader in Physics, Nayagarh College, Nayagarh, has helped both concretely with his editorial suggestions and more generally by providing me the facilities without which my efforts would have remained fruitless. From beginning to end, he has been my ground and my support.

I feel incompetent in acknowledging the role of my parents and in-laws who have constantly given me counsel and support in many ways through the years. Even their knowledge of the extent of my indebtedness to them is only approximate.

Lastly, I am highly obliged to Mr. Rakesh Goel of Kaveri Books, New Delhi, who has extended his helping hands in publishing the monograph.

Bidyut Lata Ray
Editor

Preface

The present treatise is an anthology of nineteen learned articles on various subjects of the Vedic literature, and an introduction. Each article is unique in exposing a special feature of the oldest literature. Since the Veda is not only a religious text, but also a literature of the most ancient civilization, a primordial source of human knowledge, *"Knowledge par excellence"*, people are always interested in it to discover the various branches of knowledge that underneath the sacred hymns. Hence, Vedic studies reveal that the Vedic literature comprising the Saṁhitās, the Brāhmaṇas, the Āraṇyakas, the Upaniṣadas and the Vedāṅga Sūtras, portrays well the microscopic observations of the Vedic seers on macroscopic subjects of humanism. Ostensibly, different scholars from time to time have been analysing the Vedic material with their own way of interpretations, speculations and predictions. Such hypotheses and theories put forward by the Vedic sages and studied by our scholars have opened up diverse fields of human knowledge embodied in the Vedas and the Vedic texts. The object of this project is to congregate a few of such diverse fields of Vedic studies in one Volume. In this context, different scholars have reviewed here the Vedic material from different angles. This has resulted in the exposition of the Vedic knowledge of mythology, religion, philosophy, literature, grammar, cosmology, cosmogony, space and time, sociology, astronomy, fine arts, poetry, games and sports, accent, warfare as well as system of education. Vedic science of healing by the herbs and the plants, and Vedic mathematics are the other alarming constituents of this book. Every topic here has been presented lucidly with subject-oriented informations. Our scholars have undertaken a teadeous task of exercising their capabilities in the way of extracting the very primitive speculations and conceptions made in the Vedas.

The Vedic deities are the sole belongings of the Vedas. Indeed, different branches of Vedic studies evolve with the revolution around these age-old divinities which are truly manifested in our natural phenomena. This book includes an article on the Vedic deity Aditi, the imperishable one. Due to the vastness of our ancient literature and its widest areas of human knowledge, this present volume limits the cultural contours within its pages and discourses.

In the Chapter 1 of this work, a brief introduction of the Vedic literature and its contents has been given by the editor. Chapter 2 discusses some aspects of Vedic studies. Here, Dr. G. U. Thite has analysed the varieties of interpretations of the Vedic material. According to him, two types of such interpretations prevail, one can be called fruit-oriented and the other root-oriented. The fruit-oriented Indian interpretors claim that the Veda is useful and relevant even today. The western scholars on the other hand have always been root-oriented. They consider the Vedic as well as the later Sanskrit texts to be significant for their antiquity only and not for their relevance.

In Chapter 3, Dr. Didhiti Biswas has dealt with the emergence of the *Āraṇyakas* in a great detail. The author views that the *Āraṇyakas* contain the descriptions of some rituals and also some mystic and symbolical interpretations of the rituals. The *Āraṇyakas* form the appendices to the *Brāhmaṇas*. The genesis and growth of the *Āraṇyaka* texts have been critically analysed here by the author.

Veda Vāridhi P. Rāmānujan's interest lies in Śikṣā Śāstra and Accental Semantics, which he has taken up in Chapter 4 of the book. Specifically, Semantic variations denoted by accental differences in Vedic texts are dealt with for better understanding of Vedic studies. To expose the phonetic aspects of Vedic Sanskrit is the main objective of the author here.

Chapter 5 focuses on the Vedic deity Aditi, the imperishable and a goddess of morality. Dr. Shrimanta Chattopadhyay's logical developments of identification of the divinity with Pṛthivi, Soma, Agni, Brahmaṇaspatī, Uṣas, Go (Cow) and Sky, show the speciality of the solutions of the problems raised. The discussion is cast in new dimension and hence a valuable contribution.

Vedic Mythology is the topic of Chapter 6 where the author Sri D. S. Das treats the subject starting from its root. Expressing myth elaborately, the author tries to throw adequate light on the mythical nature of the significant Vedic divinities. It is observed that mythology is closely wrapped round the Vedic gods and goddesses.

Philosophical aspect of the Vedas has been enunciated in Chapter 7 by Dr. B. L. Ray. The origin, history and tradition of Oriental Philosophy are out and out the inherent properties of the Vedic literature starting from the Saṁhitās to the Kalpas. Though the germs of Indian philosophy lie in the Vedas, they are developed the most in the Upaniṣads. Mostly, the metaphysical elements of the four Vedas, Rg., Sāma, Yaju and Atharva have been thoroughly analysed by the author.

Chapter 8 adheres to the religious aspect of the Vedas. Here the author Dr. B. K. Swain has discussed briefly the ways in which the religion is latent in the Vedas. Six fundamental principles of *dharma*, i.e., *Satya* (truth), *ṛta* (eternal order), *dikṣā* (consecration), *tapas* (austerity), *brahman* (the supreme) and Yajña (sacrifice) have been analysed by the author substantially.

Dr. P. V. Vartak has exercised a lot to draw the astronomy from the Vedic hymns. In fact, the Vedic seers had an outstanding knowledge of the celestial as well as the terrestrial phenomena, which they had reflected through their long deliberations of the *mantras*. The subject is so vast that it reserves a special berth in the train of Vedic studies and hence a separate section *'Vedāṅga-Joytiṣa'* is called into play. The naked-eye observations of the heavenly bodies are well cleaved to the Vedic hymns designed by the sages. Dr. Vartak has elaborately discussed the science of astronomy that is conceived in the Vedas and has compared the same with the modern astronomy.

Chapter 10 exhibits the subject of Games and Sports in the Veda with meticulous accounts. Here, the author Dr. P. K. Datta has attempted to discuss this unique branch of Vedic studies on the basis of dice-play, horse-race, chariot-race and gambling.

Dr. S. Biswal has taken up the topic of Space and Time in the Veda and which he has analysed in Chapter 11. Vedic cosmology and cosmogony entirely rest on the conception of Space and Time in the Vedic literature. Vedic hymns enriched with mythology, philosophy, religion, magic, materialism, cosmology, cosmogony, astronomy, et. seq. envelop truly the idea of space and time, and their characteristics. Moreover, the Universal Order 'Ṛta' is a question of space and time. Dr. Biswal has tried to account for this fundamental and alarming aspect of the creation in Vedic perspective.

In Chapter 12, Dr. Vaijayanti Shete has discussed the subject of Fine Arts in the Veda. Adherence of poetry, music and dance to the *Sūktas* displays the upliftment of the fine arts during the time of the Vedas. Author's treatment of the topic unfolds many miracle facts related to the disclosure of the elements of fine arts present in the Vedas.

The Poetic Beauty is the Ṛgveda has been expressed in Chapter 13 by Dr. K. C. Mahalik. He opines that the study of poetics is always necessary to understand the rythm of life. An, attempt has been made here by the author to expose the poetic elements of the Ṛgvedic hymns through a short analysis. Actually, such elements initially helped the entire system of hearing and remembering the Vedic mantras which, later on, came to exist in the written form.

Chapter 14 analyses Vedic Metres, which play an important role in the Vedic literature. Vedic Metres are the useful tools for preserving *mantra* - texts intact and producing the expected results of the *mantras*. When there is want of any systematic work on Vedic prosody, Dr. R. K. Panda's discourse on some salient features of Vedic metres go a long way to acquaint oneself with the *mantra* formulae designed by the Vedic seers.

Dr. Uma Chakravarty has chosen a subject of social interests. She has expressed her views on sociological grounds of the Vedic people in Chapter 15 of this book. She has exerted all her attraction on the Vedic hostile groups and individuals by analysing the movements and the settlements of the Vedic people from the period of the Vedas to the period of the Sūtras.

Prof. K. V. Sarma has presented the Atharvan roots of Āyurveda in Chapter 16. His aim here is to search for the root of Āyurveda, the science of life. How far the presently perfected Āyurvedic system are rooted in the *mantras* of the Vedic *saṁhitās*, is the problem investigated by the author, who has concluded that the tradition of Āyurveda has been developed on the basis of Atharvan medicine.

In Chapter 17, Sri V. Ramachandran Nair has extensively enumerated the Vedic system of education with a brief-sketch of Vedic people, their society and culture. Here the writer has divided the entire topic into seven parts which adhere to the course of developments of the educational system from the Vedic times to date. Every aspect of the ancient educational system like the objectives, the teacher-pupil relationships, the curriculum, the method of teaching and learning etc, have been analysed by the author with enough expositions to the subject. At the end of the article, the author has compared the modern system of education with that of Vedic period and has also marked the variants.

Warfare of the Vedic period has been discussed by Prof. N. Gangadharan in Chapter 18. The author has collected the material on the subject from the Vedic literature and has presented them to the readers in a systematic manner. He has illustrated the ethical principles of war, weapons used in war, divisions of army, strategies of war, diplomacy, etc. in a lucid and distinctive style.

Chapter 19 deals with Vedic Mathematics. Here, Dr. S. Biswal explains how the mathematical principles and the logical insights of the Vedas simplify our arithmetic and algebraic operations and hence have become the most sought attraction the world over. In course of discussions, the author has also elaborated the genesis and growth of ancient Indian mathematics and astronomy.

Lastly, Dr. Gauri Mahulikar has described the subject of medicinal herbs in the Atharvaveda with special reference to Āyurveda in Chapter 20. After thorough study of the Vedic literature, she has presented the topic with its essential elements. The discussion is quite informative and illuminative. It throws adequate light on the Vedic way of healing by the medicinal herbs and the plants. Now, the people are trying the most to understand the miracle effects of Āyurvedic system of medicine which was the only help to our ancestors to save their life from dreadful diseases.

Thus, the present work contains varieties of discussions on wide range of subjects of the Vedic literature, still many more are left to be analysed. However, most of the thrust areas, in which the general readers find their interest, are included here for deliberation.

The book ends with the brief identification of our contributors who are really the pioneers of Vedic studies.

Bidyut Lata Ray
Editor

Contents

Prolegomenon

1

Dr. Bidyut Lata Ray

The Vedas are the primordial sources of human civilization and culture. Out of the four Vedas, namely Ṛg, Sāma, Yaju and Atharva, the earliest specimen of Indian literature is the Ṛgveda, an anthology of hymns in ten books, I-X. Evidently, Vedic literature is the most ancient literature which marks the beginning of Indian literature. It is also the first full length religious and literary account of the Indo-European people. Being the earliest record of human civilization, the Vedas deal with various aspects of human life that come across or experienced by the Vedic people. It is quite encouraging to record here that copious branches of Vedic studies are now opened up by our readers, interpreters and the research scholars. Besides the history, tradition, culture and literature, we find elaborate and lucid descriptions of the 'Creation'. Vedic Cosmology and Cosmogony forward the genesis of the Universe, the earth, the water, the air and the life. The ecology and the environment depicted in the Vedas include all the natural provisions made for human existence. Vedic flora and fauna, rivers, lakes, seas, oceans, climate, mountains, forests et. sq. provide the physical pictures of the surrounding in which the Vedic people were living. The names, cities, towns and holy places have also been traced in the sacred hymns of the Vedas. Society, polity, education, science and technology in the realm of "Āyurveda" and warfare mark the significance of Vedic hymns. Above all, Matter (Pṛthvi), Energy (Agni) and Life (Savitṛ) are conceptually extolled, in the Vedic Sūktas. Ostensibly, we have a comprehensive and coherent account of the Vedic people—their life, ethos, thoughts and beliefs.

If the Vedas mark the very beginning of human knowledge and Civilization adhering to all such branches of studies like history, archaeology, cultural anthropology, sociology, comparative religion and mythology, linguistics and philosophy, cosmology, ecology, environment, science of healing and the theory of the creation, then what the Veda really is ?

The term 'Veda' means 'Knowledge par excellence', that is sacred and all pervading. The Veda represents the religion that the Āryans brought with them into India and developed during ancient times on Indian soil. In fact, the term refers to a series of texts of various contents and forms which are believed to be derived from a 'hearing' (śruti) that is a revelation. Common beliefs go in favour of the term that the Vedic narrations have been emanated from Brahman. The human authors of the Vedas were the Rishis or inspired sages who could be able to receive the Vedic mantras by a direct 'Vision'.

The Vedic texts include the Saṁhitās or 'Collections' which generally present hymns, prayers and ritual formulae. Other Vedic texts are the Brāhmaṇas, the Āranyakas (forest texts), the Upanisads, the Vedāṅgas, (ie., the auxilliary limbs of the Veda) and the Kalpasūtras. The subsidiary works of exegesis, explanation are not the part of the Veda in the narrow sense. In this context, they are no longer Śruti but *Smriti* (memory). In fact, the most ancient form of Brahmanism is the Vedism established by the four Vedas and the Vedic texts.

As there are four Vedas, there exist four Saṁhitās, viz., ṚK, Yajuḥ , Sāma and Atharva. ṚK Saṁhitā or Ṛgveda is the collection of the verses (ṛks) recited in the course of the sacrifices. The sacrificial formulae (Yajus), collected, with or without commentary form the Yajuḥ Saṁhitā or Yajurveda. Sāma Saṁhitā contains the melodies (saman). Finally, the magical formulae (atharvan) form the Atharva Saṁhitā or Atharvaveda. The Atharva was compiled in a later date and hence *trayī vidyā* or triple science is commonly referred to mean three Saṁhitās, namely, ṚK, Yajus and Saman. These texts formed the foundation of Vedism and were composed and preserved orally.

They were only preserved in human memory and passed on exactly from generation to generation with meticulous care. Vedic people were trained like that in this discipline in order to transmit the *mantras* out and out without any lapses. According to Al Biruni (11th C. A. D.), the Veda was put in written form recently in Kashmir by Vasukra.[1] Being the most ancient records of human civilization, the Vedas are still carried in the memory of human beings until only the other day and this marks how great a value these manuscripts have.

The original extent of the Vedas is vast. Only a small fraction of the extensive vedic literature existed in the pre-Vyāsa period is now available to us. Actually, there were a number of Vedas (exceeding the present ones) present during the pre-Vyāsa period. This is understood from the dictum *anantā vai Vedāḥ,* meaning the Vedas are endless. Credit goes to Vyāsa in editing the then available Vedas into Ṛg, Yajur and Sāma sections in order to help the *hotṛ, adhvaryu* and *Udgātṛ* priests in sacrifices. The Atharvaveda was a later addition. It did not enjoy the sanctity of the other Vedas even though the Brahmā of the sacrifices was considered to be conversant with this Veda. This might have been the fact that the contents of it are not in harmony with the objectives of the other Vedas. Thereafter, restrictions were imposed on the further growth of the Vedas and hence the Vedas codified by Vyāsa gained currency. These are now available to us in the form of Ṛg, Yajur and Sāma Vedas. This three-fold divisions of the Vedas is supported by the *Gāyatrī mantra* attributed to Viśvāmitra in the 3rd *maṇḍala* of the Ṛgveda. It is mentioned that *Gāyati anena trayen iti gāyatrī.*

The Ṛgveda

The Ṛgveda or "Veda of Verses" is the most ancient and most important text of Vedism. The Ṛgveda is divided into 10 *maṅḍalas,* 1028 *sūktas* (hymns) and 10552 *ṛks* (verses). As per another system of classification, the Ṛgveda is divided into eight parts (*aṣṭakas*) and each *aṣṭaka* with eight *adhyāyas* (Chapters) and these in turn into groups of five verses (*Varga*). The *maṇḍalas* are also divided in a mechanical way into "recitations" (*anuvaka*). Following Bergaigne and Oldenberg, Louis Renou points out that the hymns and the verses are arranged in the Ṛgveda according to some precise rule[2]. In Ṛgveda, we find the historical hymns, the cosmogonic hymns, and hymns in dialogue form and poetic form. The Ṛgvedic hymn is not only a song in praise of a divinity. It is a composition cast in a certain style to please the audience. They lay emphasis on benevolence. These songs of praise are sacred or profane symbolising the principal sources of Indian literary activity.

The Ṛgvedic hymns, though commonly mythological, deal with the subjects like nature, geology, geography, history, society and religions. Focussing the nature and the natural phenomena is the role of majority of the *Sūktas*. The dynastic history of the solar and lunar kings is contained in a few. This enables us to trace the history of the kings of the Ṛgveda. Many sociological aspects like the game of dice, the song of the frogs, the marriage ceremony, conversation between departed lovers, importance of farming, protection of cows and other animals, holy act of *dāna* and healthy living are the subjects of the Ṛgveda. Lastly, religious discourse is the concern of the most of the Ṛgvedic *Sūktas.*

The Yajurveda

The Yajurveda is available in its two divisions, namely the Kṛṣṇa Yajurveda and the Śukla Yajurveda. The Kṛṣṇa Yajurveda is formed of four Saṁhitās while the Śukla Yajurveda has only one Saṁhitā. The Kṛṣṇa Yajurveda is noted to have both prose and poetry in its *mantras* where the Śukla Yajurveda is purely poetry. As the Yajurveda is primarily used in sacrifices, sāyaṇa preferred this text first to comment on and then on the Ṛgveda. The *hotṛ* (Ṛgveda) priest recited Ṛgveda verses and the *Udgātṛ* sang Sāmaveda songs, the Yajurveda priest actually performed the sacrifice and chanted some formulae during performance of his ritual.

The Yajurveda depicts the sacrifices like the Aśvamedha (horse sacrifice), Agnicayana (pulling of the fire altar) and the soma sacrifice. The more ancient parts of the yajus describe the full and new moon. The Yajurveda is the ritual Veda *par excellence,* the book of prayers, except that the verses taken from the Ṛgveda remain the preserve of the hotri. The collective sacrifices recorded in the Yajurveda with the ritual minute have impressed the Indian society in some way or other for over two millennia.

Besides the sacrifices, the Yajurveda also treats of some rites relating to productive occupations like sowing, and sometimes even of domestic rites and activities. Cooking is described in Kāṇḍa IV.[3] Murthy[4] points out that the Yajurveda bears some interesting features in Iṣṭividhāna and citi nirupaṇa for expounding early mathematics and geometry. Rudra Camaka Praśna included in the fifth hymn of Vasordhārā is significant from the geological point of view as it supplies metallurgical informations. Minute ritual details play a very important role in the entire Yajurveda. This Veda witnesses the final emergence of the four castes with strictly defined and mutually exclusive rights and obligations. Folk-religion[5] elements are also traced. Popular games and pastimes are also mentioned with mystic symbolisms and they are employed in sacrifices. Some natural phenomena are explained through myths. Social customs, too, are given mythic explanations.

The Sāmaveda

The Sāmaveda exists in three recensions, viz., Kauthuma, Rāṇāyaṇiya and Jaiminīya. The second one is similar to the former in respect of the Saṁhitā, and the last one contains larger collections of melodies than the Kauthuma. In comparison to Kauthuma, the Verses of Jaiminīya are less numerous, differently arranged and subject to some sound changes. Existing six texts of the Sāmaveda are as under :

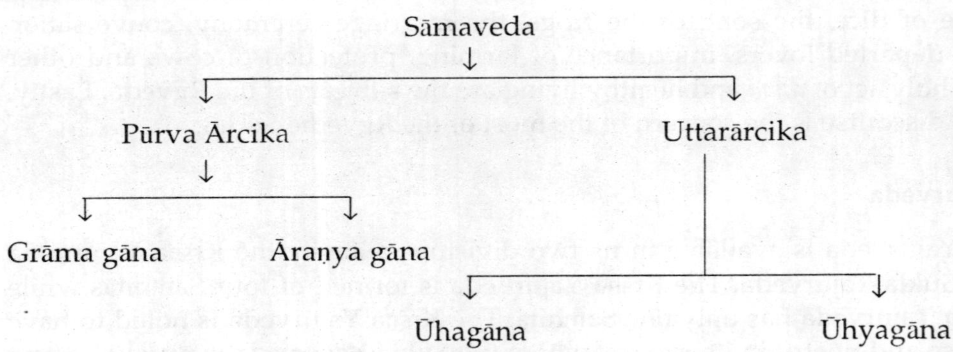

Pūrva Ārcika contains Āgneya Kāṇḍa, Indra Kāṇḍa, Pāvamāna Kāṇḍa and Āraṇya Kāṇḍa. The Uttarārcika is composed of the remaining hymns. Out of total 1875 *mantras* of the Sāmaveda, 1235 *mantras* constitute Ārcika or prayers and 640 *mantras* belong to *gāna* or songs group, some of which are based on musical notes. Most of the verses of the Sāmaveda are borrowed from the Ṛgveda, mostly from books VIII and IX, and none from the later books. Some hymns drawn directly from the Ṛgveda read different in the Sāmaveda.

The Sāmaveda is very closely connected with the Soma sacrifice. Of the three significant sacrifices—Paśu, Soma and Iṣṭi, only Soma and Iṣṭi had Sāmanas chanted. The Sāmanas were of two kinds : one group addressed to Paramāna Soma while the second group addressed to other gods. Atmospheric gods and most solar gods are found absent. Generally the hymns of the Sāmaveda are devoted in addressing the major Ṛgvedic deities with Pavamāna Soma as the core. In the Sāmaveda, we find that the prayers are the usual ones for food, prosperity and security. Soma plant has been identified with the moon. It shows the astronomical knowledge of Indian seers at that time.

The conceptions of the Sāmaveda on evolution on the earth are unique as well as based on convictions. This Veda throws light on the supreme creator and his manifestations. All that exists now and which may appear in the future are his manifestations.[6] Like the Yajurveda, this Veda holds the view that activity in the material world is only a transfer of ideas to matter. No activity or achievement is possible on earth or in heaven without prior thought or planning. Intelligence in activity creates only ideas and these-formed the creator's objective states. The Creator is the Ultimate. He is the puruṣa who bestows births of creatures first, unites with them, then the creation is manifested. Truly, the cosmos is his manifestations, rejoicing (or bestowing on us) animate and inanimate objects.[7] The cosmos is born of Activity who is united to it; the puruṣa controls it from beyond.[8]

Mentions of Agni (the fire)[9], Ṛta (the seasons)[10], Pṛthivī (the earth)[11] and Aruṇa (the sun)[12] et seq. help us to draw a few points on the geological and geographical aspects of the Veda. The terms like Samudra (the ocean)[13], Bhuvana (the earth)[14] and Bhārata (India)[15] are traced in this Veda to account for the geographical components of this material world.

Prayers, according to the Sāmaveda, are the sole means to be resorted to by us. Through these prayers, this veda extols the various universal deities for their varied activities in creating and maintaining all the living-beings to establish equilibrium in nature. All the creatures are equally treated by the supreme puruṣa, the creator. The devotees pray for their safety, security and unimpaired life.

The Atharvaveda

The Atharvaveda is a later addition to the vedic literature but not later compositions. It consists of 20 books or *Kāṇḍas* having 731 hymns and 5987 Verses. The modern subdivisions of the books are called *Prapāṭhaka* (lectures), *anuvāka* (recitations) and *daśati* (decades). The first 18 books constitute the Atharvaveda proper. These can be divided into 3 groups according to the number of verses they contain in a hymn. The rest two books are the supplements, the last one being a more recent supplement containing almost the extracts from the 8th *Maṇḍala* of the Ṛgveda. Nearly 1200 *mantras* of 20th *Kāṇḍa* (book) have been drawn directly from the Ṛgveda.

The Atharvaveda has two recensions, one of the Śaunaka and the other of the Paippalāda (the Kashmirian recension). Whitney had discovered the Śaunaka long before D. M. Bhattacharya found the manuscripts of the Paippalāda in Orissa.

In the old records, we find nine śakhās or recensions of the Atharvaveda. These are Śaunaka, Tauda, Mauda, Paippalāda, Jajala, Jalada, Caraṇavaidya, Brahmavada and Vedādarśa. However, of these, only two, Paippalāda and Śaunakīya exist with their respective texts. A large number of variations are marked when Paippalāda and Śaunakīya texts are compared. Such variants are of the nature of Kāṇva or Mādhyandina texts[16]. However, the Śaunakīya-Saṁhitā of Atharvaveda is a pure and fine editorial work. It has no parallel and hence it is commonly accepted one.

With flexibility, the books can be grouped subjectwise as follows :

(i) Charms for long life (*āyuṣyānic*).
(ii) prayers to cure diseases and demonic possession (*bhaiṣajyāni*),
(iii) Curses upon demons, sorcerers, enemies (*abhicārikānic* and *kṛtyāpratiharaṇāni*),
(iv) Charms of love (*strīkarmāṇi*),
(v) Charms to secure harmony, influence, in the assembly et seq. (*sanmanasyāni*),
(vi) prayers relating the royalty (*rājakarmāṇi*),
(vii) prayers relating to Brāhmanical power,
(viii) prayers to secure prosperity and freedom from danger (*pauṣṭikāni*),
(ix) prayers in expiation of sin and defilement (*prāyaścittānid*),
(x) Cosmogonic and theosophic hymns,
(xi) ritualistic and general hymns,
(xii) prayers devoted to marriage and funeral rites etc.,
(xiii) hymns dealing with herbs and medicinal science, and
(xiv) the Kuntāpa hymns.

The Atharvaveda is noted to be the foundation of the Indian medical science. Besides, it is the source of the science of Indian archery (Dhanurveda). The other notable aspects of this Veda are agriculture, environment (nature), cosmogony, geology, geography, sociology, castism, kingship, constitution, war and many domestic concerns. The Atharvaveda eulogises the glory of the mother Earth. There are also hymns on the aspects of time and on stars, though the stars were known by the time of the Ṛgveda as evident from the *Vedāṅga Jyotiṣa* of Lagadha. The Atharvaveda delineates the life of the common man in the ancient Indian village community—the village farmer, craftsman and others who constituted the agriculturist society of the time. It is, thus, the Veda of masses.

Tantra is the other unique and significant aspect of the Atharvaveda. In the primitive age, the non-Āryāns had their tantric culture. Following the non-Āryāns the Āryāns practised this *tantra Vidyā*. Since the applications and the consequences of *tantra vidyā* are well discussed in the Atharvaveda, it is also named as the text of *Yantra-tantra Vidyā.* There are some hymns here pertaining to magic, mystic and poetically gripping, which are exclusively and characteristically of the Atharvaveda.[17]

The Brāhmaṇas

The very name 'Brāhmaṇas' suggests that they are the 'interpretation of the Brahman' and at the same time 'Compilation of accepted interpretations' by the Brahmins. The Brāhmaṇas deal with the sacred science and interpret the Brahman. These texts are primarily concerned with the rites for which they were meant. All the sacrificial needs, procedures and the results are displayed by them. Every Veda has its own Brāhmaṇa text. The Brāhmaṇas of the Ṛgveda are meant for use of the *hotri,* those of the Yajurveda for use of the *adhvaryu,* those of the Sāmaveda for the *Udgātri* and imitating the tradition, a Brāhmaṇa has been attached to the Atharvaveda. But it is observed that only the Brāhmaṇas of the Yajurveda intimately follow the ritual being based upon the saṁhitās while the Brāhmaṇas of the other three Vedas deviate from the sequence of their respective Saṁhitās. Therefore, Renou opines that the Brāhmaṇas were initially generated as the appendices to the liturgical parts of the Saṁhitās, but later these were treated as independent texts.[18]

The Brāhmaṇas are of different sizes. One or more Brāhmaṇas have been attached to each Saṁhitā. Most of them have been subjected to addition but not recomposition. Due to the availability of a great number of Brāhmaṇas, we have a good number of commentaries on them, among which a number are ascribed to Sāyaṇācārya. Such theological explanations are found in a more systematic form in the specific texts known as 'Mimāṁsā, the true inheritor of the thought of the Brāhmaṇas.

Two principal classes of subjects noticed in the Brāhmaṇas are *Vidhi* (rules) and *Arthavāda* (the explicatory section). Myths and Legends outlined in the Vedas are found here in the Brāhmaṇas in order to focuss on the subject of Religion and Mythology of these texts. The Myths form the forte of this literature. The language in which the Brāhmaṇas depict the myths is poetic. Local or personal legends, anecdotes about sages, practices, melodies, more or less distantly reflecting historical realities have formed the folklore in toto. The cultural history about the creation is quite interesting. The origin of the caste system is found in a crude form in the Ṛgveda Saṁhitās, but it attained maturity in the Brāhmaṇic age. There is mention of women, their duty in the sacrifice as well as in the house-hold management.

The whole of the Brāhmaṇa texts has been advanced with the growth of the myths. There are six types of myths, viz., (i) theological, (ii) liturgical, (iii) social and ethical, (iv) cosmological and etiological, (v) natural and (vi) metaphysical.

In the opinion of J. Verenne,[19] the myths form a vital layer of the Vedic community's religious consciousness, but they are reflected for the first and last time in the Brāhmaṇas. Besides these, the other subjects of interest depicted in the Brāhmaṇas are the magic, the Vāc, the history, the economy, the family, the women, the social customs, the cosmogony and etiology, the ethics and the society at large. Both veiled and overt types of historical informations are gleaned from the Brāhmaṇa texts. Cosmogonic legends attached to the Prajapati cycle are traced in the Brāhmaṇas.

The elements of mystical phonetics, grammar and etymology etc. that contained in the Brāhmaṇa literature are of great importance, though for a long period they are inadequately appreciated. They are the real sources of Indian thought.

The Āraṇyakas

Karmakāṇḍa and *Jñānakāṇḍa* are the two sections of the Vedic literature in a broad sense. The first section consists of the Saṁhitās and the Brāhmaṇas while the second one bears the Āraṇyakas and the Upaniṣads. The first one is the section of work and the second one is the section of knowledge. The Āraṇyakas are the 'forest texts' which are kept away from the public and read in isolation in the forest. This is because they contain at least abstruse works having magical power.[20] Most of these texts are composite works and contain mantra, Brāhmaṇa and even elements of sūtra.

Three main and distinct Āraṇyakas, namely, Aitareya, Kauṣitakī and Taittirīya are of significance, though chants of some kinds or other adhering to the nature of the Āraṇyaka have been distinguished.

We have four distinct Saṁhitās with their individual characteristics, while the Brāhmaṇas, the Āraṇyakas and the Upaniṣads overlap with one another. Again, the Āraṇyakas and the Upaniṣads constitute a literature of transition. The Āraṇyakas move towards the forest, search for knowledge and asceticism where the Upaniṣads are based on clear doctrines. Every Saṁhitā does not have Āraṇyakas and Upaniṣads of its own, though each Saṁhitā has one or more separate Brāhmaṇas. There exist a few Brāhmaṇas which end in Āraṇyakas.

The Aitareya Āraṇyaka contains the *Mahāvrata* prayers and the ritual verses (*mahānāmni*) composed in accordance with a grammatical symbolism. Its first and last *adhyāyas* (chapters) only depict the *Mahāvrata* in a style purely Brāhmaṇical in nature. The Mahāvrata rite reinterpreted in the Aitareya and Śāṅkhāyana serves as a bridge between ritual and knowledge epochs of the Vedic religion.

There is a gradual advancement towards abstraction from the Brāhmaṇas through the Āraṇyakas to the Upaniṣads. The physical, cosmic, academic, familial and philosophical materials are traced in the Āraṇyakas in addition to the ritual elements. The concept of time given in the Taittirīya Āraṇyaka is somewhat different from that we have. According to it, the time is indivisible and eternal. The process of transition from the sacrificial to the non-sacrificial approach is the marked significance of the Āraṇyakas. The actual areas of knowledge spread over the Āraṇyaka texts are astronomy, physics, metallurgy, chemistry, geology, anatomy, physiology, psychology, philosophy, history, geography, a more systematized theology and liturgy, language, music and some other arts. During the time of the Āraṇyakas, knowledge became an essential quality for the vedic people. This hankering for knowledge expanded to cosmogonic and etiological search.

The Brāhmaṇas interpret the rituals in terms of a holistic conception of ritual symbolism whereas the Āraṇyakas transmit the messages for deep penetration of one's vision to the ritual performance and hence to retreat it in non-ritual cosmic or metaphysical symbolism.

The Upaniṣads

The Upaniṣads are, in the old sense of the word, the Vedānta, the 'end of the Veda'. They represent the way of knowledge, the *jñānamārga* while the other vedic texts deal with the way of action, the *Karmamārga*. They are the works of scientific rather than religious purport. By way of different lessons, frequently cast in the form of dialogues or in the form of fables, aphorisms and puzzles, the Upaniṣads keep an eye to introduce the learner the final objectives of the sacred teaching and hence to establish a kind of metaritualism. Due to preservation of the magical aspect in the dialogues, the Upaniṣads might be defined as dialectic on a magical basis.[21]

Both the vedic and non-vedic Upaniṣads exist. But, the former ones are of our concern here. There are 14 Vedic Upaniṣads, namely, the Bṛhadāraṇyaka, the Chāndogya, the Aitareya, the Kauṣitaki, the Kena, the Taittirīya, the Īśa or Īśavāsya, the Kaṭha or Kaṭhaka, the Śvetāśvatara, the Mahānārāyaṇīya, the Muṇḍaka, the Praśna, the Māṇḍūkya and the Maitri or Maitrāyaṇīya.

Belvalkar adds to this list the Vaṣkalamantra, a sort of hymn to Indra inspired by the Ṛgveda. Schröder[22] describes this as the precursor of all the known Upaniṣadic literature. This short text, according to one school, is called the Chāgaleya, which narrates the relations of the soul and the body by the parable of the chariot. It is named as the Arṣeya containing different opinions of the four theologians as regards to the definitions of the *brahman*. As this short treatise consists of an allegory concerned with ritual, it is also called the Śaunaka.[23]

On a broadline, the Upaniṣads can be divided into two categories, viz., prose Upaniṣads and Metrical Upaniṣads. The earliest Upaniṣads, are in prose, with some sententious verses and occasional lyrical passages. Such prose-form

Upaniṣads are the Bṛhadāraṇyaka, the Chāndogya, the Aitareya, the Kauṣitaki, the Kena, the Taittiriya and the Iśavāṣya. The second group consists of the Katha, the Śvetāśvaṭara, the Mahānārāyaṇīya, the Muṇḍaka, the praśna, the Māṇḍukya and the Maitrāyaṇīya. These metrical-form Upaniṣads are almost entirely in verse form and their connections with the Veda are not so intense.

The Bṛhadāraṇyaka Upaniṣad deals with cosmology, eschatology, ethics and other miscellaneous content adhering to metaphysical discourses. The Chāndogya Upaniṣad covers discourses on Sāman mysticism. It contains doctrines attributed to cosmology and metaphysics. The two Upaniṣads, Bṛhadāraṇyaka and Chāndogya have many passages in common like the theory of sleep, that of the five fires and of the two ways, the dispute about precedence among the sense-organs, the elixir of power, et. seq.

The Aitareya Upaniṣad depicts the creation of the world by the *ātman*, the triple birth of the *ātman*, and its pantheistic essence. Various elements of the creation are mentioned here for the first time. The Kauṣitaki Upaniṣad mentions contemporary social customs, interprets dreams and treats of reincarnation and other original eschatological doctrines and also the theory of breath and that of the *ātman*. The Kena Upaniṣad deals with cosmology as well as *ātman*. Here, the *ātman* is conceived as the indwelling spirit that impels the sense perceptions. The Taittirīya Upanisad adheres to semimystic relationships in cosmic, astronomical, intellectual, physical and spiritual elements. This Upaniṣad is splitted into the "Vine of Instructions", precepts and prayers for the use of the pupil. The last chapter of it equates Brahman with various elements like food, the vital air, mind, knowledge and bliss, but rests solely on food. The Īśavāṣya Upaniṣad throws light on the four strata of life, teaches the inefficacy of works. It says—all that matters is to know the *ātman*, which is present in all essences and overcomes all differences.

The metrical Upaniṣads include the Kaṭha, the Śvetāśvatara, the Muṇḍaka, the Mahānārāyaṇa, the praśna. the Māṇḍūkya and the Maitrāyaṇīya texts which are in the verse-form. The Kaṭha Upaniṣad deals with the episode of Yama-Nachiketa, Yama (the god of death) teaching Nachiketa about the destiny of a person after life. The identity of *atman-brahman*, and a series of attempts of state the nature of these entities have been depicted here in the Kaṭha Upaniṣad. The story of Nachiketa has been derived from a legend in the Taittirīya-Brāhmaṇa and seems to refer to an initiation into the mysteries.

The Śvetāśvatara Upaniṣad deals with the characteristics of Rudra-Śiva. Barth[24] opines that the Śvetāśvatara is a Śaiva Bhagavadgitā. According to Haur[25], the work has monotheistic approach in which the ideas of Sāṁkhya-yoga have been mingled. The basic Śāṁkhya elements of *puruṣa, prakṛti*, the three *guṇas* are all present here. Creation is described as an evolution. Sāṁkhya approach to psychology and metaphysics are clearly observed here in this Upaniṣad.

The Muṇḍaka Upaniṣad is attached to the Atharvaveda. It extols the 'high Knowledge' of the *Brahman*, from which the world emanates. Here, the author partially distinguishes *Brahman* from the individual *Ātman*. This work contains both the passages and the verses, which have closer relationships with ritual practices. Still, it adheres to mysticism to some extent. Like the Kena, Muṇḍaka betrays influence of Buddhism and also quite open Śaivite learnings.

The Mahānārāyaṇīya or Bṛhannārāyaṇīya Upaniṣad of the Kṛṣṇa Yajurveda describes prajāpati as the creative principle and analyses his creation. It is based on the pantheon of a later period. It adheres to late epic-purāṇic theophanies which include Śiva, Sūrya, Viṣṇu and Kārttikeya alongwith the goddess Durgā under various names. Demons, gnomes and goblins are freely mentioned in this Upaniṣad. Doxologies addressed to various gods bear close resemblance to epic-purāṇic content, as also rituals belonging to a later period. The myths and legends of Mahānārāyaṇīya Upaniṣad are distinctly sectarian. It holds the Great Nārāyaṇa as the divinised form of the cosmic *atman* and hence the name justified.

The Praśna Upaniṣad has a relationship with the Atharvaveda. Its text is composed half in verse and half in prose form. The replies given by the sage Pippalāda to his six pupils shape the body of its content. These questions are (a) whence comes life? (b) how many deities uphold the creature? (c) from where the vital breath derives?, (d) What is the nature of dreams? (e) What is the meaning of the sacred syllable *oṁ*?, and (f) what are the sixteen parts which constitute man? The answers explain the philosophical nature of the creation and presistence of life on earth.

The Māṇḍūkya Upaniṣad belonging to the Atharvaveda establishes the fundamental doctrine of the later Vedānta philosophy. The *Brahman* under the symbol of the syllable *om* has been described here in short sentences, since the entire work has been cast in prose-form. According to Weber, this Upaniṣad is directly attached to the Atharvaveda and is sectarian in nature. This is evident from the observation that those Upaniṣads which are directly attached to the Atharvaveda are to some extent sectarian in their contents in which respect they reach down to the time of the purāṇas.[26]

The Maitrāyaṇīya Upaniṣad deals with material of miscellaneous nature in its sixth chapter which throws much light on the social and religious life of the period. Sāṁkhya and yoga have been portrayed prominently alongwith the triad of Brahman, Viṣṇu and Śiva, and their three *guṇas* and three different cosmic functions. It has discourses on the concept of the *bhūtātman*, the phenomenal self that works under cosmic illusion, māyā, and prescribes a path for its astronomical speculations, sun worship, social morality, late practices like *haṭha-yoga* and the seven mystical sounds which is heard by a meditating man during his *yoga* practices, etc. These facts are no doubt non-Upaniṣadic in nature with an admixture of elements of folk religion rising to the surface and gaining admittance in the official canon.[27]

This Upaniṣad is nothing but a series of lessons imparted by the sage Śakayanya to the prince Bṛhadratha on the origin of life and of consciousness. Buddhist influences have been discerned, perhaps wrongly, in it.[28] The

Maitrāyaṇīya Upaniṣad contains innumerable interpolations which greatly mar the consistency of the text.[29] According to Tsuji, this Upaniṣad exceptionally contains spurious doctrines most probably alluded to Buddhism.[30]

The Kalpasūtras

Vedāṅga Kalpa is divided into four sections, namely, Śrauta (sacrificial), Gṛhya (domestic), Dharma (social) and the minor Śulva (Science of measurement). Obviously, there exist two major divisions of the Vedāṅgas : (a) religious which includes Śrauta, Gṛhya and Dharma; and (b) secular, constituting of Śulva, Śikṣā, Chandas, Vyākaraṇa, Jyotiṣa and Nirukta. Besides these, there are also ancillary texts—Prāyaścitta (expiatory), Pariśiṣṭa (complementary), Śrāddha et seq. Among different types of Sūtras composed during the Sūtra period, the Kalpasūtras are probably the most significant ones in providing the cultural history of India. These texts mainly deal with a succint and systematic account of all the Vedic sacrifices and customs of their period.

In the beginning of the Āryan Culture, the religious, domestic and social practices had no separate identity in the literature. They were jumbled of each other. With the advance of time, religion dominated the minds of the people and consequently, they tried to preserve and systematize the religious practices of the Āryan Community. This resulted in the formation of Śrauta Sūtras which bear the stamp of the Āryan character of the public life of the Āryan people. As time passed on, the Āryan and non-Āryan culture mingled together in India owing to the interactions between the people of the two communities. Thus, there was a need to distinguish the culture and traditions of the two communities. This led to the foundation of Gṛhya Sūtras which codified the rituals characteristic of the Āryan family. A third group of rules and customs emerged due to interaction between family and society. This gave rise to the Dharma Sūtras where such rules and customs have been rightly codified. The origin and development of these Sūtras gave birth to the Dharma Śāstras or the Smṛti literature.

The Śulva Sūtras form a part of the Kalpasūtras. These texts contain rules for the measurement and construction of fire-altars and sacrificial sheds, etc. It is marked that the Śulva Sūtras are closely connected with the Śrauta Sūtras as the rules of the Śulva Sūtras mostly adhere to great sacrifices contained in the Śrauta Sūtras.

Thus, the Kalpasūtras mainly deal with the Kalpa, i.e., ritual. They are devoted to Vedic sacrifices household ceremonies and customary law. The Knowledge of the Vedic Saṁhitās and the Brāhmaṇas of the respective schools are found reflected in the Kalpasūtras. Moreover, a number of sacrifices described in the Kalpasūtras are derived from the Brāhmaṇas. The principal objective of the Brāhmaṇas is to illustrate the significance of the various acts in Vedic sacrifices and to formulate ritualistic doctrines, while the Kalpasūtras are chiefly aimed at providing us a succint and systematic account of all the Vedic sacrifices and customs prevalent in the period of their formation. The texts of Kalpasūtras simply record the rituals and traditions current in their respective schools and do not give any explanation and rationale.[31]

To sum up, the Vedas contain all branches of human knowledge and understanding. Though the most ancient in style, language, nature and representation, they thrust upon the most developed strata of human mind and perceptions. The speculations are scientific and eternal. As everything was blended in one, there was no education except the Veda at that time. Facts relating to the earth and the earth bodies, both living and non-living, are the significant aspects of the most of the Ṛgvedic and some of the other vedic literature. Since, there was no classification of knowledge into different disciplines, as is done today, all such informations were jumbled up and scattered throughout the Vedas in an incoherent fashion.

References

1. Renou, L., *Vedic India*, Indological Book House, Delhi, 1971, p. 2.
2. *Ibid.*
3. *Taittirīya Saṁhitā*, 6.9.1-4.
4. Murthy, S. R. N., *Vedic View of the Earth*, D. K. Printworld (P) Ltd., New Delhi, 1997, p. 35.
5. *Tai Hirīya Saṁhitā*, VI, 6.4.3-4.
6. *Sāmaveda, Āraṇya Kāṇḍa*, VI, 3. 4. 5.
7. *Ibid.*, VI, 3. 4. 4.
8. *Ibid.*, VI, 3. 4. 7.
9. *Ibid.*, *Uttarārcika*, II, 1. 4. 1 - 3.
10. *Ibid.*, II,1. 7. 2.
11. *Ibid.*, VI, 2. 19. 1.
12. *Ibid.*, VI, 3. 3. 1.
13. *Ibid.*, V, 2. 1. 1.
14. *Ibid.*
15. *Ibid.*, VI, 2. 2. 3.
16. Gupta, S. K., "Nature of the Vedic Śākhās and Authorship of the phonetic sūtras", in proceedings of the All India Oriental Conference, XV, 1949.
17. Bhattacharji, S., *Literature in the Vedic Age*, Vol. 1, K. P. Bagchi and Company, Calcutta, 1984, p. 326.
18. Renou, L., *op, cit.*, p. 25.
19. Verenne, J., *Myths at Legends extracts des Brāhmaṇas*, Paris, 1967.
20. Oldenlerg, H., The Religion of the Veda, Berlin, 1890.
21. Renou, L., *op. cit.* p. 34.
22. Schröder, L. Von, *Mysterium und mimus in Ṛgveda*, Leipzig, 1908.
23. Renou, L., *op. cit.* p. 37.
24. *Ibid.*, p. 36.
25. *Ibid.*
26. Weber, A., *The History of Indian Literature*, p. 29.
27. Bhattacharji, S., *Literature in the Vedic Age*, Vol. 2, K. P. Bagchi and Company, Calcutta, 1986, p. 180.
28. Renou, L., *op. cit.* pp 36-37.
29. Van Buitenan, J. A. B., *The Maitrāyaṇīya Upaniṣad*, Ch. III, p.1.
30. Tsuji, N., Studies in Indology and Buddhology, etc., Tokyo, 1955, p. 93.
31. Ram Gopal, India of Vedic Kalpasūtras, 2nd edn., MLBD, Delhi, 1983, p.2.

Some Aspects of Vedic Studies

2

Dr. G.U. Thite

A very important aspect of Indian thinkers is that they seek relevance of each and every historical personality or his works. One of the most facile ways of glorifying an ancient Indian thinker, a political leader or a book is to describe him or it as 'relevant even today'. On the birth or death anniversary of a great man it is invariably said that his thoughts are relevant even today. By saying this one feels complacent that one is adequately paid tribute to that great personality. The followers and devotees also feel that their leader is aptly praised thereby. Hardly does anyone think that it is highly impossible for all the thinkers to be relevant simultaneously.

In the history of vedic interpretation we notice two main currents. By and large they can be called fruit-oriented and root-oriented. The fruit-oriented interpreters try to interpret vedic texts in such a manner as would suit their purpose and try to find out thoughts in their mind from the vedic texts. The root-oriented interpretors on the other hand, try to find out the meaning intended by the author of the text; whether it can be useful or otherwise to them. Most of the Indian interpretors are fruit-oriented because they look at the veda as a source of enternal inspiration. They claim that the veda is useful and "relevant even today'. This 'today' is also eternal. Thus for example the authors of the Brāhmana texts try to give the vedic interpretation in such a manner as would suit to their purpose namely performance of sacrifice. Philosophers belonging to different schools of thought such as Dualism, monism, etc. also try to show that the vedic texts support their views. The commentator like Sāyana also interpret the vedic texts as if they were produced in their own times and find out all the ritual and philosophical thoughts prevalent in their own times in the vedic texts. In modern days the interpretors of the nineteenth century were interested in finding out the scientific progress in their times in the vedic texts; the interpretors of the twentieth century try to update these interpretations by claiming that the progress of the twentieth century was also known in the vedic age. Thus to the scholars of the nineteenth century it was possible to discover railway in the veda and the scholars of the twentieth century could find aeroplanes in the vedic literature. The words like ecology, pollution, environmentology were not known before the seventies of this century but the vedic scholars of the last part of this century can easily find out the references to ecology and ways of removing pollution from the vedic literature. There is no wonder if someone will find out references to the diseases like AIDS and their treatment in the vedic literature even though the words AIDS was not known before 1980. So although Veda is eternal and said to contain everything which is not yet known, it is necessary for these vedic interpretors to know these things first through the newspapers.

This utilitarian outlook of many Indian thinkers leads them to relevance-mania. Thus they claim that in order to prove the importance of any work or leader it or his thoughts should be declared to be relevant 'even today'. Everything that is in the context is said to be relevant 'even today'. On the birthday or death anniversary of a great man his thoughts are said to be relevant 'even today'. While praising one great man in this manner, the relevance-maniacs forget that they have praised other great men also in the same manner previously. It is a very crude and primitive way of thinking which requires relevance today as a pre-condition for the greatness. To claim an ancient personality or a great work relevant even today is anachronistic. For how can the thoughts expressed in ancient times be useful in modern times. Moreover, if all such claims are accepted literally, the mutually contradictory thoughts of all these persons cannot be simultanéously relevant. If they were really relevant then their would be a lot of confusion and anarchy. But most of the Indian interpretors do not have a sense of history. Perhaps they are influenced by the Mimāṁsā doctrine *"na kadācit anīdṛśaṁ jagat"* which does not make a difference between the past and the present. Moreover the arguments of many Indian vedic interpretors are based not on the original text but rather on the commentaries like that of Sāyaṇa's or the translations, in English or some other language, which are based upon Sāyaṇa's commentary. Thus for example they do not understand that the translation of the Ṛgveda by Wilson or Chitrava is not the translation of the Ṛgveda but of Sāyaṇa's commentary on the Ṛgveda. It never occurs to the mind of the Indian vedic scholars that there is a basic difference between understanding Raghuvaṁśa with the help of Mallinātha's commentary and understanding Ṛgveda with the help of Sāyṇa's commentary. The language of the authors like Kālidāsa is Classical Sanskrit governed by the rules of Pāṇini and the words used by them are traditionally known. But this is not the case with Ṛgveda the grammar, the vocabulary and the weltanschauung of which is not easy to understand. Since it is very easy to understand Sāyaṇa's commentary, the Indian scholars rush to study the veda where even the angels would fear to tread. Some Indian scholars try to study veda in order to justify their philosophical thoughts or try to interpret every detail either from the point of view of astrology, sexology of modern sciences like physics, chemistry, botany, etc. All these interpretations are fruit-oriented and made in order to explain their pre-conceived notions. The basic starting point of these scholars is of course the commentary or English translations by Wilson or Griffith. The translation by Renou and many other western scholars are not within the reach of majority of Indian scholars.

A significant point in the history of vedic interpretation in India is that, upto the nineteenth century the Vedic interpretation was not a part of the syllabus of Sanskrit studies. Prior to the introduction of the British system in India, students would study the Sanskrit Śāstras like Grammar, Nyāya, Mimāṁsā, Poetics, etc. in Sanskrit Pāṭhaśālas. Whatever Vedic study was done was limited to the learning of the Veda by heart only. Most of the Vedic students used to learn a few important parts of the Saṁhitā-texts useful for household priestly rituals only. A few intelligent and hardworking students used to learn by heart one Saṁhitā text along with the Brāhmaṇa and Vedāṅga texts as well as the Vikṛkti-recitations, but no one was interested even in reading the commentaries of Sāyaṇa etc. Even in the field of Śrauta ritual which was comparatively a rare phenomenon and limited to some isolated places in South India there was no systematic provision of studying it. It used to be studied in apprenticeship-method under the supervision of the senior priests. The priests too never bothered to know the meaning of the formulae they uttered or the significance of the action they did. In Nirukta the view of Kautsa who claimed that the Veda has no meaning is refuted, but the history of vedic studies in fact has supported the view of Kautsa only; for the students of Veda recited the Vedic texts without understanding the meaning thereof. Even the discussion part of the Nirukta on the meaning of the veda used to be recited verbatim. Thus for all practical purposes Veda was only to be recited and never understood. But after the new system of education was introduced by the British, the Vedic scholars started interpreting the Veda in accordance with the needs of their times. This interpretation was of course anachronistically fruit-oriented.

A typical example of anachronistic and fruit-oriented Vedic interpretation is that of the word *rāṣṭra*. In modern Indian languages like Hindi or Marathi, the word *rāṣṭra* is a synonymn of the English word 'nation'. The concept of 'nation' itself is taken from western politics. The word *rāṣṭra* in the Vedic as well as the later Sanskrit texts is simply used in the sense of state or country. The western political science makes a clear distinction between state and nation. The concept of state depends on land, people, government and sovereignty. But the concept of nation depends upon the feeling of unity among the people. For the concept of nation in modern Indian languages the word *rāṣṭra* is used and in imitation of these languages this word is used in modern Sanskrit to mean 'nation'. For the last one hundred years we are so much acquainted with the word *rāṣṭra* in the sense of nation, that it becomes almost impossible to most of us to accept the fact that in Vedic language, this word does not mean nation at all. Therefore when a prayer is made at the time of the Aśvamedha sacrifice (e.g. VS.XXII.22) to get rain etc. in the *rāṣṭra* there the word *rāṣṭra* which is used, is to be understood in the sense of country and not as a nation. In AV XII.1 which is called Bhūmisūkta, a description of the earth in general is made. The earth is also deified there. Some of the anachronistic interpretors consider this hymn to be useful for nationalistic interpretation. But because the description is very general here and nationalism requires a particular country, this hymn cannot fully serve their purpose. The description, viz. "The earth is a mother and I am a son of this mother." (AV.XII.1.12) also cannot serve the purpose of a particular nation.

It should also be pointed out that in Sanskrit there is no word which means nature or ecology or environment. In modern Marathi or Hindi the words *nisarga* or *prakṛti* are used in the sense of the English word 'nature' which includes trees, rivers, animals, seasons, etc. Although Sanskrit authors were fond of descriptions of trees and other things they had never used any general word like 'nature' for all these things. The word *nisarga* in Sanskrit means "evacuation, voiding, excrement, giving away, bestowing a favour or grant, creation, natural state or condition, character" etc. (See Monier Williams's Sanskrit Dictionary under the word *'nisarga'*). It is the modern western critics who appreciate the descriptions of natural beauty of Kālidasa and in imitation of them we Indians also call Kālidāsa a *'nisargakavi'*. Even though the Sanskrit critics also highly praised Kālidāsa, they never praised him for this quality because the concept of 'nature' is itself western and was unknown to India. Similarly the word *prakṛti* in Sanskrit means "the original form or condition, original substance, cause source, constitution, character, temper, disposition, material world "etc. (See the same Dictionary) but never 'nature'. In Hindi and modern Sanskrit, the word *prakṛti* or *nisarga* is used in sense of 'nature'. It is therefore completely anachronistic to seek ecological awareness in Sanskrit or Vedic literature merely on the basis of the some references to trees or animals.

The ancient Indian people were animists and as such they used to think that life pervades everywhere. The so-called inanimate objects were also treated by them to do like animate or even as deities. As a part of animism they considered trees also as sentient beings. Animism is a part of primitive way of thinking. For primitive men, trees are not a biological phenomenon but rather a magicoreligous phenomenon. Therefore treatment of trees as animate beings is not a scientific proposal but rather a magicoreligous one. Otherwise trees were considered by Indians to be inanimate things only. Thus in Kādambari, while describing the hermitage of Jābāli it is said that even the inanimate trees were observing vows there; then what to speak about the sentient animals? *(niścetanāstarvo'pi saniyamā iva lakṣyante kim punaḥ sacetanāḥ prāṇinaḥ).* Here the trees are in an unequivocal manner described to be inanimate; but the anachronistic relevancialist interpretors try to understand the ancient literature in the context of modern ideology. Therefore most of the Vedic interpretors of this type can be called fruit-oriented.

The western scholars on the other hand have always been root-oriented. They treat Vedic as well as later Sanskrit texts to be simply historical documents. They consider them to be important not because of their relevance but because of their antiquity. They try to find out the 'original' meaning of the Vedic words as possibly understood by the ancient ṛṣis. Not that the western scholars are successful in every attempt in this direction. But their effort is always directed to the root or the origin. Incidentally it may be pointed out that the concept of 'originality' itself is western. There is no word is Sanskrit language in the sense of 'origin' or 'originality'. No Sanskrit author ever claims to be 'original'. He always claims to be 'a faithful expounder of the thoughts of his teacher' or 'of some great ancient author'. Even there where he is really original he will say that he is giving the thoughts 'intended' even if not expressed by his predecessor. In Sanskrit there is no word for originality. (Similarly there is no word for 'research' also in Sanskrit. In modern Marathi or Hindi the word *saṁśodhana* or *śodh* is used in the sense of research and in imitation of this—these words are used in modern Sanskrit too. But in Classical Sanskrit these words simply mean, the act of cleansing or purifying only being derived from the root *śudh,* to purify.)

The history of Vedic interpretation in the west also seems to have undergone three stages. In the first period which can be called the Creative Period, scholars like Roth, Grassman, Ludwig Bergaigne and Gelner flourished. This period came to an end with the activities of Oldenberg who was the greatest hero in this period. The second period can be called the Classical Period. In this period scholars like 'Lüders, Theime, Kuiper and Gonda flourished, but undoubtedly the greatest scholars was Louis Renou. In this period the over-enthusiastic extremist views of the scholars of the creative period were modified. While freshness an originality were the characteristics of the creative period, perfection and discipline were the characteristics of the classical period. The post-Renou period however seems to be the decadent period characterised by exhibitionism, repetitions, verbosity, obscureness, hair-splitting and much ado about nothing.

To sum up we may draw the following conclusions :

(i) Many Indian thinkers and Vedic interpretors are so found of relevance ideology that they become relevance-maniacs as it were.

(ii) The relevancialism is a part of extreme utilitarianism and is based on a complete lack of the sense of history. In other words it is anachronistic.

(iii) Due to the search for relevance the Vedic interpretations by many Indian scholars are 'fruit-oriented'. The western interpretations are on the other hand 'root-oriented'.

Emergence of the Āraṇyakas

3

Dr. Didhiti Biswas

Vedas are the earliest extant literary works of the Indo-Aryans. They are the antique store house of the ancient Indian culture and religion. Vedas are four in number, The Ṛgveda, The Sāmaveda, The Yajurveda and The Atharveda. The text of each of them varies according to their various schools or branches. The Vedas so far as the texts are concerned, are traditionally broadly divided into two parts—Saṁhitā (Mantra) and Brāhmaṇa. The Brahmanas are again subdivided into three sections—(Liturgical) Brāhmaṇa, Åraṇyaka and Upaniṣad. The Saṁhitā portion of the Veda is the collection of mantras or prayers. To each Saṁhitā is attached a Brāhmana. The term Brāhmana carries the sense of statement made by the brahmin priests, experts in theology. Upaniṣads lay much emphasis on *jñānakāṇḍa* and contain the fruits of the highest thought of the ancient Indian thinkers. The Āraṇyakas are placed between the Brāhmaṇas and the Upanisads. Āraṇyakas contain the descriptions of some rituals and also some mystic and symbolical interpretations of the rituals. As texts the Brāhmaṇas, Āraṇyakas and Upaniṣads are completely mixed up with one another. The Āraṇyakas form the appendices to the Brāhmaṇas and the Upaniṣads are either included in the Āraṇyakas or appended to them. Thus the Āraṇyakas as texts, so far as the arrangement is concerned precede the Upaniṣads and are the continuations of the Brāhmaṇas.

The origin of the Āraṇyakas and especially their scope are yet to be known. Let us now attempt here to trace the origin as well as the development of the Āraṇyakas. Before getting into this discourse let us first review different deliberations of the modern and orthodox scholars as to what they actually meant by the term Åraṇyaka.

DEFINITION

Orthodox Views

The term Āraṇyaka is conspicuous by its absence in the four Vedas and in the Brahmanas. Pāṇini takes the word *āraṇyaka* in the sense of men associated with forests and prescribes the suffix *bun (= aka)* to be attached with *aranya*[1]. It is grammarian Katyayana who first took note to this term in the sense of a chapter or treatise relating to forest[2].

Sāyaṇa, the great commentator on the Vedas, thinks that the texts Āraṇyakas are studied in the forests. His observations on this term is found in the introduction to his own commentaries of Aitareya Brāhmaṇa (AB), Āitareya Åraṇyaka (AA) and Taittirīya Āranyaka (AT). In the first place he says that the Aranyakas are the Brahmanas but to be studied in the forests—*āraṇyakavratarūpaṁ brāhmaṇam.* Again he observes that the AA forms a part of the AB and as it is studied in the forests so it is termed Aranyaka—*"aitareyabrāhmaṇe'sti kaṇḍam āraṇyakābhidham araṇya eva paṭhayaṁ syad āraṇyakamitīryate"*. It is preface to the TA Sāyaṇa communicates that there is the saying that Åraṇyakas should be studied in the forests and hence they are called Āraṇyakas,—*"araṇyādhyavanādetad āraṇyakamitīryate/araṇye tadadhiyitetyevaṁ vākyåṁ pravakṣyate"* so Sāyaṇa focuses on two features of Āraṇyaka, 1) Āraṇyakas are not separate books but a part of the Brāhmaṇas, 2) They are studied in the forest.

The association of the Āraṇyakas with forests is supported by Śaṁkara also as he remarks that the Bṛhadāraṇyaka Upaniṣad (BU) is so named because it is preached in the forest—*"So 'yaṁ ṣaḍādhyāyī arranye nucyamānatvātvādāraṇyakam*[3]. Sureśvara another commentator of the BU holds the same view in his Sambandha Vārtika[4]. Āruṇeya Upaniṣad (II) and Āruṇika Upaniṣad (II) also prescribe the recitation of the Āraṇyakas and the Upaniṣads after renouncing everything[5].

Commentators of different texts often interpret the word rahasya as the texts to be studied in the forests[6]. Pt. Bhagavaddatta[7] also holds the view that the ancient name of Āraṇyaka is *rahasya.* In support of his opinion he also cites a passage from the Gopatha Brāhmaṇa—*evamime sarve vedā nirmitāḥ sakalpāḥ sarahasyāḥ sabrāhmaṇāḥ sopaniṣatkāḥ* etc[8].

Review

From the foregoing discussion it is evident that the orthodox scholars, following the tradition, associated Āraṇyakas with forests Sāyaṇa refers to the tradition by saying *'araṇye tadadhiyitetyevaṁ vākyaṁ pravakṣyate.* It is very difficult to ascertain since when this tradition took shape. Because it is certain that the term Āraṇyaka in the sense of a treatise is a later development. Pāṇini was definitely not aware of this term in this particular sense otherwise he would not have left off by referring *āraṇyaka* in the sense of forest-dwelling men only. So it may not be wrong if we assume, that during the age of Pāṇini, the Āraṇyakas as a part of Brāhmaṇas did not acquire a separate identity and name. Since the Brāhmaṇas were never associated with forests so there was an even earlier period when the study of this portion was not restricted in the forests only. Moreover the Āraṇyaka texts themselves bear no such indication that their study should be confined to the forests only barring a single case of Āraṇaketukacayana. This cayana is discussed in the TA and here it is said that the study of this sacrifice should take place in the forests, *araṇye' adhīyīran* (TA-1.32.3). This statement will prove to be meaningless if the complete text is originally to be studied in the forest. In another place of the same text a quite different statement is found when Śanca Āhneya prescribes that Brahmajana is to be practised at any place, time or state.[9] So the entire text was not studied in the forest[10].

One more point is very important in this connection and needs some deliberation. The orthodox scholars have not indicated as to why the Āraṇyakas are to be studied in the forests. So if the association with forests becomes the only criterion to characterise the Āraṇyakas then any text which is studied in the forests should get the same designation. Thus the Upaniṣads and *araṇyageyagāna* of the Sāmaveda should come under the purview of the Āraṇyakas too.

So the teaching or studying in the forest is not an intrinsic feature of this portion of the Vedas. Probably it seems probable that the association with forest became their feature at a later period and it might happen, though we are not very sure about it, after the four orders of life was introduced. The four orders of life were first referred to in the Dharmasastras[11] which too belonged to a later period. So the nature of the Aranyaka is not satisfactorily explained by the observation aranya eva pāthyam syad' etc. because it is a later development and was not originally there.

Modern Views

The modern scholars also associate the *Āraṇyakas* with the forests and attribute to these texts mysticism and symbolical features. Macdonell thinks that the *Āraṇyakas* are of a specially theosophic character and are meant to be imparted or studied in the solitude of forests[12].

Paul Deussen holds that the *Āraṇyakas* contain the discussion on the explanations of the rituals and allegorical speculation on them and remain as the substitute for the actual sacrificial observances in the solitude of the forest. He at the same time admits that the contents of the Brāhmaṇas, Āraṇyakas and Upaniṣads are overlapping and the dividing line between the *Brāhmaṇas* and the *Āraṇyakas* and also between the *Ārṇyakas* and the Upanisads[13] is arbitrary.

This is admitted by A.B. Keith also. He declares that it is difficult to determine the scope of the Āraṇyakas. According to him the *Āraṇyakas* deal with the meaning of the offerings without necessarily assuming that it will be performed. Simultaneously he does not fail to declare that this assessment is not absolute because the rites and texts which were regarded as especially scared and to be performed outside the village are contained not merely in the *Āraṇyakas* but even in the *Saṁhitā*[14].

Winternitz remarks that the *Āraṇyakas* are of secret uncanny nature and dangerous for the uninitiated. Due to this reason they should be taught and learnt only in the forest. Moreover, he adds that the main content of the *Āraṇyakas* are no longer the rules for the performance of the sacrifices but the mysticism and symbolism of sacrifice and priestly philosophy[15]. In another place he comments that the *Āraṇakas* and the *Upaniṣads* are commonly known as *Vedānta* as they fall naturally into the end of the Vedic period as well as into the end of the period of instruction due to their difficult subject matter[16].

C. Kunhan Raja interprets the word *āraṇya* in a different way. He opines that the word *āraṇya* expresses the sense of forest in the later period and in the Vedic age it conveyed the meaning of garden only where people gathered *arani,* the sacred fuel for the rituals. The instruction in the first stage of life consists of two different types—*grāmya* and *āraṇyaka.* The first one can be imparted in the village while the second one should take place in such gardens where from the roof of the house cannot be seen[17].

Prof. Durgamohan Bhattacharya also derives the term *Āraṇyaka* from the word *āraṇya.* According to him the word *āraṇya* is derived from *araṇa* which means a faraway place, void of any locality and as such forest. A student, he thinks, before convocation used to learn the *āraṇyakavidyā* from the teachers in the forest or in a lonely place where from the roof of any residence cannot be seen *(acchadidarśa).* Moreover, the *vānaprasthins* while took resort to the forest could not make the sacrificial implements available there. As such instead of actual sacrifices they concentrated on the mental sacrifice. Thus he associates the word *Āraṇyaka* with forests in two ways—first, the students got the knowledge of the *Āraṇyaka* in the first stage of life in forest and secondly after completion of household duties when they retire in the forest they used to apply that *āranyaka-vidyā* as Vānaprasthins[18].

C.V. Vaidya points to the fact that several chapters of the AA and TA are looked upon as separate appendices as their beginnings are recited separately on the *śrāvani* day. They are called *Araṇas* by the *Vaidikas.* Then he refers to the view of V.S. Abhyankara who thinks that the word araṇa is a short form of *Āraṇyaka.* Vaidya holds that this explanation is doubtful but he tries to establish that *Āraṇyaka* might be explained as the collection of *araṇas.* This word is derivated from the root which ṛ means originally to go and thence to know and hence *araṇs* might be taken as philosophical treatise, though not found in the *Saṁhitās* and the *Brāhmanas.* In support of his view he quotes from the TA (II.11)—*brahmaṇa udaraṇamasi,* where he thinks, its sense of philosophical work is indicated.[19]

Review

The modern scholars try to justify the association of the Āraṇyakas with forest by attributing the symbolic and theosophical feature to them. Deussen, Keith and also Prof. Durgamohan Bhattacharya hold the view that the *Āraṇyakas* do not necessarily mean that the rituals are to be performed physically rather they are only concerned with the meaning of the rituals and with the contemplation also. It is true that metaphysical ideas in form of crude philosophy or symbolism are occasionally found in the *Āraṇyakas* but analysing the contents of the *Āraṇyakas* we find that symbolism is not the only and essential feature of the *Āraṇyakas*. The illustration of bad omens for death described in the AA (III.2.4) and the ŚA (XI.3; 4), the spell addressed to an amulet called *Bilva* in the ŚA (XII) have nothing to do with the symbolism. The collection of *mantras* applied in the funeral ceremony, a mere brahmanic ritual, occurs in the TA (VI). Such collection of *mantras* is also found in AV *Saṁhitā*, VS or TB. So there is nothing unique in them to designate this part as Ā*raṇyaka*.

So, it is not clear to us why these scholars hold such a view that the Ā*raṇyakas* are only concerned with the contemplation on rituals. Winternitz does not provide us with a sufficient discussion on the Ā*raṇyaka* and avoids the situation by only attributing to it two adjectives—'uncanny nature' and 'dangerous for the uninitiated'; but we fail to understand what he precisely means by 'uncanny' and 'dangerous'. It is also not clear to us how C.V. Vaidya suggested that the word *'arana'* might carry the meaning of philosophical work. Moreover, the term *'arana'* occurs in the AV (V. 22.12) *gacchamun aranam janam*. Here *arana* means a faraway place.

We cannot therefore accept fully either of the two views—orthodox or modern, so far as the true definition of an Ā*raṇyaka* is historically and in contents concerned. Neither of them can give us a satisfactory and precise answer as to the questions : what is an Aranyaka? What prompted the Vedic students to read the texts of Ā*ranyaka* in the forest? What is its actual scope? Therefore we have to look for some satisfactory explanation for clarification of the points and to see whether the definition of Ā*ranyaka* can be reconstituted. It requires study of the history of the religio-philosophical literature of the ancient vedic people.

ORIGIN AND DEVELOPMENT OF THE ĀRAṆYAKAS

The current general view is that the *Saṁhitās* are the records of nature-worship and magic formulae of the early Indo-Aryans, *Brāhmaṇas* are the books of their rituals and at the period of Upanisads only the Vedic people could reach an advanced stage of philosophical thinking. The Ā*raṇyakas* are only an intermediate step between the *Brāhmaṇas* and *Upaniṣads*.

But it is not the right conjecture. The Upanisads cannot come out of a blue and it did have a long tradition of its own. Winternitz also could not disown the existence of a philosophical school preceding the Upanisadic era. It is true that the religious practice mostly dominated the society as there was the popular belief that the rituals could fulfil their earthly desires, but simultaneously the cultivation of philosophy was also carried out by a section of thinkers however small it be. In this connection the observation made by Maurice Phillips deserves special mention—'It seems always the fate of the Hindu thinker, that he no sooner abstracts the idea of God from natural phenomena, than he loses sight of nature altogether, and merges all in God. He carries his love of unity into the highest fruition to the absolute identity of the ego non-ego, mind and matter, subject and object, the creator and the creation, God and the universe. Hence polytheism and ideal pantheism are two streams which from the earliest times have run parallel in India. As it was in the Vedic age, so it is now. Polytheism is the religion of the ignorant multitudes and ideal pantheism is religion of thoughtful few.[20]

The philosophical tradition suffered setback time and again but it cannot mean that this tradition had no continuity at all. Sometimes the link is lost to us but the existence of this tradition since remote antiquity is evident from certain facts.

First, it should be appreciated that the hymns like *nāsadīya, vāc* etc., rich with philosophical content must have a long heritage of philosophy. These hymns were so unique in their content that the Brāhmaṇas and later the Śrauta sūtras could not associate them with any ritual. So Śāyaṇa finding no other authority regarding their application in the sacrifices avoided the situation be simply declaring—*'gatoviniyogah'*.

Secondly, *Upaniṣads*, the high-ranking philosophical works borrowed some *mantras* from *Saṁhitās*. These mantras are sometimes retained in the same form and sometimes quoted with some minor variations. As for examples we may quote the verses like *rūpaṁ rūpaṁ pratirūpaṁ babhuva* (RV VI.47.18; BU II. 5.19; KU V. 9.10; JUB 1.44.1.2.); *indraṁ mitraṁ varuṇamagni-māhuḥ* (RV I.164.46; AV IX. 9.20; MS III. 1.1), *hamsah sucisad vasurantariksad* (RV IV. 40.5; VS X.24; XII.14; TS I.8.15.2; IV 2.1.5.; MS 2.6.12 : 71.14; 3.2. 1:16.1; 4.4.6 : 57.3; Maha. U.IV.9.3.; 17.8; KU II.5.2) and others. Such *mantras* were introduced in the *Upaniṣads* by phrases like *'ṛcā' bhyuktam', 'eṣā' bhyuktā', 'eṣā ṛc'* etc. These citations clearly show that Indian philosophy did not begin with Upaniṣads and there was certainly a tradition of philosophical thinking since long past and it nourished the Upaniṣadic thinkers to a large extent. It is also interesting to note that the ṛcs cited by the Upaniṣads are sometimes missing in the extant saṁhitās. The saṁhitās were in all probability compiled by the priestly class who did not give place to too many mantras not concerned with any ritual. Thus this line of thinking rich with philosophical elments has gone into oblivion in course of time.

Now thirdly, it seems to be hardly well documented that before the emergence of the *Āraṇyakas* the Vedic people were only absorbed in some rituals which actually cannot satisfy one's intellectual aspiration. Moreover, Vedic age has historically pre-supposed the Indo-European and Indo-Iranian periods and so it would not be a far-fetched suggestion that during the Vedic period there must have emerged a certain group of people who wanted to attain something beyond earthly desires. This aspiration for something else led this group of people to the path of philosophy. In this connection Winternitz remarks—'We are not, however, likely to find these oldest philosophers of ancient India among the priests, who were engaged in the science of sacrifice. For, their teachings which were directed against the plurality of gods, were in obvious contradiction to the interest of these priests[21].

So it can be suggested that the philosophical speculation of the Vedic people started long before the appearance of the Āraṇyakas and the Upaniṣads[22]. So the history of the Vedic age not only includes in itself the history of religion but the history of philosophy also.

The Religio-philosophical Development and the Āraṇyakas

Now, to find out the religio-philosophical origin and development of the ancient Indian people we will have to go back to the earliest period of the Rgvedic era. This development till the composition of the Āraṇyakas can be divided into three phase. Through these phases three schools of thought were developed, religion, philosophy and a moderate group. Before going into an elaborate description of these three phases let us first give a brief account of these phases of development. In the first phase there was no difference between the school of religion and the school of philosophy. In the second phase the existence of the three schools became eminent. Religion found shape in the prayer mantras of Samhitā, philosophy found expression in hymns like vac nāsadiya and others, the moderate group of people tried to make a compromise between the other schools and made some allegories or rituals and this attempt is recorded in the hymns like asyavāmiya, puruṣa and others. In the third phase the school of religion was developed into the Brāhmaṇa literature, the school of philosophy was recorded in some philosophical speculations in the Brāhmaṇa texts and others, the thinking of the moderate group was culminated in the Āraṇyaka text. This development can be shown in the following diagram.

	Religion	*Philosophy*	*Moderate*
First Phase	— Religion-Philosophy (Combined together in an indislinet form)		—
Second Phase	Religion (More developed prayer mantras and Yajurveda)	Philosophy (Some secptic Verses- II.12.5 III.100.3, X-21 & Vāc, Nāsadiya etc.)	Allegories on sacrifice, e.g. Asyavamiy, Purusa, Viśvakraman etc.
Third Phase	Brāhmaṇa	Philosophical speculations in Brāhmaṇas	Āraṇyaka

First Phase

In this phase, the religion and philosophy (in a very crude form) were not separated from one another and the two different schools were not yet set up. The early Aryan people had to fight against the natural calamities like storms, fire, flood and others and also against non-Aryans. They were over-whelmed with the strength and power of nature and were filled with gratitude at what they got from it. This prompted them to deify the natural phenomena and to pray and offer them oblation-sometimes with gratitude only and sometimes with the expectation that they would be endowed with more and more benefits. These two aspects—the expression of gratitude to gods and the prayer for more benefits found place in many hymns of the RV and later on made subjects of persuasion by two different groups in the second phase. One group was content with the material welfare and the other one was eager to know the true nature of gods. It is the second phase of religio-philosophical development when the first group originated the school of religion and the other one formed the philosophical circle.

Second Phase

The development of religion

In this phase the religious shcool put much stress on the fulfilment of the material welfare and it took resort to the rituals as the media to fulfil their desires. The YV can be taken as the record of religious development of this period. So far as the sacrifices are concerned they were much more simple in the RV than those in the YV. The number of priests as found the RV varies from six to eight only unlike sixteen of the YV; similarly, the number of sacrificial implements were also fewer. Among the three fires the *gārhapatya* only is mentioned in the RV. All these indicate the gradual increase of complexities in the rituals.

Philosophy

Now on the other hand, the people who concentrated more on the excellence or divinity of the gods became gradually sceptic and scrupulous regarding the plurality of gods and also regarding the utility of the rituals. There are some *ṛcs* in *Saṁhitā* where we find some occasional sparks of scepticism. In those *ṛcs* the *ṛṣis* challenged the existence of the gods : "Of whom they ask "where is he?' Of whom indeed they say, 'He is not… 'Believe in him for he, O men, is Indra" (RV II.12.5). Again in another *ṛc* (RV III.100.3) Indra is glorified in the following way—"A true one he is, if in truth he is for many say, "there is no Indra, who has ever seen him? To whom are we to direct the song of praise? Again the significance of the famous expression *'Kasmai devāya haviṣā vidhema'* (RV X. 121) is that there is no need of offering oblation to so many gods in different rituals. This scepticism searched for something else other than these deified natural forces. According to Winterints; 'These sceptics and thinkers, these first philosophers of ancient India certainly did not remain isolated. That they, too, founded schools of thought, that their teachings were diffused is proved by the philosophical hymns of the *Atharva Veda*...'[23]. Actually they were not absolutely sceptic about the existence of the gods rather they wanted to realise the true nature of the gods. Their realisation is recorded in some hymns like *Vāc Sūkta, Nāsadıya Sukta* etc. and also in some scattered verses which were borrowed in the same form or with some minor variations in the later *Upaniṣads*. To give some references we may quote some verses like *'rūpam' rūpaṁ pratirūpaṁ babhuva'* (RV VI.47.18; BU II.5.19; KU V.9.10; JUB 1.44.1.2); *'haṁsah śuciṣad'* (RV IV 40.5; VS X.24; XII.14; TS I.8.15.2; Maha, U. IV9.3.; KU II.5.2) and so on. In all these hymns and *mantras* the idea of unity among diversities is brought about. In no way these oldest philosophers can be found in the circle of exclusive ritualists or priests.[24]

Third Phase

Religion

The science of liturgy was developed in full form at the third stage. The sacrifices grew in bulk; complications and paraphernalia in performances cropped up. The rituals began to act as the tool to bring about the material welfare; The assistance of number of priests became almost indispensable for carrying out the sacrifices. It is reflected in the Aitareya Brahmana and here it is communicated categorically, 'the gods do not accept oblations from a priestless one.[25] Thus the priestly class began to enjoy a privileged position in the act of performing rituals and with the growing importance of the sacrifice they acquired a special distinction in the society. The Brāhmaṇas record the development of religion of this phase.

Philosophy

The tradition of philosophy on the other hand reached its point of culmination in the age of the *Upaniṣads*. Now, in between the philosophical hymns of the Saṁhitās and the emergence of the Upanisads elapsed a long period and the time span can be taken as the third phase of philosophy. Unfortunately we are not in a position to refer to some specific *mantras* or *ślokas* as belonging to this phase. The existence of the philosophical circle can be inferred through some rituals and some philosophical expressions in the *Brāhmaṇas*. As for example, we may refer to the *Caturhotr Cayana* of the TB (III.12.5) where water substituted the bricks to build the alter. Again the AB (V.25) speaks of the *śraddhā home*, an expiratory rite of the *Agnihotra*. If the milk for oblation gets titled in the *Agnihotra* the sacrificer should offer his reverence as an oblation. These simple rituals in the *Brāhmanas* are somewhat out of place. We assume that they caused by the contact and influence of the philosophers. Some ritualists being influenced by the other circle introduced these simple rituals. Such influence is also noticed in some more places in the *Saṁhitā* and the *Brāhmaṇas.*[26] Sometimes the philosophical terms like *braṅman* etc. are used in the line of the philosophical thinking. As for example the SB (XI 2.3.3) and the TB (II.3.11.1; 4.7.10) describe *brahman* as the first creative principle, the TB (III.12.) declares that the *ātman* is omnipresent and is not decayed through works and others. The identification of *brahman* and *Puruṣa* is also brought about in the SB (X.6.3). No doubt such example are very few in the all along description of the rituals, but we think that they indicate the parallel existence of a circle of philosophers by which the ritualists were influenced.

The prevalence of the philosophical school can further be marked by some floating lines and expressions common in more than one Upanisads, e.g. *'anoraṇīyān'* (KU 1.2.20; SVU III.20) *'na tatra suryo bhāti'* (KU II.2.15.; SVU VI. 14; MU II.2.10); *'nāyamātmā pravacanena labhyah'* (KU 1.2.23, MU III,2.3) and others. These lines might be borrowed from a common source which can be regarded as the immediate predecessor of the Upanisads or in other words the philosophy of the intermediate phase of development. So the continuous cultivation of philosophy is unquestionable though it became sometimes thin but did not extinct.

Emergence of a Third Group in the second phase

It is generally found in all societies that two extreme views cannot exist at the same time without facing an attempt to bring about a compromise between them. It happened in the case of Vedic history also. We have pointed out earlier that in the *second phase* the religious school became engrossed in the religious activities and a small circle of philosophers got absorbed in the inquiry regarding the reality of so many Gods. In this phase of religio-philosophical development we come across some hymns and *mantras* which were neither fully philosophical nor fully sacrificial but full of allegories and symbolism on rituals. They were in no way produced by the philosophers as they were of ritualistic content and in no way by the purely ritualists as these hymns show an alliance with philosophy. By observing these peculiar features it seems plausible that hymns and *mantras* were the product of some ritualists who had a philosophical bent of mind. They did not give up the rituals altogether like the philosophers but most probable became averse to the growing ritualistic complexities. They can be termed as the moderate group of people. They tried to remind us the significance of the sacrifice by means of some allegorical and symbolical hymns and there by make the other two groups closer.

Puruṣa sūkta (RV X.90); *asyavāmīya sūkta* (RV I.164); *Visvaskarman sūkta* (RV X.81:82) and some scattered *matras* possessing such trails belong to this category. The *asyavāmīya sūkta* is full of mysticism and it is somewhat difficult to grasp their true significance. Sāyaṇa while commenting on this hymn explained it in two ways—one in the sense of *Āditya* and the other in the sense of theology. In one *ṛc* we find that the poet confessed that he was ignorant and asked; 'who was that one who in the unborn's image hath established and fixed firm these world's six region' (RV I-164.6 $^{b-c}$trans. Griffith) and requested—'Let him who knoweth presently declare it' (RV I.164.7 trans Griffith). It seems that the consciousness of oneness has already cropped up but that the total faith from the sacrifice is not given up is hinted in the verses. As for example, in the *ṛc* *'dyaurme pitā janitā'* etc. (RV I-164.33) the figurative expression captures attention. Here the space between the earth and the heaven is taken as the womb that is the region of rain. Father Dyauh and the daughter *Aditi* have to depend on this rain for fertility. Moreover, symbolism on sacrifice is found in the *ṛc* RV I.164.35 where in an answer to the question raised in the previous *ṛc* it declares that 'this *altar* is the earth's extremist limit; the sacrifice of ours is the world's centre. The stallion's seed prolific is the Sama, this *brahman* highest heaven where speech abideth' (Trans. Griffith). What more, the *ṛc, indram, mitram* etc. (RV I.164.46) is undoubtedly marked with an attempt to unify all the sacrificial gods and identify them with the One Supreme Spirit. The *Viśvakarman's* hymns depict *Visvakarman* as the supreme God which points to the fact that the idea of One God became popular among this section of moderate people, but they did not show any apathy to the sacrifices as they pleaded *Visvakarman* to reveal during the sacrifice his ownself, the cause of universe (RV X.82.5) or to help in performing the sacrifice (ṚV 82.7). *Puruṣa sūkta* (RV X.90) invokes the *Puruṣa* as the original source of universe and a sacrifice is hinted at here through which the universe was created. Moreover in the sixth *ṛc* the seasons were symbolically interpreted as the constituting sacrificial elements. The last *ṛc* of this hymn, perhaps, is the most important one is this connection. Through this *mantra, yajñenā yajñam ayajanta devāh etc.* (the gods performed sacrifice with the sacrifice. These were the earliest principles) this group of people tried to remind the people of the earliest *dharma*. This mantra being found in the tenth maṇḍala is no doubt of later origin; but the philosophy referred to by the expression *tāni dharmāni prathamānyasan* is no doubt antique. Here the second 'yajña' (sacrifice) means the renunciation or in a more explicit sense self-sacrifice. This is a higher thought. The *Puruṣa* became many by self-sacrifice. Be there the idea of one God or not, it is evident that the idea of self-sacrifice of the Supreme prevailed at the root of creation at some earlier period. The sentence *tāni dharmāni* etc. carries a great value as it refers to the antiquity of symbolism in Vedic sacrifice. Symbolism and allegories are also found in the YV and in some *Brāhamaṇas.* In the VS (II.11) the invoker is found imagining his own arms as those the Aśvin, his hand as those of Puṣan and he eats as if with the mouth of Agni. Again the mind is compared with the kindling wood (II.14). The *Śraddhā homa* (AB V.25) which is already referred to is also noteworthy in this regard. This sacrifice requires no worldly materials, even no fees for the priests. In this sacrifice the sun is the pillar, the earth is the altar, the plants are the *varhis,* water is the sprinkly water and the quarters are the *paridhis*. These symbolical and allegorical portions can be taken as the origin of the earliest *Āraṇyaka.*

The Late Brahmanic Period

In the late Brahmanic period, that is towards the later part of the third phase of religious development we come across some literature dealing with the symbolic illustration of the sacrifices. As for example in the beginning of the BU we find, the different cosmic elements are reflected upon as the different parts of the sacrificial horse. The symbolic interpretation on the *Ukthа* of the *Mahāvrata* sacrifice as brought about in the AA (II) is also noteworthy. The mystic representation of the *saṁhitāpātha* while reading out the Veda (AA III.1., ŚA VII, TA VII.3) also deserves mention in this connection. These symbolical treatments however lead us to think that they were produced by the group of moderate people who again felt the necessity of making a compromise between the religious and philosophical school.

However, this moderate group was somewhat influenced by the contemporary philosophy. They introduced meditation on the rituals as well as on some words or on some syllables. By imposing such pro-philosophical elements on them they made the rituals sophisticated and thereby they as though tried to propagate that the sacrifices are not altogether devoid of any philosophical values. It must be admitted that ascription of one thing to another pre-supposes the existence of both. However, these symbolical deliberations on the rituals, though originally were appended to the *Brāhmanas,* drew much attention and were designated as *Āranyaka* in a later period.

These texts were not totally symbolic in nature; because we find in them mere brahmanical description of some rituals also which were taken as mystic; e.g. the description of the *Pravargya* (TA IV, V; SB XIV); the *Mahāvrata* (AA I, V; SA I, II) etc. The Āraṇyakas contain also some discourse which are not symbolic at all. In this connection the presages of death (AA III. 2.4-5; SA VII. 7-9), some spells for avoiding untoward incidents (SA XII), the *mantras* to be recited in the funeral ceremony (TA VI), the expiatory rites (TA III) can be mentioned. So, naturally the question arises here why they are put under the designation of the *Āraṇyaka.* This happened, according to our opinion, due to the following reasons. In the post-Brahmanic period the ritualists began to supplement the *Brāhmaṇas* in two ways—incorporating matters (i) in the tradition of the Brāhamaṇas and (ii) in the light of symbolism. Now, the symbolical portions of the Āraṇyaka which is contributed by a section of the ritualists (i.e. the moderate group of people) are the *Ārṇyaka* proper. These portions were developed following a definite course of historical evolution. The rest of the *raṇyaka* which is not basically symbolic but is mystic or magical or otherwise found its place also in the *Āraṇyakas* while the compiling of the *Āraṇyakas* as text was going on. These portions are the *Āraṇyaka* by name only, but not rigidly the *Āraṇyaka* from the point of view of historical evolution, but following the nyaya 'Pradhanayaena vyapadesa bhavanti, the whole text has been so named.

The Āraṇyakas and its association with forests

We have discussed earlier that Panini did not mention the term Āraṇyaka in the sense of treatise and the term in the sense of book was first coined by Kātyāyana. So it can very well be assumed that there was a time when *Āraṇyaka* had no special designation of its own and it went by the name of *Brāhmaṇa*. Incidentally the observations of R.L. Mitra is note-worthy. He observes, 'As sacrifices were performed long before a word of any Brahmana or Sutra had been uttered, so metaphysical speculations were carried on in the forests of India long before the names of *Āraṇyaka* or *Upaniṣad* were thought of.[27] However, it is very difficult to tell when this portion of *Brāhmaṇa* was designated as the *Āraṇyaka*. Most probably it happened at the post-Pāṇinian period. Because we think it highly documented that Pāṇini somehow missed the term *Āraṇyaka* which was incidentally an important part of the Veda. The conception of the four *āśramas* also came later as they were first referred to in the *Dharmasūtra* only. So it seems probable that the conventional association of the *Āraṇyakas* and the *Upaniṣads* with forests or more specifically with the third and the fourth order of life was brought about at a later period when the society-makers established four stages of life and prescribed that the *Āraṇyakas* and *Upaniṣads* should be studied by a forest dweller after renouncing everything.[28] The society-makers with a view to making the society disciplined, introduced the four *āśramas*. They broadly divided the span of a man's life into four stages and prescribed some duties for each of the stages. These duties were specified by studying the mental and physical attainment of a man at different stages of his life. They observed that the boys who have just crossed their childhood and are yet to enter their teen should acquire knowledge. Hence this span of life is specified by them for study and named as *brahmacarya*. After attaining youth people run after wordly happiness and prosperity. At this stage people should marry, enjoy life and perform sacrifices for various rewards. This time is named as *gārhasthya*. After completion of this period the people attain some sort of calmness and begin to meditate upon various objects and retire to the lonliness of the forest. This period is known as *vānaprasthya*. Lastly, they achieve a state when they should renounce everything and this period is named as *sannyāsa*. Observing the characteristic feature of the four sections of the Veda the society makers allotted these four sections to four *āśramas* according to the necessity felt. Thus in the first period of life the study of respective branch of the *Vedas* are prescribed. Usually these students do not get so matured to read and realise the philosophical discourse. Hence after performing sacrifices in the household life according to the rules of *Brāhamaṇas* when they should take resort to forest, they go through the *Āraṇyakas*. The experience of life and matured age and intellect help them to study the *Āraṇyakas*. The *Upaniṣads* are prescribed in the final stage of life.

That the term *Āraṇyaka* was coined after the introduction of four orders of life is an assumption only. But that the study of the allegorical meaning of the *Āraṇyakas* requires solitude and calmness leaves no doubt. Actually the sacrificial ground is not the proper place for concentration and meditation on the allegories. One need to go far away from the din and bustle of the day to day life and this remote place is indicated by *araṇya.* Thus the relation of *araṇya* and *Āraṇyaka* grows in a very natural way.

Proposed Definition of Āraṇyaka

Tracing the religio-philosophical history of India and analysing the content of the *Āraṇyakas* it seems to us that the subject-matter of the *Āraṇyakas* is almost a continuation of the *Brāhmaṇas* and so supplementary in nature and only occasionally they enter into the symbolic presentation of some rituals, most probably being influenced by having coming in close contact with philosophical thinkers. The two schools—liturgical and philosophical exist in some form or other since the Ṛgvedic age. They came in contact with each other and the *Āraṇyakas* were produced with a view to bringing the two schools closer. So the definition of *Āraṇyaka* can be suggested in the following way : those parts of Brāhmaṇas which are symbolic in nature (symbolism or rituals) and therefore preferred to be studied in the forest for some reasons or others came to be regarded as Āraṇyaka from some period of time.

CAN THE ĀRAṆYAKAS BE REGARDED AS THE TRANSITIONAL PHASE FROM RITUAL TO PHILOSOPHY ?

The current opinion is that the Āraṇyakas act as the transitional phase between the *Brāhamaṇa* and the *Upanisads*. Prof. Macdonell remarks that the *Āraṇyakas* in tone and content form a transition to the *Upanisads.* Deussen also maintains the same opinion. He holds that as the *Āraṇyakas* consist of the allegorical speculation on rituals which for the most part were not practicable and as such they emancipated from the limitation of a formal cult. So they form a natural transition from rituals of the *Brāhmaṇas* to the speculation of the *Upaniṣads.* But we are in no way ready to aceept that the *Āraṇyakas* can be taken as the transition, so far as the development of the *Brāhmaṇas* and the *Upaniṣads* is concerned.

We have shown in the foregoing discussion that the *Brāhmaṇas* and the *Upaniṣads* developed in two separate streams. The *Brāhmaṇas* were produced by the liturgical school while the *Upaniṣads* were the product of the philosophers. It seems to us a farfetched idea that a few occasional allegorical discourses in the *Āraṇyakas* form the first step to the high philosophy of the *Upaniṣads.* Actually, the evolution of the philosophical tradition and the culmination of the same in the *Upanisads* went on quite independently. The *Āraṇyakas* so far available are not many in number and the symbolic portion is not sufficient to inspire the people to the imbued with the matured philosophical ideas.

Moreover, the description of the *Āraṇyakas* as the symbolical treatise and at the same time as the first step towards philosophy cannot be possible from the point of view of logic.[29] The word symbol is explained in the Encyclopaedia Britanica in the following way : 'in its original meaning the symbol represented and communicated a coherent greater whole by means of a part. The part as a sort of certificate, guaranteed the presence of the whole and, as a concise meaningful formula, indicated the larger context.[30] Now if there is no idea of the 'greater whole' beforehand, then how the communication between the 'whole' and the symbolic object can be established in the *Āraṇyakas.* So, it is quite certain that some conscious ideas must have cropped up long before the *Āraṇyakas* and as they contradict the religious culture directly so they were cultivated in a separate circule which can be termed as the circle of the philosophers. The *Āraṇyakas* utilised these ideas with a view to popularising the rituals and also to bringing the two schools—religious and philosophical—closer.

The *Āranyakas* cannot be taken as the turning phase as well. If they were so, it would have been found in the society that the performance of and the interest in the rituals have been stopped after Upanisadic era and the entire people have been philosophical. It is too much to expect so. It is found actually in reality that after the exaulted phase of philosophy of the *Upanisads* the society again went deeply into the complexities of the rituals which have been recorded in the *Sūtra* literature. Moreover, the *Sūtra* literature cannot be taken as the mere reminiscences of the *Brahmanas.* The sacrifices of the *Brahmanas* on many occasions, are enlarged in the *Sūtras,* many new rituals were introduced and new mantras were composed to meet the growing necessity of the sacrifices.

So, the *Āraṇyakas* are neither the phase of the transition nor the turning point nor the bridge between the *Brahmanas* and the *Upanisads.* Actually they represent the phase of adjustment. From this standpoint of adjustment the *Āraṇyakas* can be taken as the bridge—not between the *Brahmanas* and the *Upanisads*—but between the two conflicting schools—liturgical and philosophical, represented by the ritualists and the intellectually advanced philosophers respectively. The *Aranyakas* tried to bring these two closer, as indicated above by making a compromise between them.

List of Āraṇyakas

The *Āraṇyakas* as texts are not systematically arranged. We find the Upaniṣadic discussion sometimes occurs in between the discourse of the Āraṇyaka and is sometimes attached towards to end of the text. So, as to the difficulty how far it should be called *Āraṇyaka,* we seek the help of our proposed definition[31] of the *Āraṇyaka* and demarcate the *Brāhamaṇa, Āraṇyaka* and *Upaniṣad* from one another.

Following this criterion some portions can be taken as *Åraṇyaka* though they were traditionally taken otherwise. Let us present here a list of texts which can be regarded as the *Āraṇyaka* according to this new definition.

To the Ṛgveda belong two *Āraṇyakas*—the *Aitareya—Āraṇyaka* and *Śānkhāyana Āraṇyaka*. Both of these Āraṇyakas deal with the *Mahāvarata* sacrifice. It is very interesting to note that though this ceremony is part and parcel of the *satrayāga* but neither the *Aitareya Brāhmaṇa* nor the *Śānkhāyana* contains any discourse on it while treating the *satrayāga*. *Mahāvrata* is taken as a mystic ceremony and the *Aitareya Āraṇyaka* contains the symbolic interpretation of the *Niṣkevalya Śastra* of the *Mahāvrata*. It is generally believed by the scholars that the last ten of fifteen chapters of the *Aitareya Brāhmaṇa* belong to later date and the *Aitareya Āraṇyaka* is just a later annexation to the *Aitareya Brāhmaṇa*. The *Aitareya Āraṇyaka* contains five chapters which themsevles are named as *āraṇyaka*, each of these chapters is divided into *adhyāyas* which are again subdivided into *khaṇḍas*, from the fourth to the sixth *adhyāyas* of the second *āraṇyaka* constitute the *Aitareya Upaniṣad* which preach the doctrine of *ātman*. Śaṁkara, on the other hand commented on the *āraṇyakas* II and III separately and named them *Mahaitareya Upaniṣad* and *Saṁhitopaniṣad* respectively. These two books which embody the commentary of Śaṁkara are available only in form of manuscript. Probably the non-ritualistic discourse of these two books leads Saṁkara to designate them as *Upaniṣads*. But so far as the true significance of the term *Upaniṣad* is concerned these two books should not be called as such. These two books unlike the *Upaniṣads* neither speak of the Absolute Reality nor do they lead one to the immediate emancipation. Moreover, Sāyaṇa himself admits in the preface of his commentary to AA II.4, that the *Karmakāṇḍa* produces the desire for knowledge and the first three *adhyāyas* of *āraṇyaka* II which deal with the meditation helps one the achieve this mental attention and a craving for the knowledge of the *brahman*. The Upanisadic doctrine is meant for the best students. For the mediocre students is recommended the meditation dealt with in AA II.1-3 and AA III, resulting in the gradual emancipation through the attainment of the *Hiraṇyagarbha*. *Karmakāṇḍa* is prescribed for the rest of the people and it bestows material prospect only. Then how is it possible that the AA II.1-3 and III should be termed as *Upaniṣads?* Perhaps the starting sentence of the third *āraṇyaka : 'athātah saṁhitāyāh upaniṣat'* misleads the commentators to take is as *Upaniṣad*. But we have noticed that the term *Upaniṣad* was used in the *Brahmanas* in sense of mysticism. Moreover, in the *Sarvanukramanı*, we find the reference to *Rogaghna Upanisad, Garbhasraāvinı Upaniṣad* etc. which have nothing to do with the Absolute Reality. Here the term is used loosely in sense of secrecy. The AA II. 1-3 deal with the allegories of *Niṣkevalya-śastra* of *Mahāvarata* and *āraṇyaka* III with that of the euphonic combination of the *mantras* applied in rituals. Due to their association with ritual we take them as *Āraṇyaka*. The last and fifth book of the AA is written in *sūtra* style and *Sāyaṇa* also does not admit its *apauruṣeyatva*. Still this book is traditionally included in the *Åraṇyaka* text and commented on.

Another *Āraṇyaka* to the Ṛgveda is the *Śākhāyana* or *Kauṣitaki Āraṇyaka* comprising fifteen *adhyāyas* each being subdivided into *khaṇḍas*. Of this *Āraṇyaka* four *adhyāyas* starting from the third one constitute the *Kauṣitaki Upaniṣkad*. The following two chapters are more or less identical with the *Aitarya Āraṇyaka* (III. 2, 3). The mental *Agnihotra* treated in the tenth chapter is completely symbolical. But the following two chapters (i.e. XI and XII) have nothing to do with the *Āraṇyaka* : and they are *Āraṇyaka* by name only. The last three chapters are spurious and added to the main text at a later period.

The *Taittirīya Śākhā* of the *Black Yajurveda* possesses the famous *Taittirīya Āraṇyaka*. It comprises ten *prapāṭhakas* which are subdivided into *anuvākas*. According to the tradition the first six *prapāṭhakas* constitute *Taittirīya Āraṇyaka* and following *prapāṭhakas* (i.e. VII-IX) constitute Taittirīya Upaniṣad and the last *prapāṭhaka* i.e. the tenth one is the Mahārārāyaṇa Upaniṣad.

Here we suggest that the first three *anuvākas* of the first *prapāṭhaka* of the Upaniṣadic portion (i.e. *anuvākas* I-III of the seventh *prapāṭhaka)* should be included in the *Āraṇyakas*.

These three chapters of the TU contain the symbolisation of euphonic combination and also some symbolic statements on pronounciation, accent etc. Śaṁkara himself correlates this portion with the *Karmakāṇḍa* by referring it as *saṁhitādiviṣayāni karmabhiraviruddhānyupāsanāni*.[32] Sāyaṇa thinks that this portion is meant for attaining introvert focussed mind.[33] Moreover the very name *śikṣāvallī* of the first *adhyāya* suggests that it is not concerned with the nature of Reality. It is not purely a *śikṣā* as well, as it contains some symbolic statements. So it has every possibility of being inlcuded in the *Āraṇyaka* portion. This is further proved by the fact that the same subject is excluded from the *Kauṣitaki Upaniṣad* and is found in the seventh chapter of the just following the concluding chapter of the Upaniṣadic portion.

The fourteenth *kāṇḍa* of the *Śatapatha Brāhmaṇa* and the first *adhyāya* of the *Bṛhahadāraṇyaka Upaniṣad* taken together are conventionally termed as the *Āraṇyaka* of the *Vajasaneya-śākhā* of the white *Yajurveda*. The last three chapters of the *Śatapatha Brāhmaṇa* deal with the *Pravargya* sacrifice which bears many peculiar traits and this sacrifice is also found in the *Taittirīya Āraṇyaka* of the Black *Yajurveda*. In the beginning of the BU we find the direction for worshipping the head of the sacrificial horse of the *Aśvamedha* sacrifice as the dawn, the eye of that horse as the sun and so on. This symbolical worship conforms to the characteristics of the *Āraṇyaka*. Now, apart from this conventional view the fifth and the sixth *adhyāya* of the BU are also considered as the *Āraṇyaka* from standpoint of our proposed definition. Because these two *adhyāyas* also contain the description of some symbolic meditation some of which are associated with ritual.

The *Jaiminīya Upaniṣad Brāhmaṇa* is popularly accepted as the *Āraṇyaka* belonging to the *Talavakāra-śākhā* of the *Śāmaveda*. This book in four *adhyāyas* is full of symbolic meditation mostly on *sāman* and its various parts. The first and the second *adhyāya* of the *Chāndogya Upaniṣad* are generally regarded as another *Āraṇyaka* to the SV. These two *adhyāyas* deal with the symbolic interpretation of *udgītha* as well as of the different parts of a *sāman*, which are essentially the constituent parts of rituals. We also bring into the purview of the *Āraṇyaka* some more portions of the same book. They are the sixteenth and the seventeenth *Khaṇḍa* of the third as well as of the fourth *adhyāya* and the entire fifth *adhyāya*. Because these portions supplemented their *Brāhmaṇa* by containing some mystic interpretations on rituals.

PROSE UPANIŚADS AND THE MODERATE GROUP

As we have pointed out earlier the Āraṇyakas contain the Upaniṣadic portion also. These *Upaniṣads* are written in prose except the Ken. Up. which is the concluding part of Jaiminīya Upaniṣad Brāhmaṇa. The prose *Upaniṣads* bear a close resemblance with the *Brāhmaṇas* and the *Āraṇyakas* and they are actually more close to them than the metrical *Upaniṣads* in treatment of the the rituals. The metrical *Upaniṣads* denounced the rituals altogether[34] and never did praise them. The prose *Upaniṣads* on the other hand spoke highly of the Absolute Reality like the metrical *Upaniṣads*, but some passages are found here which are in the same tune with the *Brāhmaṇas*[35] on rituals and they are sometimes symbolic in character like the *Āraṇyakas*.

The same line of thinking indicates that the composers of the prose *Upaniṣads* belong to the same group of people who also produced the *Āraṇyakas*. This group of people as we have shown before, was actually ritualists but with a philosophical bent of mind. Now, following the footprints marked by the Āraṇyakas the prose Upaniṣads record the further advancement of thought of these people. The use of prose form of language also confirms this assumption.

Probably it would not be out of place to point out the fact that studying the history of human civilisation it is found that when the people first learnt to channelise their emotion through language they essentially composed semi-metrical or metrical passages. As such the prose was a later development for narration of facts and was not dominated by emotion. So, the, RV, the earliest literature of India was composed in poetry. Later on, when the liturgical school found distinct shape, the thinkings of this school began to be recorded in prose; because these are nothing but some statements, descriptions and eulogies of sacrifices. So, when a fraction of ritualists watned to contribute something in pro-philosophical fashion they contributed it mostly in prose (i.e. the *Āraṇyaka*), and their matured philosophy also found shape in prose form (i.e. the prose Upaniṣads). It is very interesting to note that the prose portion of the Ken.Up. glorified the *karma* as the foundation of the mystic doctrine.[36] The prose portion of this *Upaniṣad* is thought to belong to a prior period than the metrical portion.[37]

However, the other circle of the society, the philosophers, tried to express their inner feelings and realisation from the core of their heart in poetry. This poetical tradition flowed, progressed and ultimately reached its final form in the metrical Upaniṣads following the path of the philosophical hymns of the RV and the AV.

References

1. 4.2.129.
2. Pathyādhyāyanyāyavihāramanuṣyahastiṣiti vācyam.
3. See introduction to Samkara's Commentary on Bṛhadāraṇyaka Upaniṣad.
4. araṇyādhyayanāccai tadāraṇyakamitiryate No. 9.
5. Kuticaro brahmacārī kuṭumvaṁ visṛjet pātraṁ visṛjet daṇḍamllokaṁsca visṛjet iti hovāca ata ūrdhvamamantravadākcaret trisamdhyādau snānamācaret saṁdhiṁ samādhāvātmanyācaret sarveṣu vedeṣvāraṇyakamāvartayepupanisadamāvartayet.
6. rehasyāni sāmānyāraṇyakādhītāni—Medhatithi on Manu II.140 rahasyamaraṇye paṭhitavyo grantho yaḥ tam—Maskarī bhāṣya on B. Dh. S 2.8.3.
7. Vaidikavānmaya kā itihāsa vol—III S. B. Prakashan, New Delhi, 1978—p. 224.
8. Gopatha Brāhmaṇa II-10.
9. grāme manasā svadhyayamadhīyita divā naktaṃ vā iti ha smā "ha śaucaahneya (TA II.12).
10. cf. Vaidya, C.V. History of Sanskrit Literature, p. 150.
11. Ap. Dh. S II. 9.21.1; G.Dh.S. III.2, V.Dh.S VII. 1-2 and others.
12. Macdonell, A.A., A History of Sanskrit Literature, MLBD, Delhi, Second Indian Edition, 1971, p. 28.
13. Deussen, Paul, The Philosophy of the Upanisads, Dover Publications, New York, 1966, p. 4,
14. Keith, A.B., The Philosophy of the Veda and Upanisads, MLBD, New Delhi, Second Indian Reprint, 1976, pp. 499-491.
15. Winternitz, M., A History of Indian Literature translated into English by Mrs. S. Ketkar, University of Calcutta, 1962, pp. 203-204.
16. Ibid., p. 204.
17. Raja, C. Kunhan, Survey of Sanskrit Literature. Bharatiya Vidya Bhavan, Bombay, 1962.
18. Bhāratkoṣa, Bangiya Sahitya Parisat, Calcutta, 1887 Śakābda, p. 334.
19. Vaidya, C.V., History of Sanskrit Literature, Poona 1930, p. 150.
20. Maurice, Phillips, The Teaching of the Vedas, Delhi, pp.72-73.
21. Winternitz, M, ibid, p. 198.
22. The remark of Winternitz is very important in this connection, '......netheir does the awakening of philosophical speculation come after the period of the Brāhmaṇas : It comes before this period, ibid. p. 197.
23. Winterzitz, M, ibid, p. 198.
24. Winternitz points out here, "It is much more probable that such secptics and thinkers were to be found among those who were the most obnoxious to the priests, among the 'misers', who did not believe, i.e. who did not sacrifice and gave no gifts to the priests' ibid, p. 198.

25. ā tvevā śraddhāyai hotavyam; V. 25.2, Aitareya Brāhmaṇa, Anandasram, Pune, 1977.

26. (i) *śraddhādevam yajamānam catvāri vīryyāni* TS VIII.1.8.2

(ii) *sā vā eṣā mrtāhutireva vadvapāhutir-amṛtāhutiragayāhuti... etā vā aśarīrā āhutayo yā vai kāścāśarīrā abutayo-mṛtatva,eva tābhiryajamāno jayati* AB II.2.4.

(iii) *na hotavyā atiriktā āhutayaḥ syuryadbhu-yerannadhvaryumeva juhvatamanvārabhya pratīkairanumantrayeta.* KB VII.7.

(iv) *amum aśvaṁ medhaṁ medhyam asmin arke sāyaṁ judomīmam arkam amuṣminnaśve medhe medhye prātarjuhoni* JB I.25.

(v) *Yajño vai namo* ŚB IX. 1.1.16

(vi) *so'syaiṣa sarvameva sarvaṁ hyayamātmā* ŚB IV. 2.2.1

(vii) *vidyayā tadārohanti yatra kāmāh parāgatāḥ na tatra dakṣiṇā yānti nāvidvāṁsastapasvinaḥ* ŚB X.5.4.16

(viii) *Vadṛcah...ājyāhutayo ha vā etā devānāṁ yadyajūmsi...somāhutayo havā etā devānām... yat sāmāni...meda āhutayo havā etā devānām...* ŚB XI. 5.6.4-8.

(ix) *antarviśvamidaṁ jagat/brahmaiva bhūtānāṁ jyesthaṁ/tena ko''rhati spardhituṁ/brahman-devastrayastriṁśat/ brahmannindra prajākpati brahman ha viśva bhūtāni/nāvīvāntah samāhitāh* TB II.8.8.10

(x) *śradhā devī prathamajā ṛtasya viśkvasya bhartrī jagatah pratisthā tāṁ śraddhāṁ haviṣā yajāmahe... āgāt satyaṁ haviridaṁ juṣāṇam.* TB III 12.3.2

(xi) *kaściddha vā bhasmāallokāt pretkya ātmānaṁ veda ayamahmasmīti kaścit svaṁ lokaṁ na prati jānāti agaimugdho haiva dhūmatāntaḥ svaṁ lokaṁ na prati jānāti atha yo haivaitamagniṁ sāvitraṁ veda sa etaṣmāllokā ktpretya atmanaṁ veda ayamahamasmīti, sa svaṁ lokaṁ prati jānāti* TB III.10.11.1

27. Taittirīya Āraṇyaka, cd. by R.L. Mitra, Asistic Society, Bengal, 1859, introduction, p.6.

28. See the review of the orthodox view pp. 3-6. Am

29. Winternitz, M., ibid., p. 197.

30. Encyclopaedia Britanica, Vol. 17, 15th Edition, p. 900.

31. See p. 31.

32. See preface of Śaṁkara's commentary on Ānandavallyādhyāya, Taittirīya Upaniṣad, Pune, 1977.

33. *Saṁhityāmupaniṣadi proktairupāsanai rantarmukha ekāgracittaḥ......*
Sāyaṇa's commentary on Taittiṇya VIII, 2.1., Anadasram, Pune, 1981.

34. (i) *Plavā hyete adṛḍhā yajñarupā*
aṣṭadaśoktamavaraṁ yesu karma etacchreyo
ye'bhinandanti mūḍhā jarāmṛtyuṁ te punarevāpi yanti (MU 1.2.7)

(ii) *andhaṁ tamaḥ praviśanti ye'vidyamupāsate*
tato bhūya iva te tamo ye u vidyāyām ratāḥ (IU 9)

(iii) *jānāmyahaṁ śevadhirityanityaṁ*
na hyadhruvaith prāpyate hi dhruvaṁk tat (KU 1.2.103)

(iv) *ṛtaṁ pivantau sukṛtasya loke guhāṁ praviṣṭau parame parardhe*
chāyātapau brahmavido vadanti pañcāgnayo ye ca trināciketaḥ (KU 1.3.1)

35. (i) *pura prataranuvakasyopakaranajjaghanena*
garhapatyasyodan mukha upavisya sa vasavam
samabhigayati (CU II.24.3)

(ii) *vasisthaya svahetyagnavajyasya hutva manthe sampatamavanayet* (CU V. 2.5.)

(iii) *assu vai loko 'gnirgautama tasyaditya eva*
samidrasmayo dhumo'hra rcirdiso' nagara etc. (BU VI. 2.9)

36. *tasyai tapo damaḥ karmeti pratiṣṭthā, vedāḥ sarvāngāni, satyamāyatanam* (Ken. U.IV.8)

37. Cf. Hume, Robert Ernest, The Thirteen Principal Upanisads. (P. 52)

Bibliography

Original Works in Sanskrit

1. Aitareya Aranyaka — Anandasram, 1959
2. Aitareya Brahmana — Anandasram, 1931
3. Aitareya Brahmana with commentary of Sayanacarya — S. Malaviya (ed.), Varanasi, 1983
4. Atharveda — VVRI, Hoshiarpur, 1960
5. Brhadaranyaka Upanisad — Anandasram, 1914
6. Brhadaranyaka Upanisad — Sri Ramkrishna Math, Mylapore, 3rd ed. 1979.
7. Chandogya Upanisad — Anandasram, 1902
8. Ṛgveda with commentary of Sāyaṇa — VSM, Poona
9. Śāṅkhāyana Āraṇyaka — Anandasram, 1922
10. Śatapatha Brāhmaṇa — Text with Hindi translation by G.P. Upadhyaya, New Delhi, 1957.
11. Taittirīya Āraṇyaka with bhāṣya by Bhaṭṭa Bhākskara — A.M. Shastri (ed.), Mysore, 1902
12. Taittirīya Āraṇyaka with commentary of Sāyana — R. L. Mitra (ed.), Asiatic Society of Bengal, 1959
13. Taittirīya Āraṇyaka — Anandasram, 1981
14. Taittirīya Brāhmaṇa — Anandasram, 1979
15. Taiṭtirīya Brāhmaṇa — R.L. Mitra (ed.), Asiatic Society of Bengal, Calcutta, 1859.
16. Upanisat Saṁgraha — Jagadish Shastri (ed.) MLBD, 1984.

Other Works

17. Anirvan — Veda Mimamsa, Calcutta, 1975.
18. Bhattacharjee, Sukumari — Literature in the Vedic Age (Vol. I & II) Calcutta, 1984.
19. Dasgupta, S.N. — (A) History of Indian Philosophy, 1st ed. 1922, Reprint Cambridge 1957.
20. Encyclopaedia of Religion and Ethics, Edinburg, 1909
21. Goldstucker — Panini, Varanasi, 1965 (1st ed 1860)
22. Griffith, Ralph. T. H. — Hymns of Rgveda, 1st ed. 1889. MLBD, New Revised ed., Reprint 1976.
23. Haug, Martin — Aitareya Brahmana (edited and translated) 1st Indian ed. 1922.
24. Hume, R.E. - The Thirteen Principal Upanisads, Oxford University Press, Madras, 1958.

25. Keith, A.B. — Aitareya Āraṇyaka, 1st ed. 1909, Oxford University Press, London, Reprint, 1969.

26. —do— — Ṛgveda Brāhmaṇas (Translation), 1st ed. 1919 MLBD 1971.

27. —do— — Śāṅkhayana Āraṇyaka (Translation), 1st ed. RAS, London 1908, 1st Indian ed. 1975. New Delhi.

28. Majumder, R. C. (ed.) — History and Culture of Indian People (Vedic Age)—Bharatiya Vidya Bhavan, Bombay, 1st ed. 1957, Reprint 1971.

29. Maxmuller, F. — History of Ancient Sanskrit Literature, India, 1912.

30. Maxmuller, F (ed.) — SBE, Śatapatha Brāhmaṇa, English Translation by J. Eggeling, 1st ed 1900, Indian Reprint MLBD, 1978.

31. Misra, U. — (A) History of India Philosophy, (Vol I & II) Tirabhukti Publications Allahabad 1957.

32. Oertel, H — Jaiminiya Upanisad Brahmana, Published in the Journal of American Oriental Society. Vol. XVI, 1894.

33. Radhakrishnan, S — Indian Philosophy 2nd ed. 1929. George Allen and Unwin Ltd London, eight impression, 1958.

34. —do— — The Principal Upanisads, George Allen and Unwin, 1953.

35. Sāmaśramī, Ācārya Satyavrata — Airtareyalocanam, Asiatic Society of Bengal, Calcutta, 1906.

Abbreviations

AA	:	Aitareya Āraṇyaka
AB	:	Aitareya Brāhmaṇa
AV	:	Atharvaveda
Ap. Dh. S.	:	Āpastamba Dharma Sūtra
BU	:	Bṛhadāraṇyaka Upaniṣad
CU	:	Chāndogya Upaniṣad
G. Dh. S.	:	Gautama Dharma Sūtra
IU	:	Īśa Upanisad
KU	:	Kaṭha Upanisad
Ken. Up	:	Kena Upaniṣad
Maha. U	:	Mahānārāyana Upanisad
MS	:	Maitrāyanī Saṁhitā
MU	:	Muṇḍaka Upaniṣad
RV	:	Ṛgveda
SA	:	Sankhāyana Aranyaka
ŚB	:	Śatapatha Brahmana
SVU	:	Śvetaśvatara Upanisad
SV	:	Sāmaveda
TA	:	Taittirīya Āraṇyaka
TB	:	Taittirīya Brāhmaṇa
TS	:	Taittirīya Saṁhitā
T.Dh.S.	:	Vaśiṣṭha Dharma Sūtra
VS	:	Vajasaneya-Saṁhitā
YV	:	Yajurveda.

Śikṣā Śāstra and Accental Semantics

4

Veda Vāridhi P. Rāmānujan

'नमों वाचे याचोंदिता याचानुदिता तस्यैं वाचे नामों नमों वाचे नमों वाचस्पतये नम ऋषिभ्यो मन्त्रकृद्धयो मन्त्रपतिभ्यं' (तै. आ. ७.१.१)

Introduction

In this paper, an attempt is made to describe the phonetic aspects of Sanskrit language, especially Vedic Sanskrit, for purposes of appreciating their significance and exploring ways of representing and using them for speech analysis-recognition in Computational platforms like multi-media based linguistic systems. Specifically, semantic variations denoted by accental differences in Vedic texts are dealt with for better understanding of Vedic analyses.

The Ancient Indian Science of Phonetics **(śikṣā)** is first of the six auxiliary branches of study (vedāṅga -śikṣā is likened to the nose of vedas) for the proper interpretation and understanding of vedas. The other vedāṅgas are : **chandas** (Metrics) - feet, **kalpa** (ritual Directory) - **jyautiṣa** (astronomy)-eyes, **nirukta** (Etymology) - ears and **vyākaraṇa** (Grammar - mouth (pā.śi. 41-42).

Many sages like *pāṇini, vyāsa, bhāradvāja, yājñavalkya, nārada, āpiśali, pāri* etc. have described Phonetics, and as such different śikṣā works are attributed to them. Some of these are common for all vedas while some are specific to certain veda/sākhā. Here, we shall concern with *pāṇinīya śikṣā* for further discussions. This wok is the form of sixty verses and references to them here would be by their verse number. According to panini, the purpose of the Science is to clarify the proper pronunciation of utterances (vācaḥ uccāraṇvidhi vyaktikaraṇam - pā. śi 2).

Contents of śikṣā śāstra

As per *taittirīyāraṇyaka*, śikṣā deals with the pronunciation of the character set of Sanskrit language at varṇa, svara, mātrā, bala, sāma and santāna levels. शीक्षां व्यांख्यास्यामः। वर्णः स्वरः। मात्रा. बलम्। सामं सन्तानः। इत्युक्तः शींक्षेध्यायः।। (तै. आ. ५.२.१.) What these signify is further discussed.

vernaḥ : literals (vowels, consonants etc) beginning with a. These total 63 or 64 (pā. śi. 3) twenty-one *svaras* (Vowels), twenty-five sparśas (stops), eight beginning with *ya* (four semi-vowels and four fricatives), four yamas (doubled characters under specified circumstances-explained in prāttiśākhyas), anusvāra visarga, jihvāmūlīya, upadhmānīya ḷakāra and ḻkāra pluta (pā.śi. 4-5).

svaraḥ : accent or intonation of three basic types, viz., udātta (acute), anudātta (grave) and svarita (circumflex).

mātrā : duration of utterance-hrasva (short), dirgha (long) and pluta (prolated) for vowels.

balam : covers places of origin (eight) of sound and effort of articulation (internal and external).

sāma : balanced way of pronunciation (pā. śi. 31) having acceptable qualities (pā. śi. 33, 36-37) and without defects (pā. śi. 32, 34-35).

santānah : Euphonic combinations (including their absence at specified situations).

The process of sound production

After a living 'being' (ātman) comes into contact with things through intellect, it stimulates the mind with the desire to express (its experiences). The mind triggers the body-fire which directs the inner air column. The air moving in the cardiac region produces a type of sound called *'mandra'* in the mornings having *gāyatrī* as the metre, in the thoracic region in the afternoon produces *'madhyama'* type of sound having *triṣṭup* as the metre and in the cerebral region in the evenings produces *'tāra'* type of sound having *jagatī* as the metre. This uprising air column reaches the mouth after hitting the head region and produces all the varṇas (characters or literals) which are classified in five ways. (pā. śi. 6-9).

Parameters of varṇas

svara (accent), **kāla** (time), **sthāna** (place of utterance), *prayatna* (effort) and **anupradāna** (external effort) are the five factors that characterise varnas.

svaras (accents) are three as udātta (acute), anudātta (grave) and svarita (circumflex). The musical nature of these tones is referred to by attributing specific notes in the fundamental scale of music as : udātta-niṣāda (seventh) and gāndhāra (third), anudātta-rsabha (second) and dhivata (sixth) and svarita ṣadja (first), madhyama (fourth) and pañcama (fifth).

kāla (time) is hrasva (short), dīrgha (long) or pluta (prolated) for vowels.

sthānas are eight-uraḥ (chest), kaṇṭhaḥ (throat), śirah (head), jihvāmūlaṃ (root of the tongue), dantāḥ (teeth), nāsikā (nose), oṣṭhṭu (lips) and tālu (palate) (pā. śi. 10-13).

prayatna (ābhyantara-internal effort) is of four types as spṛṣṭa iṣatspṛṣṭa, vivṛta and saṃvṛta (pā. śi. 38).

anupradāna (the external effort - bāhyaprayatna) is eleven types as vivāraḥ, saṃvāraḥ, śvāsaḥ, nādaḥ, ghoṣaḥ, aghoṣaḥ, alpaprāṇah mahāprāṇaḥ udāttaḥ anudattāḥ and svaritaḥ.

Word Accents–Hand Indication

The accents have places of indication on the right hand, udātta is indicated by the index finger placed on the root of the forefinger. Ring finger is used for indicating svarita and middle finger for pracaya, anudātta is indicated on the little finger (pā. śi. 43-44). *yājñavalkya śikṣā* gives a very detailed account of hastacālanavidhi for śuklayajurveda. It is insisted that Vedic recitation without hand indication for accents is detrimental to the utterer (pā. si. 54) while with it the reciter attains supreme bliss (pā. śi. 55). The correlation between accents, their attendant physiological effects, particularly at brain, tongue and finger-tips etc. is the subject study in neurolinguistics.

Accented word-types

There are nine types accented words as (ending in udātta) antodātta, (beginning with udātta) ādyudātta, anudātta, nīcasvarita (svarita preceded by anudātta, madhyodātta (middle udātta), svarita, words with two udāttas and the three udāttas (pā. śi. 45). Their examples are : अग्नि सोमः, प्र, वः, वीर्यम् हविषांम्, स्वः, बृहस्पतिः, इन्द्राबृहस्पती respectively. (pā. śi. 46-47). Places of accents are hṛdaya (heart) for anudātta, mūrdhā (head) for udātta, karṇamūla (root of the ear) for svarita and sarvāsya (entire mouth) for pracaya (pā.śi. 48).

The standard for the svaras (tones) are the sounds produced by : ṣaḍja-mayūra (peacock), ṛṣabha - gau (cattle), gādhāra - ajāvika (goat and sheep), madhyama-krauñca (curlew), pañcama-pika (cuckoo), dhivata-vājī (horse) and niṣāda-gaja (elephant). The standard measure of kāla is mātrā (mora) which is specified for one, two, three and half mātrās (corresponding to vowels (short, long, prolated) and consonants) is respectively that of the sounds produced by caṣa (blue jay), vāyasa (crow), śikhī (peacock) and nakula (mongoose) (pā. śi. 49).

Method of Pronunciation

The instruction for uttering Vedic characters is like a tigress applying just the right amount of pressure while carrying its cubs by mouth; neither to hurt by teeth nor let them fall (pā. śi.25) **yājñavalkya** is more specific for certain types of characters, e.g.

The consonant *ha* when originating from chest (aurasya) is to be pronounced like the sound of clouds, kettle drum (dundubhi), water springing from a deep pond or the roar of a lion, like the sound of clouds in the month of bhādrapada or the sound reaching a cave, illustrated by शुकं दुंहुहे (शु. य. सं. ३.१६) *śukraṃ duduhrē.*

For the guttural hakāra, he specifies the sound of monkeys climbing down and up in tree branches, illustrated in the hymn इहेहैषां (शु. य. सं. १०.३२) *ihēhaiṣāṃ* to stress that there should be pause between anudātta, udātta and svarita accents.

Between similar conjuncts, a pause of one mora is specified analogous to a lustful cock's utterance, illustrated by कुक्कु टोऽसि (शु. य. सं. १.१६) *kukkuṭōsi.*

For ñakāra pronunciation, he illustrates with the word युञ्जानः (शु. यः सं. ११.१) *yuñjānaḥ* that it should be like a mother kissing her son.

For nakāra pronunciation, he illustartes with the word सदुन्दुभे (शु. य. सं.) *sadundubhē* that is should be like a mare contracting and expanding her vulva on seeing a horse.

For *makāra followed by pavarga,* he cites the bellowing action of a frog's stomach region as the way of pronunciation, illustrating with the words अपां फेनेन (शु. य. सं. ११.७१) *apāṃ phēnēna.*

For pronouncing visarga, the instruction is like the puffing (exhaling), of men carrying heavy load, illustrated by अभ्यः सम्भृतः (शु. य. सं.) *adbhyaḥ sambhṛtaḥ*

For the Vedic anusvāra, the preceding vowel becomes heavy (guru) and is to be pronounced like the moans of a lustful woman illustrated by सिण्ह्यसि (शु. य. सं. ५.१२) *siṃhyasi.*

Similarly, *long vowels which are also heavy* as illustrated in वार्ध्रीनसः (शु. य. सं. २४.३९) *vārdhrīnasaḥ* and are to be pronounced like a vulture spreading his wings in air and contracting (yā. śi. uttarārdha, varṇoccārādhikārah. 59-68).

Vedic accents-types

Vedic accents are pitch or musical accents in that they involve rise and fall of voice. The *udātta* (ut-uccaiḥ... ādīyate- uccāryate), which is the main accent in a word, means 'raised' and the rise in one of pitch or musical tone. This main accent also affects the pronunciation of the following syllable, as the restoration of voice to normal level is effected during its utterance. The accent of a syllable immediately following an *udātta* is termed *svarita* which is described as a samāhāra or combination of raised and not raised *(anudātta)* voices. The main accent also affects the pronunciation of its preceding syllable, which is pronounced lower than normal and is termed *sannatara* by pāṇini. The other unaccented syllables are all *anudāttas.* Thus, out of the main accent of a word arise four different varieties of pitch, viz., *udātta, anudatta, svarita* and *sannatara.*

Words defective with regard to literals or accents or wrongly applied do not denote their intended meanings. Such an utterance becomes vajra (deadly, lethal) and destroys the utterer as in the case of the word *indraśatru* (slayer of Indra) where, due to the mistake in the accent uttered, one who was supposed to have killed *indra,* got killed by him (pā. śi. 52).

Accental Semantics

A difference in accent accounts for a difference of meaning. As an illustration, the word ***'yaśas'*** is neutral gender and means 'fame' when *ya* is acute, while the same word means 'famous' and becomes masculine when *śa* is acute. Examples are : द्युम्नितमं यशः (ऋ. सं. ८.१९.६); यशसं वीरवत्तमम् (ऋ. सं. १.१.३); त्वमिन्द्र यशा असि (ऋ. सं. ८.१०.५); etc. Similarly, the word ***'brahman'*** is neutral and means sacred utterance, the supreme being, true knowledge or penance (Cf. amarakośa 3.3.114 - vedastattvaṃ tapo *brahma, brahmā* vipraḥ prajāpatiḥ) when *bra* is acute, while it is masculine and means when *ma* is acute. For example, **ब्रह्म ब्रह्मा**ऽभेवथ्स्वयम् (तै. का. ३.९.३)

Other examples of *words identical in form but distinguished by accent* could be :

1. **ते** - *they, those* (nom, pl. of the base तद्) as in ते तें पिबन्तु जिह्वयां (ऋ. सं. १.१४.८) and ते - *to thee* (dat. sg. of the base युष्मद्), as illustrated in ये **ते** पन्थाः सवितः पूर्व्यासः (ऋ. सं. १.३५.११);

2. **दासः** *servant, slave* (substantive), as in स्त्रयं दास उरो अंसावपि ग्ध (ऋ. सं. १.१५८.५), while **दासः** servile (adjective) illustrated in यो दास वर्णमधरं गुहाकः (ऋ. सं. २.१२.४);

3. **धर्मन्** - neuter, meaning *ordinance, (solemnity, stay)* as in दिवो **धर्मन्** धरुणें सेदुषो नृन् (ऋ. सं. ५.१५.२) as against **धर्मन्** masc. *ordainer, upholder*, as in **धर्मा** भुवद्वृजन्यस्य राजा (ऋ. सं. ९.९७. २३);

4. **दामन्** - neuter, *cord, rope*, as in यद्वाजिनो **दाम** सन्दानमर्वतः (ऋ. सं. १.१६२.८.) as against **दामन्** - masc. *bestower*, as in रायो **दामा** मतीनाम् (ऋ. सं. ६. ४४. २);

5. **द्वादश** - *twelve*, illustrated by वेद मासो धृतव्रतो द्वादश प्रजावतः ऋः सं. १.२५.८) as against **द्वादश** - *twelfth* as in देवहितिं जुगुपुर्द्वादशस्य (ऋ. सं. ७.१०३.९);

6. **भूमन्** - neuter, *earth*, as in चर्मेवोदभिर्व्युन्दन्ति **भूम** (ऋ. सं. १.८५.५.) as against **भूमन्** - masc. *abundance* as in सौधन्वनासश्चिरितस्य **भूमना**ऽगच्छत; अपां **भूमानमुपे** नः सृजेह (ऋ. सं. १.११०.२.१०. ९८. ९२);

7. **युवभ्याम्** - *to you two* as in अरमिन्द्राग्नी मनसे **युवभ्याम्** (ऋ. सं. १.१०८.२) as against **युवभ्याम्** - *to the two youths*, from the stem *yuvan*, as in नमो युवभ्यो नम आशिनेभ्यः; ससान मर्यो युवेभिर्मखस्यन् (ऋ. सं. १.२७.१३, ३.३१.७.);

8. **रक्षः** - neuter, *demonhood, (injury ?)*, as in इन्द्राग्नी **रक्ष** उब्जतम् (ऋ. सं. १.२१.५) as against **रक्षः** - masc. *demon*, as in अपसेधन्**रक्षसो** यातुधानान्; यो वां **रक्षाः** शुचिरस्मीत्याह (ऋ. सं. १.३५.१०, ७.१०४. १६);

9. **वरिमन्** - *neuter, expanse* as in मितज्ञवो **वरि**मत्रा पृथिव्याः (ऋ. सं. ३.५९.३) as against **वरिमन्** - *masc. expanse*, as in दिवश्चिदस्य **वरिमा** वि पप्रथे (ऋ. सं. १.५५.१) etc.

Accents as word-category denoters

It is noteworthy here that words denote different class of objects when accented differently, i.e., accents have a link to the objects referred to by them. As a generalisation, we see words ending in udātta are substantives (cf. phiṭ sūtra of *śāntanava*-phiṣo'nta udāttaḥ), while those with initial accent are adjectives, as these amount to an implied bahuvrīhi compound interpretation, i.e. 'one or that which has (*word stem meaning*)'. This point deserves deeper consideration as it has a good potential in guiding speech recognition, in terms of supplying 'expected' categories of word and lexical category search.

Compound words in Sanskrit have their meanings derived using the grammar rules wherein the constituent nominal stem meanings, suffix meanings and the compounding (or sambandha) meanings are involved. While a same surface form of a derived word could have two or more different processes of derivation with their different semantics, the determination of the appropriate meaning in a given context may be possible by considering the accents.

Illustrations of meaning change due to accent-change

To illustrate, the word *'indraśatruḥ'* which is a compound word, has two constituents, viz., indra and satruḥ, where śatru means a killer. In the case of *bahuvrīhi* compounding इन्द्रंशत्रुः, the first word retains its orginal accent and hence *i* is acute and the word would mean 'one whose killer is indra'. Alternately, if the second word is accented, i.e. *tru* is acute इन्द्रशत्रुः (this compounding is called *tatpuruṣa)* it would mean 'indra's killer'. A Vedic episode explains how a mistake committed in reciting this word in a sacrifice by **tvaṣṭā** resulted in a counter-productive consequence यदब्रवीथ्स्वाहेन्द्रंशत्रुर्वर्धस्वेति तस्मादस्येन्द्रः शत्रुरभवत् (तै. सं. २.५.२.१).

A similar example is quoted by sage patañjali in mahābhāṣya regarding the word **'sthūlapṛṣatī'** appearing as an adjective of a sacrificial cow स्थूलपृषतीमाग्निवारुणीमनड्वाहीमालभेत, which when resolved as tatpuruṣa स्थूलपृषती (sthūlā ca sā pṛṣadvatī ca), would have *ṣa* acute and mean 'big (fat) and spotted', while as a bahuvrīhi compound स्थूलपृंषती (तै. सं. ५.६.१२) (sthūlāni pṛṣanti yasyāḥ sā) - as opposed to क्षुद्रपृंषती (तै. सं. ५.६.१२), *sthū* would be acute and mean 'one whose spots are big.' Obviously, one has to be precise in choosing the proper type of the cow (cow is big and *has* spots or *cow* with big spots).

Range of accent meanings

In general, pāṇini has referred to various aspects of speech like :
vidhi (optative),
anujñaiṣaṇā (seeking permission),
āmantraṇa (giving free choice),
nimantraṇa (invitation for a particular thing),
prārthanā (request), *āśiṣ* (benediction),

atisarga (seeking permission for a free choice),
praisa (order),
kāmapravēdana (expressing one's purpose),
adhīṣṭa (polite),
sambāvanā (probability),
anavakḷpti (impossibility),
kriyāprabandha (continuity),
kriyātipatti (condition),
kriyāsamabihāra (iterative)
samuccaya (simultaneity),
sampraśna (ascertaining by question),
hētumat (causative),
hētuhētumat (cause-effect),
prāptakāla (occasion),
icchā (desire),
āśaṃsā (hope)
abhijñāvacana (recollection),
garhā and bhāvagarhā (derogatory and that affecting action only),
parīpsā (hurry),
amarṣa (bad feeling, ire),
citrīkaraṇa (wonder),

prahāsa (ridicule) etc. while prescribing verbal tense/mood markers and describing sentence accents etc. Thus, a same word to convey different aspect from among these is accented (stressed) variously and thus, the accents are helpful in determining the speaker's intentions. (Cf. *bhartṛhari* in *vākyapadīya* on word-meaning relation,...kālo vyaktiḥ **svarā**dayaḥ...)

Experimental Indications

It is also seen in neuro-linguistic studies that the processing of natural language speech in the human brain is markedly different for noun and verb-forms and that ambiguous words with both these roles possible are processed in a peculiar fashion (e.g. a word like ***'rock'***). Details of tongue, lip and even tip of the fingers experiencing electric wave flow while thinking and problem-solving, is brought forth by modern experiments. Even changing beliefs and habits by using neuro-linguistic programming has been shown to be effective. Thus, involuntarily, a perfect system for preserving Vedic texts free of any distortion, as also to ensure perfect physical and mental health (thoroughly uniform utilisation of all regions of brain and its activities as shown by Prof. Poppel's experiments) are achieved by the study of śikṣā sāstra.

More examples/discussion

We could cite many examples of the same words being nouns and verbs in isolation, derived through different root-suffix combinations, determined on the basis of accents (e.g, तस्मात्रानादेवत्यानि सन्ति वायव्यान्युच्यन्ते (तै. सं. ६.४.६.७.); *[nānadēvatyāni] santi* - is a noun here;

अङ्गिरसः सुवर्गं लोकं यतः पुरोडाशः कूर्मो भूत्वानुप्रासर्पत् (तै. सं. ५.२.८.४); *yataḥ [purōḍāśaḥ] - yataḥ* is a noun here [mas. acc. plural in śatr ending], only *yataḥ* derived from *yad* pronoun, as its suffix *tasil* is *lit* - यतः changes verb accents;

yathā - तं नेमिमृभवो यथाऽऽनमस्व सहूतिभिः (तै. सं. २.६.११.१); आ सवः संवितुर्यथा भगस्येव भुजिः हुवे (तै. सं. ३.१.११.८); when meaning similarity or analogy, *yathā* is unaccented - यथा ; [as in these two cases] and does not accent verbs and only *yathā* derived from *yad* pronoun, as its suffix *thāl* is *lit* - यथा change verb accents).

Pānini has enumerated various circumstances for the change of default accents for nouns, verbs, particles, compounds, affixes etc. in aṣṭādhyāyi. Few examples are :

1. the word ***viśvāhā*** occurring at the beginning of the foot of a verse with four different accent patterns [with the first shown form meaning *'one who destroys all* (hostile)', while the other three forms having the same meaning as *'always, at all times'* or lit. *'on all days'*] -

(i) इन्द्रो नस्तत्र वृत्रहा विश्वाहा शर्म यच्छतु (तै. सं. ४.६.४.५); पदपाठे – विश्वाहेति विश्व – हा। इङ्ग्यं समस्तं पदम्।

(ii) ते गृहासो मधुश्चुतो विश्वहाऽस्मै शरणास्सन्त्वत्र; and तिलवथ्सा ऊर्जमस्मै दुहाना विश्वाहा सन्त्वनपस्फुरन्तीः (तै. आ. ४.७.१)। पदपाठे – (?) पदद्वयं यद्वा आरण्यकशिक्षया स्वरस्य साधुत्वम् ?

(iii) तत्रा रथमुप शग्मः संदेम *विश्वाहा* वयः सुमनस्यमानाः (तै. सं. ४.६.३)। पदपाठे-विश्वाहेति विश्वा – अहं-समस्तं इङ्ग्यं पदम्।

(iv) सिद्धामहा अवटमुद्रिणं वयं विश्वाहाऽदेस्तमक्षितम् (तै. सं. ४.२.५.५)। पदपाठे – *विश्वा*। अहा। इति व्यस्तं अनिङ्ग्यं पदद्वयम्।,

2. the word *indrāgni* (three accent patterns).

(i) तास्सृष्ट्वा **इन्द्राग्नी** अपागूहताम् (तै. सं. २.२.१.१); पदपाठे-इन्द्रग्नी तीन्द्र अग्नी।

(ii) उभा वामिन्द्राग्नी आहुवध्यै (तै. सं. १.१.१४.१); पदपाठे-इन्द्राग्नी इतीन्द्र- अग्नी।

(iii) **इन्द्राग्नी** आ गतम् (तै. सं. १.१.१४.१); पदपाठे-इन्द्राग्नी- इतीन्द्रे अग्नी।

3. the word ***dyāvāpṣthivi*** (three accent patterns).

(i) इदं द्यावापृथिवी भद्रमभूत् (तै. सं. २.६.९.५); पदपाठे-द्यावापृथिवी इति द्यावा-पृथिवी।

(ii) अन्तस्ते दधामि **द्यावापृथिवी** अन्तरुर्वन्तरिक्षम् (तै. सं. १.४.३.१); पदपाठे-द्यावापृथिवी इति द्यावा - पृथिवी।

(iii) इन्द्राग्नी **द्यावापृथिवी** आप ओषधीः (तै. सं. १.२.१.२); पदपाठे-द्यावापृथिवी इति द्यावा - पृथिवी

4. and *vājayanataḥ* (accent change causing it to be a single word or a compound word)

(i) अश्याम वाजमभि **वाजयन्तो**ऽश्यामं द्युम्नं (तै. सं. १.३.१४.३); पदपाठे-वाजयन्तः। व्यस्तं पदम् (क्यजन्तम् ?)

(ii) त्वया वाजं **वाजयन्तो** जयेम (तै. सं. १.४.४६.३); **वाजयन्तो** हवामहे (तै. ब्रा. २.४.६.४); पदपाठे-वाजयन्त इति वाज-यन्तः। इङ्गच्यम् समस्तं पदम्।

Verbal accents as sentence delimiters

The author's study of about 30000 verbal forms occurring in taittirīya saṃhitā have revealed many interesting aspects of word-meaning relations thru' accents. Verbal accents are dealt with in great detail in aṣṭādhyāyī and are quite significant in semantic extraction at sentence level. All words are unaccented except one syllable (anudāttaṃ padamekavarjam- aṣṭādhyāyī 6.1.158) is the default rule. Then, verbs are all unaccented except at the beginning of a foot of a hymn (anudāttaṃ sarvamapādādau- aṣṭādhyāyī 8. 1. 18) or when in association with the pronomial forms of yad (yadvṛttānnityam-aṣṭādhyāyī 8.1.66) or with certain particles designated nipāta etc (nipātairyadyadihanta ... - aṣṭādhyāyī. 8.1.80) or when followed by another verb (tiṅnatiṅḥ-aṣṭādyāyī 8.1.28). By default the verb is unaccented as in—पराऽस्य भ्रातृव्यो भवति (तै. सं. ३.४.६.२); पदपाठे-भवति.

A few sample illustrations of accented verbs are :

पादादौ-वेदाहमेतं पुरुषं महान्तम् (तै. आ. ३.७.७.); असि यमो अस्यादित्यः (तै. सं. ४.६.७.१);

तिङ्तिङः -ता विष्णो पाहि पाहि यज्ञम् (तै. सं. १.१.११.२) (प्रथमं - पाहि; द्वितीयं - पाहि); सर्वं पाप्मानं तरति तरति ब्रह्महत्यां (तै. सं. ५.३.॥१२.१-२); स्वेन भागधेयेनोपधावति धावति वाजम् (तैय सं. २.२.४.६); पिबन्तु मदन्तु वियन्तु सोमम् (तै. ब्रा. २. ६. ११.१०); तस्माद्यज्ञोपवीत्येवाधीयीत याजयेद्यजेत व यज्ञस्य प्रसृत्यै (तै. आ. २.१.१) तिङन्तत्रयं; यस्माद्भीषाऽवेविष्ठाः पलायिष्ठास्समर्ज्ञास्थाः (तै. ब्रा. ३.७.८.२) - तिङन्तत्रयं एकमुपसृष्टं; यथ्सञ्चरेत्युपविशेत्युत्तिष्ठते च (तै. आ. ६.६४.१); उपसृष्टं तिङन्तत्रयं आश्रावयास्तुश्रौषड्यजयेयजामहे वषट्कारः (तै. सं. १.६.११.२); तिङन्तपञ्कम् ?

यद्वृत्तात्-अग्ने यं यज्ञमध्वरं विश्वतः परिभूरसि (तै. सं. ४.१.११.१); यस्यं समुद्रं रसयो सहाऽऽहुः (तै. सं. ४.१.८.४-५)। (पदकाले आहुः); अन्यत्र-ऋषय एनसाऽऽहुः (तै. सं. ३.२.८. १-२); - पदकाले आहुः; प्राच्यां दिशि त्वमिन्द्रासि राजोतोदीच्यां वृत्रहन्वृत्रहाऽसि (तै. सं. २.४.१४.१); पदपाठे-वृत्रहेति वृत्र-हा। असि।। Here, as accented and unaccented forms both give rise to the same surface (combined) form, the study of accent change is necessary for proper vākyānta vēṣṭana during krama-pātha i.e, = वृत्रहा + असि = वृत्रहाऽसि वृत्रहा + असि = वृहाऽसि;

(निपातैर्यद्यदि... ?); अवं चोक्षति प्र चं किरति शुद्धयै (- उक्षतिं - तै. सं. ६.२.७.४); यदिं बिभीयाहुश्चर्मां भविष्यामीतिं (- बिभीयात् - तै. सं. २.२.१०.३);

हि प्राप्त्या - आपो हि ष्ठा मंयोभुवं: (तै. सं. ४.१.५.१); देवा ह्योतमैन्धेत (तै. सं. २.५.९.१) . In long prose form of brāhmaṇa texts, sentence demarcation is easily done with the accent study, kalpasūtra and mīmāṃsāśāstra also deal these considerably.

Specialities of Vedic Sanskrit

The accentual system as occurring in the Vedic texts and as described by pāṇini in aṣṭādhyāyī (vyākaraṇa) sometimes show difference and hence a set of works called prātiśākhyas specific to individual Vedic branches are also needed to study accents. [These could be included under sikṣā vedānga]. Besides these, there are also many other lakṣaṇa-granthas which describe Vedic Phonetics.

The various phonetic processes in the Vedas include, character set actually used in particular śākhās, exceptions to pragṛhyas, doubling, elision, elongation, aumements, modification, cerebralization, aspiration, euphonic combinations, distinction and unitzation (anaikya and aikya), sub-types of the accents (anudātta as dīrgha, vikrama etc. svarita as nitya, kṣaipra, praśliṣṭa prātihata, pādavrtta, tairovyañjana, abhinihata etc.), hand-signs for accents, kevala and misra anusvāras of different kinds in different śākhās, kampa, ranga-pluta, svaabhaki and its types and description of the various varṇakrama parameters.

varṇa-krama pāṭha (Vedic syllable characterisation)

As an excellent means of preserving the Vedic texts free of distortions in oral transmission, the utimate step of describing every Vedic literal is practised which is know as varṇa-kram pāṭha. varṇakrama is of five types as : śuddha varṇa-krama, svåra varṇa-krama, mātrā varṇa-kram, aṅga varṇa-krama, and varṇasāra varṇa-krama.

("kevalaḥ savarasaṃyuktaḥ m̐atrikāsahitastathā.
aṅgaṃ ca varṇasāram ca pañca varṇakramāh smṛtāḥ..").

In the last, we have the complete information of Vedic texts. This is brought out in the following verses :

"dhvanih sthānaṃ prayatno devatā tatah.
jātiraṅgaṃ variṇasañjñā vyañjanānaṃ vidhiyate.." [for consonants 8 parameters],
"acāmēvaṃ prōcymānē dhvanyādau ca yathākramam.
prayatnadēvayōrmadhyē mātrākālah prakīrtaḥa.." [for vowels 8 parameters],
"udāttāpi svaāṇāṃ tu dhvanyādin parīvarjayet.
tathāpi devatājāti guṇarekhāvidarśanam..

adhyetraṅgādyavasthāñca ṣaḍjādisvarakāraṇam.
svotpatti sthānakaṃ caiva svasañjñāñcānupūraśaḥ.." [for accents 10 parameters],
"ye dharmāḥ śuddhavarṇe to śāstroktā iha tānapi.
saṃyojya tatra tatraiva bhakti raṅgādikān vadet..
vyañjanasyāṣṭadhā dharmāḥ svarasyaiva tathāṣṭadhā.
nīcōccādi svarāṇāṃ tu daśa dharmāḥ prakīrtitāḥ..
vyañjanōccādisaṃyykta svarasyaikasya vai punaḥ.
śaḍviṃśadadīritā dharmāḥ ka ityēṣa udāhṛtaḥ... [total per syllable 26 parameters].
imaṃ budhā **varnasāra bhūtavarṇakaramaṃ** viduḥ."

These constiute the twenty-six parameters for each syllabic definition. Given below is the typical Vedic character set with these details.

''नाद ध्वनि जनित नात्युपसंहृत हनु स्थान तथाभूतोष्ठ करण संवृत प्रयत्न एक मात्रिक वायु देवताक ब्राह्मण जाति ह्रस्व संज्ञा सहित **अकार**'',

''नाद ध्वनि जनित नातिव्यस्त हनु स्थान तथाभूतोष्ठ करण विवृत प्रयत्न द्वि मात्रिक वायु देवताक ब्राह्मण जाति दीर्घ संज्ञा सहित **आकार**''.

''नाद ध्वनि जनित नातिव्यस्त हनु स्थान तथाभूतोष्ठ करण विवृत प्रयत्न त्रि मात्रिक वायु देवताक ब्राह्मण जाति विशिष्ट **अवर्ण प्लुत**'',

''नाद ध्वनि जनित तालु स्थान नात्यपसंहृतोष्ठ जिह्वामध्य करण विवृत प्रयत्न एक मात्रिक अग्नि देवताक ब्राह्मण जाति ह्रस्व संज्ञा सहित **इकार**'',

''नाद ध्वनि जनित तालु स्थान नात्युपसंहृतोष्ठ जिह्वामध्य करण वितृत प्रयत्न द्वि मात्रिक अग्नि देवताक ब्राह्मण जाति दीर्घ संज्ञा सहित **ईकार**'',

''नाद ध्वनि जनित तालु स्थान नात्युसंहृतोष्ठ जिह्वामध्य करण विवृत प्रयत्न त्रि मात्रिक अग्नि देवताक ब्राह्मण जाति विशिष्ट **इवर्ण प्लुत**'',

''नाद ध्वनि जनित दीर्घोन्नतोपसंहृत उत्तरोष्ठ स्थान तथाभूत अधरोष्ठ करण विवृत प्रयत्न एक मात्रिक भूमि देवताक ब्राह्मण जाति ह्रस्व संज्ञा सहित **उकार**'',

''नाद ध्वनि जनित दीर्घोन्नतोपसंहृत उत्तरोष्ठ स्थान तथाभूताधरोष्ठ करण विवृत प्रयत्न द्वि मात्रिक भूमि देवताक ब्राह्मण जाति दीर्घ संज्ञा सहित **ऊकार**'',

''नाद ध्वनि जनित दीर्घोन्नतोपसंहृत उत्तरोष्ठ स्थान तथाभूत अधरोष्ठ करण विवृत प्रयत्न त्रि मात्रिक भूमि देवताक ब्राह्मण जाति विशिष्ट **उवर्ण प्लुत**'',

''नाद ध्वनि जनित उत्तर दन्त मूलोपरि भाग स्थान नात्युपसंहृतोष्ठ उपसंहृततर हनु जिह्वाग्र करण विवृत प्रयत्न एक मात्रिक इन्दु देवताक ब्राह्मण जाति ह्रस्व संज्ञा सहित **ऋकार**'',

''नाद ध्वनि जनित उत्तर दन्त मूलोपरि भाग स्थान नात्युपसंहृतोष्ठ उपसंहृततर हनु जिह्वाग्र करण विवृत प्रयत्न द्वि मात्रिक इन्दु देवताक ब्राह्मण जाति दीर्घ संज्ञा सहित **ऋकार**'',

''नाद ध्वनि जनित उत्तर दन्त मूलासन्नोपरि भाग स्थान नात्युप संहृतोष्ठ उपसंहृततर हनु जिह्वाग्र करण विवृत प्रयत्न एक मात्रिक अर्क देवताक ब्राह्मण जाति ह्रस्व संज्ञा सहित **ऌकार**'',

''नाद ध्वनि जनित तालूपसंहततर हनुमूलोपरिभाग स्थान ईषत्प्रकृष्टोष्ठ जिह्वामध्यपार्श्व करण विवृत प्रयत्न द्विमात्रिक वायु देवताक ब्राह्मण जाति दीर्घ संज्ञा सहित **अव्यञ्जन एकार**'',

''नाद ध्वनि जनित तालूपसंहततर हनुमूल स्थान ईषत्प्रकृष्टोष्ठ जिह्वामध्य करण विवृत प्रयत्न द्वि मात्रिक वायु देवताक ब्राह्मण जाति दीर्घ संज्ञा सहित **सव्यञ्जन एकार**'',

''नाद ध्वनि जनित नात्युपसंहतहनु स्थान तथाभूतोष्ठ करण संवृत प्रयत्न अर्धमात्रिक आद्यंशभूत अकार, नाद ध्वनि जनित तालु स्थान नात्युपसंहतोष्ठ जिह्वामध्य करण विवृत प्रयत्न अध्यर्धमात्रिक अन्त्यांशभूत इकार, उभयांश द्विमात्रिक अग्नि देवताक ब्राह्मण जाति दीर्घ संज्ञा सहित **ऐकार**'',

''नाद ध्वनि जनित नातिव्यस्तहनु दीर्घोन्नतोपसंहतर उत्तरोष्ठ स्थान तथाभूताधरोष्ठ करण विवृत प्रयत्न द्वि मात्रिक भूमि देवताक ब्राह्मण जीति दीर्घ संज्ञा सहित **ओकार**'',

''नाद ध्वनि जनित नात्युपसंहतहनु स्थान तथाभूतोष्ठ करण संवृत प्रयत्न अर्धमात्रिक आद्यंशभूत अकार, नाद ध्वनि जनित दीर्घोन्नतापासंहतोत्तरोष्ठ स्थान तथाभूताधरोष्ठ जिह्वामध्य करण विवृत प्रयत्न अध्यर्धमात्रिक अन्त्यांशभूत उकार, उकार, उभयांश द्विमात्रिक इन्दु देवताक ब्राह्मण जाति दीर्घ संज्ञा सहित **औकार**'',

''श्वास ध्वनि जनित हनुमूल स्थान जिह्वामूल करण स्पृष्ठ प्रयत्न अर्ध मात्रिक पराङ्गभूत वायु देवताक ब्राह्मण जाति प्रथम सर्श संज्ञा सहित **ककार**'',

''अतिश्वास ध्वनि जनित हनुमूल स्थान जिह्वामूल करण अतिस्पृष्ट प्रयत्न अर्ध मात्रिक पराङ्गभूत अग्नि देवताक ब्राह्मण जाति द्वितीय सर्श संज्ञा सहित **खकार**'',

''नाद ध्वनि जनित हनुमूल स्थान जिह्वामूल कारण स्पृष्ट प्रयत्न अर्थ मात्रिक पराङ्गभूत भूमि देवताक क्षत्रिय जाति तृतीय सर्श संज्ञा सहित **गकार**'',

''हकार ध्वनि जनित हनुमूल स्थान जिह्वामूल करण ईषन्न्यूनाति स्पृष्ट प्रयत्न अर्ध मात्रिक पराङ्गभूत इन्दु देवताक क्षत्रिय जाति चतुर्थ सर्श संज्ञा सहित **घकार**'',

''नाद ध्वनि जनित नासिक विवृति विशिष्ट हनुमूल स्थान जिह्वामूल करण स्पृष्ट प्रयत्न अर्ध मात्रिक पराङ्गभूत अर्क देवताक वैश्य जाति उत्तम सर्श संज्ञा सहित **ङकार**'',

''श्वास ध्वनि जनित तालु स्थान जिह्वामध्य करण स्पृष्ट प्रयत्न अर्थ मात्रिक पराङ्भूत वायु देवताक ब्राह्मण जाति प्रथम सर्श संज्ञा सहित **चकार**'',

''अतिश्वास ध्वनि जनित तालु स्थान जिह्वामध्य करण अतिस्पृष्ट प्रयत्न अर्थ मात्रिक पराङ्गभूत अग्नि देवताक ब्राह्मण जाति द्वितीय सर्श संज्ञा सहित **छकार**'',

''नाद ध्वनि जनित तालु स्थान जिह्वामध्य करण स्पृष्ट प्रयत्न अर्ध मात्रिक पराङ्गभूत भूमि देवताक क्षत्रिय जाति तृतीय सर्श संज्ञा सहित **जकार**'',

''हकार ध्वनि जनित तालु स्थान जिह्वामध्य करण ईषन्नयूनाति स्पृष्ट प्रयत्न अर्ध मात्रिक पराङ्गभूत इन्दु देवताक क्षत्रिय जाति चतुर्थ सर्श संज्ञा सहित **झकार**'',

''नाद ध्वनि जनित नासिका विवृति विशिष्ट तालु स्थान जिह्वाग्र करण स्पृष्ट प्रयत्न अर्थ मात्रिक पराङ्गभूत अर्क देवताक वैश्य जाति उत्तम सर्श संज्ञा सहित **ञकार**'',

''श्वास ध्वनि जनित मूर्ध स्थान प्रतिवेष्टित जिह्वाग्र करण स्पृष्ट प्रयत्न अर्ध मात्रिक पराङ्गभूत वायु देवताक ब्राह्मण जाति प्रथम सर्श संज्ञा सहित **टकार**'',

''अतिश्वास ध्वनि जनित मूर्ध स्थान प्रतिवेष्टित जिह्वाग्र करण स्पृष्ट प्रयत्न अर्भ मात्रिक पराङ्गभूत अग्नि देवताक ब्राह्मण जाति द्वितीय सर्श संज्ञा सहित **ठकार**'',

''नाद ध्वनि जनित मूर्ध स्थान प्रतिवेष्टित जिह्वाग्र करण स्पृष्ट प्रयत्न अर्ध मात्रिक पराङ्गभूत भूमि देवताक क्षत्रिय जाति तृतीय सर्श संज्ञा सहित **डकार**'',

''हकार ध्वनि जनित मूर्ध स्थान प्रतिवेष्टित जिह्वाग्र करण ईषत्र्यूनातिस्पृष्ट प्रयत्न अर्ध मात्रिक पराङ्गभूत इन्दु देवताक क्षत्रिय जाति चतुर्थ सर्श संज्ञा सहित **ढकार**'',

''नाद ध्वनि जनित नासिका विवृति विशिष्ट मूर्ध स्थान प्रतिवेष्टित जिह्वाग्र करण स्पृष्ट प्रयत्न अर्थ मात्रिक पराङ्गभूत अर्क देवताक वैश्य जाति उत्तम सर्श संज्ञा सहित **'णकार'**,

''श्वास ध्वनि जनित उत्तरदन्तमूलाधोभाग स्थान जिह्वाग्र करण स्पृष्ट प्रयत्न अर्ध मात्रिक पराङ्गभूत वायु देवताक ब्राह्मण जाति प्रथम सर्श संज्ञा सहित **तकार**'',

''अतिश्वास ध्वनि जनित उत्तरदन्तमूलाधोभाग स्थान जिह्वाग्र करण अतिस्पष्ट प्रयत्न अर्ध मात्रिक पराङ्भूत अग्नि देवताक ब्राह्मण जाति द्वितीय सर्श संज्ञा सहित **थकार**'',

''नाद ध्वनि जनित उत्तरदन्तमूलाधोभाग स्थान जिह्वाग्र करण स्पृष्ट प्रयत्न अर्ध मात्रिक पराङ्गभूत भूमि देवताक क्षत्रिय जाति तृतीय सर्श संज्ञा सहित **दकार**'',

''हकार ध्वनि जनित उत्तरदन्तमूलाधोभाग स्थान जिह्वाग्र करण ईषत्रयूनातिस्पृष्ट प्रयत्न अर्ध मात्रिक पराङ्भूत इन्दु देवताक क्षत्रिय जाति चतुर्थ सर्श सहित **धकार**''।

''नाद ध्वनि जनित नासिक विवृति विशिष्ट उत्तरदन्तमूलाधोभाग स्थान जिह्वाग्र करण स्पृष्ट प्रयत्न अर्ध मात्रिक पराङ्गभूत अर्क देवताक वैश्य जाति उत्तम सर्श संज्ञा सहित **नकार**'',

''श्वास ध्वनि जनित उत्तरोष्ठ स्थान अधरोष्ठ करण स्पृष्ट प्रयत्न अर्ध मात्रिक पराङ्भूत वायु देवताक ब्राह्मण जाति प्रथम सर्श संज्ञा सहित **पकार**'',

''अतिश्वास ध्वनि जनित उत्तरोष्ठ स्थान अधरोष्ठ करण अतिस्पृष्ट प्रयत्न अर्ध मात्रिक पराङ्भूत अग्नि देवताक ब्राह्मण जाति द्वितीय सर्श संज्ञा सहित **फकार**'',

''नाद ध्वनि जनित उत्तरोष्ठ स्थान अधरोष्ठ करण स्पृष्ट प्रयत्न अर्ध मात्रिक पराङ्गभूत भूमि देवताक क्षत्रिय जाति तृतीय सर्श संज्ञा सहित **बकार**'',

''हकार ध्वनि जनित उत्तरोष्ठ स्थान अधरोष्ठ करण ईषत्र्यूनाति स्पृष्ट प्रयत्न अर्ध मात्रिक पराङ्भूत इन्दु देवताक क्षत्रिय जाति चतुर्थ सर्श संज्ञा सहित **भकार**'',

''नाद ध्वनि जनित नासिका विवृति विशिष्ट उत्तरोष्ठ करण स्पृष्ट प्रयत्न अर्ध मात्रिक पराङ्गभूत अर्क देवताक वैश्व जाति उत्तम सर्श संज्ञा सहित **मकार**'',

''नाद ध्वनि जनित तालु स्थान जिह्वामध्यपार्श्व करण ईषत्स्पृष्ट प्रयत्न अर्ध मात्रिक पराङ्गभूत वायु देवताक वैश्य जाति (अन्तःस्थ संज्ञा सहित) विशिष्ट **यकार**'',

''नादध्वनि जनित उत्तरदन्तमूलोपरिभाग स्थान जिह्वाग्रमध्य करण ईषत्स्पृष्ट प्रयत्न 'अर्ध मात्रिक पराङ्गभूत अग्नि देवताक वैश्य जाति (अन्तःस्थ संज्ञा सहित) विशिष्ट **रेफ**'',

''नाद ध्वनि जनित उत्तरदन्तमूलासन्नोपरिभाग स्थान जिह्वाग्रमध्य करण ईषत्स्पृष्ट प्रयत्न अर्ध मात्रिक पराङ्गभूत भूमि देवताक वैश्य जाति (अन्तःस्थ संज्ञा सहित) विशिष्ट **लकार**'',

''नाद ध्वनि जनित उत्तरदन्तान्त स्थान अधरोष्ठाभ्यन्तरान्त करण ईषत्स्पृष्ट प्रयत्न अर्ध मात्रिक पराङ्गभूत इन्दु देवताक वैश्य जाति (अन्तःस्थ संज्ञा सहित) विशिष्ट **वकार**'',

''नाद ध्वनि जनित उत्तरदन्तान्त स्थान अधरोष्ठबाह्यान्त करण ईषत्स्पृष्ट प्रयत्न अर्ध मात्रिक पराङ्गभूत इन्दु देवताक वैश्य जाति (अन्तःस्थ संज्ञा सहित) विशिष्ट **ओष्ठ्य स्वरमध्यस्थ वकार**'',

''अतिश्वास ध्वनि जनित तालु स्थान विवृत मध्यजिह्वामध्य करण विवृत प्रयत्न अर्ध मात्रिक पराङ्गभूत वायु देवताक शूद्र जाति (ऊष्म संज्ञा सहित) विशिष्ट **शकार**'',

''अतिश्वास ध्वनि जनित मूर्ध स्थान विवृतमध्य प्रतिवेष्टितजिह्वाग्र करण विवृत प्रयत्न अर्ध मात्रिक पराङ्गभूत अग्नि देवताक शूद्र जाति (ऊष्म संज्ञा सहित) विशिष्ट **षकार**'',

''अतिश्वास ध्वनि जनित उत्तर दन्तमूलाधोभाग स्थान विवृतमध्य जिह्वाग्र करण विवृत प्रयत्न अर्ध मात्रिक पराङ्गभूत भूमि देवताक शूद्र जाति (ऊष्म संज्ञा सहित) विशिष्ट **सकार**'',

''हकार ध्वनि जनित कण्ठोरितनांश स्थान तदधोभाग करण विवृत प्रयत्न अर्ध मात्रिक पराङ्गभूत इन्दु देवताक शूद्र जाति (ऊष्म संज्ञा सहित) विशिष्ट **(कण्ठ्य) हकार**'',

''हकार ध्वनि जनित उरोरितनांश स्थान तदधोभाग करण विवृत प्रयत्न अर्थ मात्रिक पराङ्गभूत इन्दु देवताक शूद्र जाति (ऊष्म संज्ञा सहित) विशिष्ट **(उरस्य) हकार**'',

''अतिश्वास ध्वनि जनित हनुमूल स्थान विवृतमध्य जिह्वामूल करण विवृत प्रयत्न अणु मात्रिक पूर्वाङ्गभूत अर्क देवताक शूद्र जाति (ऊष्म संज्ञा सहित) विशिष्ट **जिह्वामूलीय**'',

अतिश्वास ध्वनि जनित उत्तरोष्ठ स्थान वितृतमध्य अधरोष्ठ करण विवृत प्रयत्न अणु मात्रिक पूर्वाङ्गभूत अर्क देवताक शूद्र जाति (ऊष्म संज्ञा सहित) विशिष्ट **उपध्मानीय**'',

''अतिश्वास ध्वनि जनित कण्ठोरितनांश स्थान तदधोभाग करण विवृत प्रयत्न अर्ध मात्रिक पूर्वाङ्गभूत अर्क देवताक शूद्र जाति विशिष्ट **विसर्जनीय**'',

''नाद ध्वनि जनित नासिका विृति विशिष्ट नासिकोपरिभाग स्थान तदद्योभाग करण विवृत प्रयत्न एक मात्रिक पूर्वाङ्गभूत अर्क देवताक शूद्र जाति विशिष्ट **मिश्रानुस्वार**'',

''नाद ध्वनि जनित विवृत नासिकोपरिभाग स्थान तदधोभाग करण गकाराद्यन्यधर्म विवर्जित विवृत प्रयत्न द्वि मात्रिक पूर्वाङ्गभूत अर्क देवताक शूद्र जाति विशिष्ट **केवलानुस्वार**'',

''नाद ध्वनि जनित उत्तरदन्तमूलोपरिभाग स्थान नात्युपसंहृतोष्ठोप संहततर हनुजिह्वाग्र करण विवृत प्रयत्न आद्यंशभूत अणुमात्रिक ऋकार, नाद ध्वनि जनित उत्तर दन्तोमूलोपरि भाग स्थान जिह्वाग्र मध्य करण ईषत्स्पृष्ट प्रयत्न अन्त्यांशभूत अणुमात्रिक रेफ, उभयांश अर्ध मात्रिक संवृत करण विवृत प्रयत्न पूर्वाङ्गभूत अर्क देवताक शूद्र जाति करेणु संज्ञा विशिष्ट **हलन्ता स्वर भक्ति**'',

''र्/ल्'', ''नाद ध्वनि जनित उत्तरदन्तमूलोपरिभाग स्थान जिह्वाग्रमध्य करण ईषत्स्पृष्ट प्रयत्न आद्यंशभूत अणुमात्रिक रेफ, नाद ध्वनि जनित उत्तर दन्तमूलोपरि भाग स्थान नात्युपसंहृतोष्ठ उपसंहृततर हनु जिह्वाग्र करण विवृत प्रयत्न अन्त्यांशभूत अणुमात्रिक ऋकार, उभयांश अर्ध मात्रिक विवृत करण विवृत प्रयत्न पूर्वाङ्गभूत अर्क देवताक शूद्र जाति कर्विण्यादि संज्ञा विशिष्ट **अजन्ता स्वर भक्ति**'',

''नाद ध्वनि जनित नातिव्यस्तहनु स्थान तथाभूतोष्ठ करण विवृत प्रयत्न निरनुनासिक हृदय कमलोत्थित शार्दूल रुतोबृंहित मन्द्र ध्वनि युत पूर्वाङ्गभूत द्विमात्रिक मूर्ध स्थान जनित कांस्य घण्टा नाद तुल्य कम्प विशिष्ट मध्यम भाग, द्वितीयांशभूत एकमात्रिक नासिका बिलद्वय विनिस्सृत श्रुतिसुखाख्य अव्यक्त सूक्ष्मनाद सहित, तृतीयांश भूत एकमात्रिक सौराष्टिक नारी स्वर सम आद्यन्त्यांशत्रय निरूपित चातुर्मात्रिक वायु देवताक ब्राह्मण जाति विशिष्ट **रङ्ग प्लुत**'',

''भूमि देवताक ब्राह्मण जाति सात्विक गुण सहित तर्जिन्यङ्गुलिमध्य रेखान्यास योग्य अध्येतृदेह दैर्घ्य ध्वनि काठिन्य कण्ठाकाश कृशत्व जनित अजारुतुल्य गन्धार स्वर हेतुभूत मूर्धस्थानोद्भव **उदात्त** स्वर सहित'',

''अग्नि देवताक क्षत्रिक जाति तामस गुण सहित कनिष्ठिकाङ्गुल्याद्य रेखान्यास योग्य अध्येतृदेह ह्रस्वत्व ध्वनि मार्दव कण्ठाकाश महत्त्व जनित वृषरुततुल्य वृषभ स्वर हेतुभूत हृदयस्थानोद्भव **अनुदात्त** स्वर सहित'',

"अग्नि देवताक क्षत्रिय जाति तामस गुण सहित कनिष्ठिकाङ्गुल्याद्य रेखान्यास योग्य अध्येतृदेह ह्रस्वत्व ध्वनि मार्दव कण्ठाकाश महत्त्व जनित केकीकेकारुततुल्य षड्ज स्वर हेतुभूत हृदयस्थानोद्भव **दीर्घानुदात्त** स्वर सहित",

"अग्नि देवताक क्षत्रिय जाति तामस गुण सहित कनिष्ठिकाङ्गुल्याद्य रेखान्यास योग्य अध्येतृदेह ह्रस्व ध्वनि मार्दव कण्ठाकाश महत्त्व जनित वृषरुततुल्य वृषभ स्वर हेतुभूत केकीकेकारुततुल्य षड्ज स्वर हेतुभूत हृदयस्थानोद्भव दृढ़तर प्रयत्न **विक्रमानुदात्त** स्वर सहित",

"इन्दु देवताक वैश्य जाति राजस गुण सहित अनामिकाङ्गुल्यन्त्य रेखान्यास योग्य अध्येतृदेह दैर्घ्य ह्रस्वत्व ध्वनि काठिन्य मार्दव कण्ठाकाश कृशत्व महत्त्व समाहार जनित गजबृंहिततुल्य निषाद स्वर हेतुभूत कर्णमूल स्थानोद्भव दृढतर प्रयत्न **नित्य स्वरित** स्वर सहित",

"इन्दु देवताक वैश्य जाति राजस गुण सहित अनामिकाङ्गुल्यन्त्य रेखा न्यास योग्य अध्येतृदेह दैर्घ्य ह्रस्वत्व ध्वनि काठिन्य मार्दव कण्ठाकाश कृशत्व महत्त्व समाहार जनित गजबृंहिततुल्य निषाद स्वर हेतुभूत कर्णमूल स्थानोद्भव दृढकर प्रयत्न **क्षैप स्वरित** स्वर सहित",

"इन्दु देवताक वैश्व जाति राजस गुण सहित अनामिकाङ्गुल्यन्त्य रेखा न्यास योग्य अध्येतृदेह दैर्घ्य ह्रस्वत्व ध्वनि काठिन्य मार्दव कण्ठाकाश कृशत्व महत्त्व समाहार जनित गजबृंहिततुल्य निषाद् स्वर हेतुभूत कर्णमूल स्थानोद्भव दृढतर प्रयत्न **अभिनिहत स्वर** स्वर सहित",

"इन्दु देवताक वैश्य जाति राजस गुण सहित अनामिकाङ्गुल्यन्त्य रेखा न्यास योग्य अध्येतृदेह दैर्घ्य ह्रस्वत्व ध्वनि काठिन्य मार्दव कण्ठा काश कृशत्व महत्त्व समाहार जनित गजबृंहिततुल्य निषाद स्वर हेतुभूत कर्णमूल स्थानोद्भव मृदुतर प्रयत्न **प्रश्लिष्ट स्वर स्वर सहित",**

"इन्दु देवताक वैश्य जाति राजस गुण सहित अनामिकाङ्गुल्यन्त्य रेखा न्यास योग्य अध्येतृदेह दैर्घ्य ह्रस्वत्व ध्वनि काठिन्य मार्दव कण्ठाकाश कृशत्व महत्त्व समाहार जनित गजबृंहिततुल्य निषाद स्वर हेतुभूत कर्णमूल स्थानोद्भव मृदुतर प्रयत्न **प्रातिहत स्वरित** स्वर सहित",

"इन्दु देवताक वैश्य जाति राजस गुण सहित अनामिकाङ्गुल्यन्त्य रेखान्यास योग्य अध्येतृदेह दैर्घ्य ह्रस्वत्व ध्वनि काठिन्य मार्दव कण्ठाकाश कृशत्व महत्त्व समाहार जनित गजबृंहिततुल्य निषाद स्वर हेतु कर्णमूल स्थानोद्भव अलतर प्रयत्न **तैरोव्यञ्जन स्वरित** स्वर सहित",

"इन्दु देवताक वैश्य जाति राजस गुण सहित अनामिकाङ्गुल्यन्त्य रेखा न्यास योग्य अध्येतृदेह दैर्घ्य ह्रस्वत्व ध्वनि काठिन्य मार्दव कण्ठाकाश कृशत्व महत्त्व समाहार समाहार जनित गजबृंहिततुल्य निषाद स्वर हेतुभूत कर्णमूल स्थानोद्भव अल्पतर प्रयत्न **पादवृत्त स्वरित** स्वर सहित",

"अर्क देवताक शूद्र जाति तामस गुण सहित मध्यामाङ्गुलि मध्य रेखा न्यास योग्य ईषत्र्यून अध्येतृदेह दैर्घ्य तथाभूत ध्वनि काठिन्य कण्ठाकाश कृशत्व जनित क्रौञ्च क्वणनतुल्य मध्यम स्वर हेतुभूत (सर्वाङ्ग(स्य) स्थानोद्भव **प्रचय** स्वर सहित"

Conclusion

Thus, the various phonetic aspects dealt with in the ancient Indian śikṣā śāstras can be an invaluable source of ideas for an objective study of speech processes with the help of state-of-the-art techniques and equipments, so as to serve the purpose of developing utilitarian speech recognition systems for Indian languages. An objective set of evaluation criteria is to be developed to cover all the various śikṣā śāstra, contents (especially Sāmavedic śikṣās) and Vedic texts and their study and structural modelling etc. is to be undertaken. A phonetic database of Vedas is to be the starting point and a multi-disciplinary research involving Computer technologists, Vedic and śāstraic scholars and neuro-scientists etc. is to be initiated to get a proper understanding of the issues, their handling and Ancient Indian Phoneticians' and grammarians' contribution to Natural Language Processing and Understanding.

C-DAC has taken the lead in defining and developing Standards for representing Indian character sets on computer media through the Gist range of products (hardware and software) for various platforms. Annex G of IS 13194 : 1991 on ISCII describes the Vedic accent-marker use thru' Computers. Recently, we have rendered the Rgveda Saṃhitā and Pada-pāṭha computationally. With Yajurvēda (Trittiriya) Saṃhitā, Brāhmar.a, Pada-pāṭha, Sāmavēda (Kauthuma) Saṃhitā and many other texts in Śikṣā, Nirukta, Nighaṇṭu, Prātiśākhya, Sarvānukramaṇikā etc. available in machine-readable form, we wish to endeavour more in the area of accent-meaning analysis in the Vedic module of our *DEŚIKA* software. Nirukta, Nighaṇṭu and such other etymological works are also being integrated into *DEŚIKA* to have Vedic Concordance in a computational form to facilitate such research. Necessary software utilities could also be developed. Efforts for getting the other Vedic texts in machine-readable form are also under way and with divine support, we hope to contribute to this field significantly. We now end with śrī vedāntadeśika's concluding prayer in mīmāṃsā pādukā :

śākyolūkyākṣapāda-kṣapaṇaka-kapilāmartyavandya-pradhānaiḥ
anyairāmnāyacarcākavacadhṛtikanadgomukhadvipibhiśca.
baṃhiyaḥ kṣobhitā'pi srutitiha bahudhā jāyamānena goptrā
kālekāle bhiquptā kalahamatitarantyakṣatā rakṣatānnaḥ..

prīyatāṃ vedavedyo janārdanaḥ, śubhamastu . .

References

(तै. सं. #.#.#.#) -	तैत्तिरीय संहिता. काण्ड. प्रपाठक. अनुवाक. पञ्चाशत् संख्या
(तै. ब्रा. #.#.#.#.) -	तैत्तिरीय ब्राह्मणं. अष्टक. प्रपाठ, अनुवाक. दशति संख्या
(तै. आ. #.#.#) -	तैत्तिरीय आरण्यकं, प्रपाठक, अनुवाकं, दशति संख्या - **द्राविडपाठानुसारेण**
(तै. का. #.#.#.) -	तैत्तिरीय काठकं, प्रपाठक. अनुवाक. दशति संख्या
(ऋ. सं. #.#.#.) -	ऋग्वेद संहिता. मण्डल, सूक्त, मन्त्र संख्या
(शु. य. सं. #.#.) -	शुक्ल यजुः संहिता. प्रपाठक, मन्त्र संख्या
(pā. śi. #.) -	Pāṇinīya śikṣā. ślokasaṅkhyā.
(yā. śi. #) -	Yājñavalkya śikṣā. śikṣā. ślokasaṅkhyā.

1. *Pāṇinīya Śikṣā*, in siddhānta kaumudī + tattvabodhinī, Chowkhamba, *Vārāṇasī*, 1985.
2. *Yājñavalkya Śikṣā*, with śikṣāvallī comm., jyotiṣa prakāśa Press, Vārāṇasī, 1962
3. *The Descriptive Technique of Pāṇini* - By Prof. V. N. Miśra, Mouton & Co. 1966.
4. *Neurolinguistics, Computer and Sanskrit* By P.K. Acharya, ***Sanskrit and Computer,*** (Proc. of UGC National Seminar), Ed. by Dr. K.C. Dash, Pratibha Prakashan, 1995.

Aditi : The Imperishable and a Goddess of Morality

5

Dr. Shrimanta Chattopadhyay

Though Adolf Kaegi, quoting Max Müller, notes that there are passages where Aditi seems to be conceived as a male deity, or, anyhow, as a sexless being.[1] we, along with others, think that Aditi is a female deity. As a symbol of universalism she can at best be a sexless being but never a hermaphrodite. Aditi is said to be the first among the presiding deities in the atmospheric region : *tāsām aditiḥ prathamāgāminī bhavati (Nir. XI : 22 : 2)*. Despite her hymnlessness in the *Ṛgvedasaṁhitā*, as a female deity she occupies a supreme position. The etymological meaning of Aditi and her functions would substantiate our point.

Aditi's etymology can be traced to six roots :

(i) *dīṅ kṣaye (Dhā 1134)* to perish : from this root Aditi means imperishableness.

(ii) *do avakhaṇḍane (Dhā 1148)*

(iii) *dāna khaṇḍane (Dhā 994)*

(iv) *dāp lavaṇe (Dhā 1059)*

From these three different roots all meaning 'to cut'. the all-pervasiveness of Aditi can be reached at. Yaska also remarks : *adınā devamātā (Nir. IV : 2 : 1)*

(v) *ada bhakṣaṇe (Dhā 1011)* to eat : The meaning of Aditi as an omnivore from this root is justified by the Vedic texts : *yad yad evasṛjata tatted attum adhriyata sarvaṁ vā attīti tad aditer adititvam (Bṛ. U. 1 : 2 : 5 : =* ŚB. *x : 6 : 5 : 5).*

(vi) *adi bandhane (Dhā 62)* to bind : This root indicates that the whole world is under the grip of Aditi.

So etymologically Aditi stands for an imperishable, all-comprehending, all-devouring and all-binding goddess.

Aditi used as adjective

The term *aditi* is used as the adjective of different nouns in many a place.

(i) Adj. to sacrifice : The seer, Dırghatamas, says that the sacrifice should end uninterruptedly : *aviāsann aditim uruṣyet (RV. I : 152 : 6d)* whereon Sayana comments *akhaṇḍitaṁ anyūnaṁ etat* (meaning uninterrupted).

(ii) Adj. to Agni : Agni, the imperishable god, should make us sinless in the sacrifice-*anāgastvaṁ adite sarvatātā*.[2]

(iii) Adj. to pressing stones : Avasyu says that when Maruts are about to worship Indra, the undecaying pressing stones meet together : *grāvāṇo aditiḥ sajoṣāḥ* (*RV*. V : 31 : 5b).

(iv) Adj. to river : The wicked maliciously digs out the bank of Parusni, the unvulnerable river—*durodhyā aditim srevayanto 'cetasā vi jagṛbhre paruṣṇīm* (*RV*. VII : 18 : 81b).

(v) Adj. to Gauḥ : None should be envious of faultlessly imperishable Gauh : *Do pra nu vocaṁ cikituṣe janāya mā gām anāgām aditiṁ vadhiṣṭa* (*RV*. VIII : 101 : 15 cd).

(vi) Adj. to boat : The boat, which is broad and undecaying, should not be an object of fear : *suśarmāṇam aditiṁ supraṇītim/daiviṁ nāvam* (*RV*. X : 63 : 10bc).

(vii) Adj. to Aśvins : If the undecaying and imperishable Aśvins, two kings, put a couple on their chariot, no sin can touch them : *Do na taṁ rājānāv adite kutaś cana nāṁho aśnoti duritaṁ nakir bhyam* (*RV*. X : 39 : 11 ab).

(viii) Adj. to Dyāvāpṛthivı : The imperishable Dyāvāpṛthivı are requested to protect us : *dyāvābhūmı adite trāsithāṁnaḥ* (*RV*. IV : 55 : 1b = VII : 62 : 4a).

(ix) Adj to Varuṇa : We, says Vasiṣṭha, perform the duty of the endless Vaurṇa: *anu vratāny aditer ṛdhanto* (*RV*. VII : 87 : 7c) whereon Sāyaṇa comments *adınasya varuṇasya sambandhıni karmāṇi ānupūruyenṇa samardhyanth* (the duties of endless Varuṇa).

(x) Adj to Aśva : The imperishable horse should forgive our sins : *anāgastvaṁ no aditiḥ kṛṇotu* (*RV*. I : 162 : 22c). Since this is a hymn of Aśva Sāyaṇa explains the term aditi as *adınaḥ aśvaḥ* (the imperishable horse).

Though the term *aditi* is sometimes used as an adjective, as we have just shown, it is primarily a noun, Macdonell finds, meaning 'unbinding', 'bondlessness', from *diti* 'binding', derived from the root *dā* 'to bind'[3]. Thus Aditi is a name for the infinite which surrounds us on all sides and also stands for the endless expanse beyond heaven and earth. Here, 'We have the anticipation of a universal all embracing, all-producing nature....'[4].

Can Aditi be identified with Pṛthivı?

Aditi sometimes appears as a synonym for Pṛthivı. Let us note the following passages.

Soma, the plant or *Oṣadhi*, being born in the imperishable earth moves forward for the sacrificers : *śrathitc naptir adite* (*RV*. IX : 69 : 3b).

The sacrificer sends Soma to the sacrificial place of the earth with ten fingers: *daśa svasāro aditer upastha ā* (*RV*. IX : 71 : 5b).

Man following the path of truth finds the earth broader : *urvi gavyūtir aditer ṛtaṁ yate* (*RV*. IX : 74 : 3b).

Soma conceives near the earth : *dahhāti garbham aditer upasthe* (*RV*. IX : 74 : 5c).

In the lap of the undecaying earth the seer wishes to be well protected by Varuṇa : *avo vanvānā aditer upasthāt* (*RV*. VII : 88 : 7c).

The sacrificer polishes or reconstructs the moving Soma in the lap of the earth: *tam amṛkṣanta vājinam upasthe aditer adhi* (*RV*. IX : 26 : lab).

Śunaḥśepa when tied down for sacrificial slaughtering wanted to live more on the earth : *ko no mahyā aditaye punar dhāt* (*RV*. I : 24 : 1).

Pṛthivi gives as *rudriya* (an oblation to be offered to Rudra) : *yathā no aditiḥ karat ...... yathā tokāya rudriyam* (*RV*. I : 43 : 2 ac).

In connexion with Dyaus (heaven) Aditi appears to be Pṛthivi (earth) : *mimātu dyaur aditir vitaye*. (*RV*. V : 59 : 8a).

Aditi, the earth, expresses her greatness : *mahnā mahadbhiḥ pṛthivi vi tasthe*.[5]

Aditi is found in the sense of earth mostly in Books I and IX of the Ṛgveda and only once both in Book V and VII. Since *Somamaṇḍala* (Book IX) has a well connection with the sacrifice, Aditi, the earth, which is in most of the cases synonymous with altar, has been lauded more in Book IX.

However, even if in some passages quoted above Aditi is identical with Pṛthivi-and this has been endorsed by *Nighaṇṭu* (1: 1)-these goddesses are two, not one. In those passages Aditi figures as an adjective. Besides, since they are separately mentioned in a number of occasions[6], they are distinct from each other. Though *ŚB* identifies them : *iyaṁ vai pṛthivi aditiḥ*[7], these identifications of the Brāhmaṇas', as Muir aptly points out, 'are very arbitrary and frequently fanciful'[8].

Is Aditi equal to Soma ?

Aditi is sometimes called Soma : *antaś ca prāgā aditir bhavāsi* (*RV*. VIII : 48 : 2a). Three seers-Viśvavāra, Yajata and Māyin—were highly intoxicated and pleased as if they had achieved Aditi (*RV*. V : 44 : 11 ab). As soma is the cause of their pleasure, Aditi may have some connections with soma. However, Aditi is not identified with Soma with whom she may have some connections. Above all Aditi is referred to as the sister of Soma : *Somo bhrātāditiḥ svaṣā* (RV. I : 191 : 6b). This also does not go in favour of the contention that they are identical.

Is Aditi Agni ?

Aditi is sometimes identified with Agni : *tvam agne aditir deva*[9]. Yāska too takes Agni in the sense of Aditi : *agnir apy aditir ucyate* (*Nir.* XI : 23 : 7). Here Aditi means faultless—says Yāska : *anāgastvam anaprādhatvam* (*Nir.* XI : 24 : 2). So from the point of faultlessness both these gods are sometimes identical[10].

But these stray references cannot bracket Aditi with Agni because they differ in certain respects and above all Agni has a definite physical basis which Aditi lacks.

Is Aditi Brahmaṇaspati ?

Though Sāyaṇa surprisingly takes Brahmaṇaspati in the sense of Aditi on *RV.* X. 72 : 2—*brahmaṇaḥ annasya patiḥ aditiḥ* etc., yet it is not so, because Aditi is not the only goddess of *anna*, any god may be named as so.

Is Uṣas Aditi?

'In *RV.* there are two goddesses from an earlier heritage, Aditi and Uṣas, who are often implied in *RV* as really one and the same deity and praised eloquently in some of the hymns on Uṣas'[11]. This is maintained by Prof. Sukumar Sen who adduces *RV* IV : 55 : 3 to substantiate his point and comments that 'in fact she is identified with Aditi'[12]. But if we carefully analyse the verse : *pra pastyām aditiṁ sindhum arkaiḥ svastim īle sakhyāya devīm/ ubhe yathā no ahani nipāta uṣāsānaktā karatam adabdhe*'ǁ referred to above by Prof. Sen, we see that Aditi cannot be identified with Uṣas. This is because the said verse of Vāmadeva is addressed to Viśvedeva and in that verse many gods find mention viz. Aditi, Sindhu, Svasti, Dyāvāpṛthivī and Uṣāsānaktā. There *pastyām* (a goal for everyone) is an adjective to Aditi. Uṣas who is jointly applauded with night in this verse cannot be identified with Aditi. Besides elsewhere Aditi is said to be the contender of Uṣas : *aditer anīkam* (*RV.* I : 113 : 19c). This also indicates that Uṣas and Aditi are different from each other.

Is Aditi the cow?

Aditi is sometimes called *go* (cow)—as is endorsed bu *Nighaṇṭu* (II : 11). Pratardana says that Soma being pure like milk, is not easily available—*payo na dugdham aditer iṣiram* (*RV.* IX : 96 : 15c). Furthermore, Dīrghatamas prays that let the cows be milky : *pīpāya dhenur aditir ṛtāya* (*RV.* I : 153 : 3a)-whereon Sāyaṇa means *Aditi* by *adīnā bahusirā satī* (imperishable cow) etc.

True, Aditi is sometimes identical with *gauḥ* but this does not mean cow. In *Nighaṇṭu* (I : 4) *gauḥ* is a common name for heaven and Ādityas. Now, from heaven comes down rain which may mythologically be said to be the drop of milk which nourishes life. So there is hardly any point in Prof. Sukumar Sen's observation : 'Dyaus is a vigorous bull and Pṛthivī a speckled cow (I : 160 : 3). Here is identity as well as contrast between Pṛthivī and Aditi. Both are conceived as cow but one is speckled and the other is not'[13].

Can Aditi be identified with the sky?

Aditi in reality is popularly believed to express the infinite sky, 'not the infinite as the result of a long process of abstract reasoning but the visible infinite, visible, ... to the naked eye, the endless expanse beyond, the earth, beyond the clouds, beyond the sky'[14]. True, in *RV.* X : 63 : 3 or V : 59 : 8 Aditi may be interpreted as a synonym for the sky but Aditi can easily be taken as an adjective in those cases. The tenor or *RV.* X : 65 : 9 however is 'opposed to this identification of Aditi with the sky, as she and her sons, the Ādityas, are there mentioned separately from the other gods who are the inhabitants of the three different spheres ......'[15].

So Aditi is neither merely the earth nor the sky i.e. Dyāvāpṛthivī. Even though the term *aditī* in the dual form is enlisted in the synonyms of Dyāvāpṛthivī in the *Nighaṇṭu* (III : 30), it is curious to note that 'no passage occurs, in the *Ṛgveda* at least, where the special meaning of heaven and earth is expressed by Aditi[16]. Besides, Aditi and Dyāvāpṛthivī are mentioned side by side in *RV.* X : 66 : 4.

Though no definite identity of Aditi emerges from these various mantras, Aditi, in our opinion, is but a celestial light : *jyotiṣmatīm aditiṁ dhārayatkṣitiṁ svarvatīm*[17]. This light pervades and permeates everywhere thereby becoming a ubiquitous as well as an imperishable character. Physically 'Aditi can be conceived', Prof. Sukumari Bhattacharji observes, 'as the point in the eastern sky where the light and the sun are born'[18]. Aditi's luminous character is also proved by the fact that she is a contender of Uṣas : *mātā devānām aditer anīkam* (*RV.* I : 113 : 19c). Her frequent association with the solar gods, Ādityas, who sustain and are sustained by their mother is also indicative of her being a celestial light. Aditi can thus be styled as *gānvaḥ*, the plural form of *gauḥ*, which is synonymous with light (Nigh. i : 5). From the point of view of imperishability and pervasivenses Aditi's synonymity with Vāc (Speech), according to *Nighaṇṭu* (I : 11), is justified[19].

Surprisingly, Aditi has no hymn to her credit. Not only that, she is seldom invoked alone throughout the *Ṛgveda*. 'She, being the mother goddess, is related to each and every god and goddess and so the Vedic seer did not feel', argues Guleri, 'the necessity of assigning separate hymns to her ......'[20]. But this remark holds no ground because even the cursory study of the Rgvedic texts reveals that every god somehow or the other is connected with others and is mutually inclusive. Of course, his alternative suggestion: 'there is no particualr phenomenon which has been represented by her because she is related to each and everything, so the vedic seer did not think proper to sing separate hymns in her favour'[21]—seems to be more plausible.

Lack of definite identity may be responsible for Aditi's hymnlessness. But this is not all, for she has been named serveral times, she functions as a goddess, associates herself with others and has her share in rituals etc., that is, she has to her credit all that describes a Vedic deity. Admittedly she only lacks a *sūkta* to enjoy the full dignity and status of a goddess. So the cause of her hymnlessness lies elsewhere. The Vedic seers, we may confidently argue, have seen her as an inscrutably abstract goddess who is all pervading and whose graceful presence illumines others. To substantiate this view let us refer to one verse in which Ṛtaṁ *bṛhat*, the rhythmic greatness of the Absolute, is connected with Aditi : *aditir dyāvāpṛthivī ṛtaṁ mahad indrāviṣṇū marutaḥ svar bṛhat/devā adityā avase havāmahe vasūn rudrānt savitāram* (*RV*. X : 66 : 4). *Ṛtam bṛhat* and *svar mahat* referred to in the verse constitute the word *brahma* (*Brhat* + *mahat*) because Brahman is limitless with universal rhythm (*rtam brhat*) and great with effulgence of light (*svar mahat*). So this verse indicates a well connexion of Aditi with Brahman[22]. Cosnequently, so incomprehensible is her nature that the vedic seers with all their wonderful gift for expression have failed to adequately express it. That is why, we do not find any Aditi-hymn in the entire *Rgvedasaṁhitā.* Of course, we have a hymn of a male god Puruṣa, who can be designated as pantheism incarnated : *puruṣa evedaṁ sarvaṁ yad bhūtaṁ yacca bhavyam* (*RV*. X : 90 : 2a). This is presumably because Aditi is more inconceivable than Puruṣa. True, the goddess Vāc, another pantheistic female deity, has a hymn to her credit but there the female seer herelf reveals her nature which no other seer could possibly have done successfully. Incidentally, the female seer Aditi, the seer of *RV*. IV : 18, nowhere speaks in first person. That is why, in the case of Aditi we cannot read the seer and the deity as one, as we do in the case of Vāc.

Aditi makes us free from sins or enemy

Aditi's 'main characteristic, in conformity with the etymological meaning of the name', Macdonell observes, 'is her power of releasing from the bonds of physical suffering and moral guilt'[23]. Consequently in the verses found here and there in the *RV*. Aditi is requested to drive away our sins committed deliberately or inadvertantly[24]. Ādityas, the true successors of Aditi, are sometimes entreated to forgive sins[25]. In the hymn *RV*. IV : 3 Agni is said to have disclosed sins of human beings to Varuṇa, Sūrya, Mitra, Pṛthivī, Aryaman, Bhaga, Vāyu, Rudra, Pūṣan, Viṣṇu and Aditi. But Aditi drives away our sins (*RV*. IV : 3 : 8c). She makes the mortals free as the fisherman release fishes from his nets (*RV*. VIII : 67 : 18bc).

Pāyu, the seer, craves that the *rakṣasas* or the enemy should be offered to Aditi[26].

Aditi, the mother of royal children, should take us to a beautiful land where there is no enemy to be afraid of (*RV*. II : 27 : 7a).

From the above excerptions we see that Aditi, usually a cosmic goddess, assumes a moral character in no small degree since she drives away sin which in the Veda is frequently considered as a bondage. 'In one passage, at least, *aditi*', Hopkins comments, 'simply means freedom (1.24.1), less boundlessness than unbondage; so probably in 1. 185.3, the gift of freedom'[27].

Aditi, however as a driver of sins or faults is mentioned in seven out of ten *maṇḍalas* (omitting Books III, VI, and IX). Once more, we see that Aditi is hardly applauded alone. So to speak, solar gods almost always accompany her. Among them Savitṛ who is famous for boosting all others in their respective fields, also pushes Aditi for making the devotees sinless (RV. V : 82 : 6ab). Varuṇa of course is the true son of Aditi as he also drives away bondage and sin like his mother. 'Indeed, organization and regulation through bondage', Prof. Dandekar observes, 'is the central motif of an entire mythological complex involving *ṛta*, Varuṇa, Mitra, Aditi and Ādityas'[28].

In the passages referred to above in connection with Aditi's role in driving sin away there is only one and significant epithet *ṛtāvṛdho* (*RV*. VII : 82 : 10c) meaning promoter of *ṛta*. The term *ṛta* is not synonymous with truth because its cosmic nuance can hardly be achieved by translating the term as truth. 'The word *ṛta* is to be derived from', Prof. Dandekar finds, 'the IE root ar—'to bind', 'to unite', 'to join together'[29]. So etymologically it means a holy bond, or a systematic order which is invoked to overpower the chaos or disorder. 'One who is free', Prof. Saxema maintains, 'should not be indisciplined. The freedom presupposes the maintenance of law and strengthening of law. Freedom without law i.e. Aditi wihout Ṛta cannot be beneficial for man's physical, moral or spiritual uplift'[30].

Hence as a promoter of *ṛta* Aditi is enabled to accomplish the enormous feat of sustaining the cosmic order and none dares oppose her ordinances.

From our foregoing analysis, it is evident that Aditi takes a very important role in the Vedic pantheon and without her the whole theistic pandal would perish.

References

1. Adolf kaegi quotes Max Müller's *Lectures on the Origin and Growth of Religion as illustrated by the religions of India*. London, 1872, p. 236 f—*The Rigveda*, Delhi, 1975, Notes 225, p. 149.
2. *RV*. I : 94 : 15b; cf. *RV*. VII : 9 : 3a; VIII : 19 : 14ab.
3. Macdonell, *Vedic Mythology*, Delhi, 1981, p. 121, We, however, have not found the root *dā* 'to bind' in the Pānninean *Dhātupāṭha*.
4. Radhakrishnan, *Indian Philosophy*, Vol. I, Delhi, 1983, Rep. 1985, p. 82.
5. *RV*. I : 72 : 9cd, cf. *AV*. XIII : 1 : 38.
6. See *RV*. I : 72 : 9; III : 54: 19, 20; V: 46: 3; VI: 51: 5; ix: 97: 58; X: 36: 2, 3; 63 : 10; 92 : 11, *VS*. XVIII : 22.

7. *ŚB* II : 2 : 1 : 19; V : 3 : 1 : 4, see also VIII : 2 : 1 : 10; XI : 1 : 3 : 3.
8. Muir, *Original Sanskrit Texts,* Vol. V, Delhi, 1976, p. 41.
9. *RV.* II : 1 : 11a, cf. *RV.* IV : 1 : 20ab.
10. cf. *RV.* 1 : 94 : 15b; VIII : 101 : 15.
11. Sukumar Sen, *The Great Goddesses in Indic Tradition,* Calcutta, 1983, p. 13.
12. *Ibid,* p. 31.
13. *Op. cit.,* p. 15.
14. *The Sacred Books of the East,* Vol. XXXII, Ed, Max Müller, Delhi, 1973, p. 40.
15. Muir, *op. cit.,* p. 40.
16. Max Müller, *op. cit.* p. 255.
17. *RV.* 1 : 136 : 3. cf *'avadhrañjyotiḥ'* RV. VII : 82 : 10.
18. Sukumari Bhattacharji, *The Indian Theogony,* Calcutta, 1978, p. 160.
19. Cf. *vāgvā'ditiḥ* - ŚB VI : 5 : 2 : 20.
20. V. S. Gyleri, *Female Deities in Vedic and Epic Literature,* Delhi 1990, p. 33.
21. *ibid,* p. 33.
22. See M. P. Pandit, *Aditi and other Deities in the Veda,* Dipti Publication, Sri Aurobindo Ashram, Pondichery, Ist pub. 1958, Rep. 1970.
23. *Op. cit.,* p. 122.
24. See *RV.* I : 185 : 3abd : II : 27 : 14ab; IV : 39 : 3; VII : 93 : 7cd; X : 36 : 3ab; 12 : 8 cd; cf. *RV.* V : 82 : 6ab.
25. *RV.* II : 28 : 3cd. of. VII : 51 : Iod. Though here *adititva* is used in the sense of undecaying, it may be a synonym for *anāgastva.*
26. *Vṛścyantām aditaya durevāḥ RV.* X : 87 : 18b of. VIII : 18 : 5.
27. E.W.Hopkins, The *Religions of India,* Delhi, 1977, p. 73.
28. R. N. Dandekar, *Vedic Mythological Tracts,* Delhi, 1979, p. 330.
29. *Ibid, p.* 326.
30. "A comparative Study of Aditi in the Veda and *The Mahābhārata", Modern Evaluation of the Mahābhārata* (*Prof. R. K. Sharma Felicitation volume*), (Ed), S. P. Narang, Delhi, 1995, p. 65.

Abbreviations

Av.	=	Atharvavedasaṁhitā.
Bṛ. U.	=	Bṛhadāraṇyaka Upanṣad.
Dhā	=	Dhātupāṭha.
Nigh	=	Nighaṇṭu.
Nir.	=	Nirukta.
RV.	=	Ṛgvedasaṁhitā.
ŚB.	=	Śatapatha Brāhmaṇa.
VS.	=	Vājasaneyisaṁhitā.

Vedic Mythology

6

Dr. D. S. Das

Myth is a traditional tale common to the members of a tribe, race or nation usually involving super natural and serving to explain some natural phenomenon. The explanatory purpose of many myths is now obscure for a myth often continues to live as a tale in its own right after its explanation has been supplemented. It must be emphasised that a myth is not a specific literary work but a floating tale. Myths are often given literary treatment.

The myths of a people, taken all together is for a mythology. This term is also used to designate the study of myths. A mythology is usually taken for granted as a part of the common background of writer, and reader and most occidental writers assume that their audience will understand allusion to classical and some other mythology. It is the reflection of celestial phenomena mainly the movements of the great luminaries, knew a new revival in Germany at the beginning of the 20th century. Sir J. G. Frazer Jane Harrison, Gribort Murray and other scholars tried to explain the ancient near Eastern and Greek Myths in terms of ritual magic. The periodical death and resurrection of vegetation, Frazer claimed created the figure and the myth of dying god of which Adonis, Attis and Osris are the best known examples.

Important contributions to the understanding of myth and mythical thought have been made by many philosophers and psychologists. The new approach to myth is greatly indebted to the results of modern ethnology. The scientific study of archaic societies those societies in which mythology is or was until recently, living has revealed that myth for the primitive man means a true story and beyond that a story that is a most precious treasury because it is a sacred exemplary and significant.

Myth fulfils in primitive culture as an indispensable function, it expresses, enhances and codifies belief, it safeguards, and enforces morality, it vouches for the efficiency of ritual and contains practical rules for the guidance of man.

Myth is thus a vital in-gradient of human civilization, it is not an ideal tale but a hard worked active force, it is not an intellectual explanation or an artistic imagery, but a pragmatic charter of primitive faith and moral wisdom...these stories to be native a statement of a primeval greater and more relevant reality by which the present life, fates and activities of mankind are determined, the knowledge of which supplies men with the motive of ritual and moral actions as well as with indications as to how to perform them.

It would be hard to define myth in a way that would be acceptable to all scholars and at the intelligible to non-specialists. Myth is an extremely complex cultural reality, which can be approached and interpreted from various and contemporary view points. The definition that seems least inadequate because most embracing is this; myth narrates a sacred history; it relates an event that took place in primordial time, the fabled time of the beginnings. In other words myth tells how through the deeds of supernatural begins, a reality came into existence, be it the whole of reality, the cosmos or only a fragment of reality-an island, a species of plant, a particular kind of human behaviour, an institution. Myth, then is always an account of a "creation", it relates how something was produced, began to be. Myth tells only of that which really happened, which manifested it self completely. The actors in myths are supernatural beings. They are known primarily by what they did in the times of the beginning. Hence myths disclose their creative and reveal the sacredness (or simply the super naturalness) of their works. In short, myths describe the various and some times dramatic break through of the sacred (or the super natural) into the world. It is thus sudden break-through of the sacred that really establishes the world and makes it what it is today. Furthermore, it is a result of the intervention of supernatural beings that man himself is what he is today a mortal, sexed and cultural being. The myth is regarded as a sacred story and hence "true history" because the existence of the world is there to prove it. The myth of the origin of earth is equally true because man's mortality proves it and so on. Because myth relates the "gesta" of super natural beings and the manifestation of their sacred powers, it becomes the exemplary models for all significant human activities. Because "Holy people did it" in way that was in the first place. We must do what the gods did in the beginning. In summary, the foremost function of myth is to reveal the exemplary models for all human rites and all significant human activities alimentation or marriage, work or education, art or wisdom.

A Myth is something which occurred in the inception of human civilization. It is believed that in the primeval period human life was at a stake on earth in different ways and the gods came forward for their rescue though a number of sacrifices. Our main interest in the Ṛg. Veda centres round the various Gods who play a vital role for the growth and spread of this Ṛg. Vedic religion. The under current of this religion was purely polytheistic which comprises a gamut of gods who excelled themselves on different occasions and achieved greatness by virtue of their heroic, chivalrous deeds. In the body of that religious pantheon, their rise and fall even upgradation has not only been manifested but also extolled by the contemporary poets of those hymns.

It is presumed that in the past the vedic people selected their Gods from the Indo-European and some others on their way to India and they might have created of their own after their settlements in the sub-continent. Since agriculture and cattle rearing was the only source of livelihood they had a pastoral mode of living and perhaps, they are sun and sky Gods primarily. The Vedic Aryans most of them were cattle breeders and another aspect was added to their living, it was plunder the wealth they got from the vanquished clan of whom later became their subjects. After settlement in this sub-continent they followed mainly this agricultural way of living for which most of their earlier sky and solar Gods were linked with the pastoral life. Even some of them were retained by the same settlers with some changes in regard to their position and significance. As an agricultural clan they needed timely rain better crops and absence of any kind of atmospheric turmoils. Keeping in view of this fact solely they were in need of some solar Gods of vegetation who were to provide proper heat for germination, controlling rainfall through creation of clouds in time. Hence, to the creation of some gods of their own religious pantheon, they added the rain and thunder gods of the nomadic period. It was rather a mythical projection of the historical experience of those new settlers of Aryans' clan. The same fertility Gods and Goddesses are marked in the European mythology as they have been used by T. S. Eliot and others in their classics.

Gods are mostly mythological apotheosis of natural elements. All other mythologies present this phenomenon though myth which present the solar, lunar and consteller aspects of the sky more or less transparently. Other elements of nature are also recognizable in their mythological presentation or historical personages, local tutelary and functional divinities who either merge with existing major gods or retain their individuality. All pantheons include a cluster of demigods of different orders. In the R. V. they are presented as the Gandharvas and Apsaras. But in the last section in the Indian pantheon was added where we find certain abstractions, conceptual hierphanies or natural elements while others were purely cerebral creations. The deified natural elements appear to be the oldest stratum, then came the exhumeristic Gods, the various functional Gods. Gods thrown out the exigenies of the sacrifices. Gods created through needs at the social economic and existential level of the people and then, at the last stage came Gods who were more ideas than real gods of actual cultiritual. True though out the R. V. period we do not have any god who is totally unconnected with sacrifice, but towards the close of the period the emphasis shifted from ritual to mere concepts. (Cf. S. Bhattacharji, Literature in the Vedic Age, Vol. I, pp. 130-31).

Yaska, the 6th century B.C. theorist and etymologist divides Vedic Gods into three groups according to their habitual, celestial, atmospheric and terrestrial. Another class of people in the said period was added to these were the superior class of people represented by Brahmins who specifically practised tapas meditation which were accepted in the society's creative and preservative phenomenon and a kind of spiritual predilection. For this the Brahmins in that caste based society enjoyed a superior status a prototype of Gods on earth. The earliest stratum of Gods in the Indo-European pantheon were Dyaus, Surya, Mitra, Savitṛ Yama, Bhaga, Amsa, Daksa, Aryaman, Vivasvat, Martanda the Asvins, Aditi etc. (Cf. S. Bhattacharji, Op. Cit., pp. 131-132).

Varuṇa

Varuṇa is one of the significant deities in the Ṛg.Vedic pantheon. As a purely vedic God he has got some similarity with the Greek God Curanas that means sky or the end heaven (A.A. Macdonall, A Vedic Reader, p. 135, Vedic Mythology, Hindi translation, p. 52). We find a lot of difficulties between these 2 words (Sanskrit & Greek) so far as phonetic aspects are concerned. But the recent philologists have comparatively associated them. This deity comes from the Indo-Iranian period. It is Avestic Ahuramazda meaning the wise spirit. But some similarity is marked so far as their names are concerned (R. C. Majumdar & A. D. Pusalkar, The History and Culture of the Indian People. The Vedic Age, p. 365).

Varuṇa goes back to the Indo-Iranian as Ahuramazda who is the supreme God in Avesta and it has been translated into Sanskrit as Asuramedhas - Asura commonly known powerful. Later on Asura means as a demon. A- (na) Surah iti Asurah).

In the Indo-Iranian period those Asuras as friendly to the Aryans. But, with the change of geography, they were separated from each other. The situation made that they became hostile to them. The conversation between Sarma & Pani (Ṛg. Veda-10. 108-1-11) suggests this fact. The supreme character of Ahuramazda tallies with Varuṇa in Sanskrit. It may be guessed that the world Varuṇa is derived from Bru or to cover. It is otherwise known as the encompasser. One who covers (Vedic Mythology, A.A. Macdonell) Sāyaṇa connects Varuṇa with enveloping or confining the wicked as one of the Ādityas of seven who are the sons of Aditi of freedom. The same quality of freedom is in Varuṇa. Other Adityas revolve around him (Ṛg V. 11.28.1). He is as symbol of force for the moral and physical and cosmic sphere. We may interpret him as Rata & Ṛta (A Vedic Reader—Macdonell, p. 134-Ṛg. V.b. 41.7) and Dhṛtavṛata his ordinances are fixed. Even other gods follow his law and ordinances. For him there would be no disorder or delusion. For that he is the Lord of the universe. It is that sky or Varuṇa where Gods live. Sun and Moon are his 2 eyes. It is his glory under which other Gods come as he is the upholder of universal order. He is also the God of justice and order, lover and his blessing are in the form of rain that springs from the sky. Here he may be the God of love. The two opposite qualities love and justice have been proportionately synthesized which is rarely marked in any other mythology, where there is love there is no truth. But exceptionally truth and justice are of these contratisting qualities which have been intermingled.

Here we also make a difference that when Indra is famous for his physical valour Varuna is for spiritual values. As the God of justice he watches the conduct of all through his special spies over the whole universe.

The Varuṇa hymns in Ṛg. V. extoll his supreme ethical and religious fervour and they are highly poetic. He is described as the controller of the waters who made the rivers to flow in accordance with his own ethics. Even the seas or oceans if they don't over flow it is due to his ordinance or ruling (Ṛg. V. 2. 28. 4.5 85.6) Varuṇa has the power to move and to control both the terrestrial and the celestial. If thee is flood, if a benefit, a blessing of waters it is due to his will. The Rain water is released from clouds because of his order to make the earth vegetative and healthy and beautiful and happy. (Ṛg. V. 1. 164. 5). This water comes with also the help of Mitra (another God). The spreading of the rays of light on the earth and moving of waters are made possible by this Varuṇa simultaneously. Again the same waters move upwards by Indra when set free from movement. In the Nighaṇṭa 5th chapter, Varuṇu has been enlisted as both terrestrial and celestial God. In regard to the physical side nothing is very clear though he has been represented encompassing the whole sky. One of his multifarious activities is to watch the deeds of the people as the supreme sovereign of the sky all the deeds of day and night. During day time he watches through the Sun as his eye and at night through the Moon (Ṛg. V. 10. 30. 10). As the supreme ruler of the physical and moral order Varuṇa remains alert always. Later on his position has been degraded and the control of physical and moral has been entrusted to Yama, the death God. In this way we come to conclusion that the Ṛg. Vedic God Varuṇa has been confined to the God of ocean or Neptune.

Mitra

He occupies the 2nd position among the celestional gods. In the whole of the Ṛg. Vedic pantheon this God does not have an individual existence who is intently associated with Varuṇa. His own individual presence is in darkness. In the Ṛg. V. only in one hymn he is in praise of his qualities Ṛg. V. III - 59. As his separate character seems to be hazy, it is very difficult to assess a full impression on him. When he is addressed with Varuna in the hymn he is represented with the beneficent side of the suns power. Mitra, in the interpretation of Ṛg. V. is a friend or companion. At times he is connected with Avestic "Mithra" and in that mythology he is considered as the controller of the Morals and guardian of faithfulness. In our Ṛg. V. we see him as a solar deity who is kind and benevolent. He is also taken as a God of light being connected with the sun. Some take him as the sun God that exhibits the benevolent power of nature in the remarks of A. A. Macdonell (Vedic Mythology, Hindi translation, pp. 54-55).

The Ṛg. Vedic hymns are in praise of him who holds the heaven and earth fast and watches the people incessantly unlike Varuṇa. As one of the great Adityas he is called Yātayajña who activates the people of the universe (Ṛg. V. 3. 59. 1. 5) Even the course of the sun is regulated by this Mitra. Later on, in the Brāhmaṇas, Mitra is connected with day and Varuṇa with the night for which both of them have been contrasted like the sunrises and the evening. The sunrise represented by Mitra enables the people to work, the farmers shepherds, cowherds all start working, move and run and for this his character of Yātayajña seems to be justified. Both Mitra and Varuṇa are represented equally in regard to their qualities (Ṛg. V. 7. 60. 6, 7. 36. 2).

Savitṛ

Most of the solar deities appear to have the similar traits for which it is at times too difficult to distinguish them from one another. However, Savitṛ has got some distinctive features like that of the quickening aspect of another solar deity, sun. That Savitṛ represents the light of the sun set and before sun rise. It, as the God of inspiration (Sabitā Prasabita) dispels darkness and gives inspiration (Preraṇa). When life is dark, it is enlightened by its flash of light. It has that enlivening power of light and life and the same trait may be found in any of the writers and man who can add hope and aspiration to the needy and the uncared.

In the Ṛg. V., Savitṛ is represented as a golden deity whose complexion is golden and his car or vehicle is golden. The limbs of this God like tongue, hand and eyes all are golden. As an original solar deity he has the power of stimulation. (A Vedic reader, A. A. Macdonell, p. 11, Nirukta, R. C. Majumdar, 10 - 32. The History of culture of the Indian people, the Vedic Age, p. 367). The human life and motion is inspired, even the Śurya is installed to move by this God. According to Yāṣka (Nirukta 12. 12. Ṛg. V. 5. 81. 4) when darkness has just gone Savitṛ arrives. It is called Sun from its time of rising till setting. We may call it as the regular of the time that brings in day and night. It represents light after sunset and before sunrise for this it is called that Savitṛ which embraces the night on both sides (Uviyataḥ pareeyase). Here we mark a similarity between Savitṛ and Mitra, like Mitra he is a friend of the human world. Savitṛ is a well wisher since he embarks upon light to the mankind. As he pervades the whole space all the mortals and immortals lay rest on his lap. He has double function like ensuing rest after the sunset and waking the humanity before the sunrise (R. V. 1. 25. 2, 4.53.4) assures his position. He is called the dhrtavrata and Dhṛtakarma like Varuṇa and Mitra. He has also his rules and ordinances by which night approaches and day breaks (R. V 1. 35. 9, 1. 35. 10) He and the sun may be one but due to their subtle physical stature they are distinguished and Savitṛ guides the Sun. In (Ṛg. V. 1. 35. 10) Savitṛ is called asura-one who gives life (Asuna pranana rati dadati iti, asurah prana data suniyah srustu neta). He is the guide. In the Ṛg. Vedic period Gods were called Asuras but later on asura changed to mean a demon.

In reference to his vehicle it has been said that 5 yave is his horse of sūrya- the colour of the horse is dusky and are white footed (Ṛg. V. 1. 35. 5) and its pole is made of gold and in this car, Savitṛ is to survey the human world who live in the lustrous lap of Savitṛ. So his character is divine, inspiring and proper guiding. The god moves with the rays of the sun with his golden eyes, golden hands on a golden chariot. From the east he appears with the rays that dispel all the evil dreams and demons. The Gāytri hymns (Ṛg. V. 3. 62. 10) early in the morning make the sphere all sacred and soothing and the new thoughts are borne out of this blessing of God Savitṛ. It is his motive to make the humanity pure, sacred, active, enthusiastic and intelligent. The unquenchable thirst for knowledge is revived, and culminated by the soothing touch of this solar God specifically the morning hours stand for peace and an inkiling for learning. He, in this regard may be one of the soothe sayers and sublimative, serene. The people invoke in this serene hours that God Savitṛ to enlarge their areana of thought and action.

The study of Savitṛ further focuses light that later on he has been taken as Śurya. It is the developed from of Savitṛ. He is also called a bird who surveys the whole atmospheric regions (Ṛg. V. 1. 35. 7). The same image of the bird has been attributed to the sun in later periods (Ṛg. V. 1. 164) (Dibyaḥ as subarnagarutman) and we find that both Mitra and Savitṛ could not remain independent but have been merged in the image of the great Śurya.

Puṣan

Though Puṣan is considered to have some beneficent power and connected with shepherds and places as a shepherd God, he is rarely invoked in the whole of Ṛg. V. Literally it means "the prosperer" and the word is derived from pus to prosper (A. A. Macdonell, Vedic Mythology). So far as his physical appearance is concerned there is no such clear cut description and only thing is known that he has a bared and braided hair (Ṛg. V. 6.55.1) and whose chariot is drawn by goats and his favorite food is Karambha. He is Prashmashru hayanto. (R.C. Majumdar & A.D. Pusalkar, R.V. 6-56. 1). He has a clear knowledge of the roadways and is very active in controlling the sheep as though they are not led astray amidst jungle and brings them home safe. At another level he is described as the messenger of sun and as a charioteer, he drives the golden wheel of the sun in the down direction (Ṛg. V. 6.56.3). As the guardian of all the creatures he plays a vital role. As he is conceived to be one of the Sun Gods, he is completely ignored in the later periods. It is also understood that Pusan was the wooer of his mother and the lover of his sister (Dawn) and was was given by gods to the sun maiden Śurya as a husband. He was also connected with the marriage ceremony in the wedding hymns as narrated in the Ṛg. Veda.

Sūrya

The most transparent of Gods sun is the luminary itself and most concrete form of solar deities. The World is derived from Svar, light similar to Avestic Hvare. In avestic literature Hvare is the Sun God, he is the eye of Ahuramazda and his horses are very swift (A Vedic reader, Macdonell). In our vedic literature, he is the eye of Varuṇa and Mitra and Agni. He is the son of Dyaus and Aditi. So he is called Aditya or Aditeya. He is the light of all Gods. All flash of light has been centered round him. His rise brings light to the whole heaven and earth and acts as the inspirer, the propeller of darkness, the well wisher, the soul of movable and immovables as we find in case of Savitri (Ṛg. V. 1.11.115.1, *chitrang debana mud gadaneekan chakshu rmitrashya Varuṇa syagneh apradyaba pruthibyo Antariskhyang surya atma Jagatasta srushascha*), who follows Dawn always as human beings follow the beautiful women. The vehicle of Sūrya is drawn by variegated horses and the name of horse is Etasa and their no. is 7 (Ṛg. V. 7.63.2). He is watchful of the peoples activities like that of Varuna (Ṛg. V. 4.13.3). As the lord over other deities Surya is given the path for his traverse all over the sky by them and they are Varuṇa, Mitra, Aryaman and Puṣan. Varuṇa takes away darkness when Sūrya arrives and the illuminating actor is Puṣan who has been merged in later literature in him. The relation of sun with dawn might be mother and the child or might be she the wife from whose lap the sun shines (Ṛg. V. 7.80.2, 7.78.3, 7.75.5). Thus sun is responsible for health care and happiness of the human world. All diseases evil dreams, laziness, sickness disappear by its rays. It gives warmth, vigour enthusiasm makes the humanlife hale and hearty. It is well acclaimed as the source of life, of power, of beauty or color and charm and enchantment and thrill. The living as well as the non living, the animate and the inanimate all depend on this sun. Its heat makes the earth vegetative green, due to rain which is caused by its rays. Clouds are formed by him (7.47..4-Nirukta-7.11). So, it is called as Aba Debata. The sun when is clouded Indra wins over and rain is made possible (Ṛg. V. 10.4.35). Due to perhaps some similar trait or functions they all Mitra, Sun, Savitṛ, Puṣan, Aditya have been intermingled in the Ṛg. Vedic scripture. In the late vedic literature there are twelve adityas, the sons of Aditi come regularly in 12 months. Seven are the sons of Aditi and the 8th one was the undeveloped Martanda. All of them are the Gods of light. Among the Vedic Ādityas, Varunas, Mitra and Aryaman are supposed to be of Irarian origin while Bhaga, Daksa and Amsa seem to be deified abstractions. The 7th is the Sun and 8th is Martanda, the setting sun (R.C. Majumdar and A.D. Pusalkar, p. 368, Ṛg. V. 10.72.8). Under RgVeḍa study we come to know that the 7 horses are the 7 days of the week and the reins of horses are the rays of the sun and 12 spokes of the wheel are the 12 months as represented by 12 Aditayas. In the later period this sun worship became very popular for which a separate seat has been created.

Viṣṇu

In the Ṛg. Veda pantheon Visnu who has 3 steps (strides) occupies a sub ordinate position but in later period he has been elevated to the highest place. Only 5 or 6 hymns are offered to him for his acclamation. As a symbol of equality he is placed below the other Gods. He traverses the universe with his three long wide strides for which is called Urugayaḥ or Urukramaḥ (Ṛg. V. 1.154.1, 1.22.17, 1.154.74). All the three worlds feel rejoiced (Ṛg. V. 6.49. 13) with the bliss of Viṣṇu. He is the source of joy for the 3 worlds. Prayer is made to him to get money, wealth, good health and kith and kin. His activities can be compared with Varuna who also measures the worlds by the help of sun. Some interpret the three steps of Visnu as the motion of sun the morning sun, midday sun and setting sun. To this concept the scholars like Whitney, Maxmüller, Haug, Kaegi and Auravabha agree, whereas Macdonell, Burgein and Sakapuni differ and they view that it consists of the 3 divisions of world like the earth, the atmosphere and the sky. They also believe that the three steps must be located one on the hill where the sun rises another on the meridian sky and the third on the hill of setting sun. It may be interpreted as the year course of the sun (A.A. Macdonell). In the Ṛg. V. we find a frequent reference to Visnu's friendship with Indra- who helped him in his fight with Vrtra. It is also believed that Visnu's first 2 steps are visible when the sun is shining but the 3rd one is invisible when the sun is set and darkness approaches.

A number of hymns are there to celebrate Visnu's help to Indra for the sacrifice of Vṛtra where Indra's victories are praised. Visnu is also said to have opened the cow's stable with the help of Indra after having vanquished sambara and produced the Sun, Dawn and the fire (Ṛg. V. 7.99.4.5). In the 3 strides of Visnu lie the seeds of incarnation of Visnu in the form of Vamana or dwarf in the late puranas. But our Ṛg. V. says (1.33.6) there are 3 heavens. 2 for Savitṛ and the 3rd is in the world of Vāman (A.A. Macdonell, p. 15, A Vedic Reader).

In the 2 hymns of Ṛg. V (1.61.7) it is said that during the fight with Vṛtra Indra sought help from Viṣṇu as a friend. Who took away 100 buffaloes of Vṛtra as he had hidden the wealth of Gods behind seven mountains. Vishnu in the form of sacrifice carried Varāha for the Sacrifice of Gods. Thus gods restored their property from the demons. However, the Ṛg. V. provided enough material for later mythological elaboration of those facts in the puranic literature and we find that Viṣṇu occupies the supreme place among the Gods, earthly terrestial and atmospheric.

Asvins

The Rg. V. hymns are very long in praise of Aśvins. They may be interpreted as the morning and the evening stars. But astronomically we may conclude that they are not two but one and hence it is that morning star that represents the early hours of the day. Some scholars identify them with the twin Horse men of Greek Mythology. In the Vedic Mythology, the sons of Zens and the brother of Helen, they are considered to be the sons of Dyaus. Their character and action are more or less the same as the 2 Gods who rise through the sky with their steeds (Ṛ.C. Majumdar, A.D. Pusalkar, A.A. Macdonell, A Vedic Mythology). Some interpret that they represented the morning and evening star. They are invoked in the morning and evening (Ṛg. V. 5.77.2, Nirukta 12.5). So far as their character is concerned they are twin and inseparable, as swift as thoughts and for this quality of swiftness, they are compared with birds. They are Darśa and Nasatya (Ṛg. V. 6.63.5, 8.22.16.578.4). They travel by a golden car like Sun and all other parts of their vehicle are gold. They wear the garland or lotuses (Ṛg. V. 10.184.2, *Gamante Ashwino deba Dhatang Puskar Swaja*).

They are sympathetic to the devotees for their suffering and are accepted as the able physicans for healing diseases with remedies. They also are able to restore youth for the people. They cure physical defects and saved Bhujya from the ocean in the ship (Ṛg. V. 8.18.8, 8.22, 10). They relieved the ailing and divorced Chyavana ṛṣi from his distorted body and rejoined him with youth and longlife and made him agreeable to his wife (Ṛg. V. 1.116, 10, 10.39.8). From this reference we come to know that the Aśvins are the masters of medicine and their function was to help the poor, the needy & ailing.

Indra

He is happened to be national God of the Vedic people for whom almost one fourth of the total number of hymns are addressed to him as an important atmospheric god. Indra seems to be pre Indian (Macdonell, Majumdar and Pusalkar). In avesta, he is degraded to be a demon and he is Andra only his name comes twice in it. He is Beere Thada. In the Ṛg. Veda he is Vṛthraghn. Scholars think that there were 2 contemporary gods in both the literatures, in Indo-Iranian period the word may be derived from Ind, (Macdonell P-49). His general character is intended to be a fighting personality, a war like God. He is celebrated by heroic songs in numerous songs. He is brave, energetic, violent in his actions, he is also sensural, immoral in various ways. He is a man in lust a God in morality, both the ideals are jotted together in him. He has been represented as a voracious eater and drinks too much. There is a keen contrast between the characters of Varuṇa (Moral, ethical inspring and ideal) to an immoral, lustful, selfish but destroyer of demons. While fighting with Vrtra he drank pools of soma wine and gained the epithet somapa. It is soma that stimulates him to fight as he has an addition to soma (Ṛg. 2.55.1, 2.19.2.647.1, 6.47.2). He is accompanied by Maruts and exhilarated by soma to fight with Vṛtra. During his fight he pierces the mountains and releases the imprisoned waters like imprisoned cows. The spell of soma so intoxicates him at times that Indra never hesitates to steal. (Ṛg. V. 8.44, 2.48.2). Vṛtra has been depicted as a serpent or a dragon who keeps the water closed or imprisoned in a mountain. Indra taking soma fights bravely and kills the demon and releases water to the fields of Vṛtra. The episode is artistically described in the Ṛg. Veda (Ṛg. V. 1.32.1, 1.32.2, 1.33.4).

This myth can be symbolically interpreted as Vṛtra is the cloud which holds the cloud fast but not release. Towards the end of summer the rainy season comes, Indra the rain god pierces the clouds and causes the water to flow forth and come down in showers. Some believe that Indra is nobody but God of light. The idea of Indra came with the Aryans from Kashmir or from North western countries. He has a body head and hands. His stomach is compared to a lake while fighting with Vṛtra he drank pools of soma wine & gained the epithet soma-pa. He has an addiction to soma (Ṛg. V. 2.15, 2.19.2, 6.47.1, 2.36.8) when he is too happy his beared waves which is of green colour, he is called bright golden colour (Ṛg. V. 1.7.2.). His long arms carry the thunder bolts (Ṛg. V. 3.53.8, 6.47.18). He is well known among Gods and he is most powerful. None has acquired his might (Ṛg. V. 3.46.2). He is Shachipathin, husband of Sachi. He is the lord of might, the lord of hundred sacrifices having hundred powers. Neither gods nor men have attained to the limit of his might and fame. Agni is his twin brother and Indrani is his wife and when he was born the whole sky was illumined (Ṛg. V. 3.44.4). Maruts are his allies who help him in battles. Agni also helps him in the form of lightning. In the battle with Vṛtra he was helped by Agni, Some, Viṣṇu and Maruts. He kills the demons of darkness (Ṛg. V. 8.15.5). He also settled the quaking mountains and plains (Rg. V. 1.12.2). In one band he is a heroic fighter on the other hand protector helper friend of his worshipper. He bestows wealth on his worshipper for his liberality, he is called Maghavan, the bountiful.

From this extensive splendor and description, we come to the conclusion that Indra's character is more of a warrior than a god. Very often he is praised offered oblations. Applauded so much is these hymns that it appears as if he possessed some extra ordinary powers which were beyond the reach of any of the characters of that time. Indra may be taken for granted as a historical figure who fought bravely with the demons represented by Dasyus. The Aryans took him as their leader to crush those black skinned demons having 3 heads and 6 eyes like Namuchi or Dases and under his heroic deeds the Aryans got relief of the clutches of those people (Ṛg. V. 2.12.2, Nirukta 7.10., Ṛg. V. 10.99.6, 1.130.8). One thing is worth noting that no where in the Ṛg. V. we find Indra losing his sense or individuality from drinking, though he drank too much. It is perhaps taking soma was not considered immoral. The vedic bards are all at praise of that personality and despite all his addiction, the moral standard was maintained which reflects the human values of the period.

As an individual, Indra was quite handsome with beautiful chin and lips wearing a helmet. His weapon was the thunder bolt.

Rudra

The subordinate God in the Ṛg. V. holds the power of fears and destruction in the natural phenomenon. It is believed that the cult of Śiva Paśupati was first found in Mahenjodaro and later it was borrowed by the Aryans. Some other say that both of these appear to be contemporaries but the Vedic civilization is older to Mahenjodaro (R.C. Majumdar and Pusalkar, p. 194), If the Aryan's was indigenous yet the whole of Indus Valley might have been a synthesis of both the cultures. However it is not apt to say that the idea of Śiva Paśupati of Mahenjodaro is the proto type of Mahenjodaro of Śiva Paśupati. Rather, it appears to be an interfusion of both the characters and races. However it is very interesting to study the emphasis paid on this in regard to its part in the entire gamut of the Ṛg. Veda. He has been focused as the storm God, the father of Maruts (Macdonell, P. 56-57). In regard to his later changes he is an interesting mythical character. In the Ṛg. V. Rudra has been depicted as a malevolent deity causing death and diseases among man and cattle and therefore he is praised by the poets to spare them and their families from his wrath. It is derived from rud to weep (Nirukta. 10.5). But on the other hand he is accepted as Śiva at the time of his mirths and thereby showers blessings on mankind and some of the hymns are in praise of Rudra as a deity endowed with some healing power to the plight of humanity (Rg. V. 2.33.7, 2.33.5). So far his physical appearance is concerned it is said that he is having braided air with a brown complexion and wears golden ornaments and glorious necklace (Ṛg. V. 1.144.5) The passage also say that he has beautiful lips, hands and his arms are very attractive and body shines like sun or gold and carries thunder bolt (Rg. V. 2. 33.10), a bow and strong swift arrows in his arms and lightning might be his shaft that he throws right from the sky. As Isana and the lord of all and the mightiest of mighty he is to ward off all evil things. Another quality has been attributed to him is that he is able to make the land wet and fertile by making streams of water.

He is Rudra or Trymbaka and has an association with Maruts. At time, the word Ajaikapād is used for him and this Trymbak means one having three mothers symbolising the 3 fold divisions of the world (Ṛg. V. 7.59.12). In the Ṛg. V. (2.33.1, 1.85.1). it is also found that Rudra is the father of Maruts and it is the divine cow Parsni that gave birth to these Maruts (Ṛg. V. 1.85.2 Majumdar and Pusalkar). At another place Rudra is considered to be the greatest physician of physicians who cures diseases with his medicines (Ṛg. V. 2.33.4 Macdonell and Joas, P. 95). In the words of Weber Rudra is the harsh sound of storm. Even he is the mixed form of Agni & storm for which he is known as Śatarudrīya. Wilson in his preface to Ṛg.V. considers him to be the form of Agni or Indra. Due to this similarity, we come to interpret Agni and Rudra as one for instance he is the sun in the sky, lightnings in the atmosphere and fire on the earth. The epithet of another Paśupati attached to the same Rudra as he lives in jungle and so animals are in charge of him.

This destructive Rudra has been developed in later period into Mahandev or Mahadev. However, both the qualities of destruction and construction have been fused together in his personality.

Maruts

According to the description of Ṛg. Veda (R.C. Majumdar and P. Pusalkar, p. 372) Maruts the sons of Rudra are a group of Gods always appear in plural and are the brothers of equal size. As the Gods of storms they have an intimate relation with clouds and lightning. They represent the wind of Vāyu. It is derived from Marr or to die to crush and to illuminate to shine (Rg. V. Nirukta 11.13). Their function is to shed rain, to send rain lightning and to give thunder sound like the cow shouts following her calf. They possess golden axes ornaments, golden helmets, armlets, anklets which are special to them. Due to their association with lightning they are called Rstividyut. As the sons of Rudra they also adorn themselves with bows and arrows some time (R. V. 5.53.4). Their vehicle dazzles with lightning and the steeds are of ruddy color. Their appearance is very young, very swift like thoughts, terrible looking like lions. Thunder and roaring the winds make tremendous noise that create havoc that quake the mountains and tremble the worlds and uproot the trees and devour the forests like wild elephants.

But their benevolent nature is highly soothing and nourishing as bring rain clear the sky for the sunshine and are called the divine singers (Rg. V. 1.38.9). This rain has a healing quality and brings fertility which functions as a medicinal value like all prosperity and hope (Rg. V. 1.85.3) like Indra Maruts come to the sacrificial grass and rejoice with sweet juice or ghee (Rg. V. 1.85.6). They are also considered as the brave heroes and warriors of great battle. They are the main agents of help to Indra in his fighting with Vrtra. From this study we come to know that the Maruts occupy an important place in the Ṛg. V. pantheon and are attached with Vāyu. Later on we see that Vāyu produced Maruts, in company with them Indra gains his greatness and exploits.

Agni

In the genre of earthly gods Agni's place is second to Indra, it is sacrificial fire that became the household life of the vedic Aryans while Indra represented the external life of struggle of Aryans. Agni became a part and parcel of their household living (A Vedic Reader, Macdonell, p. 2). In the Ṛg. V. it is the Supreme deity that symbolised the immortal principle in the mortal world. It has been taken as the deathless light and the everlasting perfecter of law. Symbolically one can understand that, Agni is the everburning light- the fire in the mundane human body. In the Indo-Iranian period he was worshipped as a mighty, wise, beneficial God which may have some similarity as we find in case of the Italian and Greeks to offer to Gods in the fire. Here it may be presumed that this system or custom is related to the Indo-European tradition (A.A. Macdonell, p. 3). It was a common belief in the Ṛg. V. that Gods and their manifestations are quite complementary like the sun in the form of fire and Agni is born of the sunrise in the morning and in the setting sun it is absorbed in the evening (Ṛg. V. 7.2.1.) Agni means agile (A Vedic Reader, Macdonell, p. 3) that shows the way and its dwelling place is this earth and the foremost leading agent in sacrifice. It is the drying agent that does not moisten. In the words of Sakapuni it is derived from three roots having the meaning of shining, burning and leading. Since he is called the grhapati or the lord of the house and as the guest (atithi) has a very close association with human life than any other deity. He is the media through which offerings are sent by the human beings to Gods as sacrifice (Ṛg. V. 2.4.4). In this regard he may be a go between or a messenger.

With reference to his physique we may say that his tongue is very beautiful and by the help of his tongue Gods take their oblations. His jaws are sharp, teeth are golden, ghee is taken to be his eyes and by the help of his sharp strong teeth he destroys the demons (Rg. V. 10. 87. 2). His flames are his tail. He has the brightness like Dawn, Sun and the lightning in the clouds in the rainy season (Rg. V. 5.7.4). He despels darkness like sun. His path said to be dark. The horses of his vehicle are a black track he licks every thing by his hairy flames the forest, herbs of the earth just as the barber shaves the beard (Ṛg. V. 10. 142.4). It is his all eating nature whose flames go high up in the sky when he is fed by the oblation of Ghee (Ṛg. V. 5.15.2). Agni can be termed as elemental and personal god. His birth is from the 2 sacred fire sticks which are said to be his mothers (Rg. V. 3.29.3). Though it has a threefold presence the earth, the lightning in the atmosphere and sun in the heaven. Agni is basically one (Ṛg. V. 8.58.2). In this regard he is also termed as Tryambaka like Rudra three planes he is born. He is also called son of strength. He is *Saha Saha Sunuh,* he is also kindled in waters which are both aerialand terrestrial & this motion is marked in the Rg. Vedic terminology (Ṛg. V. 3.1.12, 3.1.13, 10.45.1, 10.1).

Agni is Apam Napal & water is the abode of Agni like the sky of Sun. It is the child of water with golden form and Golden Colour (Ṛg. V. 2.35.10). Again it has two births like "Devi Janaman" as the universe has 2 divisions like heaven and Earth. Another view says that Agni has many births as it is kindled in many dwellings (Ṛg. V. 10.5.1). He is named differently at different situation like Rtvij, Vipra, Purohita, Adhyaryu and Brahman. Unlike other Gods he possesses the qualities of wisdom, benevolence & boons bestowing. Agni is more closely associated with human life. As a great benefactor of worshipper and is more concerned with domestic warfare, offering and prosperity. Since it dwells in men animal, that refers to the eternal heat of life. On the whole Agni is the nearest way to humanity in different forms necessary for the subsistence of living. For this his worship has been done since the Vedic period to this age.

Soma

The whole of 9th maṇḍala of the Ṛg. V. has been dedicated to one of the prominent deities soma that signifies sacrifice as an established feature of the Aryan system. It is a fact that Soma is the Juice from a plant herb and is made from a tawny coloured leaves of that plant. The hymns of Ṛg. V. are in praise of this Soma Rasa (Juice) that intoxicates the Gods and men. In the opinion of the poets Soma represented as a symbol of spiritual delight that gave the gods and men, (Rasānubhuti) wine (Ṛg. V. 967. 28) gives the spiritual intoxication to all. The same cult or myth prevailed both in India and Iran. Both the Ṛg. Vedic Soma and the Zend Haoma are derived from Su, Zend, hu means to press to produce. It is believed to have come from heaven to earth to free the troubled minds of people from the earthly cares. The soma's magical powers have been attributed to God Soma by Indian and Persian bards. He has been portrayed as mighty God in both of the mythologies. The plant has been presented as worshippers and its juice is extracted for holy service. He may be the earthly or the avatar Soma and the divine soma, the symbol of light leisure, relaxation and Gods drink this juice to attain immortality. The part of which is pressed is called Amsu and honey. It was the eagle who brought Soma to the Earth, the whole of the plant is called Anwasa and when it is collected, it is called an ocean of nectar (Rg. V. 9.80.5). The ten finger involved for pressing are the ten reins.

Soma is the child of rain water. Before its use it is mixed with water or milk by which it is sweetened (Rg. V. 9.60.3). The rain drops are taken to be his mother his sound is compared to the sound of rain (R. V. 9.41.3). It is believed that Syena brought Soma to Indra. There were some birds who took interest in serving the human work like Garuda and helping Viṣṇu. The Ṛg. V. also tells that it has got an immense exhilarating power to do wonders. As a divine drink it confers on god and men a sense of immortality, as it is called Amruta, the drink of immortally. Soma has sharp and terrible weapons which he holds in his hands. He also weilds a bow and a thousand pointed shaft who helped a lot to Indra in the war against Vṛtra. If Indra is valourous and chivalrous, it is because of Soma's spell. It has also some medicinal effect narrated in the Ṛg. V. He was born as the lord of the plants (vanaspati), has generated all other plants. As a leading god he has some miraculous power (Ṛg. V. 1.91.6), as a cure for diseases he gives a healing touch, sight to the blind, strength to the weak and lame, power of speech to the mute for which he is called (Vāchaspati) & under his spell one can sing songs (Rg. V. 6.47.3). After taking soma one can think himself as the lord of everything & one can become an excellent orator. At times Soma is identified with the moon. (Ṛg. V. 10.85.5). On the whole it is the lord of wine of delight. Like Agni he is found in plants in the growth of earth and water. We get full human delight (ānanda) after a drink of it and then it becomes the symbol of inner delight.

Bruhaspati

In the Ṛg. V. Bruhaspati is addressed only in eleven times and at times he comes jointly with Indra. He is also named as Brahaman's pati or lord of prayers. He is purely an Indian deity who comes in the Ṛg. V. in earlier & later portion. The word is formed brh- meaning lord of prayer's (Vedic Mythology, Macdonell). Like Agni he is associated with sacrifice and the visible form of the priest represented the power of devotion (Ṛg. V. 2. 1. 3). He is one of the personification of moon. He is both domestic and Brahman priest. He extends help for longevity and disease free life to those who worship him. In regard to his physical appearance, we come to know that, he is sharp horned, bluebacked, golden coloured & armed with how & arrow (Ṛg. V. 2. 24. 8). He is the generator of all prayers and there shall be no fruit of sacrifice without him. His songs go to heaven who has been associated with singers (Ṛg. V. 1. 190.4). His car is drawn by swift and ruddy steeds. He is described as one of the helpers to Indra in his fight with Vṛtra. His conquest of Vala is a symbol of dispelling darkness. Which might be understood as the conquest of Indra over Vrtra (Nirukta X. 13). At times he is called as Maghavan (Bountiful) and Vairin like Indra. In regard to his birth we come to know that he was born of a celestial light & it resulted in the disappearance of darkness from the sky by his loud soar. He is described as seven fạced or *sapta sya* (Ṛg.V. 4. 50. 4). Due to his association with Agni he is called Saptaraśmi or Seveṇ rayed. (Ṛg. V. 1.146.1). He might be the prototype of Brahma.

Yama

Yama has been pictured as the first of the mortals to die. He is the God of the Mortals, but not the dark God of death as be later he came—Rather he has been presented as the benign guardian of the departed souls. No where he is entrusted with some sinister design or some malevolent traits as he was presented in later periods. As the guardian of the departed souls in the next would Yama is entrusted with the dead of his relatives. The belief of next would which seems to be a continuation of the present not hold good in the Ṛg. V. Rather it looks an illusive as the life on earth is highly coveted or wished for. The famous dialogue hymn Yama-Yamī (Ṛg. V. X.) reflects the social system which signifies Yama's sister's seduction and to which the brother refuses. In the same Ṛg. V. version there are arguments for incest as an individual request but brother's refusal is proper in regard to the social taboos.

Parjanya

Parjanya is a slightly less distinct wind god whose figure and function are broad & general with few personal traits possibly he is a harbinger of the monsoon showers. Apan the atmospheric waters are the imaginary reservoirs of the rain water in the sky. The waters some times are described as dwelling place in the highest heavens and sometimes also in the atmosphere from where they descend in refreshing fertilising showers which ensure crops and good harvest.

Dhatr and Vivasvat are extremely in distance solar Gods which mean the creative and the shining aspect of the sun respectively. Martand is the sun whom Aditi didn't like to take with her to heaven.

Female Deities

In the Ṛg. Vedic antheon female deities did not hold much ground as compared to male ones. The philosophy of female principle was certain for the act of creation, but during the vedic period it was not fully developed. However there were two significant conceptions of the heaven and earth (Dyaus & Prithiv) have been very remarkable as they were interpreted as husband and wife but described as parents in the Ṛg. V. (10. 110. 9., 4.3.11.1.55.3).

Uṣas

It is the Goddess of Dawn who seems to be an important female deity in the whole of Ṛg. Vedic pantheon. She has been addressed in about 20 Hymns some times appears in singular and some times in plural as the most resplendeul, charming, female figure in the R. V. The hymns intended to her probably are the examples of most beautiful lyrics of the time. Her physical character has been shrouded by the praise of her personification. The word Uṣas is derived from (-/Basa) meaning to shine (A Vedic Reader, Macdonell-93). Her appearance is unlike a dancer adorned with gay colourful attire & unveil her charms & enchantment while arriving. It seems as if she is decorated by her mother to give a deep spell over the whole world by a flash of light beauty. She has been portrayed as an immortal shining character whose fresh & colourful presence enables the gates of heaven to be opened & illuminates the ends of the sky (Ṛg. V. 1. 113. 16. 1. 92. 11). She is like some solar deities that activates the living being, the birds and the people. She has a close association with God and open the path of Sūrya for his Journey (Ṛg. V. 7.75.5). The Sun comes after dawn & Uṣas is an eternal phenomenon. Here Dawn is taken as his wife where as Uṣas is his mother & the process seems to be ever continuing (Ṛg. V. 7. 75. 5). In the Ṛg. V. 7. 78. 3 hymns sing of Vṣas relation with Agni who is called the lover of Dawn. But, Uṣas uses Agni to be lighted. She is called to be the daughter of Dyaus/elder sister night.

Prithvi or the Goddess of the Earth

In the Ṛg. V. Goddess of the earth is very often addressed with the sky god Dyaus for example they are eulogised as one entity- Dyāvāpṛthivī. They represent the sky and Earth as father & mother. The word is derived from pṛth that expands. It is Indra who upholds the earth, the region of torment. torture pain like the Hades (Ṛg. V. 10. 152. 4). It has a three fold existence like antarikṣa, rajas & Dyaus or heaven. It has a rare quality of tolerance and forgiveness and affection for her children (Ṛg. V. 10. 18. 10). She has excelled her power of tolerance and suffering by holding mountains, plants and everything for the well being of her children (Ṛg. V. 10. 18. 10). She is great Mahe, firm, Drudha and Luminous (Arjuni).

Aditi

Primarily it means boundlessness or non-binding. Aditi is the personification of binding. The worshipper involves her for his mukti or release from bondage of this mundane world. Diti is the mother of Daity as but Aditi is the mother of Gods. Ādityas are the sons of Gods or boundless.

She is light, virtues or Ṛta & Aditi. It is believed that Gods were first became independent of suffering and bondage or free. Mukta from the clutches of darkness. She gave birth to seven Ādityas. There are six names of Ādityas like Mitra, Aryaman, Bhaga, Varuṇa, Dakṣa & Aṁṣa. But, the 7th is not named and Āditya is the son of Aditi (Ṛg. V. 10. 72. 810. 8. 9). Martaṇḍa is the 8th son of Aditi who is undeveloped and was cast out.

Bibliography

1. E. B. Tylor, Primitive Culture - 1871.
2. Max Müller, Solar Mythology.
3. Bronislaw Malinowski, Myth in Primitive Psychology.
4. Henry A Murray, Myth and Myth Making (1960).
5. Dr. G. V. Devasthali, Religion and Mythology of the Brahmaṇas.
6. Sukumari Bhattacharji, Literature in the Vedic Age.
7. A Reader's Companion to World Literature.
8. Jyotsna Chawla, The Ṛg. V. Vedic Deities and their Iconic Forms.
9. The Encyclopaedia of Britannica.

Vedic Philosophy

7

Dr. Bidyut Lata Ray

The Vedas and the vedic texts like Brāhmaṇas, Åraṇyakas,Upaniṣads and the Kalps adhere to many metaphysical elements which, in turn, exhibit the high standard of human thinking in the most primitive period of the history of mankind. The religion, mythology, ethics, aesthetics, rites, worships, sacrifices and above all the vedic pantheon provide threads to make the string of Indian philosophy. The perceptions, speculations and logical notions of the vedic seers were framed with their philosophical insights into the every matter of this creation. The nature, the environment and the living organisms all formed the components of metaphysical attributes to human understanding of matter energy and life.

Philosophy in Ṛgveda

Ṛgvedic philosophy and religion are composed of the complex beliefs and practices of the Āryāns formed of several racial and cultural elements whose history stretched over a long period of the past. During this period, the vedic literature was developing with its components and hence was dynamic. As a result of which, the literature contains traces of the various stages of its evolution, both in mythology and in metaphysics. Therefore, the topic under discussion should be divided with precision in accordance with the specific constituents and the time when each of these arose and dominated the thought and behaviour of the Āryān people.

Religion embraces myths, rituals, magic and ethics while philosophy means the metaphysical super structure which a person can not expose clearly, but which embodies the collective vision as well as individual behaviour. Such a system of beliefs alone determines and, hence, exhibits, the religion and ethos of a person.

Ṛgveda does not narrate the myths fully and systematically, but alluded to and sometimes mentioned casually in a manner which presupposes familiarity with the current corpus of myths. Description of rituals, sacrifices and the use of the vedic *mantras* in the relevant sacrifices presupposes the knowledge of application and familiarity of the Vedic people with the hymns of the *Saṁhitās*. Some accounts of the sacrificial rituals are found in the Yajurveda. But, these accounts were intended for 'insiders'; hence they are cryptic, intended entirely for the initiated. In the later Brāhmaṇas and early Upaniṣads we trace the first impression of philosophical speculations, precisely we can say that the concept emanates from the later Vedic period, i.e., with the Xth book of the Ṛgveda. Here we meet with abstract concepts and cosmogonic and philosophical speculations. It comes down to the later Brāhmaṇas and Upaniṣads. The mythical part of the vedic religion is dealt with the Saṁhitās where the magic and ritual are reserved in the Yajurveda and Brahmaṇas. The Upaniṣads adhere to the philosophical sections.

The logic of divine intervention and that of the creation can be discovered through the sacrifices performed by the vedic people. To the sacrificing man, the creation comprises gods, demons, demiurges, spirits, Nāgas and animals. Myths expose that creation is not chao but a cosmos, that means resistances offered to the inherent harmony of the Universe and that it is possible and even obligatory to restore the broken harmony. The gods had challenged this force of destruction at first in order to maintain the creation. Once man was created on the earth the gods had entrusted him with the exalted task of preserving the creation. So man being an organic part of the creation has the sacred duty of preserving and protecting it from the destructive forces. Consequently, man must lead his life with the cosmic scheme to restore the harmony of creation. From this metaphysics follows a solemn code of ethics, because now the ritualistic attitude becomes the only valid tool of mankind to achieve the goal. The performance of the sacrifice becomes the only valid mode of living meaningfully on this earth. This attitude certainly reveal the metaphysics of correspondence between the macrocosm and the microcosm on the basis of ethics.

The deities like Indra, Varuṇa, Agni, Aśvins, et seq. are extolled in the Vedic hymns in order to save man's life from danger and disaster. They give strength to man to cope with environment in which he lives. They have released life and light for men from the clutches of danger and destruction. Light is symbolic of knowledge and understanding and of life itself. Ṛgveda ethics has the presupposition that life is precious, that it is essentially good and sweet and should be enjoyed fully as long as possible.

The theory of the creation of the world his in the hymns of the Xth book of the Ṛgveda which deals the subject in various ways like the origin, of the gods (X.72), the hymn to the unknown god (X. 121), the world derived from the primordial sacrifice (X. 82), and in more detail from the parts of the body of a primeval man sacrificed by the gods (X. 90), and finally these speculative tendencies have been expressed clearly in X. 129. Starting from a state when there was neither existence nor non-existence, the Ṛgveda (X. 129) says that a unique element was produced in due course by internal heat (tapas), then the desire (of a sexual tendency), "the first seed of thought" and then the gods. Even the gods were the parts of the order of creation. In this famous verse, Indian speculation reaches its highest point at the start. The development of an organic conception of the cosmos dwells on the philosophical point of view. Even the more direct expositions of cosmogony, like X. 129 or 121, introduçe asceticism and the sacrifice among the original factors of creation. Thus, the tenth maṇḍala of the Ṛgveda contains philosophical hymns interpreted by the scholars time and again.

B. L. Adams in his book *The Story of Oriental Philosophy*[1] has discussed germs of Indian philosophy as latent in the Vedas and developed in the Upaniṣads, culminating in the Vedanta system of Śaṅkara. Ṛgvedic hymns reveal a philosophical frame of mind in those obstinate questionings of sense and outward things. According to S. K. Das[2], the first flutter of the newfledged philosophic impulse on Indian soil clothed itself in poetry of unending charm, with abundance of myths due to fertile imagination or creative fancy. The poetic or mythical presentation of hymns of Ṛgveda has nothing *prima facie* to invalidate their claim for truth. Ṛgveda may not have made any positive contribution towards Vedanta, but it certainly prepared the field for the reception of the same. R. V. Jahagirdar[3] has analysed and interpreted the philosophical hymns of the Xth Maṇḍala of the Ṛgveda.

The seers, who composed the Ṛgveda, had a knowledge of soul as different from the body as eternal, and having the essential qualities of *sat, cit, ānanda*. Narahari gives stress on nine words, viz. *brahman, ātman, tman, satyam, aje bhāgah, jiva, prāna, manas* and *suparṇ*a. According to ṚV, (1) *Soul* is different from body; survives the destruction of the latter; (2) is eternal, neither born nor liable to destructions; (3) forms 'essence' of the body and is its controller; (4) is the experiencer of man's actions - heaven or punishment after dealth; (5) is composed of *sat, cit,* and *ānanda*. The seers of ṚV seem to know also the fundamentals of Brahman, the Upanisadic absolute. The Ṛgvedic literature presupposes a long period of development of civilization in India and represents the final stage in such an evolution. What is found enunciated in the Upaniṣad later is only what existed in the philosophy of Ṛgveda.

A. C. Bose[4] points out that there are four currents spread in Indian spiritual history , i.e., there existed 4 types of 'Ethos' basing on 4 types of castes. Each 'etha' was formed of spiritual and moral ideals.

Philosophy on Yajurveda

The characteristic material of the Yajurveda is the *Yajus*, 'the sacrificial formula'. This veda was compiled for application to sacrificial rites only. The Sāmaveda may be called a manual of song book for the Udgātā priests, for the purpose of singing in the sacrifice, while the Yajurveda contains prayer-books for the Adhvaryu priests who mutter those sacrificial prayers or formulas alongwith the performance of the sacrificial rites. The some-sacrifice is the sole concern of the

Sāmaveda but the Yajurveda supplies the formulas for the whole sacrificial ceremonial. The characteristic element of the Yajurveda, as Winternitz points out, is the prose formulas and prayers[5]. From the texts of the Yajurveda, whether they are, the prayer formulas or the "Brāhmaṇa element', i.e., the theological discussions about the sacrificial rites, it is quite evident that it is the sacrifice and not the gods that constitute the central theme of this Veda. Magical concepts are so abundant in the sacrificial rites alongwith their prayer formulas that the Yajurveda is rightly bearing magical character rather than religious[6]. The Yajurvedic priest is here playing the role of a magician[7]. Ostensibly, the religion of the Yajurveda is described as a kind of "Mechanical Sacerdotalism"[8]. The philosophy lying behind the Yajus is the achievement of material gain. According to Macdonell, the formulas of the Yajurveda have not, as a rule, the form of prayers addressed to the gods, but on the whole and characteristically consist of statements about the result of employing particular rites and mantras[9]. Oldenberg, in this connection, opines that the Yajus describe briefly what can be done through them, urge the reciter to act, or urge another object to enter into relation with him[10]. The Yajus also set forth the effect which can be realised by a rite and a prayer[11] . The ritual of the fire-altar is a more recent stratum. The Yajus concerned with this is the tool of the Adhvaryu. The Yajurveda, being the ritual Veda par excellence, is the practice manual of the Adhvaryu priest while the verses taken from the Ṛgveda are the Concern of the Hotri.

During the performance of sacrifices, the mantras are chanted by the priest with repetitions and insertions of the syllable *Oṁ*. Macdonell rightly observes that the formulas of the Yajurveda are full of dreary repetitions or variations of the same idea, and abound with half or wholly unintelligible interjections particulars, the syllable *Oṁ*[12]. Other quite unintelligible ejaculations marked during the performance of the sacrifice are *Svāhā, Svadhaā, Vaṣat,* and *Vāt.* These syllables, whether carry meanings or not, had mystical significance[13]. Further, the Yajus formulas do not aim at 'worshipping' gods, but at influencing them, at compelling them to fulfil the wishes of the sacrificer[14]. Through the Yajus, the priest even tries to have control over Nature as well as the supernatural powers[15]. Apart from ritual, the Yajurveda also deals with *sṛṣṭiyajña.* Agni prayed in this veda represents knowledge of *Sattva, rajas, tamas*. Vedic conception of ultimate world, much in advance of present-day science, is current in the Yajus. Studying the myth and metaphysics in perspectives of vedic and purāṇic myths and the concepts of *saṁsāra, punarjanma, karma,* and *dharma,* G. A. Deleury points out that Indian metaphysics is basically a re-interpretation of sacrificial system[16].

The sacrifices like the Aśvamedha, (horse sacrifice), the Agnicayana (piling of the fire altar) and the Soma sacrifice are elaborately treated in the Yajurvada. The horse sacrifice is interrupted frequently by other rituals, of the other sacrifices mention should be made of Darśapūrṇamāsa, Rājasuūyra, Sutrāmāni and the special animal sacrifice. The new and full moon sacrifices depicted in Kāṇḍas I and II are significant. we also trace the references to human sacrifice in most ancient civilizations. The Aztecs had it. This was there in Babylon and Egypt. Powell refers to human sacrifice at Samain[17].

The Puruṣa hymn of Ṛgveda (X. 90) describes the ritual slaughter of the puruṣa and thus refers to human sacrifice. The paruṣa, the supreme being, is here mentioned as the Cosmic oblation which is the potent cause of creation. Like the myths of Ymir or the later Mithraic myth it is cosmological or etiological in character. This ritual 'Purusamedha' appears as symbiotic and explains the curious etiology of the significant social phenomena of the rise of professions. Next, we trace another interesting rite 'the Sarvamedha'. Theoretical implications are observed here in this rite to offer his *all* as sacrificial fees by he sacrificer at the and of the rite. In this respect, Bhattacharji holds that the rite has a philosophical basis. It is the utter unreality of this proposition which adheres to metaphysical symbolism, i.e. the ritualist is given a philosophical interpretation of his ritual act; self-abnegation is upheld as the underlying principle of sacrifice[18]. In other world, this section anticipates the Brāhmaṇa and Āraṇyaka Sections for interpreting rituals on the basis of underneath metaphysics. The very last chapter of the Yajurveda Saṁhita (Ch. 40) reiterates the metaphysics of the Sarvamedha attitude.

Agni hotra is the simplest and the shortest of rites. It is significant for upholding the Sun in the firmament. In the Nahua mythology "creation is held to be impossible except through sacrifice : the sacrifice of the sun dismembered among human-kind ......the sacrifice of men to restore the Sun's original unity".[19]

The Vedic divinities are also given philosophical touch in addition to their natural manifestations. For instance, Agni is consecrated of the gods, the piler of the fire of, men[20]. Taittiriya Saṁhita[21] describes 'Virāja' as "dividing itself stayed among the gods with the holy power (brahman) among the Asuras with food". Agni, Indra and Sūrya were regarded as the three pre-eminent gods of the three regions - earth, atmosphere and the highest heaven respectively. Yajurveda treats penance as a value and a creative force. When the gods supplicated prajāpati for offspring he said, "As I have created you by penance, so seek ye offspring through penance[22]. The Cow has been described with rich symbolic significance that even the dust of its footprints are said to fulfil the purpose of the sacrifice. With the ritual language, the philosophical thought is charged with cosmic significance.

Philosophy in Sāmaveda

The Sāmaveda Saṁhitā plays an important role in the history of vedic thought where magic, music and sacrifice were blended together. Both sacrifice and melody are magical in character and hence their combination in the Sāmaveda reveals the magico-religious features of the Vedic religion.

The Sāmaveda presents two different concepts, namely, (i) all that exists and that may come in the future too are nought but the puruṣa known as Savitā or

Viṣṇu. All activities belongs to him and he manifests himself as all creatures and the worlds (ii) He creates man in his own image as a subtle being endowed with all seven principles of activities, who degenerates to lower forms by shedding one activity after another in the subtle world until he is devoid of all seven activities and reduced to the state of inanimate matter. The eternal divinities raise him from the lower strata to the upper, i.e. the stage of man. In this form, he longs to go back to his heavenly home and prays constantly the almighty for the same. Finally attains his goal through trials and tribulations. Thereafter when he is gilled with worldly desires, he returns to the earth by birth and then undergoes the fortunes of earthly existence. He does not mingle with the creator at any time.

Both the views mentioned above are concident on one point that the conception of a Jiva makes it easy to explain the processes of creation. However, the creator desires to continue the process of creation through diverse activities, with increasing sense of perceptions. Activity alone ensures existence. The Sāmaveda stresses on the prayers as the sole means to attain an unimpaired life on earth. The prayers are meant to keep constant touch with the creator. Various hymns have been composed for praying different deities to secure a wealthy, healthy, painless, peaceful and long life in this world. According to Sāmaveda, *prāṇa* is born of Agni in the brain (hill) to whom Agni gives command (direction) to produce oblation to the brain, which is stabilized by him through the nerves (Vāyu)[23]. Indra preside over the sense organs in compassion and skilfully allots (the sense activities of men) to them[24]. Prajāpati (Kāyā) is fond of the home (brain) and guides consciousness to the mother bestowed on the world through activity[25]. Soma nourishes with the motley sense activities; the sense activities nourish men by arousing them. In the sacrifice, the five sense activities of men are guided by the deity in order to bestow vigour in men[26]. The brain above helps the sense organs as desired by them by stimulating ideas[27]. Rudra, the nervous system controls us in life, presides truly in life over both brain and sense organs[28]. Regarding the birth, the Sāmaveda says that it is the dharma of yonder world which unites with us and grows together with existence. The father (Activity) unites with the brain, concealed like a tortoise. Agni has faith in mother who is the preceptor to Mind[29].

Universally it is believed that words have a creative power[30]. The biblical account of creation through words or its Upaniṣadic equivalents where Prajāpati desires and expresses his desire which leads to creation. Words symbolize the manifest world. Music on the other hand "brings us into harmony with the non-manifest".[31] According to poet Tagore, "Music begins where words end".[32] It is the non-manifest invoked to achieve the desired end, hence music helps. In addition to this, music song as the Sāmans, within a conventional and specified range of melodies, to specified rhythmic beats and to known and shared myths expressed in the hymns, produces ecstasy, indispensable to any shamanistic practice.[33] The sound of the sweet music often heralds the approach of the supernatural. Sweet melody is essentially attributed to the other world. Chanting of the Sānmans leads the performer to a collective semi-hypnotic state. Then, philosophical thoughts prevail. The *stobhas* of the Sāmaveda bear the disyllabic *huva, hau, hoi, hovi, havu,* et seq. The stobha in the means of modification applied to the ṛe whilst it is joined with the melody.[34] The Sāmans, when chanted, induce psychological influences in the minds of others and as a result of which the enemies, demons, ghosts and monsters are brought to control during the performance of rites or sacrifices. Thus the chant is a means not only for pleasing gods but also for imposing upon devils. Therefore, the *Udgātṛ* sings the sāmans in the most mysterious forms. The song moves in specially rapid rhythm to generate the particular psychosomatic condition conducive to trance-like experiences. The chanting of the Sāmans by a group links with the folk-songs, which are gradually established in the community with the process of religious evolutions and attachments.

The conceptions of Sāmaveda on Evolution on earth are unique but at the same time most rational carrying the stamp of conviction. The views of the Sāmaveda on the theory of Evolution coincide in many respects to those of the Yajurveda. The creator is the puruṣa whose presence is felt every where in this vast and illimitable space.[35] Truly, the cosmos is his manifestation, rejoicing animate and inanimate objects.[36] All this here is the puruṣa, all that exists and also that may come into existence in the future are his manifestations.[37] The cosmos is born of activity who is united to it; the puruṣa controls it from beyond.[38] Ostensibly, in creative activity, there is at first a descent from intelligence to inertia or matter, rather quick and then a slow or measured ascent of the combination of both as life-process or manifestation[39].

Philosophy in Atharvaveda

Philosophical thoughts gleaned in the Atharvaveda are best reflected in its cosmogonic and metaphysical hymns which are quite common in the latest sections of the Ṛgveda books I and X. Such hymns of the Ṛgveda are cryptic, verging on mystic esoterism probably shared and jealously guarded as a cult secret in a mystic brotherhood. Yet these are the first ever attempt to unravel the many confusing strains of reality. There are a large number of hymns on the knowledge of Brahman[40] or Ātman. Ṛgvedic names like Bṛhaspati, Brahman, Prajāpati, Virāj and Ātman are also traced here on the Atharvaveda, while a few new names like Vena, Rohita and Skambha appear in this veda. Thus, the level of abstraction or metaphysical speculation is reflected here. The sense of mystery in creation and its source is very well expressed in a hymn of the Atharvaveda[41]. The knowledge of the mystery is equated essentially with the knower's identity. The idea of the supreme spirit is given in hymn X. 8. Bloomfield, analysing the hymns of the Atharvaveda, opines that the priest of this Veda was truly a Brahman, for he had already been engaged in the metaphysical speculations. He was a superior theologian. Ostensibly, the Atharvaveda itself was called Brahmaveda[42].

Time is depicted in two outstanding hymns of this Veda[43]. Time is the primordial element, it is Brahman ..... as Brahman it contains the Supreme being (*parameṣṭhin*). Everything (living or own-living) begins from Kāla (Time), all sacred lore flew from it, all activities and manifestations are embodied in it, and hence it conquered all regions with the power of *brahman* and attained the Supreme Nature of being termed as the Supreme-God. The metaphysical concept of time is explained here as the invisible, creative, eternal entity in which the cosmos is inherent[44].

The terms like *Virāj, Skambha, Jyeṣṭhabrahman, Brahmandana, Prāṇā,* etc. are extolled in the Atharvaveda to scatter the mystic concepts as well as the creative principle[45]. *Viraj* symbolises the creative principle closely connected with sacrifice, while Brahmandana represents the rice mess for or of Brahman. Another creative principle is 'Rohita' who created heaven and earth[46]. Rohita stands for the sun, the white sun of the black (mother), the calf of the night who climbs the sky[47]. Aditi and Rohita, both are mentioned in here[48]. We observe a mystic account of gods, elements, truth, abstract principles, good and evil, theft, crookedness, et seq. that grasped man[49]. So, the wise men consider man as *Brahman* where in all the divinities dwell as Cows in a Cowpen.[50] Puruṣa is another word used here to mean man. Puruṣa is attributed to ambrosia and death. Puruṣa symbolises the ocean which contains the body of man.[51] He, who knows Brahman in Puruṣa, knows Parameṣṭhin.[52] Man is the ultimate purpose of the creative process.

Cosmogony dealt on the Atharvaveda has a metaphysical approach, which they share with the very last metaphysical hymns of the Ṛgveda. The hymns of the Atharvaveda are blended with both magic and religion. Mysticism is the fundamental approach here to understand the reality. The power of the magic is felt with the three basic notions of the Vedic people: (i) the desire for material prosperity in general, (ii) the consciousness of powerful and evil hostile agents and (iii) an attitude of self-confidence or self-reliance of the priests. There were charms and prayers in the Atharvaveda which were used to remove the effects of all kinds of evils due to defects in sacrifice, mental deliquency, debts, incurred and not paid back, cheating at play and doing harm to "Air or Earth or Heaven"or doing wrong to them.[53] The Atharvavedic charms and spells have both auspicious and harmful character. According to Macdonell, the hymns of this veda are meant to appease and bless as well as to curse.[54] Thus, they contain a double aspect.

Many hymns of the Atharvaveda also testify to a vivid consiousness of sin.[55] The truth is spoken of as one of the elements that sustain the earth.[56] Both the Ṛgveda and the Atharvaveda regard sin as a 'pollution' which afflicts a person and clings to him like a disease and misfortune. Therefore, man pray god to save him from the curse of sin.[57] Sin can be transferred from gods to men and from men to men.[58] Sin is inherited from the father, mother and other relatives, apart from committing it one-self.[59]

Ṛta represents the cosmic 'laws' and 'order' that governs he entire creation, the Universe. This cosmic significance of the Ṛta is marked in the Ṛgveda[60] as well as in the Atharvaveda[61] to some extent. In the Ṛgveda, Ṛta alongwith *'satya'* and *'tapas'* is acknowledged as one of the three principal constituents of the universe. Thus, the myths, rituals, magics and mysteries, all at a time envelop the cosmogony and metaphysics which require exploration with sincere investigations to open up doors for the emergence of new philosophy.

References

1. Adams, B.L., The Story of Oriental Philosophy, New York, 1932, Chapters 1-8.
2. Das, S.K., The Spirit of Indian Philosophy, CR 42, Jan. 1932.
3. Jahagirdar, R.V., Speculation on Vedic Speculation, J. Bombay. Vin. 4, Nov. 1935.
4. Bose, A.C., Four Currents in Indian Spiritual History, Prabuddha Bharata, Calcutta, August, 1936.
5. Winternitz, M., A History of Indian Literature trans. S. Ketkar, Vol.1, Calcutta University Press, Calcutta, 1927, p. 177.
6. Gaden, A.S., "Nature (Hindu)", the Encyclopaedia of Religion and Ethics, Vol. 8, p. 311
7. *Ibid.*, p. 313.
8. Macdonell, A. A., "Magic (Vedic)", The Encyclopaedia of Religion and Ethics, Vol. 8, p. 183.
9. Macdonell, A. A., A History of Sanskrit Literature, Delhi, 1958, p. 184.
10. Oldenberg, H., The Religion of the Veda, Berlin, 1890.
11. Renou, L., Vedic India, Indological Book House, Varanasi, 1971, p. 16.
12. Macdonell, A. A., op. cit., p. 183. Also if. Uma Gupta's Materialism in the Veda, Classical Publishing Company, New Delhi, 1987, p. 97.
13. Winternitz, M., op. cit., pp. 185-186.
14. *Ibid.*
15. Macdonell, A. A., op, cit. pp. 183-184.
16. Deleury, G. A., Myths and metaphysics: relation between Vedic and Purāṇic myths and the concepts of *Saṁsāra, punarjanma, karma* and *dharma*, Summary of papers, 21 Aloc, 1961, pp. 194-196.
17. Powell, T.G.E., The Celts, p. 155
18. Bhattacharji, S., Literature in the Vedic Age, Vol. I, K. P. Bagchi & Company, Calcutta, 1984, P. 213.
19. Sejourne, L., Burning Water, London 1957, p. 59.
20. Taittirīya Saṁhitā, V, 4.9.2.
21. *Ibid.*, V, 6.8. 2-3.

22. *Ibid.*, VII, 1.5.2.
23. Sāmaveda, Ågneya Kāṇḍa 1.1.2.3.
24. *Ibid.*, 1.1.4.10.
25. *Ibid.*, 1.1.5.9.
26. *Ibid.*, 1.2.1.2.
27. *Ibid.*, 1.2.1.3.
28. *Ibid.*, 1.2.2.7.
29. *Ibid.*, 1.2.4.10.
30. Levi-Strauss, C., The Raw and the Cooked, New York, 1964, p. 22.
31. Rees, A. and B., Celtic Heritage, London, 1961, p. 137.
32. Bhattacharji, S., op. Cit., P. 173.
33. Rees, A. and B., op. Cit., p. 137.
34. Hoogt, J. M. van der, the Ṛgvedic chant studied in its textual and melodic form, Wageningen, 1929, p. 26.
35. Sāmaveda, Āranya Kāṇḍa, VI, 3.4.3.
36. Yajurveda, 31.4.
37. Sāmaveda, Āranya Kāṇḍa, VI, 3.4.5 Yajurveda, 31.2.
38. Sāmaveda, Āranya Kāṇḍa, VI, 3.4.7.
39. Ganapati, S. V., Sāmaveda (ed.), Motilal Banarsidass, Delhi, 1982, p. 228.
40. Atharvaveda, V, 6 on brahman.
41. *Ibid*, VII, 66.
42. Bloomfield, M., Hymns of the Atharvaveda, Introduction, pp. xiii, xix.
43. Atharvaveda, XIX, 53 and 54.
44. Bhattacharji, S., op. Cit., p. 302 & fn. 104.
45. Atharvaveda, VIII, 9,10; X, 7. 35, 38; X, 8; XI, 5.21; XI, 4.20.
46. *Ibid.*, XIII, 1.6.
47. *Ibid.*, XIII, 3.26.
48. *Ibid.*, XIII, 1.
49. *Ibid.*, XI. 8.
50. *Ibid.*, XI. 8. 32.
51. *Ibid.*, X, 7.15.
52. *Ibid.*, X, 7. 17.
53. Gupta, U., Materialism in the Veda, Classical Publishing Company, New Delhi, 1987, p. 106.
54. Macdonell A. A., *op. cit.*, P. 185.
55. Atharvaveda, VI, 111. 3; IV, 6. 1-2.
56. *Ibid.*, XII, 1.1.
57. *Ibid.*, X, 3.8; and Ṛgveda, VI, 74.3.
58. *Ibid.*, VI, 113.1; VII, 64; and Ṛgveda, X, 37.12.
59. Ṛgveda, VI, 74.3; and Atharvaveda, V, 30.4; VI, 116.3.
60. Ṛgveda, X, 190.1.
61. Atharvaveda, VIII, 9.13; 16-17

Vedic Religion

8

Dr. Brajakishore Swain

Introduction

In the Vedas the very term dharma is used conveying the sense of religion. Sometime it is translated as law. Both the terms usually convey the one and the same sense from the Vedic point of view.[1] In the history of law the most important early specialization is that which separates what a man ought to do from what he ought to know. A great part of the religious literature, including the creation of the universe, the structure of heaven, hell, and the world or worlds and the nature of the Gods, falls under the last head, what a man ought to know. Law-books (*dharmaśāstras*) first appear as a subdivision of the first branch, what a man should do[2]. In the Vedas, dharma has an intellectual acceptance as the moral conduct and the spiritual build. The basis of dharma, then, is the moral law with spiritual discipline guiding life. Therefore dharma has been conceived as the ideal form of conduct.[3] As a matter of fact it (dharma) is also said as eternal law. Lord Viṣṇu upholds it.[4] Agni has been said as the chairperson of the *dharmasabhā* where law is to be determined[5]. This is very lucidly revealed in the Atharva Veda (xii. 1. 17) that *pṛthivī dharmaṇā dharmaṇā dhṛtām.* This idea has been taken in Mahābhārata-Karṇaparvan 69-59, *dhāraṇād dharmamityāhuḥ.* For upholding of this universe the vedic seers have taken pain to identify six fundamental principles of dharma viz. truth (*satya*), eternal order (*ṛta*), consecration (*dīkṣā*), austerity (*tapas*), brahman and sacrifice (*yajña*)[6]. In this article an humble attempt has been made to analyse these six fundamental principles of dharma.

Truth

Truth is the oral form of dharma. The Vedas place it first and ritual last. In every case the problem has been to find out this truth and not to stick to belief. The vedic sage has been the seeker after truth. His sincerity and freedom of mind have been responsible for the maintenance of the philosophical and spiritual outlook. In the Vedas, we find reference of thirtythree deities as the manifestation of truth[7]. The head of those deities is Savitṛ that is why Savitṛ has been invoked as *satyadharmā* (AV. I. 24.1)[8]. Prayer and ritual of the right type comeout of a truthful life and true heart. The path of religious progress is the path of truth. In

Muṇḍaka Upaniṣad (iii. 1. 6.) it is revealed that by truth is the divine path laid out, by which sages, having obtained what they desire, ascend the supreme abode of truth.[9] The same Upaniṣad (iii. 1. 5) also clarifies that the *ātman* is to be realised through truth (*satyena labhyaḥ*). It declares with confidence that truth alone triumphs and not untruth. One can find the very core of the vedic religion as truth if he enters into the basic text with intuition. There, it is revealed that, truth in its moral sense is truthfulness, integrity, in a metaphysical sense it signifies reality. This way *satya* becomes *sat*. *Satya* applies conduct. Sat is an object of search of knowledge or realisation and vision.[10]

In the Yajurveda (xxxii.8) it has been recorded that the sage has his vision of *sat* in which the Universe is united as men in the home.[11] Sage to sage, the knowledge passes like the information about an unknown land from traveller to traveller (RV. x. 32. 7)[12]. A traveller, who has yet a long way to go, may remain silent about *sat*. But with *satya* it is different. *Satya* is our concern at every moment of life. Therefore, truth as a value of life is abiding and ultimate. In Yajurveda it is held that one has to speak the truth for spiritual disquisition.[13]

Eternal Order

Ṛta : Eternal order is the second fundamental principle of Vedic religion.[14] In practice, this term is not, at present, used. However, its negative *anṛta* i.e. disorder has been used from ancient time.[15] In its moral aspect *ṛta* is cognate with truth.[16] In the *aghamarṣaṇa sūkta*[17] it is revealed that there are three gradual states of action. They are *ṛta, satya* and *tapas*. Here the beginning point of action is *ṛta* whereas the ending point *tapas*. Both *ṛta* and *satya* (Rg. x. 190.1) are spoken of as being born in the beginning of things out of perfect spiritual order. *Satya* upholds the earth whereas *ṛta* upholds the heaven.

In its moral aspect, however, ṛta is wider than truth. It includes justice and goodness. It is the synonymous with dharma as an ethical concept. This way rta is opposed to evil. That is why it is spoken of as stern and fierce i.e. *ugra*.[18]

Like satya, ṛta forms an essential part of the conception of the divinity. The God is told *ṛtavān* in the Vedas : the guardian of law.[19] Here ṛta has a wider implication than morality. It stands for cosmic order i.e. immutable law of nature, by which the universe becomes systematised and integrated. On account of its eternal nature it avoids chaos and confusion. In Rg. iv. 40.5 and YV. x. 24 divinity is identified with ṛta.[20]

With reference to ṛta we find a co-ordination between natural law and moral law. Good life, which is lived according to ṛta as moral, is cognate with cosmic law governing nature. The man of faith is, of course, one who has understood and accepted the eternal law. The atheist is one who does not believe in the eternal values and does not stand for goodness. We are told of relation of Vṛtra with Indra. It is construed that Vṛtra, whom Indra destroys, is the power of darkness and evil who obstructs the working of ṛta. Thus awareness of the working of eternal law in nature and life is ṛta. Varuṇa is the presiding deity of ṛta. He holds together the cosmos through ṛta : natural law. The natural law is nothing but discipline of life through moral law. From aesthetic point of view ṛta is the discipline of form that makes beauty (Rg. iv. 23.9)[21].

Both satya and ṛta have represented in the Vedas as Brāhmaṇa and Kṣatriya respectively. Of these two, Brāhmaṇa corresponding to truth (satya) represents the cultural force. Kṣatriya, corresponding to ṛta, represents the political power. In Rg. viii. 35. 16-8 we find a good reference of three fold interest of life where it is revealed that "strengthen the power of knowledge and strengthen intellects, strengthen the ruling power and strengthen heroes. Give strength to the milch-cow and strengthen the people."[22] It is observed, here, that three types of men emerge—, the brahmana, the philosophical man, the ksatriya, the political man and the vaisya, the common man. While the last will produce the wealth of the nation, the second will work for order and security and the first will carry on the intellectual and spiritual interprise. In this system the 1st group needs protection. Special effort is to be directed to the encouragement of the first two groups of society (YV. vi.3)[23]. Thus brāmaṇa and kṣatriya are found to make up between them the religious and political idealism of vedic time.

Two types of virtues are stressed in the Vedas. They are wisdom and valour. They correspond to brāhmaṇa and kṣatriya respectively. There are prayers, on the one hand, for intellectual power (*dhı*), wisom (*kratu*), efficiency (dakṣatā, spiritual vigour (*varcas*) and higher intellect (*medhā*); on the other hand, there are prayers for strength (*saba*), valour (*vırya*), manliness (*nṛmnā*), spiritual power (*ojas*), conquering power (*sahas*), wrath (*manyu*), fearlessness (*abhaya*) and vigour (*bala*) (Rg. x. 148.4)[24]. Social organisation becomes perfect when the two powers brahmana and ksatıiya work in harmony (Rg. YV. xx. 25).

Consecration

Consecration, austerity, prayer and ritual are four fundamental principles of dharma. These, generally, come under the category of philosophical-religious interest of which brāhmaṇa is the executive authority. The first tow of these, consecration and austerity, are chiefly directed at the realisation of ultimate truth. These refer to detailed systems of self culture for spiritual advancement. (YU. xix. 30)[25].

Relation between teacher and student is identified through consecration. But consecration is not merely a formal initiation. There is a deep personal contact between the teacher and the pupil under instruction (*śiṣyatva*). While giving the initiation, the Āchārya carries the pupil with him (AV. xi. 5. 3.)[26]. The initiation is nothing but the path of transition from darkness to light, from humanity to divinity, from untruth to truth.

As a matter of fact there is something positive in the instruction that the Āchārya gives to his disciple. Instruction is like the guidance that a man who knows a land gives to one who is a stranger to it. God has given everybody the opportunity and ability to acquire knowledge with his own endeavour, but one receives guidance under instruction and goes directly forward. This instruction is nothing but a guidance to a traveller who is actuated by a desire to visit and see the land.[27] This instruction gets the essence of initiation if it comes to a desciple from a teacher. Therefore, the initiative lies with the pupil. He is not a passive recepient, but an active agent in the acquisition of knowledge. In the YU, it is revealed that by self-realisation *(vrata)* one obtains conservation *(dikṣā).* By consecration one obtains grace *(dakṣinā).* By grace one obtains reverence and by reverence is truth obtained (xix. 30).

Austerity

Austerity is termed as *tapas* in the Vedas. It is the physical involvement of the individual in religious life. From it the creation begins. (*tapaso 'dhyajāyata*). This creation is nothing but the creation of result from action. *Tapas* is the unflagging, unsparing effort in the achievement of higher things. The infinite pains one has to take to do something are really worth while. Tapas lies at the beginning of all great things.[28] Truth (*satya*), and order (*ṛta*) are born at the beginning out of perfect spiritual ardour. Even Gods and sages perform noble things though tapas.

Tapas has some sort of social transformation. It is taken into account at the beginning of life as discipline for the student of the Vedas. This is known as *brahmacharya.* Whatever knowledge a student may acquire from his teacher or text he can only satisfy his teacher by tapas.[29]

However, tapas has many forms of application. The persons who live worthily practise *brahmacarya.* If a king intends to protect his state he has to undergo brahmacarya. The ācārya desires to have his students through brahmacarya. A maiden gets a handsome husband through brahmacarya. It is observed that austerity, in the vedic age, construed to have manifested in brahmacarya[30]. In the Vedas, it is revealed that brahmacarya lies at the centre of divinity. Only because of brahmacarya the Gods get-rid-of death (jīvanaṁ vindudhāraṇāt).

Austerity, in form of brahmacarya, is the discipline of body and mind for attending the fitness for knowledge. Control and sublimation of sex energy are invitable for it. For this, physical cleanliness is meticulously attended to. It is known from the Vedas that the *brahmacārin* is the worshipper of Saraswati, the divine mother, at whose breast he prays to be privileged to feed.[31] That is why an Āchārya is to be a married man and to live with his family and the *brahmacārin* is adapted to it.[32]

Brahman

Brahman has been construed as the Vedas and the Supreme also. The *brāhmaṇa* portions analyse Brahman whereas the *āraṇyaka* and *upaniṣad* portions explain the very core idea of the Supreme soul. Thus Brahman has been understood differently in course of time. However, in its primary sense Brahman means prayer. Then it means the body of *mantras* in the Vedas meant for prayer. Then the term implies the Vedas as books of prayer and wisdom. In the Vedas we find a deity named *Brahmaṇaspati* who plays a role as the lord of prayer.[33] The Brahman stands for the object of the prayer, the divinity especially contemplated as an impersonal reality.

In the *Dharmasūtras*, we are told that, Brahman i.e. Vedas as the basic source of dharma. Smṛtis and custom come next if they do not contradict the Brahman.[34] As the basic source of dharma, Brahman stands for the activities associated with the search for Reality and Truth. In the post vedic period, under the influence of Upaniṣads etc. it is known as *jñānayoga*. This has been termed as svādhyāya i.e. *brahmayajña*.[35] Among the five *Mahāyajñas*, which have been originated in the *smṛti* literature, *brahmayajña* has been placed first to be performed by the householder as a daily work[36]. Unless it is done, then Yajnas become fuitle. Mention may be made here that the men who carried the Vedas in their heads deserve well of society, and a traditional social law gives them a previleged position for which they are immune from capital punishment.[37] As a matter of fact for to kill a brahmana is to obstruct the oral tradition of a Veda (*Brahman*) carried on by him.

Sacrifice (Yajña)

Yajña is the vedic ritual of offering libation or oblation on the sacrificial fire, lighted on an altar. In the *yajña* whatever the names of the deities worshipped the ritual is the same. The vedic ritual, as it were, is picturesque, accompanied by chanting and singing of hymns and also acting. Being a great public institution the *yajña* has developed complicated ritual which adds to the attractiveness of the ceremonial side of prayer. The core idea of dedication rests in the yajña.[38]

In course of the development of vedic culture the conception of yajña has much been widened by the adoption of five systems of *Mahāyajñas* (great sacrifices) in which in addition to the usual *Agnihotra*, the study and teaching of the Vedas (*brahmayajña*) service of the guest (nṛyajña), giving food to the lower creatures (bhūtayajña) and offering of oblation to manas (pitṛyahña) are recognised as great sacrifices. But the spirit of yajña in the Bhagavadgita differs from that of the forms determined in the Vedas.[39] If the spirit is accepted, then the material parts of yajna, related to the fire, fuel and the oblation are to be taken not only literally but also symbolically and figuratively. Here this yajña is to be recognised as material sacrifice, but there is to be taken into account the yajña of tapas in which the fire of restraint is lighted and the senses are to be the offering.[40]

Due to the contact of Brāhmaṇa portion of the Vedas with the upaniṣadic portion, spiritualisation of the concept of yajña has been evolved. However the institution of the yajña as ritual has its specialities of its own. it emphasises the realistic elements of the vedic religion. In the way of ritual-based religion of the Vedas colour, sound, fragrance and all other finer things of the senses have their full play. The glorious luster of the blazing fire, the sweet perfume of the burnt ghee, the blades of grass, the cooked offering and all other materials of yajña have their direct and purifying effect on the minds of the worshipper.[41] According to upanisadic stand point yajñas make *cittaśuddhi* which enables the performer to get liberation.

Conclusion

(a) Thus Vedic Religion, on the one hand ritual-based and contemplation-based on the other. Ritual-based religion leads one to heaven whereas contemplation-based religion makes one's soul liberated. (b) Vedic Religion has two different forms viz. *karman* (action) and *guṇa* (endowment). Of these two, karman is external whereas *guṇa* is internal. The basis of karman-form of religion is the Brāhmaṇa portion of the Vedas whereas Āraṇyakas and Upaniṣads are identified basis of the guna-form. (c) Although dedication is the cardinal characteristic of Vedic Religion, still, in its ritual-based form dedication of material things is the medium through which one is to be privileged to access the heaven. In its contemplation-based form, dedication of body (both gross and subile) is the medium through which one gets liberation (*mokṣa*), for body is the point of bondage, as it were. For these two ends of life six fundamental principles of religion are to be followed.

Notes and References

1. In the hymns of the Rgveda the word (dharma) appears to be used either as an adjective or a noun (in the form of dharman, generally neuter) and occurs at least about sixty times by itself and about eighteen times in combination with particle 'vi').

   P.V.Kane : *History of* Dharmaśāstra. Vol;. I, Pt. I (B. O. R. I., Poona, 1968) p. 1.
2. Maine, H. S. : *Early law and Custom* (B. R. Publishing House, Delhi. 1985) p. 18.
3. Bose, A. C. : *The Call of the Vedas* (Bharatiya Vidya Bhavan, Mumbai, 1988) p. 38.
4. *Rgveda* . I. 2. 18.
5. *Ibid.* VIII. 43. 24.
6. *satyaṁ bṛhad ṛtam ugram dīkṣā tapo brahma Yajñaḥ pṛthivīṁ dhārayanti/AV.* XIII. 1. 1
7. *yuvāṁ devāstraya ekādaśāśaḥ/*

   satyāḥ satyasya dadṛśe purustāt / / Rg. VIII. 57. 2

8. *savitā satyadharmā/ AV*. I. 24. 1
9. *satyamava jayāte nānṛtam//*
   satyena panthā vitate devayānaḥ// Muṇḍakopaniṣat. III. 1.6
10. *Bṛhadāraṇyakopaniṣat* . I. 3. 28.
11. *venastatpaśyannihitaṁ guhā sad*
    yatra viśvaṁ bhavatyekanīḍam/
    tasminnidam sa ca vi caiti sarvaṁ
    sa otaḥ protaśca vibhūḥ prajāsu// YU. XXXII. 8
12. *akṣetravit kṣetravidaṁ hytprāṭ*
    sa praiti kṣetra vidānuśiṣṭaḥ/
    etad vai bhadramanuṣāsanasyota
    sruit vindatyañjasīnām // Ṛg. X. 32. 7
13. *YU*. XXXII. 8
14. The law of which Varuṇa is the custodian is called the Rta. Rta literally means the course of things. It stands for law in general and the immanence of justice. This conception must have been originally suggested by the regularity of the movements of Sun, moon and stars, the alternations of day and night, and of the seasons. Rta denotes the order of the world. Everything that is ordered in the universe has Rta for its principle.

    Radhakrishan, S. : *Indian Philosophy*. Vol. i. (Blackie & Son Pub. Pvt. Ltd.) p. 78
15. Ṛg. I. 105. 6
16. *ṛtamiti satyamiyat// Śat. Br*. VI.7.3.11
17. Ṛg. X. 190. 1
18. *satyam bṛhad ṛtamugram// AV*. XII. 1. 1
19. Ṛg. I. 147. 1.
20. Vide the *aghamarṣaṇasūkta* of *Ṛgveda*.
21. *rtasya dṛlhā dharuṇāni santi*
    purūṇi candra vapuṣa vapūṁṣi/
    ṛtena dīrghamisananta pṛksa
    rtena gava ṛtamavivesa//Rg. IV. 23. 9.
22. *brahma jinvatamuta jinvataṁ dhiyaḥ*
    kṣatraṁ jinvatamuta jinvataṁ nṛn/
    dhenūrjinvatamuta jinvataṁviśaḥ// Rg. VIII. 35. 16. 18.
23. *Yatra brahma ca kṣatrañca samyañcau carataḥ saha/*
    taṁllekaṁ puṇyaṁ prajñesṁ yatra devāḥ sahāgninā// YU. XX. 25.
24. *imā brahmendra tubhyaṁ śamsi*
    da nṛbhyue nṛṇāṁśūraśavaḥ/
    tebhirbhava sakraturyesy cakannuta
    trāyasva gṛṇata uta stin// Ṛg. X. 148.4
25. *vratena dīkṣāmāpnetidakṣiṇām/*
    dakṣiṇā śraddhāmāpneti śraddhayā satyamāpyate // YV. XIX. 30
26. *ācārya upanayamāne brahmacārinaṁ kṛṇute garbhamantaḥ/*
    tam rātrīṁ tisra udare bibharti tam jātaṁ draṣṭumabhi samyati devāḥ// AV. XII. 5. 3.

27. *Ṛg* X. 32. 7
28. *na ṛte śrāntasya sakhāya devāḥ// Ṛg*. IV. 33. 11
29. *icchanti devāḥ sunvantaṁ*
    sa svapnāya spṛhayanti/
    yanti pramādamatandrāḥ//Ṛg. VIII. 2. 18.
30. *brahmacaryana tapasā rājā rāṣṭraṁ vi rakṣati/*
    ācārya brahmacaryena brahmacāriṇamicchate//
    brahmacaryṇa Kanyā yuvānaṁ vindate patim/
    brahmacaryeṇa tapasā devā mṛtyumapāghnata//
    indra ha brahmacaryeṇa devebhyaḥ svarābharat // AV. XI. 5. 17-19.
31. *yaste stanaḥ sasaya ye mayebhūr*
    yena viśvā puṣyasi vāyāni/
    ye ratnadha vasuvid yaḥ sudatraḥ
    sarasvati tamiha dhatavekaḥ// Ṛg. I. 164. 49
32. Bose, A. C. : *The Call of the Vedas* (Mumbai, 1988) intro. p. 58.
33. Keith, A. B. : *The Religion and Philosophy of the Veda and Upanisads*. Vol. II (Motilal Banarasidas, Delhi, 1976) p. 438.
34. *Vedo dharmamūlaṁ. tadvidāṁ ca smṛtiśile. Gautamadharmasūtra*. I. 1. 1.
35. *svādhyāye vai brahmayajñaḥ. Śat. Br*. XI. 5. 6. 2.
36. Kane, P. V. : *History of Dharmaśāstra*. Vol. II, pt. I (Poona, 1974) pp. 696-704.
37. *Śat*. Br. II. 5. 7.
38. Majumdar, R. C. : *Vedic Age* (Bharatiya Vidya Bhavan, Mumbai, 1968) pp. 442-452.
39. Ghurye, G. S. : *Vedic India* (Popular Prakashan, Mumbai, 1979) p. 59
40. Bhatkhande, S. M. : 'Sacrifice in the Bhagavadgītā' in *Sacrifice in India : Concept and Evolution* (Viveka Publication, Aligarh, 1987), pp. 116-120.
41. cf. *ātmā pitustanur vāsa ojade' bhyañjanam. Rg*. VIII. 3. 24.

Vedic Astronomy

9

Dr. Padmakar Vishnu Vartak

Astronomy means the scientific study of the heavenly bodies while Astrophysics means the study of the physical structure of the planets and stars. We find the roots of both these sciences in the Vedas. Science means the knowledge gathered by experience.

Astronomy is called in the Vedas as Jyotiṣa which means a science of the luminaries in the sky. Joyti means a flame. A flame from the sky is nothing else but a star or a planet. The planets are also included in the Jyotiṣ Sāstra and studied well in ancient India; because the planets also give light though reflected from them.

It is usually taught that the science of astronomy is developed by the Arabs and Egyptians or other west-Asians, because they had to travel in the deserts with the help of the stars. If it was so there should have been marked knowledge, even today, about astronomy in that region. But evidently it is lacking. Even today the Muslim world cannot predict their ceremonies like Id earlier. They run here and there and have to change their ceremonious day often. The fact clearly shows their ignorance in the field of astronomy.

On the contrary, the Hindus calculate their ceremonies at least two years before. This tradition of the Hindus is seen from the remote past. The astronomical data is seen recorded in the world's most ancient literature the Vedas which belong to the Hindus from India. So we can say that the Vedic people are the fathers of astronomy.

Even then, today every scholar thinks that the science has been developed in the western countries like Europe during last 500 years. This is ridiculous. Science with all its branches appears to have the roots in the Vedas. Veda is a precious and prestigious heritage of India. Veda means the knowledge. The knowledge means knowing the truth, the reality. The ancient Indians revealed the ultimate truth and they kept that knowledge in the Vedas. Because the Veda stored very important knowledge, the seers wanted that a single word or a syllable or a single letter should not be changed. Hence they made their students cram over all the verses in 'to and fro' manner. Thus the Vedas are preserved for thousands of years. It shows the importance of the knowledge stored in the Vedas. If those were ordinary poems they would not have been stored like this. Brahmins spent their whole life retaining the Vedas on their tongues. If we explore the Vedas with the help of the modern astronomy we find the astronomical records of at least 25000 years, showing that much antiquity of the Vedas.

If we study the Vedas we find a graph of the development of the astronomy. First the Vedic sages were attracted towards the sky because the sky had no support at all but was loaded with the stars. Therefore, Ṛgveda 1-24-7 says, "The pure and allert king Varuṇa presents a heap in the bottomless sky above the world. The rays of light placed inside the dome come down though the source or the base in above.[1]" The sages went on observing the sky day and night and recorded that "These stars well-placed above are visible at night but where do they go during the day? Bright moon comes at night. Varuṇa's rules are unbreakable." (Ṛgveda 1-24-10)[2]

Atharva Veda 13-2-17 as well as 20-47-14 state that "The stars run away with the night, just like the thieves, for the Sun to see the world."[3] The sages went on studying the sky at night and came to the conclusion that "The Suns are powerful than the Moon and the Earth is greater than the Moon. The Moon is kept in the lap of the stars."[4] This conclusion is recorded in Ṛgveda 10-85-2 as well as Atharva Veda 14-1-2-. These verses prove that the sages revealed that the stars are the Suns and the Sun is a star. In clear words it is stated that the Suns are more powerful that the Moon and the Earth is bigger than the Moon. Is this not the root of astronomy as well as astrophysics?

The vedic people found out that the Moon travels on a specific path of the stars. They observed that the stars do not move, therefore they coined a name Nakṣatra means the one which does not move! Na Kṣarati Iti Nakṣatra' is the definition given by sage Vyāsa in his Mahābhārata at Śānti Parva 290/36. The epic Mahābhārata is honoured as the fifth Veda. The name 'Nakṣatra' itself stores a specific meaning and hence it is scientific, but the modern name 'star' has no meaning at all and hence it is unscientific.

After confirming the path of the Moon among the stars, the sages observed that the Moon comes near a particular star in a particular time, say a day. Accordingly they selected the stars and constellations at a certain interval on that star path and named those stars. On this observation they based their unit of time and called the day by the Nakṣatra near which the Moon resided. They named all the twenty eight Nakṣatras on the path of the Moon. The Ṛgveda mentions the following Nakṣatra : Aghā i.e. Maghā and Arjuni at 10-85-13, Revati and Punarvasu at 10-19-1. Revati is also mentioned at Ṛg. 5-11-14 and 4-51-4. Tiṣya is mentioned at 5-54-13, Chitrā at 4-51-2. Tiṣya at 10-64-8. All the 28 Nakṣatras are not seen in the Ṛgveda but as seven are mentioned it is clear that the sages knew all the 28 Nakṣatras. The word "Nakṣatra" is used in the Ṛgveda at 1-50-2, 10-68-11, 7-86-1 etc.

Taittiriya Samhitā of the Black Yajurveda gives all the 28 Nakṣatras at 4-4-10, thus :

Kṛttikā (having its Deity Agni), Rohiṇi (Prajāpati), Mṛgas'irṣa (Soma), Ārdrā (Rudra), Punarvasu (Aditi), Tiṣya (Bṛhaspati), Ås'leṣā (Sarpa) Maghā (Pitṛ), Phalguni Pūrvā (Aryamā)., Uttarā Phalguni (Bhaga), Hasta (Savitṛ), Chitrā (Indra), Svāti (Vāyu), Vis'ākhā (Indra and Agni), Anurādhā (Mitra), Rohiṇi or Jyeṣṭhā (Indṛa), Vichṛti (Pitṛ), Pūrvā Āṣādhā (Āpa), Uttarā Āṣādhā (Vis' vedevā), S'roṇā (Viṣṇu), Śvaviṣṭā (Vasu) S' atabhiṣaja (Indra), Pūrvā Proṣṭapadā (Aja Ekapāda), Uttarā Proṣṭhapadā (Ahirbudhnya), Revati (Pūṣan)., As'vayujau (As'vinau), Apabharaṇi (Yama).

The Deity of the Nakṣatra is given in the bracket :

While observing the movements of the Moon they noticed that the Moon goes on increasing in size till it becomes full in about 15 days. Then it begins decreasing in size till it vanishes in about the next 15 days. They observed minutely this waxing and waning of the Moon and revealed that the moon increases or decreases in one day by one unit called as the Kalā. The sages found out the reason of the disappearance of the Moon. On realising that the Moon disappears when it comes near the Sun, they named the day when the Moon is not seen in the sky at night as Amāvāsyā. This name itself is very scientific. It has two components, Amā and Vāsya Amā means together. Vāsya means residing. When the Sun and the Moon reside together the days is called as Amāvsyā. In the modern science in this science-age all the scientists call that day as the New-Moon-Day. It is quite ridiculous because the Moon never becomes new. The same old Moon is seen again. Thus it appears that the Vedic sages were more scientific than the modern scientists.

After the Amāvāsyā every day the Moon goes on increasing in size by one Kalā each day. When one Kalā of the moon was seen, the day was called as Pratipadā, when two Kalās of the moon was visible it was called as Dwitiyā, when three Kalās were seen the day was Tritiyā, when four Kalās were visible the day was named as Chaturthi. On the Aṣṭami day half moon is visible, on Dwādaśi three-fourth moon was seen and when the full moon was seen it was called as *Pūrṇimā* Imā means the Moon, Pūrṇa means full. The full-moon-day was called as the Purnimā meaning 'of the full-moon'. After the full-moon day the moon begins waning day by day, one Kalā each day till it vanishes. According to the Kalās the day was named as Pratipadā, Dwitiyā, Tṛtiyā etc. till Amāvāsyā. These days were used to count the days. The days were called as the Tithis.

The sages noticed that at a ṛegular interval the full moon appears and at a regular interval the moon vanishes. Therefore they fixed a period from one Amāvāsyā to the next Amāvāsyā as one Māsa. As the period belonged to the Moon they named that period as Māsa because Māsa means the moon. Some sages held this period of one Māsa from a full-moon to the next full-moon.

They divided the Māsa into two halves namely Pakṣa. The name is very poetic as well as scientific. Pakṣa means a wing of a bird. A bird flies with its two wings, in the same way the Time flies with the two wings of a month. Therefore the name Pakṣa. There are two Pakṣas. In the first Pakṣa after Amāvāsyā, the moon-light goes on increasing day by day; hence it is named as Śukla or Śuddha. The second half is called as KṚṢNA Pakṣa because the moon-light goes on decreasing and darkness goes on increasing in it.

Later on the sages began naming the Māsas relying on the Nakṣatra near which the full moon resided. If the full moon is near Chitrā Nakṣatra the month is called as Chaitra, if the full moon is near Kṛttikā, the month is called as Kārtika and so on. A Nakṣatra which is seen just after the sun set at the eastern horizon and which appears in the sky whole night is selected to name that month. The word 'Māsa' is used in Ṛgveda at 10-68-10, in the sense of moon.

While the sages were observing and studying the Moon and the Nakṣatras, they noticed some stars which were seen moving. Thus they discovered the five planets. It was the height of their keen observation to distinguish the planets and the stars requires minute and precise studies for years together, rather centuries together. This very fact shows that the knowledge and observations must have been transmitted through many generations. The five planets are mentioned at Ṛgveda 1-105-10[5] and 10-55-3[6] as five gods. They were offered oblations as seen from Taittiriya Brāhmaṇa 3-1-4-6.[7] Ṛgvedic 'Vena' is same as the planet Venus and is given one full Sūkta 10-123 in the Ṛgveda. The planet Bṛhaspati is described in the Ṛgveda at 4-50-4, 10-67 and 10-68. Thus it is clear that the Vedic sages had made distinction between the planets and the stars.

They were counting days according to the Tithi and Nakṣatra and were using the lunar months; but then they observed that a certain type of weather appears at a certain interval and there is a cycle in this change in the climate. They observed that the Moon is not responsible for the change in the weather. They further noticed that the climatic variations depend on the position of the rising Sun on the eastern horizon. When the Sun goes towards south there is cold and when it goes towards the north there is heat. They noticed that there is a regular swing of the rising Sun on the eastern horizon from the north to the south and back again from the south to the north. They called this journey of the Sun as 'Ayana'. They named the southward-journey of the Sun as 'Pitṛyāna' (10-88-15) and northward 'Devayāna' (10-18-1). The seers noticed that rains started with the beginning of the Pitṛyāṇa. (Ṛgveda 6-322-5).[8]

Ṛgveda 1-95-3 states that "Agni or the Sun is the controller of the seasons and it presents first the East and then the other directions : following it.[9] In this statement two facts are clearly presented; the first is that the seasons, Ṛtus are controlled by the Sun. This is a fact well accepted by the modern science. The second fact is that the east is presented by the Sun first. It is quite clear that the Sun rises at the east and shows that direction clearly to begin with and gradually it shows other directions by its light.

Accordingly they recognised the directions depending on the Sun. The place where the sun rises is called as Udichi or Pūrva. When we stand facing the rising Sun, the right handed direction is called as the 'Dakṣiṇa' Dakṣiṇa means the right hand. Paṣchima means the back, so the direction at the back of a person who stands facing the rising sun is called as Paschima. After labelling the Udichi or Pūrva, the Prśchima (the west) and Dakṣiṇa (the south), the remaining is called as the Uttara which means the remaining. This establishment of directions is very scientific and is universal. Even if you go on any other planet, you can fix the directions following this scheme of Ṛgveda. Magnetic needle used by the modern scientists to fix first the north, may not be useful on other planets.

After confirming the two Ayanas, the sages further studied and they found the seasons called as Ṛtu. Vasanta, Greeṣma and Śarad are the three Ṛtus mentioned in the Ṛgveda at 10-90-6.[10] Hemanta is mentioned at 10-68-10[11] Five Ṛtus and twelve Māsas are mentioned at 10-90-15.[12]

Taittiriya Samhitā of the Black Yajurveda at 4-4-11 gives all the six Ṛtus which are further bifurcated into two months each. Thus there are two months Madhu and Mādhava constituting Vasanta Ṛtu. Śukra and Śuchi composed the Greeṣma Ṛtu consisted of Nabha and Nabhasya. Varṣā Ṛtu means the rainy season when the sky is covered by the clouds hence these names Nabha and Nabhasya. Īṣa and Ūrja constituted Śarad Ṛtu. Saha and Sahasya were the two months of Hemanta Ṛtu. Śiśira Ṛtu was composed of the two months Tapa and Tapasya.

Here it is very important to note that these are the seasonal months and the seasons depend on the Sun. These should not be mistaken as the lunar months saying Madhu Means Chaitra; but this mistake is done by many scholars. Usually all the scholars hold that Madhu Māsa is the Chaitra Māsa because Sāyaṇāchārya has said so in his commentary on the Taittiriya Samhitā.[13] Sāyaṇāchārya was not wrong because at his time Madhu Māsa coincided with the Chaitra Māsa. That was the condition between 500 AD to 1500 AD, but now it has changed. This change occurred because of the Precession of Equinoxes. But we will deal with the problem of the Precession of equinoxes in detail later on. Here I want to stress the point that Madhu-Mādhava etc are the seasonal months and not lunar months. The seasonal months are the solar months and that is made clear by the Viṣṇu Purāṇa 2-8-70 saying Dwau Māsau Arkajau Ṛtu द्वौ मासौ अर्कजौ ऋतुः : meaning that the two solar months form a Ṛtu.

The regular cyclic changes in the climate were closely observed and the period from one rainy season to the next rainy season was taken as one Varṣa i.e a year. Varṣ means to shower. Varṣā is the Ṛtu of rain showers, and a period from one Varṣā to the next Varṣā is called as Varṣa the year. They closely observed the climatic changes during a year divided the year into six seasons or Ṛtus namely Varṣā. Śarad, Hemanta, Śiśira, Vasanta and Greeṣma. At times Hemanta and Śiśira were fused together and only five Ṛtus were counted because both the

Hemanta and Śiśira are of cold climate. Aitareya Brāhmaṇa 1-1 and 2-7-10 mention like this.Varśā and Śarad may also be fused together because both shower rains.

Ṛgveda sages began their new year with the rainy season as is seen in 2-24-5, 7-103-1, 7,8,9.

2-24-5 states, "The ancient prayers of Brahmaṇaspati release the future waters for you by months and years. Then without any effort the heaven and the Earth enjoy each other's water.'[14]

Here the cycle of water is described because the same water goes in the sky in the form of vapour and comes down on the Earth in the form of the rains.

Ṛg 7-103-1 states, "Frogs sleeping for a whole year began croaking to please the rain God like a Brahmin practising a rite at the beginning of the new year." This shows the beginning of the new year with Rainy season.

Ṛg. 7-103-7 states, "When the rainy season approaches, on that first day of the new year frogs develop every where." Here again the new year is shown beginning with the rainy season.

Ṛg. 7-103-8 states, "The frogs are croaking like a Brahmin reciting the annual prayers after drinking Soma. A priest who officiates at a sacrifice perspires profusely, similarly the sweating frogs come out immediately after it rains." Here a metaphor is used. Annual prayers were recited at the beginning of the new year when the Brahmins used to sweat profusely. It shows that the new year began at the onset of the rainy season, when there is lot of humidity and heat.

Rg 7-103-9 states, "These great frogs follow the orders of the God. They follow the rules of the twelve months and the Ṛtus. At the end of the year troubled by the heat the frogs come out of their burrows when the rainy season begins." The Ṛc shows clearly that there was extreme heat at the end of the year and the new year began with the rains.

Rg 7-101 and 7-102 are in praise of the rainy season. Similar Suktas praising the summer of the winter are not seen in the Ṛgveda, suggesting that the Varṣā had a special significance and that was the beginning of the new year.

Taittiriya Brśhmaṇa 3-10-4-1 states that Vasanta is the head of the year, Greeṣma the right wing and Varṣā is the tail end.[15] This verse shows that with Varṣā the year ended, so the year must have been beginning with the Varṣā. When Vasanta came into importance, Varṣā was given the place of the tail end, to show the ancient tradition of the new year day in the rainy season. It is for this reason that the Taittiriya Samhitā states that "the Ṛtu-pātra (urn of seasons) has two mouths. Who knows the real mouth of the seasons ?"[16] This jumbling suggests that there were two methods of beginning the new year, one from Varṣā and other from Vasanta.

It was probably the Yajurveda and its followers who induced a new method of beginning the new year with the Vasanta Ṛtu. Those sages gave importance to

Yajnas. Yajnas could not be done in the rainy season. Hence they performed the Yajnas in the Vasanta Ṛtu wherein the weather was the best. For that reason they began their new year in Vasanta. This is reflected in Taittiriya Samhitā 7-4-8 and Taittiriya Brāhmaṇa 1-1-2 [17] which say, "Oblations be given to Agni in Vasanta because it is the mouth of the seasons." Taittiriya Samhitā begins the list of the seasons with the Vasanta at 4-4-11 and 1-4-14, suggesting Vasanta at the beginning of the new year.[18]

The system of taking Vasanta the first season and beginning the new year with Vasanta became very popular and the system of beginning the new year with the rainy season became obsolete. Even then its existence is registered by keeping it at the tail end.

The year beginning with the Varṣā Ṛtu was called as Varṣā while the year beginning with the Vasanta was called as Saṁvatsara.

The Ṛtus depended on Ayana. Varṣā Ṛtu began with the beginning of the Pitṛyāṇa. Śiśira Ṛtu began with Devayāna. Hemanta ended with Pitṛyāṇa. Greeṣma ended with Devayāna. When the Sun was near the middle of the east it was either Vasanta or Śarad depending on the Ayana Deva and Pitṛ respectively.

With Tithi, Nakṣatra, Māsa, Ṛtu and Ayana their Panchanga was complete. This is actually an eternal calendar. Now-a-days we depend on the calendars hanging on the walls. If we are unable to see a calendar we cannot fix a day or a date or a month. If we go out of our place for & few days we forget the day, date and month easily. Suppose we are going on a ship and it wrecks throwing us in the sea, we may land on some isolated island not inhabitated by human beings. In such circumstances we will forget the day, date and month and will never tell it any time in the future. But if we know the ancient. Indian Vedic style of Panchānga we can fix the Tithi, Nakṣatra, Māsa by looking at the sky at night, and we can fix the Ṛtu and Ayana by looking at the rising Sun's position, on the eastern horizon. We can carry all the transactions on the basis of that Panchānga. As far as the earth and the sky exist this Panchānaga will exist.

One more advantage of this Panchānga is that by knowing a Tithi we can understand the time of high-tide of the sea; by knowing the date of a modern calendar we can never fix the time of high tide. Let me give here the method of calculating the time of high-tide. Take three-fourth of the Tithi and add to it minutes three times of the Tithi. For example Purṇimā means 15th Tithi. Its three fourth is 11 hours and 15 minutes. Three times Tithi is 45 minutes. Adding we get 12O' clock as the time of high tide at noon as well as midnight. Thus the Tithis are very useful for fishermen as well as those people residing near the sea.

Rāśi or the signs of zodiac were established by the Ṛgvedic people. They were twelve in number. They had divided the year into 12 months and so each month they observed the sky and constellations. Nakṣatras were 27 or 28, they had to be gathered in twelve groups now called as Rāśi. Rāsi means a heap of stars. Ṛgveda

4-33-7 tells about Ṛbhus that— "Ṛbhus enjoyed hospitality in the twelve Dyun (sections of the sky) of the unscret Sun and then getting up with thunderous sound (Raṇan) they made the land fertile by bringing rivers, producing plants in dry lands and making low lands watery."[19]

This Ṛc has two-fold significance. First point to note is that the Ṛbhus rested for twelve months and then produced plenty of water, so the year was marked by rainy season, the new year began with the rains. The second point is that they rested in 12 Dyun. Dyu means heaven or sky. The sky is always one and only one. Even then a plural form is used so that it indicates twelve sections of the sky studded with the stars. Every month a separate portion of the sky is visible. Naturally separate stars are seen every month. Those stars and sky-sections are called as Dyun. Evidently Dyu denotes the Rāśis.

The same Ṛc is explained by Ṛg 1-164-12 and Praśnopaniṣad at Prasna 1, Maṁtra 11 where it is stated that the year has five parts and twelve figures in the sky.[20] The twelve figures in the sky are nothing else but the Rāśis or the Dyuns. Thus it is seen that piling of 28 constellations was done into twelve Rāśis during Ṛgveda period. It is wrong to say that the Rāśis came to India from western countries.

The twelve Māsas were the regular feature, but occasionally there arose the thirteenth Māsa[21] which is mentioned at Ṛgveda 1-25-8. This is because they used lunar as well as solar-seasonal months. A period of one year was fixed from one rainy season to the next, or from one Vasanta to the next. They used both the methods for some time but then they noticed that after five or more years the Ṛtus did not adjust with the lunar months. They noticed that in five years time the season shifts by two months. So they deviced an ingenious system of Adhimāsas. Taittiriya Samhitś tells at 5-6-7 that there are twelve Māsas in one Samvatsara or thirteen Māsas in one Samvatsara.[22] Taittiriya Brāhmaṇa 3-8-3 also tells the same thing. The Adhimāsa was named as 'Saṁsarpa'. This name is mentioned in Taittiriya Samhitā along with Aṁhaspatya at 1-4-14. Madhava's commentary tells that Saṁsarpa is an Adhimāsa while Aṁhaspatya is Kṣaya Māsa.

Twelve lunar months, each of 29.53058 days from one lunar years of 354.367 days. The solar year is of 365.25 days. Thus there is a deficit of 10.88 days every year. To remove that deficit they took Adhimāsas two at a time after every five years.[23] This system is reported in the epic Mahābhārata Virāta parva 52/3. Probably these two Adimāsas were Saṁsarpa and Aṁhaspatya. Using this system for a few years they noticed that there arises an over correction and the seasons miss the lunar month again. Hence they deviced one Kṣaya Māsa. In the later period this Kṣaya Māsa was held as Aṁhaspatya as is mentioned in Madhava's commentary.

From Vedaṅga Jyotiṣa onwards the sages started taking one Adhimāsa after two years, five Pakṣas and two and one-eighth day.[24]

Stars were Named Scientifically

The vedic names of the stars are quite scientific. Jyeṣṭhā is a vedic name of a star in Scorpio, which is known in the modern astronomy as Antares. The word Antares means the rival of the Mars. This star looks red in colour like Mars and is of the same size of Mars, hence the name. The name Antares shows that the Greeks saw it with naked eyes, saw its similarity with the Mars and coined the name Antares. On the other hand the Vedic seers call it Jyeṣṭhā, which means the eldest and the biggest. Why was it called the eldest and the biggest? If we see with unaided eyes it is the 17th star in the rank according to brightness and size. Then why is it named as Jyeṣṭhā? The reason is found in the modern astronomy which describes it as " a red giant approaching stellar senility". It is 300 times bigger and 2000 times brighter than our Sun. It is the oldest among the 28 constellations, and is the biggest. Hence it is called as Jyeṣṭhā. The modern astronomy discovered the real nature of Antares only after the progress in nuclear physics. Then will it be wrong to conclude that the vedic sages were advanced in the nuclear physics? Otherwise how could they name the star so accurately?

The name Mūla or Mūlabarhi is also very scientific. It was held that it was the root or the centre of the Universe. It is now proved by the modern astronomy that the centre of our Galaxy is really situated at the star. Mūla means the root and Barhi means the fan. Our Galaxy is really fanned out from the star as is discovered now by the modern astronomy. How could the sages found out that the Galaxy is fan shaped and its root is at the Mūla Nakṣatra? This fact again proves the far advanced nuclear physics, in India in ancient era of Vedas.

The Vedic names of the planets are also scientific. Bṛhaspati or Guru means the great or biggest. The modern astronomy has now proved that the planet is really the biggest in our solar system. Modern science calls it Jupiter, but this name has no science in it. With unaided eyes how could the seer realised that it is the biggest planet? Naked eyes show Venus as the biggest and brightest, but is not called as Guru. Therefore it is sure that the sages knew that Jupiter was the biggest even though it looks smaller than the Venus. Venus is called as Śukra meaning very bright. Śani means slow and Saturn is really the slowest planet among the five they had discovered. Śani's another name Maṅda also means slow.

Some stars other than those on the path of the Moon are also named scientifically. The star Crux was named as 'Triśaṅku' Triśaṅku means Three Śaṅkus. Śaṅku is a number - Lakṣa (10^5), Koti (10^7), Abja (10^9) Kharva (10^{10}), Nikharva (10^{11}), Mahāpadma (10^{12}), Śanku (10^{13}), Jaladhi (10^{14}), Antya (10^{15}), Madhya (10^{16}) and Parārdha (10^{17}).Why did the sages discover such huge numbers ? Parārdha means 18 zeroes on 1. Such great numbers must have been discovered for astronomical calculations. For easy calculations they developed bigger units also. That is the reason why Divya Varṣas are told. Divya means astronomical. One human year multiplied with 360 becomes a Divya Varṣa. Thus one Divya Varṣa means 360 human years of 365.25 days. These are astronomical measures.

Śaṁku means 10^{13}. Three Śaṅkus means 10^{13} x 3.3 Śaṅku Mahāyojanas comes to 204 light years. (one Mahayojana means 40 miles). One Śaṅku miles means 1.7 light years. One light year means a distance covered by light in one year at the velocity of 186000 miles per second. Thus Tri Śaṅku Mahāyojanas or 204 light years is a distance between the Earth and that star Triśaṅku. The modern astronomy gives information that Crux i.e. Triśaṅku star is at a distance of 205 light years. Difference between 204 and 205 is negligible. So we have to accept that the ancient Indian sages knew the distance between the earth and that star very well.

Agasti means the star Canopus. It is the brightest star in the southern sky. The star is named after the sage Agasti. A legend tells that Agasti sat near the sea at the shore and drank whole of the sea. The story indicates that Agasti is on the sea-shore. Sea means Jaladhi, Jaladhi means 10^{14}. Jaladhi Mahāyojanas means 680 light years. Astronomy books state that Canopus is 650 light years distant from the earth. There is negligible difference between 650 and 680. So we have to accept that the distance was known to the sages who named these stars. (The original concept behind these thoughts about Triśaṅku and Agasti is of my friend late Mr. Pant M. B.)

Star Names Went From India Abroad

Usually the scholars hold that the names of the stars are imported in India from western countries, but this supposition is absolutely wrong and baseless. On the contrary the names went from India to the east as well as the west. For example, the Great Bear. Ṛgvedic sages called any star Ṛkṣa. Ṛkṣa has two meanings (1) an animal called as Bear and (2) a star, a bright object in the sky. Later on the sages found a group of seven stars moving around the North Pole and called that group of stars as Saptaṛkṣā, seven stars. Later on they named each of the seven stars from that group e.g. Atreya, Vasiṣṭha, Kaśyapa, Bhāradvāja, Viśvāmitra, Goutama, Jamadagni. A minute star is seen near Vasiṣtha which is named as Arundhati, who was the wife of the sage Vasiṣṭha. All these details did not go to the western countries. Only the name Ṛkṣa went there and the people over there took the first meaning 'Bear' of that word. Hence they started calling it the great bear. Actually we cannot see the figure of a bear in that group of stars, we have to assume it. The vedic seers changed the name from Ṛkṣa to Saptarṣi is reported in Śatapatha Brāhmaṇa at 2-1-2-4.[25] Please note that the Śatapatha Brāhmaṇa is dated at 3000 years BC by the great scholar Late Mr. S. B. Dixit. He showed the evidence in Śatapatha that "Kṛttikās do not move from the east," is a statement in it and that was the condition around 3000 BC. This change in the name could not go to Europe so that they stuck up to the old name Ṛkṣa and called it Bear. However, the change in the name went to for east to South America where the new name was accepted. The South Americans called it as the seven brothers and a sister. This is surprising because Saptarṣis are not visible in the south America, so that they could not have conceived the names; the name must have gone to South America from India. There are evidences of Indian culture in the south America.

Venus is a name of the brightest planet. Formerly in India it was named as Vena after a famous king from the Ikṣvāku dynasty viz. Vena. This king Vena is 62nd ancestor of Rāma. After naming the planet Vena, thousands of years passed and naturally Vena was forgotten. Therefore a new name was given as Śukra in the memory of a great sage Śukrāchārya. This change in the name of the planet did not reach the western countries so they are still calling it Venus from the original Saṅskṛta name Vena. Śukra also means the bright and it is really so.

Two stars near the Milky-way are called as the Dogs - Canis Major and Canis minor. But these names are given by the Ṛgveda. Ṛg 10-14-11 describes Pathirakṣi Śvānau. These two dogs are the two bright stars near Patha, the Milkyway. Thus it is proved that the names went from India to Europe. Śvānau means two Dogs. Later on the bigger star Canis Major was renamed as Vyādha. This star Vyādha is supposed to be the God Rudra. This name is again very scientific because the God Rudra is always accompanied with his wife Umā Gauri. The name shows that the sages knew that it is twin star. The modern astronomy has now discovered that the star is really a binary star or a twin star. Out of the two stars one is very small called in modern astronomy as a white dwarf. Umā Gauri is an appropriate name for white dwarf. This new name did not go to Europe, they stuck up to the old name Dog. Some scholars may not agree that Canis major is Vyādha, even then the fact that the name Śvānau the Dogs went from India to Europe will not change and the fact that Vyādha is a binary star will not alter. It shows that the sages had knowledge of astrophysics.

This naming and renaming of the stars in ancient India is a strong evidence to show that astronomy as a science was active and progressive in ancient India.

Ṛg. 10-14-11 uses the word Patha[26] for the Milkyway, but the Milkyway is described at Ṛg 1-164-43 under the name Śakamayam Dhūmam.[27] It is said here that "I see smoke of cowdung far away. From that insignificant faint (smoke) I see equality. That spotted sky cloud is developed by the Mighty. These are the original supporters or the existing things." The sage noticed a smoke like strip far away in the sky. He realised equality from that insignificant faint thing because mighty gods developed that faint sprinkled thing alongwith the bright stars. The sage discovered that the sprinkled smokes are the original existing thing from which the world came into being. The sage here tells about the Galaxy which really gave birth to our world according to the modern astronomy. It shows that the Galaxy or the milkyway was studied by the sages.

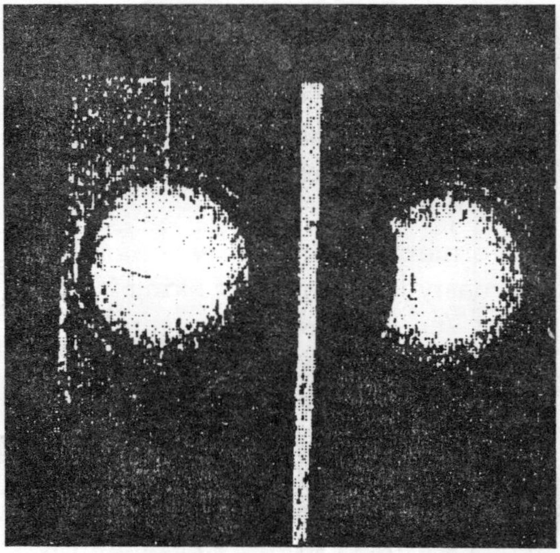

Fig. 1 : A part of the Sun eaten up by Demon Svarbhānu Ṛg 5-60-7

Fig. 2 : Total Solar Eclipse the Sun split into two parts as told by Vyāsa in Mahābhārata Bhiṣma 17/3 Ṛg 5-40-5, 6

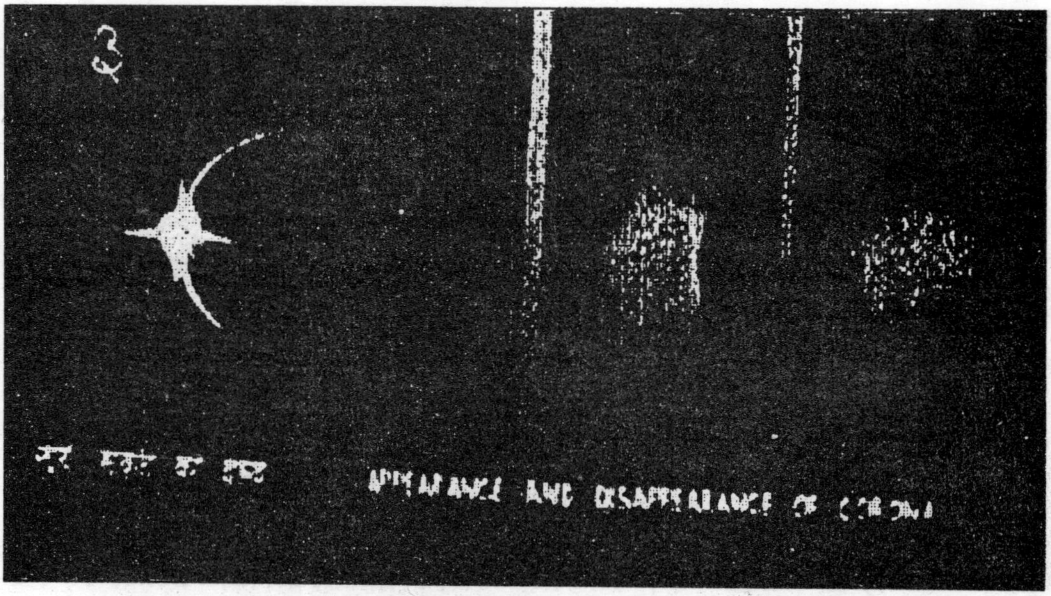

Fig. 3 : Eye of the Sun is again established in the sky. Ṛgveda 5-40-8

Dhūmā i.e. the milkyway is also described by Vālmiki in his Rāmāyaṇa[27] at Ayodhya 41-12.

Sun Spots : There are dark patches on the Sun called as Sun spots. It is taught in classes that the sun spots were observed with naked eye since 165 BC by the Chinese, but the first man to study sun spots with a telescope was Galileo. In the nineteenth century an amateur German astronomer Heinrich Schwabe came to the conclusion that the number of sun spots reaches a maximum every eleven years. Though the Chinese are credited with the observation of the sun spots in 165 BC I would like to point out that the sun spots were first observed by the Indians as far back as Ṛgveda and Vālmiki Rāmāyaṇa because Valmiki has described the sun spots in a speech of Rāma. Ṛgveda 1-140-1 talks about Yoni of the Sun.[28] Yoni means a place of birth, vulva or vagina, a mine. If we see a photograph of a sun spot [Fig. 4(a) & (b)] it does resemble like a vulva. Sunspots do give out flames like Yoni gives out a child. So the simile or the metaphor of Yoni to sunspot is perfect, proving that the sages had observed the sun spots as far ago as Ṛgveda.

Solar Eclipse is described in the Ṛgveda 5-40-5 to 9. Ṛc 5th states "Oh Sun, when you are afflicted by the demon Svarbhānu the people having no knowledge of physics (Akṣetravit) become dumb because the planets (Bhuvanāni) get covered by darkness."[29] [See Fig. 2 and 4]

The word Svarbhānu is important. It is composed by three words e.g. Svar which means the sky or the heaven, Bha which means light and Anu which means following or follower. Svarbhānu means Rāhu or Dragon's head. Rāhu is actually a shadow of the Moon because the Moon comes between the Sun and the Earth. It is a follower of the sunlight (bhā) in the sky. It is a follower (Arm) because where ever there is light there is shadow. The shadow is also present on any other planet if the Moon comes between that planet and the Sun. Therefore the sage has used the word Bhuvanāni, suggesting many planets. The sages knew that Rāhu works on all the planets. Thus the reason of the solar eclipse was found by sage Atri.

Ṛg 5-40-6 says, "Oh Indra, Svarbhānu's present illusion in the sky is beyond the usual rites of the Sun. The Sun disappears (Gūḷham) by the darkness, but Atri discovered that (Māyā) i.e. illusion) with the help of an instrument called as 'Turīya'."[30] Rāhu, the shadow, causes an illusion that a demon has eaten some portion of the Sun and then the demon has eaten up the whole of the Sun. This Māyā or illusion was removed by the sage Atri. For that purpose Atri used an instrument Turīya but it is not described in the Ṛgveda. Even then the narration proves that in Vedic era the sages were advanced to prepare and use some instrument to discover astronomical facts and phenomena.

Ṛg 5-40-7 tells, "Oh Atre, when you are alive do not make me gulped (Fig. 1) (Ni Gārīt). You are a friend worshipping the Truth. You and king Varuṇa both

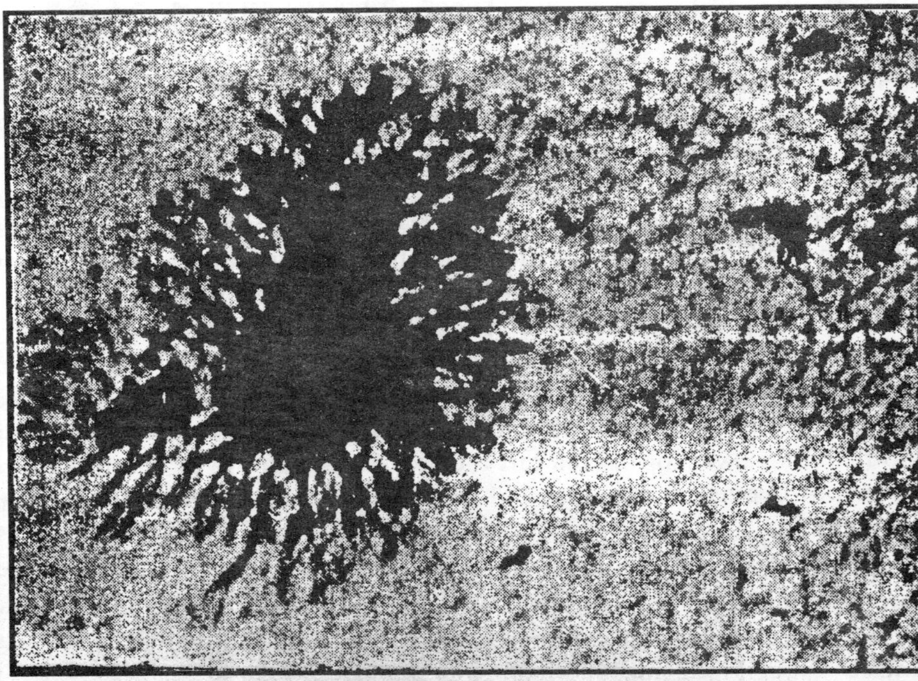

Fig. 4 (a) : Yoni of the Sun (Sun spots) Ṛg. 1-140-1

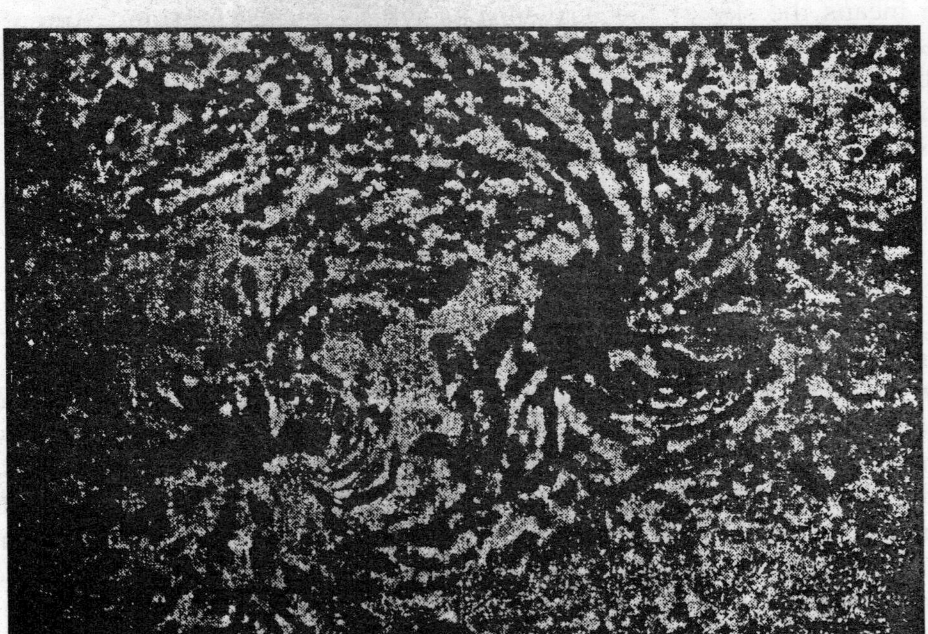

Fig. 4 (b) Yoni of the Sun (Sun spots) Ṛg. 1-140-1

protect me here in this world, (said the Sun)[31] "Here the Sun is personified to tell the greatness of sage Atri by a request to him to protect him with the help of Varuṇa. Varuṇa is the supreme entity controlling the sky as is shown in Ṛg 1-24-7[1] and 10.[2]

Ṛg 5-40-8 states "Combining the knowledge with the covered (Kiriṇā) and politely serving (Saparyan) and approaching the heavenly bodies (Devān), Atri unveiled (Aghukṣat) the bad illusion (Apa Māyā) of Svarbhānu and established (Ādhāt) the eye of the Sun in the sky."[32] (Fig. 3)

With his great knowledge Atri studied the heavenly bodies and discovered the effects of Suarbhānu (Rāhu). Exactly as he forecasted the Sun's eye was seen again in the sky. This 'eye' of the Sun is nothing else but the famous Diamond Ring which appears in the sky at the end of the solar eclipse.

5-40-9 Ṛgveda states, "Sages Atris found out what was that Demon Svarbhāmu who afflicted the Sun by darkness. Other sages could not do that work."[33] Atrayah is a plural form of the word Atri suggesting that there was not only one person but a team studying the phenomenon of solar eclipse. Probably many years or rather many centuries the study was conducted and then only the conclusion came out.

Thus it is proved that the studies of solar eclipse were being done in India in the remote past of the Ṛgvedic era.

Precession of Equinoxes

World famous scientist Gamow was surprised to see that the ancient Indian sages had noted the precession of equinoxes. Earlier we have seen that the sages noted the two Ayanas of the Sun namely Pitṛyāṇa and Devayāna. They arranged the seasons, Ṛtus, accordingly. They had mastered two streams of the Time reckoning namely solar-seasonal and Lunar months. By the name of a lunar month we can fix the position of the full moon and then the Sun's position in the Makṣatra path. By the Ṛtu and Ayana we can fix the position of the earth in relation to the Sun. This was very ingenious system by which we can fix the time perfectly. If it is stated that it was Hemants Ṛtu and Chaitra Māsa we understand that the fact must be at lest 8000 years old. This is the case of Rāma's birth.

The sages had developed the seasonal months. Nabha, the first month of Varṣā Ṛtu began with the Pitṛyāṇa or Dakṣhiṇāyana which means the southern journey of the Sun. It is fixed on the 22nd June according to the modern scientific calendar. Their Śiśira Ṛtu began with the Devayāna or Uttarāyaṇa which means the northward journey of the sun. It is fixed on the 22nd December according to the modern scientific calendar. Their Mādhava Māsa began on the Vernal equinox which is fixed to the 21st March according to the scientific calendar, which comes in the middle of the Vasanta Ṛtu. At the mid-Sarad Ṛtu began their Urja Māsa which comes on the 23rd September of the scientific calendar. These are the four nodes/very important in the astronomy. Two Solstices namely the Winter and the Summer which come on the 22nd December and the 22nd June of the scientific calendar and two equinoxes which fall on 21st March Vernal equinox and 23rd September the Autumnal equinox. These four nodes were known to the ancient sages and they were keen to record the position of the sun on any of these four nodes, the position of course on the path of Nakṣatras.

Because the sages were recording the Sun's Nakṣatra on a node they must have the knowledge that the positions are changing. This change of position of the sun on the equinox or solstice is called as the 'Precession'. The Vedas do not mention any name for the Precession, but knew the existence of the precession so that they carefully recorded the Nakṣatra of the Sun on the solstices.

Taittriya Brāhmaṇa 1-5-2-6,7 state, "Kṛttikā is the first Nakṣatra and Visākhā is the last Nakṣatra of the Devayāna. Anurādhā is the first and Āpabharaṇi is the last yama Nakṣatra. Deva-Nakṣatras turn (the sun) from the south. Yama-Makṣatras turn from the north."[34]

This is a straight forward translation of the verse and its meaning is also straight forward that Nakṣatra Kṛttikā turns the sun from the south while Anurādhā turns the sun from the north. In the modern language it means that Kṛttika was at the Winter Solstice and Anurādhā was at the Summer solstice. That means the northern course of the sun started with Kṛttika and the southern course of the sun started with Anurādhā. Āpabharaṇi was the last Yama Nakṣatra and Kṛttikā was the first Deva Nakṣatra that means the Winter solstice was between the two. In the modern language the winter solstice, then, was at 26° 40′. At present on 22nd December 1997 the sun was at 246° 20′. The Precession has an anticlockwise direction. Thus it reversed from 26° 40′ backwards to zero degrees and then backwards to 246° 20′. That means from zero or 360°, it traversed back to 246° 20′. This comes to 360° minus 246°20′ that is 113° 40′. This is to be added to 26° 40′. The result is 140° 20′. Thus the winter solstice has receded by 140 degrees and 20 minutes. The rate of the precession is 72 years per degree. So we have to multiply 140.35 degrees with 72 years. It comes to 10103.76 years. That means that the incident has occurred 10103.76 years ago. Subtracting 1997 AD we see the date of the Taittiriya Brāhmaṇa as 8106 years Before Christ.

Viśākhā is the last Deva Nakṣatra and Anurādhā the first Yama Nakṣatra. It shows that the Summer solstice was at 213 degrees 20 minutes. On 22nd June 1997 at the summer solstice the sun was at 66° 48′. The solstice has receded from 213° 20′ to 66° 48′. The total shift is 146° and 32′. Multiplying by 72 years (the rate of the precession) we get 10548 years ago. Subtracting 1997 AD we get 8551 years BC as the date of Taittiriya Brāhmaṇa.

We got two dates 8106 BC and 8551 BC. The mean comes to 8328.5 BC. Thus

8328 BC must be the date of Taittiriya Brāhmaṇa. At the most we may say that 8328 years BC is the date of Taittiriya Saṁhitā.

Here I have taken the rate of precession as is confirmed by the modern astronomy. In the past the sages were holding that the sun recedes by one Nakṣatra in one thousand years. So approximately they were correct. At the rate of 72 years per degree the rate per Nakṣatra comes to 960 years.

I have shown here the date of Taittiriya Saṁhitā or Taittiriya Brāhmaṇas 8328 years BC, but many scholars are afraid to accept such an ancient date. Why should there be any fear to accept the mathematical result? The only reason is the preconceived notion that the culture could not be so advanced in so ancient a period. With this fear many stalwarts in the field of astronomy and ancient history tried to manipulate the verse and tried to show that the Vernal equinox was at Kṛttikā, and calculated the date to be 1640 BC. Those astronomers were totally wrong to hold the Vernal equinox at Kṛttikā because if it was so the sage would not have said that the Deva Nakṣatras turn from the south. The sage has used the word 'Pariyanti'. The verb Pariyanti has the root परि + इ pari plus I (1 P) which means to turn or to reverse. It is used as causative too. If the vernal equinox was at Kṛttiki, then the verb becomes meaningless. The vernal equinox is situated at the middle of the Devayāna. Therefore there is continuous northward motion of the sun, there is no chance of any turning there at the vernal equinox. Hence the verb Pariyanti would have no meaning at all. Such a nonsensical verb could not have been used by the wise sage. It is also senseless to say that a Nakṣatra at the vernal equinox turns the sun from the south, because the Vernal equinox is at the centre, on the equator. If Kṛttikās were at the vernal equinox, the sage would have said, "Deva Nakṣatraṇi Viṣuveṇa Pariyanti" instead of "Dakṣiṇena Pariyanti'. But he does not say so. He is firm at his statement. Therefore we must agree that the Winter solstice was at Kṛttikā, and the date is 8328 BC. Vālmiki has used this verb in his Rāmāyaṇa at 6-54-35 in the sense of turning.

The modern astronomy has accepted that the rainy season in India begins at the Summer solstice and the same is stated in Ṛgveda 6-32-5.[35] So the sages knew very well the two solstices and were careful enough to note the Sun's Nakṣatra on the solstices.

Vālmiki Rāmāyaṇa, Ayodhyā 63/14, 15 also state that when the Sun is going towards south the rainy season begins.[36] Śuśruta Saṁhitā 6-6 tells that there are two Ayana e.g. Dakṣina and Uttara. Dakṣina contains Varṣā, Śarad and Hemants Ṛtus while Uttara contains Śiśira, Vasanta and Greeṣma.[37]

Yaju Pātha 5-7 tells that in Udagayana, which begins with Tapa or Śiśira there is diminution in the nights while days are increasing. In Dakṣiṇa Ayana exactly the reverse happens i.e. days decrease and nights increase.[38]

There evidences definitely show that from Summer solstice to winter solstice there was Pitṛyāṇa or Dakṣināyana and from Winter solstice to Summer solstice there was Devayāna or Udagayana or Uttarāyana.

The same is the concept exhibited in all the later literature like Mahābhārata, all the Purāṇas etc that Pitṛyāṇa begins with the Summer solstice and Devayāna begins with the Winter solstice. But neglecting all these evidences the experts twisted the meaning and told that at Kṛttikā there was Vernal equinox, only to bring the period later. For that purpose they used the support of Śatapatha Brāhmaṇa 2-1-3 where it is stated that Vasanta, Greeṣma and Varṣā are Deva Ṛtus while Śarad Hemanta and Sisira are Pitṛs.[39] It is wrong to give importance to only one book neglecting many others. The evidence of Śatapatha should be neglected. I say so because Yājnavalkya, the author of Satapatha was deadly against the original Yajurveda. He had studied it from his teacher Vaiśampāyana who his maternal uncle. But later on he quarrelled with the uncle for his remuneration in one Yajna and in a fit of anger he vomited out the original Yajurveda which he had learned from the uncle. Then he composed another Yajurveda and named it as Śukla Yajurveda. Then he himself wrote Śatapatha Brāhamaṇa. With this enemnity in his mind he deliberately perverted some concepts. Among those convertions one is the change in Devayāna which he held to begin with Vasanta Ṛtu and Pitṛyāna which he held to begin with Śarad.

I say confidently that sage Yājnavalkya was wrong in his concept because the same Yājnavalkya in the same Śatapatha 6-2-2-18 states that the first night of a year is of Phālguni Pūrṇanāsi with Vasanta.[40] If Phalguna Purṇimā is in Vasanáta, the Sun must be in Uttarā Bhādrapadā, directly opposite to the full moon. Then how can he say that Kṛttikā is at vernal equinox? Therefore Yājnavalkya was wrong and the scholars depending on him were wrong and so the date they have fixed is also wrong.

Yājnavalkya was wrong in one sense but he had shown the northern and southern hemisheres of the earth in that verse. It is astronomically significant.

Let us ...now see, how other literatures have recorded the Nakṣatras of the solstices or equinoxes.

Taittiriya Saṁhitā 7-4-8 and Taittiriya Brāhmaṇa 1-1-2 state that Agni should be oblated in Vasanta because it is the mouth of Ṛtus. In the night of Pūrvā Phalguni oblations should not be given because it is the last night of the year. Oblations be given in the night of Uttarā Phalguni because it the first night of the year.[41]

This statement show that Phālguna Māsa coincided with Vasanta Ṛtu at the time of Taittiriya Saṁhitā. It means that the sun was in Bhādrapadā in Vasanta.

At present the same is the condition. But nobody will dare to say that Taittiriya Saṁhitā is composed at present. Then when was it composed? Of courses in the remote past when the condition was the sáme. It could have happened before one complete cycle of 27 Nakṣatras of the precession. At the rate of 960 years per Nakṣatra a cycle of 27 Nakṣatra must have taken 25920 years. Deducting 2000 AD we can say that the date of Taittiriya Saṁhitā is 23930 BC.

Ṛgveda 1-161-13 states, "who aroused the Ṛbhus?" The Sun replied, 'the Dog because today is the end of the year.'[42]

Here Ṛbhu means the clouds because the clouds are born (bhu) due to motion (Ṛ). Ṛgveda 1-161-11, 12, and 4-33-7 show Ṛhu as clouds. Śvānam means the Dog which is nothing else but Mṛga Nakṣatra. Thus the meaning of the Ṛc is "who aroused the clouds? Mṛga, because it is the end of the year".

Clouds are aroused means clouds began showering rains, on the Mṛga Nakṣatra. It was the end of the year. Therefore it seems that on Mṛga the rainy season began at the end of the year. At present the rainy season in India begins on Mṛga. The same was the condition in the past at the time of Ṛgveda. So one Nakṣatra cycle is completed by the precession at the rate of 960 years per Nakṣatra Hence the period of Ṛgveda comes to 23920 BC.

Ṛgveda 4-57-5 requests Śunasirau to shower water from the heavens on the earth.[43] Śuna means dog, Sirau means two heads. These heavenly dogs are just near the Mṛga Nakṣatra. So this verse also shows that the rainy season, then, began with the Mṛga, the date being 23920 BC.

Both the above Ṛcs tell that the Summer solstice was at Mṛga. After some period the Summer solstice shifted back to Kṛttikā due to the anticlockwise precession. That is also recorded in Taittiriya Brāhmaṇa 3-5-7-1 which states that Kṛttikā invites the rainy season[44] The T.B. also states at 3-1-4-5 that the plants and trees grow because of Kṛttikā,[45] of course because Kṛttikā produced rains.

Kṛttikā is a faint constellation consisting seven very minute stars. Even then all the seven stars are named in Taittiriya Brāhmaavṇa 3-1-4.[46] The name are (1) Ambā (2) Dulā (3) Nitatni (4) Abhrayanti (5) Meghayanti (6) Varṣayanti (7) Chupuṇikā. All these seven names are related to water and the three names clearly indicate rainy season Abhrayanti means the one bringing Abhra i.e. white clouds having no water. Meghayanti means the one bringing the black water loaded clouds called as Megha. Varṣayanti means the one causing Varṣā the showers of rains. Thus the names suggest that there was rainy season beginning with Kṛttikā. It shows that the names were given when Kṛttikā was at the Summer solstice that means the Sun on 21st June then resided in Kṛttikā. We have seen above the date 23920 BC when the Varṣā Ṛtu began with Mṛga Nakṣatra. The solstice shifted back to Rohiṇi and Kṛttikā. Two Nakṣatras are shifted at the rate of 960 years per Nakṣatra. So 1920 years have passed. That means 22000 BC is the period when the Nakṣatra is given these names.

Taittiriya Brāhmaṇa 3-1-4-5 states, "The stars of Kṛttikā are hairless but by producing plants they become hairy."[46] The plants are called as hair of the Earth in Muṇḍaka Upaniṣad 1-1-7[47] and Aitareya Upaniṣad 1-2-4.[48] Śatapatha calls Kṛttikā as hairy at 2-1-2.[49] Taittiriya Brāhamaṇa states in 3-5-7-1 about Kṛttikā that it is the head of a hump of the sky, the supporter of the Earth, therefore it showers rains because that important location in the sky holds good rains.[50] This important location is the Summer solstice.

Before Kṛttikā, the summer solstice must have been on Rohiṇi. I do not find in the Vedas a direct proof for it, but the epic Mahābhārata which is supposed to be the fifth Veda has given that fact in Vana Parva 230/10. There sage Vyāsa has narrated an important astral fact which which happened in the remote past. He tells that the Nakṣatra Abhijit slipped down in the sky.[51] Vyāsa tells the fact in enigmatic language but I have deciphered it. Vyāsa has told that Kṛttikā contested with Abhijit and went to the summer solstice when Abhijit fell downwards. The time is very remote in the past. At that time Brahṃā started counting time with Dhaniṣṭhā as the first in the Nakṣatra list. Still in the past Rohiṇi was the first in the Nakṣatra-list. This story reveals that fact that when Kṛttika went to the summer solstice the Nakṣatra Abhijit started falling. It shows that the star began the fall around 22000 BC. At this time Brahmā made Dhaniṣṭhā the first, because Dhaniṣṭhā was at the Vernal equinox then. Kṛttikā was not given the honour though it had approached the summer solstice. Before this time says Vyāsa that Rohiṇi was held the first. It shows that around 22960 BC Rohiṇi was at the summer solstice. This story indicated that the vernal equinox and the summer solstice were held important then.

The story also proves that in so ancient a time a 24960 years BC, the sky was minutely observed, otherwise a fall of one star could not have been noticed. Few thousand years before the incident they must have been watching the stars.

The story is not a fantasy because out of innumerable stars only one is told to have slipped and that is Abhijit which is now called in the modern science as star Vega. And it is reported in all the important books on astronomy like Encyclopedia Astronomica by La Roussae, Popular Astronomy by Patrick Moore, Newcomb's Popular Astronomy etc. that Star Vega did fell down to become the Polar star around 13000 BC. The modern astronomy does not tell when the fall started but the Mahābhārata tells that the fall began around 22000 BC.

Ṛgveda 1-164=19 sates,[52] "Oh Indra and Soma, you two like harnessed horse rotate to support the world." These two rotating and supporting the world ....

cannot be anything else but the solstices or equinoxes. Indra is the deity of Jyeṣṭhā Nakṣatra and is the Rain God. That means Jyeṣṭhā was at the Summer solstice. At the same time Soma who is the deity of Mṛga Nakṣatra was at the winter solstice. The date of this fact comes to 10280 BC.

Mūla Nakṣatra is given the deity Niṛti. When Mūla was at the summer solstice the Indian sages discovered that the winds from the Naiṛtya brought rains in India. Therefore Niṛti was the deity allotted to Mūla. Here it is interesting to note that the epic Mahābhārata also has given the fact at Udyoga 82/10 where it is told that when Kṛṣṇa departed for peace talks there appeared storm, lighting, with darkness due to clouds and heavy rain caused by the south-west winds. (Vāto Dakṣiṇa Paśchima:[53]). The Meteorological science accepts that India gets the rains due to the south-west winds. This discovery of the rains due to south-west winds can be dated as 11240 BC when Mūla was at the summer slostice.

Just before this the sages had noticed that the rainy season begins with Pūrvāṣādhā at the summer slostice, the date being 12200 BC. Hence they fixed the deity of Pūrvāṣādhā as Udaka, the water.

Ṛgveda 3-57-2 states, "Indra and Pūṣā milch the clouds"[54]. Milching the clouds means bringing the rains and that work was done by Indra and Pūṣā who are the deities of Jyeṣṭhā and Revati. The rainy season began with Jyeṣṭhā and ended with Revati. The date of this fact comes to 9360 BC to 10280 BC.

Mitra is the deity of Anurādhā and Varṇa that of Śatatārakā. Mitra brought the rains so is called as the friend. Varuṇa stopped the rains at proper time. In the Kārtika Māsa with the Sun in Anurādhā the rainy season began and in Māgha Māsa on Śatatārakā it ceased. Its date comes to 8400 BC.

Viśākhā has a twin deity, Indra and Agni. Indra is the rain God while Agni is heat. Both are together at the summer solstice. So I think that the deities are allotted when Viśākhā was at the summer solstice causing heat and rain together. The date is 8000 BC.

A Nakṣatra is named as Āpabharaṇi in Ṛgveda. Āpa means water. Bharaṇi means to fill. How can a Nakṣatra from the sky fill up water on the earth? Of course by producing rains. So it is seen that the name was given when Āpabharaṇi was at the summer solstice inducing rainy season. Its date is 20840 BC.

Vālmiki Rāmāyaṇa tells that the Kula-Nakṣatra of Ikṣvākus was Viśākhā. Viśākhā is supposed to be a poisonous Nakṣatra; then why Rāma tells proudly that his Kula Nakṣatra is Viśākhā? (Yuddha 4-51, 52)[55]. The only possibility is that when Rama's Kula began with Ikṣvāku reigning there was Viśākhā at the Vernal equinox. Its date is 14120 BC to 15080 BC. Ikṣvāku was the son of Manu in whose life there was the great deluge described by many books. Modern science geology accepts that the great deluge did occur around 15000 BC.

Vālmiki Rāmāyaṇa tells that Daitya-Kula-Nakṣatra was Mūla.[55] (Yudh. 4/52, 53). It shows that Daitya Kula began with Mūla at the vernal equinox during 17000 BC with Hiraṇayakashipu or Bali.

Vālmiki Rāmāyaṇa tells that the rainy season then began with Aśvini Pūrṇimā. On Aśvini Pūrṇimā the full moon is near Aśvini Nakṣatra that means the Sun is diagonally opposite near Chitrā. Thus Chitrā was at the summer solstice, the date being about 7000 BC.

During this period the planets were weli studied and they were recorded at the important incidents. Thus Vālmiki records that at the time of Rāma's birth the moon and Jupiter were in Karka Rāsi and five planets were in their exalted positions.[56] From this date I could fix the exact date of Rāma's birth as 4th December 7323 BC.

The Mahābhārata also records the position of planets at the important incidents, but it has used an illusive enigmatic language. By deciphering that language I could fix the dates of 60 incidents from the Mahābhārata.The exact date of the Mahābhārata war is 16th October 5561 BC.

Viṣṇu Purāṇa 2-8-76 to 79 state that day and night become equal when the Sun resides in the first quarter of Kṛttikā and Moon in the fourth quarter of Viśākhā. Similarly the day and night becomes equal again when the sun resides in the third quarter of Viṣākhā and the Moon in the head of Kṛttikā.[57] The day night become equal at the Vernal and Autumnal equinoxes. From this data we can calculate the date of Viṣṇu Purāṇa as 1652 BC.

Suśruta Saṁhitā 67 tells that Māgha Māsa and Śiśira Ṛt simultaneously,[58] its date being 1640 BC. But it at 6-10 also states that Varṣā Ṛtu coincided with Bhādrapada and Āśvina Māsas.[59] This shows the date as 4000 BC. Probably this was the the first edition which was revised later in 1640 BC.

Maitrāyaṇī Upaniṣad 6-14 states that Dakṣiṇāyana extended from Maghā, to Śraviṣṭhā Nakṣatra's midpoint. This shows its date 1909 BC.

Kauṣitaki or Sāṅkhāyana Brāhmaṇa (1/3) tells that in the middle of the rainy season give oblations looking at Punarvasu Nakṣatra; but in this period in the first fortnight, Śukla Pakṣa, the does not unite with Punarasu. Therefore give oblation on Amāvāsyā which comes after Āṣaḍha because on that Amāvāsyā there is Punarvasu. The combination of Amāvāsyā, Punarvasu and rainy season gives fulfilment of all desires. This data shows the date of Kauṣitaki Upaniṣad to be 2320 BC.

Matsya Purāṇa 204/5 suggests to donate in Varṣā Ṛtu on Trayodaśi with Maghā Nakṣatra. Trayodaśi with Maghā occurs in Śrāvaṇa and Bhādrapada Māsas. Śrāvaṇa and Bhādrapada Māsas coincided with the Varṣā around 2000 BC.

Śrimad Bhāgavata Purāṇa tells that the day, equals the night when the Sun resides in Meṣa and Tulā Rāśi. This gives the date between 1600 BC and 2000 BC.

Vedāṅga Jyotiṣa gives winter Solstice on Dhaniṣṭhā, the date is 1640 BC. Garga gives summer solstice at Sārpānta[60] at 120 degrees, the date is 1640 BC Parasara gives summer solstice at mid-Aslesa,[61] date is 1159 BC.

Varāhmihira gives the summer solstice at Karkādya[62] at 90 degrees and the winter solstice at Makarādya or 270°, so his date is 520 AD.

Thus there are abundant records of the positions of the sun in Nakṣatras on solstices or equinoxes from 24000 BC to 520 AD. No body could have written those positions by imaginations. We have to believe in those records and accept the dates arrived at by calculations.

Comets are mentioned in Ṛgveda 8-43-4 where it is said that the attractive Dhūmaketus go speedily with wind near the Sun and work separately for Agni.[63] This description is correct because the comets are near the sun and they go with great speed with wind. Comets are gaseous in nature according to the modern astronomy. The exact function of the comets is not yet known to the science. Sages also did not know their function so it is said that they work for Agni, the supreme authority working behind this Universe.

Vālmiki Rāmāyaṇa states that Rama saw a Dhūmaketu near Mūla Nakṣatra[64] (Yudha.4/53). In a metaphor Valmiki has used Dhūmaketu at Sundar 19/9.[65] A club or bar shaped comet was seen near the Sun (Araṇya 23) Mahabharata also mentions a Dhūmaketu in Puṣya Nakṣatra[66] at Bhiṣma 3/12.

The Week Days : The Indian system of the week days reveals a great astronomical knowledge. Usually it is supposed that the Chaldeans prepared the system of week days but it is absolutely wrong a notion. Ṛgveda the most ancient literature of the world mentions week days at 1-164-2,3. Here it is stated that the chariot of the Sun is pulled by seven horses and seven sister like cows[67]. Evidently these are days and nights. It is stated at 1-164-5 that the garment of year is woven with seven fibres.[68] The seven fibres of the year are seven week days. Ṛg 1-164-12 speak about a wheel of seven having six spokes.[69] It is a wheel of seven days and six Ṛtus.

Vālmiki Rāmāyaṇa Ayodhyā 26/4 tells that on the day of Bṛhaspati[70] with Puṣya Rāma had to go in the forest. The day of Bṛhaspati means Thursday. I have fixed the date of exile of Rāma as 29th November 7306 BC when it was Thursday.

Māhābhārata Ådi Parva 160/7,[71] Kātyayana Gṛhya Sūkta 3-5-2[71] mention Vāras. i.e. week days. The order of the week days is given in Atharva Jyotiṣa[72] 93 as well as Yājnavalkya Smṛti,[73] Āchārādyāya 295. The order is Sun, Mon, Mars, Budha, Guru, Śukra, Śani. This order is very important because it show the deep knowledge about planets and astrophysics. The sages honoured the Sun as Ātman and the Moon as Mind. Hence they gave them the first and second places. Then alternately they used one external planet and one internal planet to name weekdays. The internal planets are inside the orbit of the earth while the external planets are outside the earth's orbit. The modern astronomy gives the order of the planets according to their distances. From the sun closest is Mercury (Budha), then Venus (Śukra), then the earth and the Moon, then Mars (Mangala), then Jupiter (Guru), then Saturn (Śani). Mercury and Venus i.e. Budha-Sukra are the internal planets and all others are external.

This system of seven days a week began at the time of Taittiriya Samhitā about 8000 BC out of the Yajna system. Taittiriya Samhitā advises to be Dikṣit for six days and then one day off.[74] (T.S.5-6-7). Accordingly people used to perform Yajna every day for six days. For counting these six days they offered oblations to each of the five planets, one each day. The Moon was the most important because it was thought to be the mind. So it was offered on the first day. After the six days one day was taken as off day but as the sun was held to be the Ātman it was given oblation on that day also. The planets were held as the gods according to Ṛgveda 1-105-10 and 10-55-3,[75] therefore they were given oblations. (Tait Brā, 3-1. 4-6) (Vājasaneya Saṁ 22-30)

Ṛg 1-164-15 states,"all the seven originated at a time, but the Sun came into existence first, independently, others were born later."[76] This statement applies to the week-days as well as the planets. Astronomy accepts that the sun was born first and immediately from it the planets were born. Similarly all the seven week days came into existence at one time, but sun was taken as the first.

Taittiriya Samhitā 7-4-7 mentions a yajna of 49 days. It was performed by Vasiṣṭhā to defeat Sudāsa. 49 days' Yajña cannot be explained on any other method of counting the days but the week day system.

The Genesis of the Universe

When the modern science advanced much the scientists started thinking in 20th century, how the Universe came into existence. It requires a lot of knowledge to arise this question in mind. This problem is dealt with quite efficiently in the famous Nāsadīya Sūkta of Ṛgveda 10-129. Its first[77] Mantra states. "There was no Sat present nor Asat present at that time of the genesis of the Universe. There was no Raja (Planets or Particles) no Vyoma (sky or space). There was nothing else too. Then what covered on? Where? For whose shelter? What was that profound and unfathomable Ambha?"

Sat means the existing things. Those were not present then. Asat means which is not Sat. All the imaginary things are Asat but they were also absent then. Raja means the planets or the particles. Modern science admits that at the genesis of the Universe there were no particles at all. Planets were also absent then. But this nothingness as is told by Veda is not at all conceived by the modern astronomy till this date. The modern astronomy assumes the presence of space and some gas then. How those two came into being is not considered by the science. But

Veda considers that. Veda tells that to begin with there was nothing but then some thing appeared some where. The thing appeared is named by the sage as 'Ambhas'. It was fathomless and very vast. For whose benefit it appeared is not understood by the sage, it is not yet understood by the modern science as well.

The sage tells that Ambhas appeared at one place. This is not yet coroborated by the modern science directly. But indirectly science accepts that concept. A great scientist Hubble says, "The galaxies are running from each other at the velocity of 60000 miles per second."For this reason the theory of expanding Universe is accepted all over. If we reverse the concept we can imagine that the galaxies are coming closer to each other at the speed of 60000 miles per second as we go in the past. Therefore there must be one place where all the galaxies were in the past. That one place is told by the sage.

The word Ambha coined by the sage is very scientific because the root Ambh means to sound. The matter which had appeared then was very dilute and was moving. A moving matter always produces some sound. Hence the name Ambha is scientific. The modern name for the similar matter is YIEM but it is not scientific because it is coined by fusing Yl from the Yale University with the initials of the two researchers E and M.

Scholars expert in Sanskṛta say Ambha means water. But we must remember that the sage has clearly stated in the first line that there was no Sat. Water is Sat, so it cannot be presented at the beginning of the world.

The modern astronomy says that the premordial gas present at the origin of the Universe was uniformly distributed throught space and its density was 10^{-22} times that of water. This premordial matter is named as Ambhas by the sage.

The sage did not understood what was that primitive matter, so he puts a question "what is that fathomless Ambha?" What is that matter is still not understood by the science.

Mantra 2 says, "There was no death present, immortal was also not present. There was no day nor night. It was only one thing breathing without air with its own energy. Really there was nothing else."[78]

Modern science admits that there was no sun, no planet. Naturally there could not have been any day or night. There was no life at all. Hence there was no death. But when I say that there was no life at all. Hence there was no death. But when I say that there was no death, one may assume that there were immortals present. Therefore the sage tells that there was no immortality as well.

There was only one thing breathing without air, with its own energy, says the sage. This statement is admitted by the world famous astronomer Mr. George Gamow. After studying pulsating stars he states in his book 'Birth and Death of Sun' thus; "Observations of the Doppler effect in the spectral lies of Cephoid variables actually prove that these stars are, so to say, 'breathing' that is, their surface layers are periodically rising and falling." Simile of breathing is used by the present renowned scientist just like the ancient sage.

As soon as we hear a word 'breath' we think of air. Therefore the sage makes it clear that 'it' was breathing without air, because there was no air at all at that time before the genesis of the world. The modern science agrees that there was no air then.

The sage further says that it was breathing with its own energy. This is also approved by the modern science because Gamow says, "the pulsations came as a result of a conflict between the nuclear and gravitational energy producing forces in the steller interior." Thus the energy was its own coming from within.

The sage says that there was only that one thing, nothing else. This also is agreed to by Gamow who says that there was only one uniform layer of that matter in the space. Sir Bernard Lovell states that there was only one fire ball from which the whole Universe appeared after the Big Bang. Sir James Jeans says that there was only one uniform layer of that matter. Thus all the three scientists agree fully with the sage.

Mantra 3 : There was darkness. In that darkness something mysterious was present to begin with. It was impossible to understand it. It was all "Salila' i.e. undulating. Ābhu which originated from the surrounding matter was wrapped up by some light matter. That one took birth from the greatness of the Heat.[79]

It is correct to say that there was total darkness then, because there were no stars at all. Even today the space is full of darkness, in spite of light from the sun and the stars. The statement of the sage that "in the darkness there was some thing mysterious which could not be understood" still holds truth because even today it is not understood by the modern science. All the scientists agree with Helmholtz that in early stages of development of the world all the stars were extremely rarefied and cool spheres of gas. Being cool there was no emittance of light. Hence it was a mystery in the darkness.

Gamow says, "At the dawn of the Universe the stars were dilute and they occupied all the space forming a continuous gas layer. Later due to some instability inside the continuous gas broke up into a number of separate clouds or gas drops." In that 'one' there was instability, separation and cloud formation so that there must have been some undulations, which are described by the sage in one word 'Salila'.

Gamow says that the Gas drops were enormous having diameter of two to three light years, and a mass of 10^{30} kilograms. These gas drops were formed from that one layer of gas occupying all the space, according to Gamow. The concept is told by the sage in one word 'Abhu' which means 'a thing which comes into being from the surrounding matter.' आसमन्तात् भवति इति आभुः ।

The sage tells that the Abhu was covered by the light matter (Tuccha). It is true to the modern science which says that gravitation forces do work in the gas drops which then contract and become ordinary stars. When the gravitation forces work there in collection of the dense matter at the centre and the light matter accumulates at the periphery. Hence it gets wrapped with the light matter as told by the sage in words "Tucchayana Ābhu Āpihitam".

The sage further says that it came into existence due to the greatness of the Heat. It is true because modern science says that the original cool spheres of gas became hot and luminous as a result of their gravitational contraction. (The Contraction Hypothesis of Hermann von Helmholtz).

Due to the heat there arose atomic reactions and explosion occurred due to energy in the interior, producing the Universe. Thus the Heat is very important in the genesis of the Universe as told by the sage.

Mantra 4 : A small seed in the mind becomes a great desire similarly, the sages conceived, 'Sat came into being from Asat.'[80]

The present Universe and all its matter came into existence from the matter which is not now present. (Asat)

Mantra 5 : Its strands or rays scattered, whether they were oblique or ascending or descending ? Some became germ-holders and become enormous. Those who surrendered or remained aloof became small.[81]

It is scientifically true that from the gas drops some matter scattered in the form of strands. When they became luminous light rays scattered from them. Were those strands or rays oblique or going up or downwards ? The sage tells in this question that there were no such directions as oblique or up or down. At present also in the space there are no directions at all. And all the possible directions are also possible for the rays or the strands to scatter. Again the sage tells the scientific truth here.

The sage tells that the germ-holders became bigger because they took efforts. Others who kept themselves aloof, holding themselves remain small. This is quite true scientifically. Some matter was thrown out from the Abhu in the form of strands. Some portion out of it came together to form germholders. Germ means nucleus. Around that nucleus matter started gathering so that they became bigger and bigger. To attract the matter is doing efforts. So it is said that Prayati Prayastāt. A hypothesis developed by Pierre Simon de Laplace, Carl von Weissacker, Kuiper and Terhar tells that the sun contained one per cent dust, particles of which came together to get solidified, while the remaining 99 per cent were gases which went away due to the centrifugal force leaving behind the solid mass of dust. This solid mass attracted other dust particles from the surrounding and grew bigger and bigger till they became planets. It is observed that when a small mass bumps against a large mass, the small mass gets merged with the large. In the same way the small planets got absorbed into the large ones which became enormous. The same hypothesis is put forth by our sage using the words 'Svadhā' and 'Prayati', for the small planets and the large planets respectively.

Mantra 6 : Who knows definitely from where the Universe came. Who can profess on the genesis of the Universe? Due to its origin even the Gods have become subsequent, then who can tell or know from whom it is born?[82]

In spite of the great knowledge the sage says that nobody can know from where the Universe has come. Even the modern science fails to know it definitely.

Mantra 7 : The entity from whom the Universe is born supports it or not ? The supreme controller in the supreme space knows it or not ?[83]

Here a principle is told by the sage that a thing which produces other supports the other. For example, the Moon is originated from the earth and the earth supports the moon due to its gravitational attraction. The sun gives birth to the earth and supports it by gravitation. Similarly the galaxy produces the sun and supports it. In the same way the Universe is produced by that Supreme authority and that supports it. That supreme authority is in the super space. That must be knowing about the genesis of the Universe. Saying so the sage questions whether He knows it or not? In this question he suggests that there may be a still higher authority.

Thus the Nāsadiya Sūkta deals with the problem of the genesis of the Universe very scientifically only in seven Mantras. His thoughts are similar to the ultra-modern scientists of the later half of the 20th century.

Aitareya Upaniṣad gives similar thoughts about the genesis of the Universe. In Anuvāk 1 it states "There was only one Atman at the beginning. Nothing else was moving then. He thought of producing worlds."[84] To say that Atman 'thought' is a very good thought now agreed to by the modern noble laureatte Sir Bernard Lovell who says that to begin with there was only one Fireball, then Big Bang took place and the Universe was born. He further states that had there been a mistake of a fraction of a second, there would have been no formation of Hydrogen and then the world in the present form would not have been born. As there was no mistake at all, there must have been knowledge and thought. The same is told by the sage Aitara.

Anuvāk 2 states that there developed four Lokas namely Ambha, Marichi, Mara and Āpa. Ambha is beyond the Heat and Light (Diva). Marichi or stars are in the space or sky. The earth is Mara, and Āpa comes later.[85]

Here the sage Aitara shows that Ambha means space and gas together. The modern science also assumes that some premordial gas in the space was already present. That gas in the space is called as Ambha by the sage. Aitara tells that the Earth came first and then the water. This concept is different than that of Taittiriya Upaniṣad which holds that first Āpa came into being and then Pṛthvi. The modern science agrees with the Taittiriya and says that first the Earth was full of liquid which gradually disappeared leaving the earth bare. It is for this reason that the earth in its three-fourth part is covered by water. Though the modern science agrees with Taittiriya we cannot say that Aitareya is wrong, because new evidences give support to Aitareya. In the case of the planet Mars it is discovered that there is Mara but there is no water, the Āpa. Water may occupy Mars in future. Therefore first Mara and then Āpa is is correct.

Taittiriya Upaniṣad, Brahmānandavalli Anuvāk 1 states that from Atman first the space came into existence, from it Vāyu, from it Teja, from it Apa and from it Pṛthivi came into being.[86] This thought is in line with the modern science. Further it tells that from Pṛthvi, the earth, arose plants, from the plants arose the food and from food arose the life. This also is true to the science. In Anuvāk 8-4, it tells that whatever is in this life is present in the Sun.[87] This is the height of the knowledge because now the modern science has accepted it. The subatomic particles present in the living animals are present in the Sun. In Śikṣāvalli, anuvāk 10, the Taittiriya Upaniṣad records the statement of Triśanku that just like the Sun I also the pure immortal.[88] This also is in accordance with the science.

Taittiriya Upaniṣad, Śikṣāvalli Anuvāk 5-1 states that "Bhu, Bhuva and Suva are the three 'Vyāhṛti's. In those the son of Mahāchamas added the fourth namely Maha. That is the Brahma, that is the Atman.'[88]

Mantra 2 states, "Bhu is this earth. Bhuva is the atmosphere. Suva is that Loka." In the Anuvāk 3 Mantra 3 it is told that Pṛthivi is close to us, Dyau (Suva) is distant, but the space, Ākāśa, is continuous (Sandhi), Vāyu is connected to both the earth and Dyau. "From these statements it becomes clear that the earth is Bhu, Atmosphere is Bhuva, and the uppermost layer of atmosphere is Suva or Dyau. Dyau means bright, and really the uppermost layer of our atmosphere is bright, beyond that Dyau there is darkness. So the sages knew that there is light in the Suva or Dyau which is approved by the science. Vyāhṛti is the word composed of Vi Ā Hṛti. Vi means special. Ā means towards us. Hṛti means to achieve, achievable thing. The sages wished to achieve this earth, the atmosphere and its hightest layer the Suva. Till the Vedic era that much was the knowledge. But later on the son of Mahāchamas discovered the space beyond the Suva. It was very vast, so he named that space as Maha. Further it is said "Maha is Ādityā". It suggests that Āditya, the sun is situated in Maha. Science is sure that the Sun is situated in Maha. From the descriptions it appears that Maha is the space in the solar system in which all the planets rotate around the sun.

Still later than Mahāchamas, are added Jana, Tapa and Satyam. It appears that Jana means the space outside our solar system but within our galaxy. Tapa is the space outside our galaxy. Satyam is the whole Brahma. Thus the sages had achieved the knowledge of the entire space in Brahma.

Here it is important to note that the word Ākāśa is very scientific. Root Kāśa means to manifest, to appear, to shine. Ā is a prefix which shows reverse action.

Hence Ākāśa means the thing which never manifests, never appears, never shines. The space is really such a thing. On the contrary there is Prakāśa which strongly shines, appears.

Muṇḍaka Upaniṣad 2-1-5 states that from the Parabrahma Agni came into existence. One straw of that Agni is the Sun.[89] This statement shows that the sage knew that the Sun is negligible in the Universe. The same is proved by the modern astronomy.

Muṇḍaka 1-2-4 tells that there are seven tongues of Agni namely Kāli, Karāli, Manojavā, Sulohitā, Sudhūmravarṇā, Sphullingini and Viśvaruchi.[90] These appear to be the seven energy bands. Kāli is the ordinary sun light. Karāli means having many hands to work. It is electricity. Sulohitā means infrared (Lohita means red, Su means beyond.) Sudhūmravarṇā means ultraviolet because Dhūmra means smoky violet, Su means beyond (violet). Manojava means having a speed of mind. Mind has the highest speed faster than light. The light takes 8 minutes to come from the sun to the earth, but our mind reaches the sun instantaneously. The sage tells that such an energy having velocity faster than light does exist. Dr. ECG Sudarshan, Seracuse University, New York, alongwith Dr. V.K. Deshpande proposed the hypothesis about the particles faster than light in 1956. They named those particles as Tachyon. Manojava is a right name for those particles.

Sphullingini means having vibrations which are exhibited by atomic energy. Viṣvaruchi means the energy which likes to devour the Universe. The black holes is a similar energy which may gulp the whole world in a moment. Praśnopaniṣad 3/8 states "Āditya is Prāṇa, it helps Prāṇa in the eyes. The goddess in the Earth helps the Apana in the man by attraction."[91] This is a straight reference to the gravitation attraction of the Earth. Gravitation attraction of the earth does help Apana in defaecation, urination, parturition.

Adi Sankaracharya, in his commentary on this verse says, "If the famous goddess of the Earth did not help our Apana by attracting us downward, due to weight, Gurutva, of the body we would have floated in the sky or would have fallen anywhere in the space,"[92] How perfectly Śankarācharya has described the effect of non-gravity is under-stood by seeing the condition of astronauts in the space.

In Vedic Astronomy we must consider the epic Mahābhārata. Because it is supposed to be the fifth Veda. Sage Vyāsa was an intelligent scientist, He describes a solar eclipse at Bhiṣma 17/3 that "the sun rose and was split into two parts. It was throwing out firy flames enormous in size (Bhūya) instead of raya.[93]" In Bhisma 19/39 he tells 'the sun lost its brilliance.'[94] The modern astronomy approves this description. Scholars mocked at Vyāsa criticizing that the sun cannot be split into two parts. But the splitting happens, not like a fruit cut in two slices, but in a different way. We can see a black disc in the centre and a bright corona around it (Fig. 2). Are not these two parts of the Sun? It is also proved by the science that at the time of the total solar eclipse the sun does sow huge flames of height as far as five to ten lacs of miles. So Vyāsa was a great astronomer.

Vyāsa has described three more planets beyond the Saturn in his Màhābhārata under the names of Śveta, Śyāma and Tīvra[95] at Bhīṣma 3/11, 15, 26. Their position in the Nakṣatras are also given. Seven planets excluding the Sun, Moon, Rāhu and Ketu are mentioned at three places[96] viz. Bhīṣma 17/2, Droṇa 137/22 and Karṇa 37/4 or 26/34 (BORI). I have calculated the exact date of the beginning of the great war as 16th October 5561, BC, and on this date Śveta is found at the place of Uranus by calculations, Śyāma is found at the place of Neptune and Pluto's position is found occupied by Tīvra. Thus mathematically it is proved that Vyāsa did know the three planets. The names used by him are realistic because Śveta means greenish white and Uranus is actually greenish white in colour. Śyama means blue and Neptune is blue in colour in reality. So it is proved that Vyāsa had seen the two planets. Tīvra is also named as Tīkṣṇa, both the words mean minute. It is also called as Nakṣatra at Bhīṣma 3/30.[97] Nakṣarati iti Nakṣatra is the definition. The star was found stationed at one spot in Kṛttika for a long time, so Vyāsa thought it to be a Nakṣatra, but later discovered it as a planet. Thus it is proved that Vyāsa knew all the three planets supposed to be a discovery of 18th and 19th and 20th century. Neelakaṇṭa a commentator of Mahābhārata calls Śveta as Mahāpāta. Pāta means orbit. Its orbit was greater than the Śani or Saturn hence this. Neelkaṇṭa was in 16th century, at least one hundred years earlier than Herschel who is supposed to have discovered the planet Uranus in 1761 AD. Neelkaṇṭa calls Śyāma as Parigha. Parigha means circumference. A planet situated at the circumference of our solar system is named as Parigha. Neptune is really so felt Neelkaṇṭa, hence he used that name. Neptune is discovered by the modern science in 1846 AD. Including Uranus and Neptune alongwith the originally known planets, Budha, Sukra, Mangala, Bṛhaspati, Śani, Vyasa has mentioned seven planets in Bhīṣma 17/2 and Karṇa 37/4. Pluto is supposed to be discovered by a French scientist in 1930, but Late. Shri B. V. Ketakar from Maharashtra, India, had already written a research paper and sent it to Paris in 1911 AD. Pluto was known to Vyāsa in 5561 BC.

Vyasa had invented a method to give positions of planets from the position of the Sun at the Vernal equinox. This system may be called as Sāyana because the sun's position has an Ayana, a motion, in anticlockwise direction. At his time the Vernal equinox was in Punarvasu Nakṣatra so it was supposed to be zero point. From that zero, Puṣya was the first Nakṣatra, so it was held as Aṣvini, which is the first Nakṣatra in the Nirayana system. There is a difference of eight Nakṣatras between Aśvini and Puṣya, and the same is reflected in the two positions of the planets given by Vyasa for each planet at one time. No sensible person can say that a planet is situated at two Nakṣatras at one time, but Vyāsa the author of one lac Slokas writes so. He gives the positions of planets thus : Śani in Pūrvā

Phalguni and Rohiṇi, Guru in Śravaṇa and Viśākhā, Mangala in Maghā and Anurādhā, Moon in Maghā and Anurādhā, Śyāma (Neptune) in Pūrvā Proṣṭhapadā and Jyeṣthā. There is a difference of eight Nakṣatras in these twin positions. Therefore it is certain that Vyāsa has used two methods having their zero point eight Nakṣatras apart. Sāyana Nakṣatra is eight Nakṣatras earlier, as stated in the Mahābhārata.

Vyāsa had the knowledge of slipping of the star Vega i.e. Abhijit which had occurred around 13000 BC. He also had noticed that Arundhati overtook Vasiṣṭha and went ahead of him. (Bhiṣma 2). Saptarṣi are the seven stars in Ursa Major. Its shape is like a kite with a tail. In the sky we see that the square of the kite is towards the west while its tail is towards the east. Vasiṣṭha is the middle star in the tail. Just to the cast and a little below i.e. towards the north of it, there is a minute star named as Arundhati, (who was the wife of sage Vasiṣṭha). Therefore it is said that Arundhati is ahead of Vasiṣṭha, now, but this was not the position before Mahābhārata. Vyasa says Arundhati was behind Vasiṣṭha but then went ahead. Many scholars say that such a change in the position is impossible. But it is possible according to the modern astronomy, which has discovered the positions of the seven stars one lac years ago, one lac years hence and two lacs years in future. These maps show changes in the positions of the seven stars. Arundhati is far distant than those seven stars and so it is quite possible that it might have changed the position in relation to Vasistha, before 5561 BC.

Vyāsa has recorded that there were two eclipses in one month[98], one lunar and one solar, just before the Mahabharata War. He appears to be correct mathematically. On 16th October 5561 BC the great war began when the Sun was in Uttarāṣādhā at 279 degrees, and Rāhu was at 273 degrees. Therefore it was a total eclipse. It was Mārgaśirṣa Amāvāsyā and not Kārtika as is supposed generally without considering enigmatic verses. That Pakṣa consisted of 13 days only, as is stated by Vyāsa (Bhiṣma 3/28) So 13 days earlier there must have been Pūrṇaimā, full moon. 13 days earlier the Sun must be 13 degrees earlier at 266 degrees, in Pūrvāṣādhā Being full moon day the moon must be diagonally opposite to the Sun. So the moon was at 86 degrees. Therefore it was Mārgasirṣa Māsa. Ketu is always diagonally opposite to Rāhu. Rāhu was at 273° so Ketu was at 93°. The moon was at 86° while Ketu at 93°, seven degrees away, therefore there was an eclipse but not total or partial caused by Umbra, the dark shadow of the earth; but was Penumbral eclipse wherein the moon becomes faint only. Vyāsa describes this pallor of the moon at Bhiṣma 2/23.[99]

Vyāsa records the opinion of sage Vasiṣṭha about the genesis of the Universe in the Mahābhārata, Śānti Parva 302 thus : One kalpa means 48 millions of Divya years. It is Brahmadeva's one day. His night is equally long. So day and night means 96 millions of years. These are the Divya years. One Divya year means 360 human years. So multiplying by 360 to 96 million we get 34560000000 years i.e.

34 Abja 56 Koti years or 3.4 billion years. After 3.4 billion years the shapeless Śambhu activates and becomes Jyotirūpa i.e. He assumes a form of a great flame. From that originate five Mahā-Bhutas - Åkaṣa, Vāyu, Teja, Āpa, Pṛthvi. On 29th August 1975 all the newspapers published new discovery of Sir Bernard Lovell who proved that one billion years ago there was only one fire ball in the space. It exploded and innumerable stars got birth. Due to the speciality of that Big Bang, there arose the Universe and the life. Thus there is marked similarity between the thoughts of Lovell and Vasiṣṭha as recorded by Vyāsa. Now Sir Lovell says that the time may go much back than one billion years. So it appears that the ancient sages are more correct in their astronomical researches.

Considering all these advances in the astronomy one may question whether there were telescopes and may say that without the telescopes astronomical research is impossible. I have found an evidence to show that telescopes might have been present then alongwith microscopes. Mahābhārata records 'Avyakta-lochana' and 'Avyakta Darśanat' at Śanti 308/10, 12.[100] This certainly points to microscopic and telescopic vision., because the microscopic living things are told in Śānti 15/26. Ādi Śankarāchārya also tells in Aparokṣānubhūti 81 that minute things appear big with the help of Upanetra.[101] It is told in ancient literature that Yajnas were ignited by keeping Suryakānta Maṇi in the sunrays. This definitely suggests the convex lens. Śankarāchārya and other sages are much older than the 16th century when European scientists started work.

There may be or may not be any physical means to see at a long distance but there was certainly Yogic vision called as 'Divya Dṛṣti' with the ancient sages in India. Pātanjala Yoga Sūtra, Vibhuti Pāda 26 says,"Bhuvana Jnānam Sūrya Saṅyamāt." It means that if a Yogi performs Dhāraṇā-Dhyāna-Samādh on the Sun be gets knowledge of the world - earth and heaven together. The combination of Dhāraṇa, Dhyāna and Samādhi is called as Saṅyama. On performing Saṅyama on the Moon, a Yogi gets knowledge of the arrangements of the stars. By Saṅyama on Dhruva i.e. the polar star a Yogi gets the knowledge of the motion of the polar star. (Sukta 27 and 28 of Vibhuti Pāda). How could sage Patanjali observe the motion of the polar star in so ancient a time as 5000 years BC? The polar star was supposed to be a fixes star having no motion at all till recent time in the European astronomy. But Patanjali clearly speaks about its movement and Purāṇas tell the stories of change of the polar stars. This show that Yogic Dṛṣti was used in the research of Jyotis in the sky.

Velocity of Light was known to the India in the 15th century AD accurately. Sāyaṇāchārya or 15th century comments on Ṛgveda 1-50-4, that "It is remembered that the sun light travels two thousand two hundred and two Yojanas in half a Nimeṣa." One Yojana means 9 miles and 110 yards i.e. 9.0625 miles. The Mahābhārata Śānti 231 tells fractions of a day in which half a Nimesa seems to be 0.106666 seconds. If calculated on this data the light comes to 187084.1 miles per second. According to Michelson it is 187372.5 miles per second.

Sir Monier Williams gives one Yojana as 9 miles. With this if we calculate the velocity comes to 186413.22 miles per second. The well accepted popular scientific figure is 186300 miles per second. In any case the velocity of light told by Sāyana is almost the same as the modern science. The modern science calculated the light velocity in the 20th century, 500 years later than Sāyaṇa.

Ṛgveda 1-164-34,35[102] and Yajurveda 23-59-61, 62 state that the Vedi is the last boundary of the Earth and the Yajña is the centre of the earth. It leads to the inference that the Vedic sages knew very well that the earth is spherical, that is why every where the planets are called as Grahagola. Gola means sphere.

There are many other evidences but from these few given above we are convinced that Astronomy and astrophysics was far advanced in Vedas. Hence Śikṣā 41-42 rightly states that Jyotiṣa, Astronomy is the eye of the Vedas. We should be proud about this heritage of the knowledge and study it on the basis of the modern science. The unintelligible verses may become intelligible with the help of the science.

References

1. ऋग्वेद 1-24-7 — अबुध्ने राजा वरुणो वनस्योर्ध्वं स्पूतं ददते पूतदक्षः।
नीचीनाः स्शुरुपरि बुध्न एषां अस्मे अन्तर्निहिताः केतवः स्युः ॥७॥
2. ऋग्वेद 1-24-10 — अमी य ऋक्षा निहितास उच्चा नक्तं दहश्रे कुह चिद्दिवेयुः।
अदब्धानि वरुणस्य व्रतानि विचाकशत् चन्द्रमा नक्तमेति।।10।।
3. अथर्ववेद 13-217 20-47-14 — अपत्ये तायवो यथा नक्षत्रा यन्त्यक्तुभिः सूराय विश्वचक्षसे ॥17॥
4. अथर्ववेद 14-1-2 — सोमेनादित्या बलिनः सोमेन पृथिवी मही।
ऋ. 10-85-2 — अथो नक्षत्राणामेणामुपस्थे सोम आहितः॥
5. ऋग्वेद 1-105-10 — अमी ये पञ्चोक्षणो मध्ये तस्थुर्महो दिवः।
6. ऋ. 10-55-3 — आ रोदसी अपृणादोत मध्यं पञ्च देवाँ ऋतुशः सप्त सप्त।
7. तै.ब्रा. 3-1-4-6 — बृहस्पतये स्वाहा, निष्याय स्वाहा।
वाजसनेय सं. 22/30 — चंद्राय स्वाहा, दिवापतये स्वाहा।
8. ऋग्वेद 6-32-5 — ससर्गेण शवसा तक्तो अत्यैरप इन्द्रो दक्षिणतस्तुराषाट्।
9. ऋग्वेद 1-95-3 — पूर्वामनु प्रदिशं पार्थिवानामृतून् प्रशासद्विद धावनुष्टु॥
10. ऋ. 10-90-6 — सत्पुरुषेण हविणा देवा यज्ञमतन्वत।
वसन्तो अस्यासीदाज्यं ग्रीष्म इध्मः शरद्धविः ॥6।
11. ऋ 10-68-10 — हिमेव पर्णा मुणिता वनानि....।
12. सायणाचार्य — मधुः चैत्रो मासः। माधवो विशाखे मायः।
13. ऋ. 2-24-5 — सना ता का चिद्भुवना भवीत्वा माब्दिः शरद्भिः दुरो वरन्तः वः।
अयतन्ता चरतो अन्यदन्यदिधा चकार वयुना ब्रह्मणस्पतिः ॥5॥

14. तै. ब्रा. 3-10-4-1	तस्य ते बसन्तः शिरः। ग्रीष्मो दक्षिणः पक्षः। वर्णाः पुच्छम्। शरदुत्तरः पक्ष हेमंतो मध्यम्॥
15. तैत्तिरीय सं. 6-5-3	उभयतोमुखमृतुपात्रं भवति कोहि तद्वेद यहतूनां मुखम्।
16. तै.सं. 7-4-8 तै. ब्रा. 1-1-2	बसंते ब्राह्मणोऽमिमादधति...मुखं वा एतहतूनाम्।।6॥ यद् वसंतः।
17. तै, सं. 4-4-11	मधुश्च माधवश्च वासंतिकावृतू शुक्रश्च शुचिश्च ग्रैष्मावृतू। नभश्च नभसश्च वार्षिकावृतू। इषश्चोर्जश्च शारदावृतू। सहश्च सहस्यश्च हैमंतिकावृतू। तपश्च तपस्यश्च शैशिरावृतू। सहश्च हैमंतिकावृतू। तपश्च तपस्यश्च शैशिरावृतू।
18. ऋ 4-33-7	द्वादश द्यून्यदगोह्यस्यातिथ्ये रणन्नृभवः ससन्तः। सुक्षेत्राकृण्वन्ननयन्त सिन्धू-धन्वातिष्ठन्नोणधीर्निम्नमापः॥
19. ऋ 1-6-4-12 प्रश्नोपनिषद् 1-11	पञ्चपादं पितरं द्वादशाकृतिं दिव आहुः परे अर्धे पुरीणिणम्। अथेमे अन्य उपरे विचक्षणं सप्तचक्रेषकर आहुरर्पितम्।
20. ऋ 1-25-8	वेद मासो धृतब्रतो द्वादश प्रजावतः वेदा य उपजायते॥
21. तै. सं. 5-6-7	द्वादश रात्रिदीक्षितः स्यात् द्वादश मासाः संवत्सरः। त्रयोदश रात्रिर्दीक्षितः स्यात् त्रयोदशमासाः संवत्सरः।
22. महाभारत विराट 52/3,4	पंचमे पंचमे वर्षे द्वौ मासावुपजायतः।।3 एषामभ्यधिका मासाः पंच दिनद्वये।
23.	गते वर्षद्वये चैव पंचपक्षे दिनद्वये। दिवसस्य अष्टमे भागे पतत्येकोडधिमासकः।।45
24. शतपक्ष ब्रा. 2/1/2/4	सप्तर्षी नु ह स्म वै पुरर्क्षा इत्याचक्षते।
25. ऋ 10-14-11	यौ ते श्वानौ यम रक्षितारौ चतुरक्षौ पक्षिरक्षी नृचक्षसौ।
26. ऋ 1-164-43	शकमयं धूममारादपश्यं विषूवता पर एनावरेण। उक्षाणं पृश्निमपचन्त वीरास्तानि धर्माणि प्रथमान्यासन्॥
27. वाल्मीकि रामायण अयोध्या 41/12	विशाखास्तु सधूमाश्च नभसि प्रचकाशिरे ।। 12
28. ऋ 1-140-1	वेदिषदे प्रियधामाय सुद्युने धासिमिव प्रभरा योनिमग्नये।
29. ऋ. 5-40-5	यत्त्वा सूर्य्य स्वर्भानुस्तमसाविध्यदासुरः। अक्षेत्रविद्यथां मुग्धो भुरनान्य दीधयुः।।5
30. ऋ 5-40-6	स्वर्भानोरध सदिन्द्र माया अवो दिवो वर्त्तमाना अवाहन। गूढहं सूर्य्यं तमसापव्रतेन तुरीयेण ब्रह्मणाविन्ददत्रिः।।
31. ऋ 5-40-7	मा मामिभं तव सन्तमत्र दूरस्या द्रुग्धो भियसा नि गारीत् त्वं मित्रो असि सत्यराधास्तौ मेहवतं वरुणश्च राजा।।7।
32. ऋग्वेद 5-40-8	ग्राव्णो ब्रह्मा युयुजानः सपर्य्यन् कीरिणा देवन्नमसोपशिक्षन्। अत्रि सूर्यस्य दिवि चक्षुराधात्स्वर्भानोरप माया अद्युक्षत्

33. ऋ. 5-40-9	यं वै सूर्यं स्वर्भानुस्तमसाविध्यदासुरः। अत्रयस्तमन्वविन्दन्नहि अन्ये अशक्नुवन्॥9
34. तै. ब्रा. 1-5-2-6,7	कृत्तिकाः प्रथमां विशाखे उत्तमं। तावि देवनक्षत्राणि। अनुराधा प्रथमं आपभरणीरुत्तमं। तानि यमनक्षत्राणि॥ यानि देवनक्षत्राणि तानि दक्षिणेन परियंति। यानि यमनक्षत्राणि तानि उत्तरेण॥
35. See 8	ततः प्रावृनुप्राप्ता....
36. वाल्मीकि रामायण अयोध्या 63/14,15	परेताचरितां भीमां रविराविशते दिशम्।
37. सुश्रुत 6-6	अयने द्वे भवतः। दक्षिणं उत्तरं च। तयो दक्षिणं वर्णा शरद् हेमन्ताः। उत्तर च शिशिरं वसन्त ग्रीष्माः॥
38. यजुः पाठ 5-7	स्वराक्रमेते सोमार्कौ यदा साकं सवासवौ। स्यात्तदादि युगं माघस्तपः शुक्लो अयनं हि उदक्॥5 प्रपेद्यते श्राविष्ठादौ सूर्याचंद्रमसौ उदक्। सर्पार्द्धे दक्षिणार्कस्तु माघ श्रावणयोः सदा॥6 धर्मवृद्धिरणां प्रस्थः क्षपा-ह्रास उदग्मतौ। दक्षिणेतौ विपर्यस्तौ षण्मुहूर्त्ययनेन॥ 17
39. शतपथ ब्राह्मण 2-1-3	वसंतो ग्रीष्मो वर्षाः ते देवा ऋतवः। शरद्धेमंतः शिशिरस्ते पितरोः। स यत्रोदमावर्तते देवेषु तर्हि भवति। यत्र दक्षिणावर्तते पितृषु तर्हि भवति।
40. शतपथ 6-2-2-18	एषा हसंवत्सरस्य प्रथमा रात्रिर्या फल्गुनी पूर्णमासी
41. तैत्तिरीय संहिता 7-4-8 तै. ब्रा. 1-1-2	वसंते ब्राह्मणोऽग्रिमादधीत मुखं ता एतत् ऋतूनाम्॥6॥ यद्वसंतः॥ न पूर्वयोः फल्गुन्यो-रग्निमादधीन। एषा वै जघन्या रात्रिः संवत्सरस्य यत्पूर्वे फल्गुनी। एषा वै प्रथमा रात्रिः संवत्सरस्य यदुन्तरे फल्गुनी॥ मुखत एव संवत्सरस्याग्निधाय।
42. ऋ. 1-161-13	सुषुप्वांस ऋभवस्तदपृच्छतागोह्य क इदं नो अबूबुधत्। श्वानं बस्तो बोधयितारमब्रवीत्संवत्सर इदमद्या व्यखत।।
43. ऋ.. 4-57-5	शुनासीराविमां वाचं जुषेथां यद्दिवि चक्रशुः पयः। तेनेमामुप सिञ्चतम्॥5
44. तै.ब्रा. 3-5-7-1	अग्निर्मूर्धा दिवः ककुत् पतिः पृथिव्या अयम्। अपारेतांसिजिन्वति दिवि मूर्धानं दधिषे सुवर्षाम्॥
45. तैत्तिरीय ब्राह्मण 3-1-4-5	त्रक्षा वा इयमलोमकाऽसीत्। ततो वा इयम् ओणधीभिर्वनस्पतिर्भि सलोमका प्रजायता॥
46. तैत्तिरीय ब्राह्मण	अंबायै स्वाहा दुलायै स्वाहा।

3-1-4-1	नितल्यै स्वाहा अभ्रयंत्यै स्वाहा।
नक्षत्रेष्टी कृत्तिकेष्टी	मेघयंत्यै स्वाहा वर्णयंत्यै स्वाहा।
	चुपुणीका यै स्वाहा।
47. मुंडकोपनिषद्	यथोर्णनाभिः सृजते गृह्णते च यथा पृथिव्याम्ओषधयः संभवन्ति। यथा सतः
1-1-7	पुरुषात् केशणेमानि तथा अक्षरासंभवतरित विश्वम् ॥7 ॥
48. ऐतरेय उपनिषद्	कर्णो प्रविशन् ओषधिवनस्पत्स्यो लोभानि भूत्वा त्वचं प्राविशत्। त्वचो
1-2-4, 1-1-4	लोभानि लोभभ्यः ओषधिवनस्पतयः।
49. शतपथ ब्रा. 2-1-2	यत्कृत्तिकास्त छै सलोभ
50. Sec 44	
51. महाभारत वन	अभिजित्सार्धमाना तु रोहिव्या कन्यसी स्वसा।
230/8-11	इच्छन्ती ज्येष्ठतां देवी तपस्तप्तुं वनं गता॥
	तत्र मूढोस्मि भद्रं ते नक्षत्रं गगनात् च्युतम्॥
	कासं त्विदं परं स्कंद ब्रह्मणासह चिन्तय॥9
	धनिष्ठादि तदा कालो ब्रह्मणा परिकल्पितः।
	रोहिणी ह्यभवत्पूर्वमेवं संख्या समाभवत्॥10
52. ऋग्वेद 1-164-19	इन्द्रश्च या चक्रशुः सोभ तानि
	धुरा न युक्ता रजसो वहन्ति॥
53. महाभारत उद्योग 82	अनभ्रेऽशनिनिर्घोषः सविद्युत्समजायत।
	अन्वगेवं च पर्जन्यः प्रावर्षद्विधने भृशम्॥5
	प्रामश्नाद्धास्तिपुरं वातो दक्षिणपश्चिमः। 10।
54. ऋ. 3-57-2	इन्द्रः सु पूषा तृषणा सुहस्ता
	दिवो न प्रीताः शशयं दुहुहे।
55. वाल्मीकि रामायण	विभते च प्रकाशेते विशाखे निरुपद्रवे॥5॥
युद्ध सर्ग 4	नक्षत्रवरमस्माव्यमिक्ष्वाकूणां महात्मनाम्।
	नैर्ऋतं जैर्ऋतानां च नक्षत्रं अभिपीडयते॥52
	मूलो मूलवता स्पृष्टो छूप्यते धूमकेतुना।
	सर्वं चैतद्विनाशाय राक्षसानामुपस्थितम्॥53।
56. वाल्मीकि रामायण	ततश्च द्वादश मासे चैत्रे नावमिके तिथौ॥5॥
बाल काण्ड सर्ग	नक्षत्रे अदिति दैवत्ये स्वोच्चसंस्थेषु पंचसु।
	ग्रहेषु कर्कटे एग्ने वाक्पताविन्दुनाराह॥
57. विष्णुपुराण	मेषादौ च तुलादौ च मैत्रेय विणुवस्थितः।
2-8-76 से 79	तदा तुल्यमहोरात्रं करोति तिमिरापहः॥76
	दशपंचमुहूर्तं वै तदेतदुभयं स्मृतम्।
	प्रथमे कृत्तिका भागे यदा भास्वांस्तदा शशी॥77

	विशाखानां चतुर्थे अंशे मुने तिष्ठत्यऽराशयम्। विशाखानां यदा सूर्यश्चरत्यंश तृतीयकम्।।78 तदा चंद्रं विजानीयात् कृत्तिमा शिरसि स्थितम्। तदेव विणुवाख्योऽयं काल पुण्योऽभिधीयते।।79
59. सुश्रुत संहिता 6-7	तत्र माहादयः द्वादश मासाः। द्विमासिकं ऋतुं कृत्वा षट् ऋतवः भवन्ति। तेषां तप तपस्यै शिशिरः।
60. गर्ग	यदा निवर्तते अप्राप्तो धनिष्ठामुत्तरायणे आश्लेषां दक्षिणायने अप्राप्तस्तदा विद्यान्महद्भयम्।
61. पराशर	यद्यप्राप्तो वैष्णवमुदग्मार्गम्प्रद्यते दक्षिणम् आश्लेषां वा महाभयम्।
62. वरामिहिर बृहसंहिता	आश्लेषार्धाद् दक्षिणमुत्तरमयनं रवेर्धनिष्ठाधम्। नूनं कदाचिदा सीद्येनोक्तं पूर्वशास्त्रेषु॥ अप्राप्य मकरमर्को विनिवृत्तो हन्ति सापरां याम्याम् कर्कटकमसम्प्राप्तो विनिवृत्तश्चोत्तरां सैन्दीम्॥ 4
63. ऋग्वेद 8-42-4	हरयो धूमकेतवो वातजूता उप द्यवि। यतन्ते पृथगग्नयः।।4॥
64. Sec. 55	
65. वाल्मीकि रामायण सुन्दर 19	धूप्यमानां ग्रहेणेव रोहिणीं धूमकेतुना।।9॥
66. महाभारत भीष्म 3-12	धूमकेतुः महाघोरः पुण्यमाक्राम्य तिष्ठति।।12
67. ऋग्वेद 1-164-2	सप्त युञ्जन्ति रथमेकचक्रमेको अश्वो वहति सप्तनामा।।2 इमं रथमधि ये सप्त तस्थुः सप्तचक्रं सप्त वहन्त्यश्वाः। सप्त स्वसारो अभि सं नवन्ते यत्र गवां निहिता सप्त नाम।।3
68. ऋ. 1-164-5	वत्से बष्करोऽधि सप्त तन्तून् वि तलिरे कवय ओतवा।।5
69. Sec. 20	
70. वाल्मीकि रामायण अयोध 26	अद्य बार्हस्पतः श्रीमानुक्तः पुण्यो नु राघव।।9
71. महाभारत आदि 160/7	एकैकश्चापि पुरुषस्तत्प्रयच्छति भोजनम्। स वारो बहुशिर्वर्णैर्भवत्युसुकरो नरैः।।7
कात्यायन गृह्यसूत्र 3-5-2	तत्रोदयनम् आपूर्यमाणपक्षे पुण्याहे तिथिवारकरणे नक्षत्रे च गुणान्विते।।2
72. अथर्वज्योतिष 93	आदित्यः सोमो भौमश्च तथा बुध बृहस्पति। भार्गवः शनैश्चरश्चैव एते सप्त दिनाधिपाः॥
73. याज्ञवलक्य स्मृति आचाराध्याय 295	सूर्यः सोमो महीपुत्रः सोमपुत्रो बृहस्पतीः। शुक्रः शनैश्चरौ राहुः केलुश्चैते ग्रहाः स्मृताः॥

74. तैत्तिरीय संहिता	षडरात्रीदीक्षितः स्यात् षड् वा ऋणवः संवत्सरः।
5-6-7, 7-5-6	षडहैर्मासान्संपाद्यहसत्सृजति।
75. ऋ. 1-105-10	अमी ये पञ्चोक्षणो मध्ये तस्थुर्महो दिवः। देवत्रा नु प्रवाच्यं.... ॥
75. ऋ. 10-55-3	आ रोदसी अपृणादोत मध्यं पञ्च देवाँ ऋतुशः सप्त सप्त।
76. ऋ. 1-64-15	साकंजानां सप्तथमाहुरेकजं षडिद्यमा ऋषयो देवजा इति।
77. ऋ. 10-129	नासदासीन्नो सदासीत्तदानीं नासीद्रजो नो व्योमा परो यत्।
नासदीय सूक्त 1	किमावरीवः कुह कस्य शर्मन्नम्भ किमासीद्गहनं गंभीरम् ॥9 ॥
78. ,, ,, 2	न मृत्युशसीदमृतं न तर्हि न रात्र्या अन्ह आसीत्प्रकेतः।
	आनीदवातं स्वधया तदेकं तस्माद्धान्यन्न परः किंचनास ॥2 ॥
79. ,, ,, 3	तम आसीत्तमसा मूलहमग्रे अप्रकेतं सलिलं सर्वमा इदम्।
	तुच्छग्येनाभ्वपिहितं यदासीत्तपसत्तत्महिनाऽजायतैकम् ॥
80. ,, ,, 4	कामस्तदग्रे समवर्तताधि मनसो रेवः प्रथमं यदासीत्।
	सतो बन्धुमसति निरविन्दन् हृदि प्रतीष्या कवयो मनीषा ॥4 ॥
81. ,, ,, 5	तिरश्चीनो विततो रश्मिरेषामधः स्विदासीदुपरि स्विदासीत्।
	रेतोधा आसन्महिमान आसन्स्वधा अवस्तात् प्रयतिः परस्तात् ॥5 ॥
82. ,, ,, 6	को अद्धा वेद क इह प्रवोचत्कुत आ जाता कुत इयं विसृष्टिः।
	अर्वाग्देवा अस्य विसर्जनेनाथा को तेद यत आबभूत।।6 ॥
83. ,, ,, 7	इयं विसृष्टि यतः आबभूत यदि ता दधे यदि वा न।
	यो अस्याध्यक्षः परमेव्योमन्सो अङ्ग वेद यदि वा न वेद ॥
84. ऐतरेय उपनिषद्	आत्मा वा इदमेक एवाग्र आसीत्। नान्यत् किंचन मिषत।
1-1-1	स ईक्षत लोकान्नु सृजा इति ॥
85. 1-1-2	स इमाँल्लोकान सृजत। अभोमरीचीर्मरमापोऽदोंभः परेण दिवं द्यौः
	प्रतिष्ठाष्ठान्तरिक्षं मरीचयः।
	पृथिवी मरो या अधस्तान्ता आपः ॥
86. तैत्तिरीय उपनिषद्	तस्माद्वा एतस्मादात्मन आकाशः संभूतः।
ब्रह्मानंवल्ली अनुवाक्	आकाशाद्वायुः। वायोरग्निः अग्नेरापः अद्भ्यः पृथिवी।
87. तैत्तिरीय उपनिषद्	स पश्चायं पुरुणे। यश्चासावादित्ये।
ब्रह्मानंदवल्ली अनुवाक्	स एकः। स य एव वित्।
88. तै. उपनिषद	अहं वृक्षस्य रेरिवा।
शिक्षावल्ली	उर्ध्व पवित्रों वाजिनीव स्वमृतमस्मि। ... इति त्रिशंकोर्वेदानुवचनम्।
अनुवाक् 10	
89. मुंडकोपनिषद् 2/1/5	तस्मादग्निः समिधो यस्य सूर्यः
90. मुंडकोपनिमद् 1-2-4	काली कराली च मनोजवा च सुलोहिता या च सुधूम्रवर्णा।
	स्फुल्लिंगिनी विश्वरुची च देवी ऐसायमाना इति सप्त जिन्हाः ॥4 ॥

91. प्रश्नोपनिषद् 3/8	पृथिव्यां या देवता सैषा पुरुषस्यापानम् अवष्टभ्यान्तरा.... ।
92. शांकर भोण्रा	तथा पृथिव्यामभिमानिनी या देवता प्रसिद्धा सैषा पुरुषस्य अपानमपानवृत्तिभवष्टभ्याकृष्य वशीकृत्याध एवापकर्णणेनानुग्रहं कुर्वती वर्तत इत्यर्थ। अन्यथा हि शरीरं गुरुत्वात् पतेत् सावकाशे वा उद्गच्छेत।
93. महाभारत भीष्म अ.	द्विधाभूत इव आदित्य उदये प्रत्यदृश्यत।
भीष्म अ. 17/3	ज्वलन्त्या शिखाया भूयो भानुमानुदिते दिवि॥
94. महाभारत भीष्म 19/39	निष्प्रभोऽभ्युदियात्सूर्यः सघोषो भूश्चचारह।।39
95. महाभारत भीष्म 3	श्वेतो ग्रहस्तथा चित्रां समतिक्रम्य तिष्ठति॥ 11
	श्यामो ग्रहः प्रज्वलितः सधूमः इव पावकः।
	ऐन्द्रं तेजस्वी नक्षत्रं ज्येष्ठामाक्रम्य तिष्ठति॥97
	कृत्रिकासु ग्रहस्तीव्रो नक्षत्रे प्रथमे ज्वसन्
	वपूण्यपहरन्भासा धूमकेतुरिवस्थितः॥29।
96. महाभारत	दीप्यमानाश्च संपेतुः दिवि सप्तमहाग्रहाः ।।2
भीष्म 17/2	प्रजासंहरणे राजन् सोमं सप्त महाग्रहाः।।22
द्रोण 137/22	निःसरन्तो व्यदृशन्त सूर्यान्त सप्तमहाग्रहाः॥4
कर्ण 37/4	निश्चरन्तो व्यदृश्यन्त सूर्यान्तसप्त महाग्रहाः।।34
97. भीष्म 3/30 महाभारत	कृत्तिकां पीडयन् तीक्ष्णैः नक्षत्रम्॥30
98. महाभारत भीष्म 3	चतुर्दशीं पंचदशीं भूतपूर्वां च षोडशीम्।
	इमां तु नाभिजानामि अमावास्यां त्रयोदशीम्॥25
	चंद्रसूर्याविभौ ग्रस्तावेकमासे त्रयोदशीम्॥29
99. महाभारत भीष्म 2/23	अलक्ष्यः प्रभयाहीनः पौर्णभासीं च कार्तिकीम्॥23
100. महाभारत शांति	तदा प्रकृतिमानेष भवत्यव्यक्तलोचनः।।10
308/10, 12	पतः केवलधर्मासौ भवत्यव्यक्त दर्शनात्॥92
101. अपरोक्षानुभूति आदि शंकराचार्य	सूक्ष्मत्वे सर्व वस्तूनां स्थूलत्वं च उपनेत्रतः।
102. ऋग्वेद 1-164-35	इयं वेदिः परो अन्तः पृथिव्या अयं यज्ञो भुवनस्य नाभिः। 35

Games and Sports in the Veda

10

Dr. P.K. Datta

The Veda is the storehouse of knowledge to contain many facets of Vedic Studies. The daily life of the Aryans is basically found in their occupations like agriculture, cattle-rearing, various amusements etc. The work is an enterprise to achieve the desired objects of revealing Vedic Seer Poets in some aspects. The Scholars come across frequently a few hymns to bear testimony of scattered ideas in Vedic knowledge.

The Vedic tradition had a great regard for manual labour for which the people preferred agriculture as their most honourable occupation. The seer poets prescribed for the down-trodden persons as defeated by gambling dice to take up agriculture for pretty better way of life.

In ṚV X. 34.13 termed akṣahymn the disappointed gambler finds a new way of earning for his livelihood in agriculture which was treated to be the most honourable occupation among the early Aryans. Yaśka, a great etmyologist finds a sort of censure in dice-playing and at the same time finds out a measure against the evil by means of a praise for agriculture noted in the Nirukta VII.3.

The winning of a race was essential to the Aryans for getting the woman of their choice. It was one of their favourite amusements like races of horse, chariot etc; the other being the throwing of dice. The heroic deeds are recorded befitting to a brave warrior to be ever memorable in the Victorious ages of history. In fact the hymn in ṚV X. 102 is a full-fledged battle Song sung in praise of brave deeds of a hero and his heroic wife with the aid of the bull and club harnessed to the chariot. A sort of act is interestingly described to depict the rapid movement of the chariot of the heroic lady. Viśpatā is so remarkable in an Aryan period to take part in such action.

There is a reference to frogs in the clefts of the earth as designated iriṇa to compare them with the brahmins. They croak to wake to activity at the beginning of the rains. The frogs are invoked as well-swimmers to come there by crying loud in favour of bringing rain. They must swim at ease after spreading their four legs. They remain also afloat. The Swimming was one amidst the games in ancient India.

A wooden pole termed Kārṣma interpreted by Sāyaṇa in ṚV I. 116.17 is to indicate the goal for the Chariot-race as one of the favourite amusements. The other amusement is dice-playing to inspire a person for the enjoyment of Victory in ṚV X. 34.1. The deity Savitṛ wished to give his daughter Sūryā in marriage. All gods assemble withdesire to marry her. It was settled that they should race up to the Āditya and the one who would win, will get Sūryā. The gods ran the race, and the Aśvins Won. They asked Sūryā to get into their chariot. So the winning of the race as sports is a target in view of gettings daughter among the Aryans. The ṚVI. 119.5 confirms the victory of Chariot-race for the Aśvins to win Sūryā. Therefore, the Vedic Aryans enjoyed amusements in the race for horse chariot as well dice-playing.

A comic picture for race in horse chariot is noted in the hymn of Mudgala-ṚV X. 102 according to the view of Geldner. The interpretation is unsound as so stated by Bloomfield. It is a case of woman warrior charioteering her husband's war chariot. It depicts a herioc act of victory by a brave woman charioteer, Mudgalānı as Indrasenā by name to drive her husband's chariot through the battle-field, when a bull and a log i.e.—club are harnessed to the chariot for want of mares in his encounter against king Sūbharva in order to victory for cows. The charioteering was one amidst the sports.

The name of one Swift mare is preserved as Viśpalā in ṚV I. 116.15 where upon it is noted that a broken leg was replaced by the Aśvins in a race. Pischel finds here a race in honour of Vivasvant, but such the equation is denied even by Sieg to accept the theory of Viśpalā, the wife of King Khela. Pischel also seeks to suggest that the races were run in honour of gods. But according to the TS I.8.15; KS XV. 8; VS X. 19; TB I. 7.9 and ŚB IV.2.3 the formal race is generally a feature of the ritual noted at the Rājasūya or royal consecration. There is also a reference to horse race in ṚV I. 116. 17 where the gods ran a race to win over Surya.

Khela is a god, Vivasvant on whose honour the races were run explaining the phrase as ājā Khelasya at the race of Khela. A man is meant as King Khela whose Purohita was Agastya. An iron leg to Viśpala was offered by the Aśvins at a contest. A case of Viśpalā is laid down in a race as heroic deed of woman to win over the enemy's booty. To run a race for horse was treated as game during the Aryan period.

The hymn of ṚV X. 34 is the lamentation of a disappointed gambler presumably the sad soliloquy of the Seer Poet himself, recollecting his past sad life. This hymn is treated to be the soliloquy of a penitent sinner having lost all happiness of life by means of his irresistible attraction of dice-playing. Such the soliloquy of a gambler seems more probable to him as a part of ballad wherein epic story was told like that of Yudhiṣṭhira or Nala. The first stanza of the hymn is to be the praise of Victory of dice-playing. There is a formula to apply it as a process of Victory in such playing. The stanzas like 7, 9 and 12 also bear the testimony of praise to gambling. Yāska, a reverend author of Nirukta finds praise in the first Stanza, but considers other stanzas to be contempt to dice-playing.

The stanzas 3 and 4 of such a hymn are clearly censurable. The dice-playing is really a Vice-Practice in ṚV X.34.11. Hence the term Vṛṣala is noticeable as an outcast. The defeated gambler reaches the highest disgrace being lost all sympathy of his kith and kin, who forsake him in utter distress. But knowing not him, they put him to prison as referred to in ṚV X.34.4. In order to release him from the deplorable condition the Seer Poet comes forward with a sympathetic advice corroborated in Stanza 13. It gives up the practice of dice-playing by instructing the mind in agriculture. So the hymn is really intended to raise a voice blaming the dice-playing.

Yāska finds a sort of censure in such the playing and at the same time finds out a measure against the evil by means of a priase for agriculture in Nirukta VII.3. Śaunaka, a reverend author of the Bṛhaddevatā announces such the hymn as a priase for victory of dice-playing. Śaunaka and Yāska both find praise of agriculture in Stanza 13. The introduction of Akṣa-Sūkta in the collection of the Ṛgveda indicates an example of a well-thought didactic fọr social welfare and also a warning against the evils of dice-playing to be ever memorable of the revelation. The dice-palying is all-destroying.

The hymn begins in a dramatic way by expressing the simultaneous excitement of the joy for victory and grief of defeat. The dice-playing inspires a gambler for the enjoyment of Victory. But in Pathetic words the disappointed gambler describes his distress and domestic unhappiness caused him due to defeat at the games of dice. The distress of the disappointed has reached to the climax, when he has been foresaken by all as father, mother, brother etc. No body has pity on him. The ṚV.X. 34.4 indicates a gambler to be imprisoned if he fails to repay the loan as borrowed.

The severe attraction of gambling can not be resisted and therefore the disappointed gambler is tossed between good and evil thoughts. He is helplessly devoid of sense to check himself to refrain from the impulsive gambling. The mind of a gambler is tossed up and down with hope and despair. The dice are monarchs of their own jurisdiction being omnipotent like the sun without bowing down to anybody. But the Kings bow down to the dice with great reverence. They even honour such the games as referred to in the Stanza 8. It was customary of this playing at the Aśvamedha or Horse Sacrifice.

The Frog-Song in ṚV VII. 103 is regarded as funny, a Parody on the Sacrificial Poem and malicious Satire against the brahmins. It is also observed as a magic incantation being employed as a rainspell. The frogs can bring forth water and so that they are praised and invoked as fore-runners by bringing rainy water in a world. After beginning to fall the rain, the pairs of frogs are pleased. Being cooled by the shower of rain by Parjanya, they jump; and dark as spotted and tawny frogs croak in company of each other as if one frog endears the other. The jumping is hereby treated as sports in the Veda.

In this hymn apparently quite secular poem has got mixed amidst the Sacred songs and Sacrificial chant of the Veda. The ṚV IX. 112, a Satirical Poem in the midst of Sāma Songs derides the manifold desires of making. The Frog Song gives us a clear picture of the rain-god to come and proclaim his showering of rain in his thundering voice for the welfare of the animal and plants. The Brahmin Pupils recite the words of a teacher in various ways of modulation. The frogs, too modulate their croaking voices. So the modulation is a real practice to protect the health through pronunciation as noted in this Song. The Sāma Songs are recited by the Priests sitting at the Soma-Sacrifice so-called atirātra.

The frogs are just like Brahmins bent on penance and observe vow of austerity by invoking gods to attain special wishes. The constant and repeated croakings of frogs as if in the promise of rain god are considered to be the invocation of the god for showering of rain. The vow of austerity is a hard work as observed on penance for healthy protection in the Veda.

The lakes are full to the brim if the rain appears. The frogs are invoked for crying loud in favour of bringing rain. They are praised as harbinger of rain. Pischel in Vedische studion 2.223 makes a reference to frogs in the clefts of the world comparing with the Brahmins that the frogs coraking as awake to activity at the beginning of rain. In AV I V. 15.14 the frogs are invited as well swimmers to cry loud for bringing the rain. They swim easily by spreading their four legs wide so still remain afloat. The Swimming is one practice against the sports in the Vedas on many facets of Vedic Studies prevailing so far.

The River Song on ṚV III.33 presents the introduction of the origin of the rivers while describing the rapid flow of the Vipāṭ and the Śutudrī. From the lap of the mountains they having risen with the intention to go towards the Sea are flowing rapidly in close company with each other amidst profuse water. The Śutudrī and the Vipāś are going towards the same destination. They being swelled by water are proceeding towards the ordained place. Such the proceeding is regarded as one of practise for rapidity of flow. The rivers relate about their origin on account of heroic exploits of Indra who has slain Vṛtra, the obstructor of rivers. Thus the exploits are rememberable for ever against the games as we sports in ancient India.

The rivers observe that Viśvāmitra must have been tired of coming from a great distance. They want to oblige him by restraining their rapidity in a manner of a suckling mother or a young lady stooping before her husband. The Bharatas have crossed the rivers. The rivers have been turned as being dug by the thunder to flow profusely towards the sea themselves. There is a germ of such facets noticeable in the Veda.

A legend or drudgery of labour and reward for work in ṚV X. 51, 52 are the sources of fleeing Agni to escape from the swelled water. The gods want to pacify and please Agni to do his duty by carrying nourishment for the gods.

They offer him an enternal life as a reward for the duty to carry oblation to god in peaceful bent of mind. The laborious duty would likely be enormous and exceedingly large called lion's share for practice in health care. Agni in order to lessen the burden of laborious duty at length demands a lion's share of the oblation offered by the devotees to gods in Sacrifice.

The demons of drought, the great enemies of Indra are pierced and crushed by the discharge of Indra's thunderbolt in ṚV I.32. The clouds are considered as mountains as well cities either or fortresses of the Asuras in ṚV II. 14.6; VIII. 17.14 etc. There appears a dint of mightly god by destroying completely all the weapons of Vṛtra caused the water to flow down. All such are devoured in delight of Vitals of living beings. The mightly work is a seed of sports related to a vivd encounter of Indra in ṚV VIII. 96 for accomplishment in flowing down the rivers through conquest of water occupied by the dasyus.

Some was the famous plant which was used for the preparation of the libation of Soma made at the Vedic Sacrifice. Little is actually known of the some plant, though its twigs or shoots are described as brown i.e.—babru or aruṇa in ṚV VII. 98.1, X. 94.3 to mean ruddy as well tawny termed harita in ṚV IX. 92.1. The original Soma Plant is conceived of identical with the Haoma of the Avesta of Ancient Iran. The pant was prepared for use by being pounded with either stone or mortar. The pounding with stones was the normal method of procedure as usual one in the Ṛgveda. The process of Pressing the Soma was one of methods as practised at sports recorded in the Vedas.

The TB III. 10.9.12 speaks of Yajñopavīta. It seems to denote the weaving of the brahmanical priest over the left shoulder at the Sacrifices. It was originally a thread that was worm, but a garment of cloth or deer skin. The weaving is so-called amongst such the practices in the Vedic studies.

Uṣas appears before the sun as the mother in ṚV I. 113. 1-2. The Åditya in ṚV I. 164.10 only does not feel tired while holding his three mothers like earth, heaven and sky as well as three fathers viz. presiding deities as Agni, Vāya or Indra and Sūrya. Like a female person the rays of the sun make water to conceive in producing something. They make water sprinkle on earth in view of showering rain over it. The sprinkling is regarded as one of sports to take care on health. The showering is considered to have cooling properties for the welfare of the animals as well plants on the record of such practice.

A young woman having four braids of hair, a fairy pleasing figure wears magnificent dresses as laid down in ṚV X.114. 3. The altar of the Sacrificial place is the woman. Four angles of the rectangular altar provided with ghee are her four braids of hair. The pleasant and fair sacrificial things are her dress. From the study of the nature of the method it appears that teh Vedic syllables in mystical utterings occupy a hidden idea in them. The process for sacrificial performance is an epithet of practice as a unique feature of facets noted in this topic.

The severe tremoving rays as laid in ṚV I. 35.7 flying wings so-called Suparṇa raśmi spread over three Worlds. The rays are well moving all over the world. They appear in a sky having different forms. The movement was among the most popular practices in ancient India in taking care of health as one of playing. It even formed a part of sports. The term asura is a life giver to mean Supreme Soul. The longevity depends upon such the playing as a sort of games and sports on many facets of Vedic studies.

The wid range of the Uṣas pervades the world so as another frequent epithet of the dawn is Uruki. She is addressed as the remover of darkness in ṚV IV. 2.,19 whereas in ṚV VIII. 10.1 she is also the lover of the Sun. The proper feeling of passion is one side of health care by treating such a practice as nॱted in the palying. The daily seige of the east is being every evening by the Solar powers who role of their brightest treasures in the West as laid down in an allegorical story of dialogue hymn in ṚV X. 108. Here is a germ of adjudication to take care of playing or practices of health in games and sports prevailing in ancient India amidst many facets of Vedic Studies.

The marriage procession proceeds past the spectators. At the presence of the immates, relatives and even the spectators assembled, some magic formulas and charms are exployed for the healing of various diseases. All such sorts of activity reflect the performance of magical charms prevailing as practices to games etc during the Aryan period. The clasping of the hand of a bride by the bridegroom in reciting mantras and for prayer to gods to retain long life, good health etc. is also a form of facets.

The hymn VII. 55 of the Ṛgveda begins with a prayer for friendship and blessings of Vāstoṣpati. Vasiṣṭha is represented as a burglar attacking the house of his father Varuṇa only for seeking to obtain what he may have regarded his own. He also appears in his father's abode at night in a dream when he is to face the barking dog called Sārameya whom he pacifies by uttering mantras. The poet addresses the house-guard dog and wishes it to chase after thieves and dacoits. The singer wishes all the people and the women lying all around the floor in carts or on planks i.e.—bed steads who give out sweet perfume may fall fast asleep. It is a case of his visit to father's dwelling in a dream at night as Sāyaṇa suggests. There is sort of mention to desire to be culled to sleep. The dwelling is deemed to belong to a lover's joint family where Viśpati is the head of such family whereas parents live together. Thus the action may be traced as a practice of playing during the Aryan time.

The hall was clearly used for dicing, when the assembly was not transacting public business in AV V. 31.6; VII. 12.1-2; VIII. 10-.5; MS IV. 7.4; TS I. 7.6.7; VS III. 45; XVI. 24; XX. 17; TB I. 1.10.6; ŚB II. 3.2.3; V. 3.1.10 etc. A dicer is called Sabhāsthāṇu as Pillar of the assembly hall, because of his constant presence there in MS I. 20.2; VS XXX. 18; TB III. 4.16..1. It may refer to gambling as non-political activity. But the authors like Macdonell and Keith on the Vedic Index of names and Subjects P II, P 426 state Sabhā as the name of an assembly of the Vedic Indians as well as of the hall where they met in assembly. We may trace one's acquiring fame in a word "Sabhāsāhena" as laid down in ṚV X.71.10 to such an action. There contains a clear reference to serious activity in the Sabhā i.e.—hall serving as a meeting place for social affairs as well amusement like gambling etc.

The Aryan people had a normadic race with brown clour and blue eyes to have a common homeland starting living in central Europe by extending up to the caspian Sea. There was a parallel human race too. They were pastoral normadic rearing sheep, cattle and horse. The Aryans possessed horses and horse-chariots for war, no doubt, but they must require to build up flotilla of boats in large numbers for the purpose of conquering marshy lands, hilly places and clearing forests; they were to prepare good number of implements. The Vedic Aryans enjoyed amusements in the race for horse chariot, and also dice-playing to such the games and sports in the Veda.

The gambling is an evil against warning of dice-playing to be ever memorable as all-destroyer. The severe attention of it can not be resisted. The dice are monarchs of their own jurisdictions as omnipotent like the Sun without bowing down to anybody. But the Kings bow down to the dice with great reverence. Such the palying was the prevalent at the horse-sacrifice.

Really the dice-playing is a Vice-Practice referred to in the ṚV X. 34.11. Jāra stands for a lover having no sinister sense in the early Vedic text. The gambler feels the severe pain of defeat just as if an arrow pierces his heart whereas at the same moment a great pleasure appears before the winner who tastes the flaver of honey sweet gift. A sad experience puts forth an abominable feeling of the loser and at the same time an enthusiastic praise of gambling by the winner. The gambler bewaits his fate, but he can not overcome the powerful attraction of gambling.

The gambler is called hereby Vṛṣala by indicating the dice-playing to be a contemptible practice, and he is at the moment taken to be an outcast. A pitious feeling arises in the mind of a gambler at the Verge of ruin. He also finds a new way of earning for his livelihood in agriculture which was treated to be the most honourable occupation amidst the Aryans. He implores upon all the powerful dice to set him free from their harmful attraction. Then the so-called gambling my be given up.

The gambler resolves to turn over a new leaf in order to earn his honest living from farming. The Vice of dice-playing may occur to his enemies. This is the solace for a broken hearted dicer to stop the cause of lamentation for the loss of all and at the same time getting a penacea to rid of this evil practice. Thus there is a long teatment of games and sports in the midst of facets in the Veda.

Space and Time in the Veda

11

Dr. S. Biswal

The history of science reveals that the knowledge of science begins with the understanding of the nature surrounding us. In this respect our Vedic seers are best known of their profound knowledge in the environment in which they lived. Therefore, the Veda is the primordial source of human knowledge in scientific studies and investigations. We find magical elements blended with mythology, religion, philosophy and materialism. Truly, the primitive man was a hardboited realist and a tough-minded materialist ostensibly, his beliefs, thoughts, speculations, perceptions and practices of rites and sacrifices of magical nature are the expressions of the most ancient materialistic thoughts which can properly be called the archaic materialism. It is thus natural that such archaic materialism first embodied and enumerated in the Veda in the form of magico-religious phenomena is bound contain the germs of science. Hence, it is also justified to call this as the nascent science or pre-science.

The *Ṛta*[1], as conceived in the Veda, is the first display of the consciousness of the law that governs the nature. The belief in the magical efficacy of *mantra* and *yajña* as the means to have control over the courses of the nature and even over gods underlie an attitude of the Vedic Āryāns akin to that of science. According to Frazer[2], magic is the next kin to science, because both have in common "The general assumption of a succession of events determined by law". Needham's view reveals that the science and magic were mingled together in the earliest phase[3]. Therefore, he calls magic 'pre-science' or 'proto-science'. Further, he adds that the phase of this 'magico-scientific tradition' is significant and which was the crystallization of prinitive shamanism.[4] In the evolution of human reasoning, in search for causality in nature for controlling it in order to achieve vital problems, magical elements came first and then the science. Understanding the happenings in nature was initially imperfect through magic and which gradually became perfect when man tried to solve the innumerable and vital problems of life[5]. The first solutions were expedients but that must do for the beginning. Different branches of science sprouted and grown during the Vedic age truly laid the foundation of the ancient Indian sciences, rich in qualities, quantity and variety and even comparable to the ancient Greeks.[6] Among these, the most fundamental and alarming aspect is the concept of space and time from which this creation emanated. M.Vannucci[7] points out that the analysis and measurements of the multiple aspects of Ṛta in space and time, is the true meaning of the word Ecology (the science of the house). House here means the living and non-living environment of which man is a part, whether he wants it or not. The natural elements, viz., fire, wind, water, air, seasons, birth, growth, old age and death of plants and animals, reproduction and reproductive cycles, floods, landslides, avalanches, earth quakes and intellect are all expansion of the divine and they all fall with in the realm of the eternal law and order (Ṛta) or, alternatively, temporary disruption of Ṛta means disorder.[8] This order or disorder is again a question of space and time.

Space

Vedic hymns enriched with mythology, philosophy, religion, magic, materialism, cosmology, astronomy, etc. seq. envelop truly the idea about space and its characteristics. Space is all pervading, unlimited and ever expanding. It is that medium which accommodates the manifest universe. It is characterised by the qualitiy of sound according to Taittiriya Upaniṣad. It gives rise to the earth through Vāyu, Agni and Āpas. The Vedic seers had attributed the earth and the sky with Dyāvā- pṛthivī in many sūktas.[9] On the basis of the Vedic conceptions, the Āryāns related the earth with the space or sky. Ghosh[10] opines that the Heaven (Div), the Earth (Pṛthivī) and the Firmament (Antarikṣa) form a triplet interlinked with one another. Kramvish,[11] while studying the triple structure of creation in the Ṛgveda, suggests that the Antarikṣa has been created by the separation of heaven and earth through Demiurge. In Amarakosh, as pointed out by Lewis Rice, there are 21 synonyms used for the sky in *Vyomavarga*[12]. These are Dyo, Divau, Abhram, Vyoma, Puṣkaram, Amabaram, Nabhaḥ, Antarikṣam, Gaganam, Anantam, Suravartma, Kham, Viyat, Viṣṇupadam, Ākāśa, Vihāyasa, Nāka, Tārāpatha, Sabdaguṇaḥ. Meghadvāram and Mahābulam. Pandurangi has discussed the concept of Space and Time in Indian philosophy[13]. In the Vaiśeṣika Darśana of Maharṣi Kaṇāda, the physical quantities (abstracts) have been enumerated as *Dravya, Guṇa, Karma, Sāmānya, Viśeṣa* and *Samavāya*[14]. Here Dravya[15] includes solid, liquid, energy, gas, plasma, space or the length vector, time, soul and mind. Vaiśeṣika Darśana claims that plasma, space and time[16] are eternal and all pervading.

The Nyāyavaiśeṣika[17] school considers both space and time as primary and separate categories of being. These are treated as eternal entities. Space and time are all-pervasive in the sense that they are co-extensive with the entire matter, all events and actions, and a new word *Vibhu* is employed to describe it.[18] The term *dik* is used to indicate space while *ākāśa* represents the locus of sound. *Purvamimāṁsā* uses space to mean a substance which is an evolute of sound. Thus, these systems do not use *ākāśa* to mean space. Different views are noticed about space and time in *Mimāṁsā* and in *Sāṁkhya*. The process of evolution of primordial matter has been related to space and time in the Sāṁklya school. Dvaita school considers space as separate entity from which time is derived. The space is called *avyākṛtākāśa* and *dik* is a natural division of it. In Indian philosophy the reflection of *Brahman* is the space. Being *avidyā*, space is not real; its effects are not also real. According to Taittirīya Upaniṣad[19], the internal mind is recognised as *ātman*, a reflection of the *Brahman* as per the Advaita school. This reveals that the universal mind is nothing but *ākāśa*.

Modern science defines space as a medium through which light is propagated and is bent at celestial objects[20]. In the Vedic literature, the sky or space has been given the utmost importance. The sky has been termed as *Brahman*, the Supreme Authority from which the sun, moon, planets, stars, earth, and living organisms and non-living objects of the world have been created. Here the sky is considered as real and eternal while the rest of the creation is perishable. The sky is infinity. All sorts of knowledge and understanding of nature are followed from the sky. Ākāśa or void (space) is intangible and is the beignning of everything. According to Renou, it is called *Dyaus* in the veda[21]. It refers to the father of gods. For the most part, the sky is invoked jointly with the earth by the name *Dyāvāpṛnthivī*[22] which is a composite word designating the parents of the gods and of the worlds, and has some importance in the ritual.

Time

The book X of the Ṛgveda provides abstract ideas like *lābha* (gain), *Kāla* (time), *manya* (anger), *Kāma* (desire) and *Śraddhā* (faith). Atharvaveda contains two outstanding hymns to Time[23] with a total of fifteen stanzas. Poets and wise men ride on the time-horse. Here time is compared with the horse. Thus, the poets and the wise men attain immortality. Time is the first of the gods. A full jar is placed in time, we observe it as myriad-shaped. Time rests in the highest heaven; There is no power higher than it. *Kāla* is the primordial element. It is *Brahman*, the Supreme Being (*Parameṣṭhin*). The entire creation was originated from *Kāla*. All sacred lore flew from it. Time embraces every thing, every existant. The sacrifices, the rites, the gods, the demigods and the sages are all possessed by the *Kāla* with the power of *Brahman*, all regions including space were conquered by Time and thus *Kāla* attained the throne of the Supreme God. Ostensibly, the above definition forwards in the metaphysical concept of time. It is the invisible, creative, eternal entity in which the cosmos is contained. In the same manner, Kronos (time) was defined in ancient Greece. But Zurvan (time) in the Nuzi tablets of 13th-12th centuries B. C. is still older. Mithraism revived the cult of Aeon (time) and a Luristan plaque preserved in Cincinnati museum shows Zurvan with tiwns. Zurvan later became the cardinal god of Zervanism. Some other mythologies have also deified Time. In Indian mythology, such deification has been synchronized with the wake of prajapati who symbolizes Time, the creator.[24]

The Dvaita School does not accept the *akhaṇḍakāla*[25]. Each moment is all-pervasive but not eternal. Every moment perishes to make room for the next moment. Time is envisaged as a close associate of continuous evolution of matter and is known intuitively. According to Advaita school, time like space is an aspect of *avidyā*[26] and hence its effects are not real. Evidently, time is not real.

Atharvaveda IX and X indicate markings of the calendar and measurement of the year and seasons. Ṛgveda mentions the course of the sun as 360 days.[27] Hints are given to determine the calendar, mainly for fixing solstices and equinoxes[28]. Many astronomical references are traced in the Vedas, particularly in the Yajurveda, which show that a system of astronomy, based on practical observations of moon and stars, existed for providing the calendar to enable the priests to perform *Yajñas* in the right times of the day and of the year. The duration from Sunrise to Sunset was called a day and that from sunset to sunrise was called a night. Each was divided into 15 *mahurats*. These *mahurats* were named differently for each day and night of the dark and bright fortnights of a lunar month. In addition to this, three divisions of a day, viz. Pūrvāhna, Madhyāhna and Sāyāhna were known. The duration of a day was also roughly divided into five divisions, namely *Prātaḥ, Sangava, Madhyāhna, Aparāhna* and *Sāyāhna*. The duration of time for a lunar month was 30 days, each of which was named separately. Two schools of Vedic people had reckoned the month differently. One group had reckoned a month from full moon to full moon, and the other from new moon to new moon. Twelve months formed a year spreading over 6 seasons. The months of a year were known as Madhu, Madhava, Shukra, Shuchi, Nabha, Nabhasya, Isha, Urja, Sahas, Sahasya, Tapas and Tapasaya. Six seasons were named as Vasanta, Grishma, Varsha, Sharad, Hemanta, and Shishira. The names of the months were later changed to the present names with the discovery of the *Nakṣatras*. A solar year was also formulated in due course. A thirteenth month *Amhaspati* was introduced to regulate calculations. A solar year was supposed to consist of 366 days. A *Yuga* was formed of 1830 civil days 62 (synodic) months of moon, 30 omitted *tithis*, 2 intercalary months and 5 mean revolutions of the sun. Vedāṅga Jyotiṣa comprising the rules for calculating astronomical results was framed for each Veda. This text was authored by Leghadha. Rough calculations of solar and lunar elements were given in the Vedāṅga Jyotiśa. No calculations were given there for planets.

A period of 5 years was called a *Yuga* and the names assigned to these 5 years, wre Samvastar, Parivastar, Idavastar, Anuvastar and Idvastar. A correct table consisting of the units of time given by sage Maitreya is noted below :

TABLE OF TIME UNITS

2 *Paramāṇus* of time make one *aṇu*

3 *aṇus* of time make one *transareṇu*

3 *trasareṇus* of time make one *truti*

100 *truṭis* of time make one *Vedha*

3 *Vehas* of time make one *lava*

3 lavas of time make one nimeṣa

15 nimeṣas of time make one Kāṣṭa

30 Kāṣṭa of time make one muhūrta

30 muhūrtas of time make one divā-rāti of 24 hours/

Comparing with the present time-units, we get 1 *nimeṣa* = $\frac{16}{75}$ second, where 1 hour has 60 minutes and 1 minute has 60 seconds. With the concept of nimeṣa, Sāyaṇācārya, while commenting on a hymn of the Ṛgveda[29], gives us a definite value for the velocity of light in half-*nimeṣa*. Sunlight travels 2,202 *Yojanas* in half-*nimeṣa*. The calculation is done as under.

$$1 \text{ yojana gives } \frac{100}{11} \text{ English miles}$$

$$\frac{1}{2} \text{ nimeṣa gives } \frac{8}{75} \text{ second}$$

so, in $\frac{8}{75}$ second, light travels 2202 yojanas in 1 second, light travels

$$2202 \times \frac{75}{8} \times \frac{100}{11} \text{ miles}$$
$$= 1{,}87{,}670 \text{ miles}$$

Thus, the velocity of light is 1,87,670 miles/second. The modern accepted value of 1,86,000 miles/second for the velocity of light is close to the above value. It confirms the accuracy of the time-units prescribed by the Vedic seers.

After vedic period, the *Siddhānta Jyotiṣa* period of Indian astronomy came. The *Siddhānta Jyotiṣa* is a system containing the rules for calculating time, motions, of planets, etc., from the beginning of the Universe to the end. Five such Siddhāntas are known :

(i) Brahmā Siddhānta

(ii) Vaśiṣṭha Siddhānṭa

(iii) Romaka Siddhānta

(iv) Paulisa Siddhānta

(v) Sūrya Siddhānta

out of these, the last one is the most scientific one and hence widely acclaimed. Its calculations are based on recorded co-ordinates of Nakṣatras. Its time of composition is about 280 A.D.

Space (*dik*) and Time (*Kāla*) combinedly form the Space-Time continuum and possess conjunctive relation with the matter of any state or Mass (*bhūta*).

Ostensibly, *bhūta, dik* and *Kāla* become the fundamental physical quantities which are now known as Mass, Length and time in physics, ie. in the science of measurements.

References

1. Ṛgveda, III, 6.6-10; I, 44. 14; IV, 3.9;
2. Frazer, J. G., The Golden Bough, Abridged ed., Macmillan, London, 1959, quoted in 'Materialism in the Vedas' by Miss Uma Gupta, Classical Publishing Company, New Delhi, 1987, p. 128.
3. Needham, Science and Civilization in China, Vol. I, pp. 108-209.
4. *Ibid.*, pp. 93, 117, etc.
5. Sarton, A History of Science, quoted in 'Materialism in the Vedas', p. 130.
6. Sircar, Hindu Achievement in Exact Science, quoted in 'Materialism in the Vedas', p. 131.
7. Vannucci, M., Ecological Readings in the Veda, D. K. Printworld (P) Ltd., New Delhi, 1994, p. 89.
8. *Ibid.*, p. 123.
9. Ṛgveda, X, 192. 3 and Yajurveda, 40.8.
10. Ghosh, E. N., "Studies in Ṛgvedic deities—astronomical and meteorological", JASB 28, 1932.
11. Kramvisch, stella, "The triple structure of creation in the Ṛgveda", History of Religious, University of Chicago, 2, 1962-63, 140-175 and 256-285.
12. Rice, L., Amarakosha of Amarasiṁha, (in Kannada), Mysore, 1970, p. 407.
13. Pandurangi, K. T., "The Concept of Space and Time in Indian Philosophy" in Scientific Heritage of India, Mythic Society, Bangalore.
14. Dongre, N. G., Physics in Ancient India, New Age International Publishers Limited, New Delhi, 1994, p. 12.
15. *Ibid.* and fn. 2
16. *Ibid.*, p. 13 and Fn. 3.
17. Murthy, S. R. N., Vedic View of the Earth, D. K. Printworld (P) Ltd., New Delhi, 1997, p. 99.
18. *Ibid.*
19. Tai ttirīya Upaniṣad, Sixth Anuvāka of Śkṣāvalli.
20. Hawking, S. W., A Brief History of Time, Bantam, New York, 1994, p. 198.
21. Renou, L., Vedic India, Indological Book House, Delhi, 1971, p. 67.
22. Atharvaveda, 6. 40. 1.
23. *Ibid.*, XIX, 53 and 54.
24. Bhattachariji, S., Literature in the Vedic Age. Vol. I, K. P. Bagchi & Company, Calcutta, 1984, p. 302 and fn. 104.
25. Murthy, S. R. N., op. cit., p. 100.
26. *Ibid.*
27. Ṛgveda, I, 155.6 et. al.
28. *Ibid.*, 136 and 137
29. *Ibid.*, I, 50.4.

Fine Arts in Veda

12

Dr. Vaijayanti Shete

Vedas accumulated enormous material by a deep intuitive awareness of the essential unity and inter connectedness behind the omnipresent, Omniscient pheneomena. Between them they express the collective wisdom and history of the entire race, socio-religious ideals, beliefs, joys, sorrows, aspirations and achievements. There is also a fascinating array of diversions amusements together with ṛṣis aesthetic versatile genius. Repeatedly scholars have commented and admired our age old past, though much emphasis is not put over the art-side. No doubt it is essential to ponder over such factors that will appeal the present age, present problems! The continued progress and advanced development throughout the years, perhaps unfold a miracle, some unsolved querries in the art-historical mileu. With this notion in the mind let us have some observations on the vibrant, life-affirming faith embeded in the vedic encompass.

Attempts have been made to show how from very small beginning various theories evolved dilate upon the kindred matters recorded in our tradition. On the other hand the earliest evidences of Indian painting are found in the Ramagarh-caves dt. 2nd century A.D. But it is to be borne in mind earlier works being unexplored does not prove the absence of art. All the sister arts were rooted in the society from long period ago and may be ascertained through number of references. It would not be out of place here to resume the different possible grounds for the execution of fragments of arts came down to us.

Taking a peep into the remote past we met with to an exceedingly charming concept of uṣas-dawn (ūshā sūkta) represented youthful, well decked, like a dancer, appearing in the east. She is a living personality,

> ''रश्मिभि व्यंक्त:
>
> अधि पेशांसि वपते नृतूरिवोपोर्णुने वक्ष सुस्वेव वर्णहम्।
>
> ज्योति र्विश्तरमै भुवनाय कृण्वन्ली गावो न व्रण व्यशषा आँवर्तन:॥ (Rv I 92.4)

of course, each and every time uṣas dancing figure triggered to mind the relevant vedic aesthetic sensibility. It is a charming imaginative word-picture immortalised on the walks of an art-gallery also appealing to mind the feminine grace unveiling the form etc. The word art denotes beauty, life pleasantness, the typical standing posture all the guidelines those which are quite common when an artist modells an art-form!

Another vedic quotation Rv. I.161.2 highlights fair women clothed by their father.

सुधृष्टमे वपुष्ये इन रोदसी पिता यत्सीमभि रुपैरवासयत्॥

Nevertheless Yujurveda (YV) ascertains the feminino beauty is the line

पुरान्ध्रयोषेत्याह। योषित्येव रुपं दहाति।

तस्सास्त्री युविति: प्रिया भानुका। TB III 8.13.2

In one of the hymn Indra's epithel as dancer occurs. VI 29.3 Dancing incorporates the beauty of body movement and the rhythm. Later on Siva's dancing image is much popular it is carved in so many sites i.e. Chidambaram even it is remarkable to admire dancing Ganesh carved in medieval period though it is a rare form. The genesis of dancing image is tracable in vedas. Thus symbolism yields to vedic people's love and fondness for dancing in the open air (Rv. x. 76.6) vedic hymn mainly comprises the spontaneous out-pourings of the surrounding splendour and grandeur apart from it's integrity to religiosity.

Music both vocal and instrumental was well-known. Among musical instruments percussion instruments like the drum (dundubhi) wind instruments—flute and stringed instruments, like the lute (viṇā) are listed. In the Yama's abode music was going on so also maruts, the storm gods, are described as playing wind instruments.

Also cp. Rv. VIII 68.7.5—

य: पूर्व्याम् अनुष्टुलिम् ईशे कृर्ष्टानां नृतु:। पुरुद्धतं पुरुष्टतं गायान्य श्सनश्रुनम्। इन्द्र द्वनि व्रर्वाननं VIII. 92.

Yv. distinguishes between different muscial instruments Yv. xxx.19.

शब्दा आरं बराधानं महरो वीणावादम्।

"means for sounds the beater on the kettle drum sublimity, the viṇā player. Musical instruments have due place in sculptures and paintings. Various types of viṇā's are visible in so many cites e.g. Bodhugaga. Amaravati. Similarly in the Vāmanāvatara story hailed from Bhandarkar Orietdal Institute set of paintings, all the celestials are showering flowers dancing and playing kettle drums etc. It is a common narrative in puraṇic episodes.

AV. invokas a war drum especially war drum is made up of a tree and gourd. It makes loud-noise, whetting voice, thunder, resounding. It is headed with cowhide and speaks clearly is a stretched one.

cp. AV. V 20. मुच्चैर्धोषों दुन्दुभि: सत्वनायं न्वानस्पत्य:॥

"इसे नभसी अनाराघोष उरस्तु"

हारणस्य अण्निेन दुन्दभिन्न च।

Affinity with patterns from thropomerpic expression is a clue to the existence of image worship and the practicing art. We came across the epithets like hiraṇya pāṇi, hiraṇy-hastaḥ, sushipra, suniṭha etc here and there throughout the vedic text. We positively may remark that the concept of saguṇa-mūrti was postulated in the mind of a vedic seer,

RV 1.35.9 हिरण्पाणि: सविना विचर्षणि: ।

Rv. 1.35.10 हिरण्यहस्सो असुर: सुनीय: and so cu.

is then only understandable it is note-worthy at this juncture that the epithet suniṭhaḥ is used referring to Buddha's hair later on cp. icnographical description of Buddha in Brhat sumhita. It means trimmed hair.

पहमाङ्कित करचरण प्रसन्नमूर्ति: सुनीचकेशश्च ।
पदमासतोपविष्ट: पितेव जगतो भवति बुद्ध: ॥

Vardhamihira's Brhat samihta is noticeable in this context ch and tha.

To substantiate the possibility of idol-making—are changeable

कं इमं दशभिभमेन्द्र क्रीणानिद्येनुभि: ।

is highly remarkable. The reference suggests a sort of bartẹring, selling and purchasing of the image of India in the exchange of milch-cow.

There is also another ṛc which resembles to it's import cp. Rv. VIII 1-5.

महे चल त्वामद्रिव: परा शुस्काय देयाम्। न सहस्त्राय नायुताय वज्रिवो न शताय शतामछ ।

The very rich group of workmanship is represented in vedic words to note them a pusta-a doll made with a plaster etc. wrapped with wood, cloth, leather, iron laksha b. varaschana-chisel and ishika

b.c. taṅks stone chisel d. shilva art e. Pratimā-the original is upamāna f. kārartisan g. vaidehika-art teacher, h. Taksha-carpenter i. kumbakār potter j. pala gaṇda-plasterer k. rangājiva-painter or dyer l. kāshtatat-wood-splitter etc.

Another valuable contribution in outlining the assumption of sculpture, Sāyana's explanation on the word 'pratima' is a hall mark.

देवता-प्रतिमा! तथा प्रतिमा हवि: प्रतियोगित्वेन मीयते निर्भीयते इति प्रतिमा देयता।

Sāmaveda's Sadviṁsha Brāhmaṇa (v.10) may not be overlooked in this context. It is fascinating to pinpoint distinguished emotions in case of deities kept in the temples, our historical past reflects on the distinct feelings expressed in various images cp.

देवतायतनानि कम्पन्ते। देत्रता प्रतिमा हसन्ति रुदानी नृत्यानी स्फुटानी खिधान्ति उन्मीलन्ति निमीलनी।

these pratimas laugh, cry, dance, smile fade, blossom forth. Really such jotings lead to consider highly expertise in composition.

The devamāna or the mansion of the god's is mentioned in hym. x.135.7

इमं यमस्य सादनं देवमानं यदुत्यते।

mūrtipoojā seemed to be the practical outcome from the saguṇa descriptions in passage like-Yv.

त्र्यम्बकं यजामेह चत्वारि शृङ्गा त्रयो अस्य पादा

व्दे शीर्षे सपर्‌तहस्तासो अस्य हिरण्यश्मश्रुः ॥

However the import of such scattered occurrences have kept on changing time to time.

The entire history can be seen as a constant process of challenge and response if we peep into the Rv. I. 164.9.

The concept of Devi is found emerging out, Aditi is conceived as the mother of all. She is symbolised as the earth which envices the great principle of motherhood and fertility for perceptible and imperceptible world. The principle of motherhood remains everlasting and effective through her creative potency. There are seven manifestations viz. mind, (Prāna) life. The mother inculcates fine gross elements such as pṛthvi, apa teja, vāyu, ākāsha. They turned into different emerging factors by group of seven mothers, who were none but seven sisters according to the vedic seers cp. Rv. I.164-3, I.164.8. By the time of puraṇic era, they were termed as seven mātṛkas, personifying powers of the seven typical devas. The mother principle got emphatic recognition in the vedic literature. Then in order feminine personification, the universal life force reappeared in the Brahmanic civilization in the for of Umā-Haimavati, she reveals herself in the kena-upaniṣad for the first time. She plays the role of a guru of the male gods, like Agni, Indra and Prajāpati.

In Rv. I. 89.10 अदितिर्घो रदितिरनारिक्षमदितिर्भाता स पिता स पुत्रः। अदिनिजतिमदितिजेनित्वम्।

Yv. 25.6 3 — follows the re. and AV. vii. 6.2 . महीमू षु मातरं सुव्रतानाम्रतरय पानीभवसे हवामते''

The divinity is invoked as feminine significant principle e.g. dity in every order of ṛeality. She is described as the mighty mother in iv. IX. 3

मातरं नाम महीम् अदिलिं नाम

This feminine power became the object of work in tantra. Markandeya purana invoke her in the words—

या देवी सर्वभूतेषु मातृरुपेण सांस्थिति।

नमस्तस्यै नमस्यै नमस्तस्यै नमो नमः॥

Mātṛkā worship through tender love, corresponding to the tender caressing of a child is expressed through a mystical symbolism in which the loving sages called 'vana'—शिशुं रिहानी मतयः'

Rv. IX . 85. 11.

Rv. 1. 164. 49→ यस्ते सानः शशयो यो मयोभूतर्येन विश्वापुष्यसि वर्ण वार्याणी

Av.-vii. 10.1→विश्वा पुष्यासि वार्याणि सस्स्वति...

etc. focus on the child feeding at the breast of the of the Divine mother Saraswati. This motherly is carved in so many places like Khajurāho, Koṇark still another vedic analogy attracts the mother child's inborn close-relationship.

तं माता रेजिदू स एश्सिह मातरम्'

एकः सुपर्णः स समुद्र आ विवेश

speaks of a mother kissing the child while in response. He kisses his mother. The poet confesses that he visualised the exchange of love between child and mother suparṇa (the beautiful winged bird) is a symbol for the Deity. It is interesting to observe the gods, compared to the child loved by or loving the mother. Later on Almighty, the child reappears in vatsala rasa, which form the part of bhakti cult, child kṛṣṇa symbolises the ideal of Divinity. Thus mātṛkā-worship, scattered all over the country has survived down to our times.

Transmigration of Indra's fight itself is breaking down to the birth of Mahiṣāsura in Rv. x. 189.2—

अनाधरति् रोचनास्य प्राणादयानती।
व्यरव्यन्मदिषोदिषम्''।

Mahiṣa, the king of Asura is pitted against Indra—the god of Devas. Rv. represents the fanciful description of Mahiṣa as an asura going round heaven and wishing to penetrate into the region of Indra, Mahiṣa as asura batters against that region of Indra and for a time being succeeds in penetrating the order of heaven. This is referred to as इंद्रोभूत महिषाक्य

and yet, interwining, through a golden thread, Rudra's imagery in the hymns may not be excluded from the sphere of polytheism. Polytheism being the reaction of the free poetic soul to the a esthetic appeal which makes to imagine. Hence it delights in the glory of colour and form. In accordance with poetic and artistic forms in the sacred pricinct. Rudra's representation is creative and vital. Rudra's physical features are described in number of times—He has a hand Rv. II. 33.7 व्रवस्य ते रुद्र मृकंया कुहेस्तो यो अस्ति भेषजो जलषः Rv. II 33.3 श्रेष्ठो जातस्य रुद्र। श्रीयासि तवस्तमस्तवासा वज्रबाहे। His limbs are firm cp.-Rv. 2.33.11—सुहिश्‍ श्रतुं गर्तसदं युवान'' मृगं न भमिनुपह नुमुग्रम्।

Nevertheless, he has beautiful lines 2.33.5—सुहवो, सुशिप्रो while his braided hair (Rv. I. 114. 15) are similar to pūśana. His colour is babhru and he is decked with golden ornament 2.33. I necklace, niṣka 2.33.10 also he mounts on a car 2. 33.4. अहिन्बिर्भर्षि सायकानि धन्वार्हनिष्कं राजत विश्वरूपम। Vs. 16 adds a more features to him. He is thousand eyed, Av. 11. 2. 7—अस्त्रा नीरुशिखण्डेन सहस्त्राक्षेण वाजिना

VS 16.6 -असौ यास्ताम्रो अरुण हत बभ्रु । 7- मख्रिीवा विसोहिगतः।

He has a belly, a tongue and teeth.

AV. 11.2.6 अडेभ्यस्त उदराय जिह्वाया आरयायि ने।

His belly is black AV. 15.1.7.8

He is blue necked vs 16.7 and blue tufted Av. 2.77.6

His complexion is red and copper like vs. 16.7

Rudra is invoked as ruddy (asura) boar of heaven

cp. I.114.5—दिवो वराह मरुषं कपर्दिनं त्वेष रुपं नमसा नि ह्वयामहे।

He is called a bull—2.33.7—भा वृषभ चक्षमीयाः।

He is attired in a skin

(Vs. 3.61, 16)

he dwells on mountain VS. 16.24

Rudra's bow and arrow are strong and swift

(2.33.10.11, op. cit.)

5.42.11—तमु ष्टुहि यः। स्वंषु सुघन्वा यो विश्वस्यक्षयति भेषजस्य

10.125.6—अहं रद्राय धनुरा तनोमि ब्रह्माद्विषे शखे हन्तवै ह।

vii.46.1—इमा रुद्राय स्थिरधुन्वने गिरः क्षिप्रेषेव देवाय—हिग्मायुधाय

His lightning shaft (Vidyut) discharged from the sky traverses the earth (7.46.3)—या ते दिधुयवसृष्टा दिवस्परि क्षमया चरति परि सा वृगवेजु नः

AV and later vedic texts claimed Rudra's various weapons—bow, arrow, belt, club frequently.

(cp. AV. I 28.5; 28.1; 6.93; 15.5)

Shiva's Tripurāntaka firm-holding a bow and an arrow is again and again appreciated by Shilpa texts. However Shiva's manifestation in Gudimallam, possessing a bow and an arrow is unforgetful. Rudra's names like Śarva and Bhava. Bhava are assigned to in VS 16.18-28 but these two names occur in AV also 2.27.6, 6.

In the tenth maṇdala (10.125.6) the ṛṣi claims that the god is thread of a bow at the time of Tripurasura fight Sāyaṇa beings to comment in the words त्रिपुरासुर विजय संग्रामे।

In VS 37.8 other firms are enumerated like Iśāna, Mahadeva, Paśupati. Iśāna form is blended in five facets of Shiva. It is ākasha, it witness functions of Buddhi. Vishnudharmotaro purāṇe epitomises Iśāna as the fifth face. ईशानं पञ्चम मुखम् p. 48 Aduyaya Rudra is invoked as a boar of heaven. Also he is called a bull.

Afterwards a bull becomes Shiva's vehicle. Sometimes he is called Uṣiṣin having a crown or a head gear. VS calls him Śitikaṇṭtha—white or blue throated Rudra-Shiva is not only maleficent like or demon but he is bountiful as well as an auspicious god. His heating powers are especially brought to the notice. He is a physician. His epithets jalāsa-cooling bheshaja are noteworthy. Rudra is spoken of clad in an antelop's (kārṣṇya vāsana). Thus Rudra is embodied with ascetic as well as warrior's features.

cp. लिग्भमेको विभूर्ति हस्त आयुध:।

शुचिरुग्रो जाणषभेषज:। (Rv. viii.89.5)

Yv. pays homage to Rudra the God of death also God of well being in the words

नम: शङ्क्वे च पशुपतये च।

नम: उग्राय च भीमाय च।

Here to borne is a mind, Rudra Shiva's assimilation in a trial or religious pantheon is not out of place.

By illustrating Viṣnu's hymns we may assert the polytheistic creeds maintained by individual initivative personification.

Notwithstanding that the statistical standard puts viṣnu minor deity in the Ṛgveda. However viṣṇu three strides are frequently glorified from vedic to puranic network. Fundamentally viṣṇu's Urugāyatva and Urukramatva puts him on a high esteem; He assumes vast body which is known by tri-vikram form though he was a child cp. Rv. I.155.6

बृहच्छरीरी विभिमान ऋकभिर्युवा कुमार: प्रत्येत्याहवम्''।

Viṣṇu traverses the terrestrial spaces, two-steps are visible to men, on the other hand the third one is beyond the mortal kern. Rv. I.155.5

व्दे इदस्य क्रमणे स्वर्दशोऽमिख्याय मर्त्यो भुख्यति। तृतीमस्य नकिरा दर्धषति वृयस्वन पतघना: पतत्रिण॥

See also Rv VII 99.2

This vedic narrative is expanded in vaman story in the puraṇas, though infused in Aiteraya Brāhmaṇa and Śatapatha Brāhmaṇa, with a slight innovation, viṣṇu's wide going feature evokes fine visual equivalents in the painting set housed in Bhandar Oriental Museum. It established visual discourse in which viṣṇu's most distinctive achievement is celebrated. This outstanding feature of viṣṇu is attributed to India sometimes (cp. vi. 69.5 गुरु चक्रमयि) keeping consistency with vedic germs developed later on in visual paraphenalia the sun and the savitṛ and purushasūkta are to be taken into consideration, The sun in a chariot drawn by a single horse (etaṣa) is represented. On the contrary the sun's image is visualised mounted on a chariot to which seven horses are yoked represented at Modhera is not missing. From the point of considerable anthropomorphism, the prayers for savitṛ-god throw light on physical features, namely possessing broad-hands (ii.30.2) wearing tawny garment (iv.35.2) iv.352—आगन्नृभूषामिह रानधेयमभूत्सामस्य

we are all aware of the puruṣasūkta Rv. x. 90—13

चन्द्रमा मनसो जात्क्षो सूर्यो अजायत

मुखादिन्द्ररवाग्श्रिव प्राणाद्वायु रजायत''

नाभ्या आसीदनारिक्ष शीर्ष्णों धौ: समवर्तन। etc.

parallel to the vishwarupa darashana an impressive form so also evaluated many times by the art-historians. Even it is surprising that an artist has transmitted this form with a grandeour and elegance which is ever remembered. Virātarupa juxtaposes divine form in dyu, sun, moon, wind, earth water, fire;

Human form—Barahmana, kshatriya, vaishya and shudra

Animal form—cow, goat, curd, ghee, sthavararupa—earth, food samidha etc. All the universe came out of this cosmic form same tone is expressed in Bhagavadgita

ब्राह्मार्पण ब्रह्महली: ब्रह्माग्नौ, ब्रह्मणा दुत्तम्।

ब्रह्मैव तेन गन्त्य ब्रह्मकर्म समाधिना

or यज्ञेन यज्ञं अयजनां देवा: [10.10.16]

Proceeding ahead in vedic poetry and music the media of expression, corroborating to polytheism particularising a definite plastic form 'suparnas (beautiful winged birds) allegories philosophical over tone on the on looker's mind. The distinguished two birds seated on a tree looking forward, disclose some mystery behind the manifestation of the universe.

Thus crystalised ideas already retained in the vedic culture, could discern by the occurrence of the word Shilpacitra and their further explanation enunciated is Brahmaṇas.

Usually in present time the word shilpa indicates sculpture but vedic cannotation is slightly different. Shilpa is a common term suggestive of all arts including crafts. Hence all products which need strikingness and expertise may be termed as shilpa. Aitereya Brahmana vi.5.1 makes mention of Śayana's interesting remarks

शिस्पशष्दान् च आश्चर्यकरं कर्म ब्रूते

is defined as following—

शिस्पानि शंसन्ति देवशिस्पानि एतेषां लै शिस्यानां अनुकृतिः शिस्पं अधिगमंयते। हस्ति कंसो वासो हिरण्यं अश्वजारीरथः शिस्यण्। शिष्यं हास्मिन्नधिगमयते य एवं वेद यद् एव शिस्प। आत्म-संस्कृतिर्वाव शिस्पानि। छंदोमयं वा एतद् यजमान आत्मानां संस्कृरुते।

Shilpa is classified into two groups :

devashilpa and manushashilpa. The word shilp hints bahurupali according to Sāyaṇa. Kaushitaki Brahmana explains शिघो बहुरूपः and prescribes that Shipa is applied to dance and instrumental music, In the śathapatha Brāhmaṇa the word shilpa is taken to mean the art of modelling, painting etc.

मन्त्रस्य शिस्यपदं व्याचस्टे यव्दा इति। प्रतिरूपं प्रतिकृतिः। वै शब्देन रणेकप्रसिद्धि रुच्यते। वैकिका हि हरि तुरत्रादि प्रतिरूपं शिस्यं दूत्यादुः। [III 2.15]

Also गव्दै प्रतिरूपं तत् च शिस्यम्।

pratirupaktva hints at semblance Rv. refers to रूपं रूपं प्रतिरूपं कबभूव। and the word like sthuṇa which means an image of iron according to the lexicographer—Amarec, strengthens the literary evidences.

Thus in all, supports to the anticipation of the image making in ancient times. At this juncture, it is relevant to bring to notice the controversial views regarding the art of idol-making, known to vedic people. Some scholars like Williams and Müller remark 'Vedic religion knows no idols though early worshippers clothed their gods with human forms in their own imaginations. Idol worship was a secondary formations. While Bollensen speaks strongly on the other side-Indian did merely imagination assign human forms to god but also represented them in a sensible manner. Thus a painted image of Rudra II. 33.9 is described with strong limbs awful having brown complexion etc. He is painted with shining colours. There is a word 'sandṣa' in vedic which properly denotes an image of god.

Taittiriya Āraṇyaka takes note of this word TA x.1

न संहशे तिष्ठसि रुपं अस्य न चक्षुषा पश्यति कछान एतम्।

Sāyaṇa has remarked on it and it may be carefully observed in this context.

किं च अस्य परमात्मर्नां रूपं नीष्पीतादिकं संदर्श प्राणिनां दृष्टिविषये न तिष्ठति।

Thus such references are highly expressive while presuming the existence of art.

It is supposed that religious and social forces were determinants of functional awareness, so also an art-activity is subservient to reigion or it is emphasised that an art of or building or construction is a bye-product of religious practices. But vedic religion was not onesided, vedic seer was versatile. In one of the hymn (cp. Rv.x.71.11) four methods of religious practice are mentioned recitation, 2, singing, 3-path of knowledge, 4-yayña in śakvari measures. One seapks of the existing thing and one lays down the rule of Yajña. This is how the categorisation was made. And the person measuring the यज्ञ yajña was part and parcel of the on going function. No doubt the advanced stage of construction is exhibited in various shapes of vedic altars like garudācayana. Apart from the sutra period Rv.x.107.10 highlights decorative motifs, still survived down, and the parts of temple like well-decorated vitānan still observed in Dilwara-temple amazingly though so late in construction was not unknown to vedic time x.107.10.

भोजायाश्रय सं मृजन्त्याशु भोजायास्ते कन्या शुम्भमाना।
भोजस्येदं पुस्करिणीव वेश्म परिष्कृतं देवमानेव चित्रम्।।

This is an exquisite type of a building.

Sāyaṇa comments on—

बोजस्य हृदयाह्लादकरं वेश्म गृहं भवति। कीदशम् पुष्करिणीव। पुष्कराणि पदमानि यरयाः सन्तीति पुष्करिणी सरसी। सा यथा पदमहंसादिभिरतंकृता भवति लव्दत् परिष्क्रतं विनानादिभिरख्क्रृतम्॥

Also see AV VI 106— आयेन ने परायणे दूर्वा रोहनु पुष्पिणी।

उत्सो वा तत्र जायतां-हदो वा पुष्परीकवान्।

(Rv.iv.30.20, Rv. 10.101.8)

(Av.ix.3.21) या ब्दिपक्षा चतुष्पक्षा षट्पक्षा या निमीयते।

Rv. projects the types of houses comprising two wings, four wings, six wings, eight wings and ten-wings. The plans were worked out according to appropriate measurements. Atharaveda also refers to dwellings places through the word shala and dharm cp. Av. viii. 6.10 and 11.14.6

They who dance around the dewellings in the evening

The reference to word 'harmya' hints at substantial structure, vṛtra was detected in a dark harmya तमसिहस्य (Rv. v. 32.5)

Rv. viii.40.12 Sun's rays penetrate from above the harmya to note हर्म्येत्रः vii 7.6.2 implies the considerable height of the building of the harmya class or it's position on the top of a house. In latter treatises the word harmya designates a room on the upper part of a house, samarāṇgaṇa—sutradhara throws light on the harmya—18.9.

Indra is said to be destroyer of harmyas perhaps of the asuras

Rv. ix. 71.4,78.3

सिञ्चति हम्यस्य सक्षणिम्।

हम्यस्य शत्रुपुररस्य

The strength and stability of vedic houses is pointed out by the word dhruva

cp. Rv. III. 54.20 ध्रुवक्षेमासः निधात्व्स्थानाः।

Rv. II.41.5 राजाना वननि, द्रुहा ध्रुते सदस्यत्तमे। सहस्रास्थूण आसीत।

Shilpashastras describe special class of building called as dhruva.

cp. vishwakarma prakash 2.103

and Samarāṅgana Sūtradhara 23.6—

ध्रुवं धन्यं जयं नन्दं खरं कान्तं मनोरमम्।

ध्रुवे जयं आप्रोनि

The epitheta like drdha, drmhita, dur, duroṇa etc. are presumably used in relating to fort 'Durgaṇi śyasi' applied to puras (cities) signified firmness in case of fortifications. One single reference to the hundred cities made of stone-aśmamayasi "Rv. iv.30.20

शतमश्मन्मर्यानां पुरामिन्द्रो व्यासार [sayaṇa अश्मन्मर्यानां—पोषाणैनिमितानां पुरा नगराणां

strengthens the views that at least the walls of the forts were constructed with hard materials,

Rv vii. 15.14 leads to suppose that forts consist of a series of concentric walls at that time. The expression shubhra Rv. vii. 36. 16 indicates the whiteness or shining character of the building probably it denotes the white washed walls of the city or some shining materials of which walls or houses were built. Materials used for construction is referred to occasionally. Measurements are prescribed for a structure. It gives rise to the inference for the systematic building operation and not just a haphazard action. Doors and pillars are worshipped.

Rv.III.8 युवा सुवासा परिवीन आगात्स ह श्रेयान्भवति जायमानः ।

युक्त-हढाङ्गा अष्टाश्रयादिख्क्षणत्वर्क्षनः ।

Rv. refers to satabhuji—100 pillars or walls (I.166.8). The rules for selection of soil, reference to assembly, the reference to chhardi, roof of a house—Rv. iv.2.5. पृथुबुदनः सभावान्

and also chaṣāla davara, dena-khani etc. form the nucleus for the ancient architectural development.

The word Trivarutha in Rv. viii. 18.21

त्रिवरुथं मरुतो यन्त नश्छर्दिः ।

त्रिवरुथं शीतातपवर्षाणां निपारकं यव्दा त्रिभूमिकं छर्दिः गृहम्।

in connection with dwelling place suggests according to Sāyaṇa shelter, protection, against sun, rain and cold or a three storeyed abode.

The word Tridhātu is applied to buildings in shilpaashastras either in the sense of seven parts or the materials

cp. shilparatna ch. 16. 121.23 मांस मेचकवर्णं स्यानचर्म नीरूं न संयायः ।

त्वक् कृष्णवर्ण मित्यादः प्रासादे रुपाधानवः ॥

Rv. vi. 46.9 Sāyaṇa explains as Tribhūmi—Three courtyards several references to pillars are located all through the Rgveda namely sthuṇa, stambha, skambha, viskambha, showing free-standing pillars and pilasters while other words such as upamit, meta, upamat, Dharuna are used for only support. Many gods are compared to pillars in respect of support they offered to the invokers

cp. Rv. I.59.1 बैन्धातरं नृक्षितीनां सथूणेव जनां ुपामिघयन्थ ॥

वंशधारणार्य निखानः स्तम्भः यथा गृहउपरिस्यं वंश धारयति।

Rv. III. 31.12. विस्कभन्तः स्कम्भनेना जनित्री आसीना।।

iv.5.1 सभायत् उपमित् रोधः। सागु सौत्रो धातुः ।

The svarus or chips mentioned in the context are nothing but the part inserted under a rope girding the lower part of the yupa. On the other hand chaśala or a ring is set on the upper part, it forms a head piece, the chaṣāla was prototype of the capitals of pillars.

The credit for giving shapes goes to Tvashtā. He is rupakṛt (TB II.5.7.4)

RV. compares Travshtā to a wood carver.

त्वष्टारँ रुपाणि विकर्वन्तं विपाश्चित्।

त्वष्टा रुपाणि पिंशतु

RVI 1889

त्वष्टा रुपाणि हि प्रभु: पशून्विवाश्र्वान्समानसे

तेषां न स्फातिमा यण।

In course of centuries he is called Takshaka or a mason engaged in building operation. His role is to chip wood on stone or brick. Tvashtā is the son of Vishwakarmā, while Ribhus were his disciples, Shilpa literature describes him the master architect Mayamatam v.20.

Rv. never talks of Vishwakarma's special association with structural activity. The building of a temple or a house forms a part of religious ceremony. Hence, vastoṣati (Rv. vii.5.4.53)

is invoked wherein he requested to offer an excellent abode—svabeśa

Thus while plunging into the vast corpus of vedic ocean, an observer is somewhat bewildered since Indian architecture or rather to say Indian art-tradition is marked by distinct changes and contrast, in comparison with the present-day advancement in all plastic arts. The traditional practising art and the astonishing development even in the medieval period appears complex. Sometimes a connoissuer feels a transplantation of an alien art form on our soil, rather to have comprehensive understanding in the art-realm! In this context it is more logical to approach in a sympathetic attitude.

A pattern of subteterian architecture is emerging in the process may be traceable from Rv. as well as Av., Av. vi. 106-2

अपामिदं न्ययनं समुद्रस्य निवेशनम्। मध्ये-हदस्य नो गृहा:"

throws light on a house in the water "The down course of the waters, the abode (niveshana) of the ocean, in the midst of a pool are our houses"

The construction of a lake, dam, well, canal was known to vedic time canal is as if their vatsa, vedic term kulya brings to light the embankments and canals. There is discourse between ṛṣi and two personified rivers. The sage approaches to the rivers with a wagon and a car and requests them to bend low since he may easily cross the water.

cp. III.33.9 ओषु स्वसार: कारवे श्रृणोत

ययौ वो दूराद् अनसा रथेज॥

III.3.10 आ ते कारो श्रृणवामा वचांसि।

ययाथ दूराद् अनसा रयेन:

In the course of time the personification of the rivers usually known as Gaṅgā and Yamunā, or nadidevatās, with a water vessel still persists at Amaravati. They adorn the entrance of a temple in medieval architecture.

Rv 3.55 : be speak to us Vishwakarma's iconographical form which is a literacy parallel to one of visual parallel.

कंबासूत्राबुपात्रं बहति करनले पुस्तकं ज्ञानसूत्रम्।
हंसारुढ़स्त्रिनेत्रः शुभमुगुटः शिरं रुर्वतोवृद्धकायः॥
त्रैलेक्यं येन सृष्टं सकलसुरगृहं राजहर्म्यादि हर्म्यम्।
देवाऽसौ सूत्रघोर जगदा खिल हिनः पालु वो विश्वकर्मा॥
विश्वाय विश्वरुपाय नमस्ते विश्वमूनेये।
विश्वकर्म सुभंगस्य विश्वविधा विनोदिने॥

The ṛcs furnish vishwarija image resemble to an image exhibited in Mathurā Museum. It reveals emergence of Shiva from Agni's flames. In the beginning of creative process, Shiva manifested, came out of Vishwakarma's mouth. Viṣhnu emerged out from Vishwakarma's arms. The celestial world is created from Vishwakarma's head and so on.

RV also mentions some colours like Rohita (red), kṛṣṇa (black), Shukla-white. TA mentions supportive output to the description of colours when it describes the seasons.

TA 1.3.4 :

शुक्रवासा रुद्रगणः। ग्रीष्मेणावर्तने रुद्रः।
विश्वरुपाणि वासँसि। आदित्यानां निबोधन।
तदमा पीत इव दृश्यते।

The description focuses light on all round picture of the variegated forms, sights and colours which the world put on the different seasons. To illustrate the white is attired to summer, Rainy season is yellow in appearance, sharad ṛtu is of golden colour and fresh. Hemant is red. Artists have blended seasons in Rāgamālā paintings, of course to create the excitement, as well as to suggest the time factor. The usage of ample colours denotes the various sentiments. For example to suggest Sṛṅgāra colour is used or to give an idea of calmness colour is found.

Landscape yields the environment in Mālwā, Mewār, Pahari set of paintings. It is again to stop a while when an art-lover visualises the different sets of kṛṣṇa-legend paintings. Especially when an onlooker go through the kṛsṇa, pranks, depicted by various artists, the kāliyādaman story has many versions. It is found in Ajanta painting, Bhāgavata puraṇa set of paintings and so on. Now the Kāliyā-nāga legend is familiar to us chiefty through the purāṇas. However instead of repeating the entire story it is enough to mention herein about the origin of this legend. The earliest known source about the kāliyā damana narrative seems to trace in RV viii. 96.13-15 :

अव द्रासो अंशुभतीमतिष्ठदियानः कृष्णो दशभिः सहस्त्रैः ।

In these verses it is told that swift maving kṛṣna stood on the Amśumali River also with 10,000 demons. Indra caught him snorting in the water Ṛṣi tells that he has seen kṛṣṇa standing there as the (sun) in a cloud and appeals for conquering Him to showerers. Indra aided by Bṛhaspati smote his ally. Then the swift moving one assumed his own body Sāyaṇaś commentary draws the attention—He mentions it is a historical legend of course, metaphorically 10,000 demons might have been responsible for the many hooded kāliyā serpents who infested the River Yamunā

Also Kṛṣṇa with the help of his brother Balarāma vanquished black serpent and drove him along with his followers from that poisonous river, it is specially to mention here that Indra's fight with Vṛtra is always glorified in veda. He killed ahi–a serpent who lived in waters. This achievement of Indra is assimilated in Kaliyā legend Indra and viṣṇu belongs to solar clan kṛṣṇa is considered as incarnation of viṣṇu. Thus with a slight innovation RV may be said the earliest document for kāliyā legend.

Compare sāyaṇa's commentary on ṛc 13.

अत्रेतिहास समाचक्षते कि. । कृष्णओ नामासुरो दशसहस्त्र संख्यै-रसुरैः परिवृत्तः सन्नंशुगर्त नामधेयाया नघाऽत्रीरेः अनिष्ठत्। तत्र तं कृष्ण मुदकमध्ये स्थित मिन्द्रो बृहस्पलिका सहागच्छान्। आगत्य तं कृष्णं तस्यानु-चरांश्च बृहस्पति रुहायो जधानेति।

Apart from several references for wonderful, striking, excellent meanings, all embracing all comprehensive domain of the tradition borne to us the practical evidence for sketching the figure of course, AV being much related to social customs, specifically refers to the picture of a person who wished to gain the love of a woman. He made a picture out of clay (AV, V.14)

AV, VI.13 : A woman acts in similar manner and makes an elligy of the man

(Also AV, III, 25)

Going ahead on the same track, the illustration of a svarūpa (shape) in AV, *IV*, 17.2. draws reader's mind. Moreover, Av inculcates the description a tree along with roots branches etc. pertaining to different colours.

Av. mentions white, red, black, swarthy colours in viii.7.1.

''या बभ्रवो याश्च शुक्ला रोहिणीरुत पृश्जयः ।

असिवनीः कृष्णा ओषधी सर्वा अच्छावदामपि ।।''

Ample references to the words citra (rūpa) ā kṛti, shilpa etc. bring us near to another aspect of vedic society. Rūpa denotes form, shape, outer appearance in Rv.1. 164.44.

Also means colour in Rv vii, 97.6—नभो न रूपमरुषं वसानः ।

IX, 16.6 पुनानो रुपे अत्यये रुप्यमाणे।

The word shilpa is expressive of glorious thing, wonderous deed, skill while the word citra which means a painting in present day context, only indicates brightness, touching the heart, excellence etc.

Rv., x.100.12—स चित्र चित्र चित्तयनमस्मे।

Rv., I, 48.11—चित्रस्तेभानुः आश्चर्यभूतश्चायनीये वा।

Av. invokes in VI. 41—

''मनसै चेलये धिय आकूतय उत चितये।
मत्यै श्रुताय चक्षसे विदोम हविषा वयम्।''

to various divinities which directs to the process of imagination and intuition "To mind, to thought, to device (dhi), to design, to intention, to opinion, (mati), to instruction (cruta) to sight we pay worship to divinities with oblation" If we think over little while, it explores how the journey of an art-expression continues when there is 'bhavanā' for designing an art-form it may be poetry, or a painting or a sculpture, it is deeply rooted in the mind. An artist feel quit-voice by summoning all the energies of the mind centres down to one point, involves fully away" from all distractions conceives the mental frame, with his workmanship having a broad out look and along with a developed training through abhyāpa, vyavahāra etc. By synchronizing all the processes a visual form emerges out. It is a reaction responding to the unity of whole. It is transformed for all to see and enjoy. It is to recollect at this point Mammata's kāvyaprakāsha wherein he elaborately launch into kāvyahetu and kavyashikshā.

It comprises multi-dimensional units extending from genious to competence all the while.

It is a pleasant surprise to know and to understand the Indian point of view striving at a standard practical approach. Herein to piece together Mimamsaka's definition of bhāvanā will be highly appreciable.

cp. भावना नाम भार्वनुर्भावायीनु भेवनानुकूलो व्यापार विशेषः।

To mean bhāvanā an activity, the composite entity appearing one and indivisible, though actually it is deciphered into number of units.

Vedic poetry is always changed standing in mystic experience, admist the religious background. The ṛṣi urges living presence of the divine in the beauty and nobility. It came out of a joyous and radiant spirit-Ṛṣi himself talks about the adequate expression into a hymnal form entangled in purity, austerity and power. It is compared to the fresh, clear streams gushing out of a rock, mountain.

Rv.x.68 :

गिरिभ्राणो नोर्मयो मदन्ते।
बृहस्पति अत्यक्ताऽन्वन्॥

It is everlasting, years donot age, for months, not also days wearout

"न यं जरन्ति शरदो न मास न धावा"

with such a delicate mind vedic man looks around the nature.

The beautiful pictures of life and nature seem to carry some deep hidden meaning. Having carried forward whole heartedly (Rv., II, 13.7) the source of beauty couched in the concept of ṛta.

cp. Rv. II.13.7 :

"यः पुष्पिणीश्व प्रस्वध धर्मणा
ऽधि दाने व्यश्वनीधारयः।
यधासमा अजनो दिधुर्ता दिन
उरुरुर्वा अभिनः सास्युक्श्यः।।"

The eternal law manifests itself in nature, making its beauty and glory rich

"you who by enternal law has spread about flowering and seed bearing plants, and streams of water

you, who generated the matchless lightnings in the sky, you, vast, encompassing vast realms are a fix subject for our song"

Thus, in evoking words the ṛsi glorifies the surrounding, it highlights the landscape environment, which we met with in ample set of paintings. Viṣṇudharmothara purāṇa calls it satya type of citra in adhyayai 41.

The similar exciting element is found in Av-again. The representation of flora and fauna in natural sketch is quite evident.

(cp. Av vi. 52)

While projecting the earth Av. makes a mention of some colours. cp. Av. 12.1.11—

"गिरयस्ते पर्वता हिमवन्तो
अरण्यं ते पृथिवी रसोनम् अस्तु।
बभ्रकृष्णा रोहिणी विश्वरूपा
ध्रुला भूमिं पृथिवीम् इन्द्रगुप्ताम्।।

So, the earth is pleasant due to hills and snow-clad mountains. Also woodlands add to it's beauty. Thus, the earth comprises all colours like brown, black and ruddy.

It has become some what of common nature in these days to speak of the ancient Hindus as having achieved distinction in philosophy. But, our traditional literature makes a substantial contribution to both historical and asethetic sides. The exposition is throughout on a highlevel in the midst of suggestions. It is greatly valuable for the student of art.

The Poetic Beauty in Rigveda

13

Dr. K. C. Mahalik

Rigveda is the oldest book not only of the Aryan race, but of the whole world. Some Mantras of Rigveda have the charming beauty of poetry which enrich the poetic product of vision or imagination of Indian Literature.

The present article is an humble attempt to analyse some Vedic Mantras of Rigveda, as the beauty of poetry from various stand points to understand the vedic studies more scientifically and reasonably.

The study of poetics is always necessary to understand the rythm of life. Poetic plays a vital role to regulate and reflect the activities of Literature and its impact on human life. All the poetic elements are combined to produce supernormal pleasure named "RASA". Rasa is a pure blissful experience, which thrills all the external and internal organs.

The beauty of Poetry is another name of Rasa. The origin and development of poetry or Rasa is a special class of Literature which has its root in Rigveda[1]. The Vedic Literature has remained a neglected branch of study, though the Literature on its own essentially represents a very important part of Indian Spiritual Lore.

The great poets are seers, one who has spiritual insight and can see truth that others can not[2]. Here it needs be mentioned that Kavi and ṛṣi are greater poets than others. A ṛṣi or a Kavi[3] is a visionary and the epithet is mostly used after the deities or the deified ancestors. The world Kāvya has been used four times in the R. V. III,[4] where it means powerful hymns of vision.

Both Skanda and Sāyaṇa agree to interpret the word as a "stotra", while Velankar would understand it as priestly acts which also include offering of "Stotras with oblations, "Viśvāni Kāvyāni Vidvān"[5] where Viśvāni Kāvya means hymns containing knowledge.

The beautiful description of Goddess Uṣā fulfils the poetic charm of Ṛgveda.[6] It beauties can be well compared to that of a beautiful princess. The charm of Goddess Uṣā rising in the eastern horizon from an unending reddish carpet can again be compared to that of a diamond necklace of the princess.

The poet is of the opinion that all these miracles and charming beauties of Goddess Uṣā is definitely meant to attract her better Love, the Sun God, just like a woman attracts her mate posing her naked body before him.

In the Mandukasukta of Ṛgveda[7] also explains the poetic beauty that the croacking sound of the frogs at the advent of the rainy season, which is followed by other frogs repeatedly becomes so enchanting to hear for the masses, is just like the imitation of the disciples while learning from their Gurus.

Not only that the poets of the Vedic age have gone to the extent of bringing about genuine reforms[8] in the married life.

On the marriage altar how oath is taken by the married couple and the blessings of the husband to his wife to most fortunate and to lead a conjugal life of inseparable sanctity of the coining words of the Vedic age and to be imbibed for innumerable generations to come, were controlled by the rishis.

Here it may be explained in the light of R.V. III. 62.8,[9] where the poet examplifies the image of a lover taking delight in the beloved's words. The poet invites Indra to enjoy his words - Vadhū yu (one who attracts after a woman) the image clearly points to a passionate enjoyment which is all possessing in Ṛgveda.

Truely speaking we may not find the refined poetry of Kalidāsa, the philosophical vigour of Kapila, the voluptuous mysticism of Jayadev and epic simplicity of Vyāsa and Valmiki in Ṛgveda, but we can get enchanting heart touching songs of hymns which contains the wisdom and thoughts in expression of poetic beauty.

To distinguish between the individual soul and the ultimate soul the ṛṣi is of the opinion[10] that man is the individual soul enjoys his life to the taste and fancy of his animate nature, completely ignoring the aims of the ultimate soul, that is within him. To put this idea in philosophical way, the poet says that there is a couple of bird setting on the branch of a tree, miracuously enough. One of the birds eats every thing as the individual soul, where as the other is sitting silently symbolising the ultimate soul.

Further the poet also explains the poetic beauty of Ṛgveda by the image of Swan.[11] In here two meanings under line this image. On the one hand melodious sound of the Swan is appropriated to the melody of the hymn while on the other Swan lends its gaitey and majesty to the form and the meaning of the hymn.

The Vedic culture and the Vedic reforms as depicted in the Ṛgveda, in such a picturious manner that, those were the monopolly of the ancient Indian culture influencing the entire human race then and now.

References

1. T.G. Mainker. Rigvedic Origin of Classical Poetics, pp. 10-49.
2. Dḥvanyālokaḥ ch. 3 (a Pāre kāvyasaṁsāre kavireva Prajāpatiḥ .)
3. ete vai kavaya yad ṛṣayaḥ (Sat. Br. 1.4. 2.8)
4. Ścotanti dhārā madhuno ghṛtasya Vṛsā Yatra Vāvṛdhe Kāvyena. (RV. III. 1.8)
   mahāṅ ugro vāvṛdhe vīryāya samācakre Vṛsabhaḥ kāvyena. (RV. III. 36.5.)

ā devānaṁ abhavaḥ ketur agne mandro viśvāni kāvyāni vidvān. (RV III. 1.17)
ghṛta Pratika vrviyā vyadyand agnir viśvanikavyāni vidvān. (RV III. 1.18)

5. Pari viśvani kāvyā nemiścakram ivābhavat (RV. II. 5.3)
6. कन्येव तन्वा शाशदानां राषिदेवि देवमिय क्षमताम्।
   संस्मयमाना युवतिः पुरस्ताद् विवक्षांसि कृणुसे विभाती (ऋग्वेद)
7. य देषगमन्यो अन्यस्य वाचं शाक्तस्येव वदति शिक्षमाणः।
   सर्वं दतेषां समृधेव पर्व यत्सुवाचो वदथ नाध्यप्सु (ऋग-7.163.5.)
8. गृभ्णामि ते सौभगत्वाय हस्तं मया पत्या जरदस्त्यिर्थासः
   भगो अर्यमा सविता पुरंधिर्महयं त्वाद्दर्गाहय पत्याय देवाः (ऋ. 10.85.36)
9. tāṁ Juṣasva giraṁ mama vājayantim ava dhiyam vadhū yur iva Joṣāṇam.
10. द्वासुपर्णा सयुजा सरवाय समानं वृक्ष परिषस्वजाते।
    तयोरन्यः पिप्पलं स्वादुत्त्यनश्चन्नन्या अभिचाकशीति'' (ऋग् 164. 20)
11. ''हंसा इव कृणुथ श्लोकम्'' (ऋग् 111. 53. 10)

Vedic Metres

14

Dr. R.K. Panda

Introduction

Metres play an important role in the Vedic literature. They bear some special significance not only from the point of view of Vedic poetry but also from the point of sacrifice. They are said to be particular formulas in which *mantras* with reference to different deities are composed and useful tools for preserving *mantra*-texts intact and producing the expected results of the *mantras.* The significance of *mantras* is easily understood from the following words of Bharatamuni. There is no word without metre; nor is there any metre without words.

In this chapter I have tried to throw some light on some salient features of Vedic metres. We have to admit the fact that there is no availability of any systemetic work of Vedic prosody in Sanskrit as we see in case of classical metres.

Significance of Metres

Metres occupy a significant place in the *Brāhmaṇa*-texts in which they are referred to sometime as a group and individually. The metres in which the *Mantras* were embodied, came to assume the utmost importance in the exposition of the science of sacrifice. Metre was considered as one of the three important factors viz., *ṛṣiçhandas* and *devatā* necessary for the study of the Vedic literature. A person, who does not know these three factors and makes their use in actual practice, is said to be a *mantrakaṇṭaka.*

The preference for metre of the Vedic bards seems to be natural, because they could express their feelings in better way through metres. Secondly, as the Vedic hymns were composed for sacrificial purposes, with a view to propitiate the gods, nothing could please the gods better than prayers sung in the particular metres. Thirdly, the metrical limitations served a most practical purpose, that of preserving and remembering easily what was composed, especially when writing was not in vogue.

Meaning of the Word Chandas

The word *chandas* is derived from cadi *ālhadāne*. Yāska derives the word from *chād* to cover and *chandas* is so called because it is the covering of the Vedic texts.

By metaphor the texts of the Veda themselves came to be called *chandas* because their external form was metrical. Thus *chandas* became a synonym of Veda. The etymology of the word is given in several ways. However, the striking note in these etymological explanations of the word *chandas* is that the *chandas* is capable of covering or protecting one from the evil and thus full of potent power.

Vedic Prosody

The science of Prosody held an important place in Sanskrit literature. In the history of Sanskrit literature, from time, to time, at various stages prosody has been employed with diversity of forms and variety of usages. On the grounds of prosodial employment, the entire Sanskrit literature can be broadly classified into two sections:

Vedic and Classical

Like all other Śāstras, prosody also has its sources in Vedic literature. So many scattered references of prosody, generally appear in almost all parts of the huge volumes of Vedic literature. But there are a few number of works in all Vedic sections, consisting of noteworthy discussions on prosody. They are : *The Ṛk- Saṁhitā*, the *Taittirī*a *Saṁhitā, Aitareya Brāhmaṇa, Daivata Brāhmaṇa Ṛk Pratiśākhya, Rgveda-Chandonukramaṇi, Nidāna Sūtra, Upanidāna Sūtra, Chndaśāasatra, Sarvānukramaṇi, Ṛgvedānukramaṇi* of Venkta mādhava, *Atharva Veda Brhat Sarvāṇukramaṇi, Agni Purāṇa, Jayadeva Chandas* and *Vṛtta Muktāvali* . Prosody is included among the six Vedāṅgas, and is designated as the foot of the Veda. The work which is regarded as a Vedāṅga, is Poiṅgala's *Chandasśūtra,* the earliest extant work on prosody. Though the work is regarded as a Vedāṅga, it discusses mostly classical metres.

Prominent Metres of the Veda

The most prominent of the Vedic metres are :

Gāyatrī	8	8	8			
Uṣṇik	8	8	12			
Purauṣṇik	12	8	8			
Kakubh	8	12	8			
Anuṣṭubh	8	8	8		8	
Bṛhatī	8	8	12		8	
Satobṛhatī	12	8	12		8	
Paṅkti	8	8	8		8	8
Prastārapuṅkti	8	8	8		8	
Virāj	10	10	11	or	11	11
Triṣṭubh	11	11	11		11	
Jagatī	12	12	12		12	

There are of course, many sub-varieties of these metres, formed by altering the order of the various feet. The metres of the different verses in the hymns of the *Ṛgveda* are all exhaustively given in the *Sarvānukramaṇi* of kātyāyana extract from which are as a rule, quoted by Sāyaṇa at the commencement of his commentary on each hymn. Restricting overselves to the seventh *maṇḍala,* we find that the *Triṣṭubh* metre prevails mostly thoughout the book with a very few exceptions of other metres.

Salient Features

The principle of considering a whole letter, whether short or long as a unit for matrical scanning underlines Vedic prosody. According to this principle, a letter regardless of its quantity, forms the basis of a metrical line and the number of letters in a line alone distinguishes one such line from another. The chief representatives of the Vedic metres, which may be called *Akṣara Vṛttas* in view of this principle, are the *Gāyatri Anuṣṭubh,* the *Triṣṭubh* and the Jagati. They respectively contain 8, 11, and 12 letters in each of their lines. *Anuṣṭubh, Triṣṭubh* and *Jagati* have 4 such lines in their stanzas, while *Gāyatri* is evidently the oldest of these and *Anuṣṭub* represents only an attempt to bring *Gāyatri* to the level of *Triṣṭubh* and *Jagati,* by having four instead of three lines. Similarly, a *Jagati* line seems to have originated as an extention of the Triṣṭubh line by a single letter, where, however, the nerotory of the two long letters at the end of the Triṣṭubh line was sought to be broken by the introduction of a penultimate short, in the *Jagati* line. Here perhaps was the beginning of a consciousness of the new type of musical rhythm which brought into existence the classical *Varṇa Vṛttas.* From here the Vedic poets may have worked backwards and tried to introduce the alternation of short and long letters in the last part of the *Triṣṭubh- Jagati* line, namely letters 8-12.

The introduction of the *Jagati* line of 12 syllables may have also an additional cause, namely, the extention of the *Gayatri* line by a half. This newly invented line, i.e. the *Jagati* line, could thus be freely associated with the *Gāyatri,* while the other *Triṣṭubh* lines we would not so easily mingle with it. We actually find many a *Jagati* line which by the construction of its lst part of 4 letters indicates unmistakably that it was bu an extention of an original *Gāyatri* line augmented by 4 letters.

The *Jagati* line may have also paved the way for the introduction of strophes and particularly of mixed metres. It is noteworthy that the real mixed metres, i.e. those that were really intended to be such (and not those that were unconsciously turned into such ones) are generally based on a combination of these two types of lines namely, the *Gāyatri* and the *Jagati.* Thus we have *Bṛhati* and *Satobṛhati,* which are meters of 4 lines like the *Triṣṭubh,* as well as *Uṣṇiḥ, kakubh* and *Purauṣṇiḥ* which are metres of 3 lines like the *Gāyatri*. On the other hand, a combination of lines of 11 and 12 syllables in the same stanza represents an unintentional mixture occasioned by an inconvenient word; but most of such cases of unintentional mixture are only apparent ones. For, lines which appear to have only 11 syllables, are not really so in the midst or those of 12 syllables, certainly intended to be regular lines of 12 syllables by their poets. But the changed pronunciation of some words and the compulsory observance of the *Sandhi* for certain vowel-combinations in the later days have brought about the deficiency of a syllable or two in them. Similarly, an increase of a letter or two in only one or two out of the 4 lines of a stanza indicates an unintentional but a real mixture of the two types of lines caused by an inconvenient word or expression, or, by a poetical licence according to which sometimes two short letters occurring one after another were so quickly pronounced as to take the time which was normally allotted to the pronunciation of one letter, short and long. A different kind of mixture of two types of lines is sometimes observed in the Triṣṭubh stanzas where lines of 11 syllables are mixed up with those of 10 syllables and these letter connot be reasonably regarded as original lines of 11 syllables through reasons mentioned above. Two main types of such lines of 10 syllables are generally noticed: one in which a syllable is dropped owing to some kind of poetical licence or misunderstanding; and the other where the line is from the very beginning conceived as divisible into two equal and parallelly constructed parts of 5 syllables each.

Vedic poets gave us three main metres, the Anuṣṭubh, the Triṣṭubh and Jagati. These three were turned into 33 or more by the post-Vedic poets with the help of the newly discovered music of sound-variation. It is quite obvious that at the start these three metres alone were adapted to this new music and various permutations and combinations of short and long letters were introduced into their lines, with the result that in theory a very large number of the different kinds of lines of 8, 11 and 12 letters became possible. In actual practice, however, the poets adopted only a few each of these three classes and the pendantic prosodist could not impose more on them. Yet he surely enticed them to a wider field of choice by showing the possibility of shorter or longer metrical lines treated with the same kind of music. The *Prātiśākhas* had already suggested the possibility of such metres when they gave different names from *Gāyatri* to *Utkṛti* to Vedic stanzas containing from 24 to 104 letters in them. Indeed, the length of the lines in these Vedic stanzas of the different classes mentioned by the *Prātiśākhyas* was not uniform. The class name was given on the basis of the total number of letters in a stanza, whether the lines were threl or more, or whether they were of uniform length or not. Longer lines containing more than 13 to 14 letters (e.g. The irregularly extended *Jagati* or *Triṣṭubh*) are unknown to Vedic poetry in general; yet a combination of a number of lines of varied length, usually of the *Gāyatri* and the Jagati type gives rise to longer stanzas having a total of 56 letters or more. A few varieties of the Vedic metre were turned into a very large number of sub-varieties with the help of the newly discovered metrical music based on the alternation of short and long letters or sounds.

An important feature of the *Varna Vṛttas* is the *Yati* (the metrical pause) introduced in the middle of a line. This in not regularly noticed in the case of the *Triṣṭubh* and the *Jagati* lines in the Vedic stanzas.

Following the Vedic tradition, the classical poets and earlier prosodists have adopted *Gāyatrī* as their shortest stanza and *Utkṛti* as their longest one. Only, in the case of *Gāyatrī,* they had 4 lines of 6 letters each instead of 3 lines of 8 letters each, and this was in conformity with the general principle of having 4 lines for a stanza of a *Varṇa Vṛtta* which alone is the legitimate descendent of the Vedic metres.

All these Vedic metres are based on the *Svarasaṅgita* (the Music of voice-modulation) where the time-element plays no important role in the production of the metrical music. The musical difference between a short and a long letter was not yet made use of for the sake of music in the Vedic metres, a letter whether short or long, being considered as the metrical unit for the construction of lines. But, since short and long letters had to be used in different orders in a line in actual practice, the consciousness of this musical difference could not be avoided for long. Very likely it was first perceived in the process of extending the *Triṣṭubh* in to the Jagati line. The penultimate syllable of a *Jagati* line is always short while that or a *Trṣṭubh* line is generally long. The music produced by the alternation of short and long letters at the end of the *Jagati* line was in course of time carried a little further back, i.e. upto the second metrical break in the line, and the last 4 or 5 letters of the *Triṣṭubh* and the *Jagati* lines were unconsciously, or at least without any idea of compulsion, adapted to this music which is generally known as the lambic rhythm. This same tendency is seen in the latter part of the *Gāyatrī* line, with this difference, namely, that it was more regular in the 2nd line of a hemistich shether of the *Gāyatrī* or of the *Anuṣṭubh,* than in the first. The opposite kind of rhythm or music i.e. the Trochaic, produced by the alternation of long and short letters in succession must have naturally been perceived and employed in course of time, but still without any idea of regularity or compulsion. We find a large number of *Gāyatrī* lines in the *Ṛgveda* which are adapted to this kind of rhythm or music, i.e. the Trochaic. Yet, on the whole, it must be concluded that Trochaic was not as popular as the Iambic with Vedic poets and that the Trochaic was employed as a short of check and sometimes to slur over a vowel. Even this restriction of having four, quarters, each with eight syllables, is not adhered to in some cases. Considering other varieties of the metre, as given in the *Ṛk-Prātiśākhya* (xvi-27/30) and *Piṅgala Chandah--Sūtra* (III.23/5), the only principle universally followed is that of having 32. This number 32 can be arrived at by lessening the number of quarters and increasing the number of syllables in the lines, e.g. according to *Piṅgala-Sūtra* (III.28), an *Anṣṭtub*h may contain three *padas* and 32 syllables (8+12+12). Sometimes the number of syllables in a line is lessened and the number of lines increased (e.g.5+5+5+5+5+6(?7)=32 syllables (*Ṛk-Prātiśākhya*, xvi-30). In short the Anuṣṭubh metres in the early Vedic literature appears in a chaotic condition, on the monotory produced by the more usual Iambic rhythm. This is particularly noticed in the case of the hemistich of *Anuṣṭubh* stanzas, where one *Gāyatrī* line follow another in quick succession. Here we find a general tendency to introduce a long letter both in the 7th place of the first line and in the 3rd place of the 2nd. This manipulation serves a double purpose. It prevents the similar and hence monotonous ending of the two lines forming the hemistich and supplies also a change or variation in the 1st, before the reappearance of the Iambic rhythm at the end of the 2nd line of the hemistich.

This same tendency to introduce variety is also noticed in the case of the *Triṣṭubh* and the *Jagati* lines. The Vedic poets were gradually becoming conscious of a different kind of music, which could be produced by the alternation of short and long letters. By the end of the saṁhitā period, the earlier metrical music based on the modulation of voice to different pitches and tunes seems to have been generally given up in preference to the kind of music based on the alternation of short and long sounds. The older music was taken up for a special treatment and development by the schools of the *Sāmaveda* and the growth of the different *Rāgas* and *Rāgiṇis* in the Indian music must surely be traced to their original and early efforts. The Gāthās in the Brāhmaṇa literature are found existing in the three different prominently Vedic metres, namely, the *Anuṣṭubh*, the *Triṣṭubh* and the with occasional metrical lapses or licences.

Piṅgala defines four different groups of *Viṣama Vṛttas* viz. *Vaktra* group, the *padacaturūrdhva* group, the *Udgatā* group and the *Upasthitapacupita* group. These are arranged in accordance with the ascending order of the number of syllables which their first lines contain. The chief metre of the second group of the Viṣama Vṛtas is *Padacaturdhva*, the four lines of which respectively contain 8,12,16 and 20 letters in them. The peculiarity of this group is that there are no restrictions whatsoever, about the use of short or long letters at the different places in their lines. In this respect it closely resembles the Vedic metres. The number of letters which is divisible by 4, in the different lines also show the influence of the *Gāyatrī* and the *Jagati* lines. Among the *Visama Vṛttas*, the *Vaktra* and the *Padacaturūrdhva* groups show the influence of the Vedic metres.

(1) The Vedic metres are much less regular than the classical metres. There is no hard and first rule regarding the quantity and order, of the several letters. The total number of syllables is the only criterion of distinguishing one metre from another.

From the metrical point of view, the Ṛgveda is made up of hymns, each of which consists of a certain number of verses and each verse consists of two or more feet, and each foot consists of a certain number of syllables.

Significance of Anuṣṭubh Metre

The *Anuṣṭubh* metre occupies a unique position in Vedic Prosody. The word *Anuṣṭubh* itself is used in more than one sense. In works on Vedic and Classical Sanskrit Prosody, the word *Anuṣṭubh* is used, not for a particular metre, but for the class of metres wherein there are four lines (*pada* quarter), each *Pada* consisting of eight syllables (cf. Triṣṭubh and Jagati- which also are class-names of metres).

According to Ait. Br. (III.47), the metres having carried the oblation to the gods, get tired and stand at the back of the sacrifice, just as a horse or a mule stands having carried its load. One should give to them the *devikā*- offerings (i.e. oblations to the minor deities after the sacrificial cake of the animal offering to Mitra and Varuna. To Dhātṛ he should offer a sacrificial cake on twelve potsherds. Dhaar is the *Vasaṭ* call. Then he should offer *Caru* to Anumati, Raka, Sinivale and Kuhu, who are identified with the metres *Gāyatri, Tṛṣṭubh, Jagati* and *Anuṣṭubh* respectively.

In his introduction to Brāhmaṇas Haug points out that the power of the Hotṛ priest at a sacrifice lay in his being able to use the sacred words frequently personified by *Vāk*. The sacred words, pronounced rightly by the *Hotṛ* prist, effect, by the innate power of *Vāk,* the spiritual birth of the sacrificer, shape his body, secure leaver for him, cause him to live a hundred years, and procure him wealth and offspring, will stay his enemies and destroy the conseqnced against a of his sins. But pronounced against a man by the prist or his enemies world will curse him unless he finds other words more powerful to counteract the hostile spell. The influence lies mainly in the form or metre in which the given words are uttered; hence the importance of metre, terms and words. Each metre is specially influential in the securing of some particular bon. The *Gāyatri* metre is the most sacred and is the proper metre for Agni. It expresses the idea of *Brahma*. Therefore the sacrificer must use it when he wishes anything closely connected with *Brahma*, such as acquirement of sacred knowledge. The *Triṣṭubh* expresses the idea of strength and royal power; It is the proper metre by which Indra is to be invoke. The *Uṣṇi* is to be employed by a sacrificer who aspires for longevity. The *Jagati* is to be used by an aspirant of wealth. The same idea is expressed by the *Paṅkti* metre. The *Bṛhati* is to be used when a sacrificer is aspiring to fame and renown. The *Anuṣṭubh* is the symbol of the celestical world. He who seeks a place in heaven should make his prayer in it. The aspirant of abundance of food should employ the *Virāja* metre.

Conclusion

Thus in the evolution of Vedic prosody, the Vedic Saṁhitas from the rudimentary stave of prosody. After *sutra* period the work of porosody got decreased. After the *Vṛttamuktāvali* works on Vedic porosody have almost disappeared. Even in classical period also many qualities of Vedic prosody have dominated. Besides the number of syllables, the syllabic instants also are given importance in the classical prosody. Measuring the length of syllabus is rare in Vedic prosody. But is is a determining factor of metres in classical period. Foot division is taken from the Vedic porosody.

Thus the prosody has undergone several stages of development findings its ultimate fulfilment in *Kāvya* literature. In this process, Vedic prosody has transferred its structure into classical prosody. The sanctity of the subject has been transformed into a literary charm. In fact, the decadence of Vedic prosody is not decay but a change of phase. Since the Vedas are the eternal streams of knowledge, the prosodial laws that govern the Vedic compositions are also everlasting.

References

1. Arnold, Vernon, *Vedic Metre,* Motilal Banarasidass, Delhi, 1967.
2. Dange, S.S. (Edited) *Sacrifice in India Concept & Evolution,* Viveka Publications, Aligarh, 1987.
3. Mimamsak, Yudhisthira, *Vaidika Chandomīmāṁsā.*
4. Mukherji, Amulyadhan, *Sanskrit Prosody: Its Evolution,* Sarasvat Library; Calcutta 1976.
5. Murty Rani Sadasiva. *Vedic Prosody, Its Nature, Origin and Development,* Vohra Publishers & Distributors, Allahabad, 1988.
6. Sukthankar, V.S, *Vedic Metre in Ghate's Lecturer on Ṛgveda.* Oriental Book Agency, Poona, 1926.
7. Velankar, H.D. Ed., *Jayadāman* (A Collection of four Prosodial Texts), Haritoshamala Publishers.

Vedic Hostile Groups and Individuals

15

Dr. U. Chakravarty

Introduction

The Vedic Aryans' identification of the enemy or objects of their hatred changed concurrently with the development of their settlement in the new land. In the first phase of settlement in the new land. In the first phase of settlement they had to fight with the obstructing aborigines whom they called *dāsa-s* or *dasyu-s* when they fought under the leadership of Indra, their war god. In short and precise style the Ṛgvedic poets narrate extensively these conflicts with their defeated enemies. Sometimes different Aryan groups also fought against each other the Indra-worshippers against the non-Indra-worshippers. The Dāśārajña war is the best example in this regard.

Concurrently with the advancement of settlement in the land where they had migrated sacrifice became the cardinal issue of life. The term *devāsura* emerged to signify aryans and non-Aryans (*dāsa-dasyu-s*). This change is more mainfest in the *TAIS* and the Brāmaṇas which belong to the second phase of the Vedic literature. Both the devas and the asuras were, however, Prajāpati's children. Prajāpati favoured too much his weaker group of sons, i.e. the devas and was partial to them against the stronger group, i.e. the asuras. Nonetheless actual fights were not necessary for the suppression of enemies. Through prescribed ritualistic processes like performance of sacrifices, chanting hymns etc. the enemy could be overpowered.

By the age of the Vedāṅga literature belonging to the last phase of the Vedic epoch society had taken a definite shape under the guardianship of ritualists. There hardly remained any enemy to be actually fought against; what remained was individual rivalry, and the ritualists prescribed ritualistic means to overcome these rivals. Life became very realistic. The veil of mythology (cf. *devāsura*) was totally shed for ever.

SAṂHITĀ PERIOD

The Ṛgveda

The *Ṛgveda,* the sole source of knowledge to be gathered about the earliest phase of Vedic life, bears a religious stamp all along. The other aspects of life like, social, familial, historical and the like are to be inferred from the imagery used in the verses and sometimes of course from the texts directly. Consequently, there remains the possibility for drawing wrong conclusions. Today, as a considerable amount of works on the subject has been published, things have become much easier than it was with our predecessors, our pathfinders.

The Aryans entered India in different waves. We are mainly concerned here with the Vedic Aryans who belonged to the last wave of this long stream of migration. Their war god (war hero?) was Indra. They drove horse-drawn chariots and used the invincible weapon *vajra* against their enemies. These two privileges put them in an advantageous position and earned them numerous victories over their enemies, both Aryans and non-Aryans.

We shall deal first with the stories of enmity between Aryans and non-Aryans and then with the hostility between different Aryan groups.

Aryans *vs* non-Aryans

Dasyu-s, Dāsas and also the *paṇis* stand mainly for the non-Aryan enemies. In fact, it is very difficult to distinguish the *dasyu-s* from the *dāsa-s*. Beneveniste (1969, [Eng. tr. 1973, p. 260]) in course of his discussion on the ethnic interpretation of the dasyu (India) and *dahyu* (Iran) observes : "In India, *dasyu* may be taken as an ethnic. The *dasyus* are a foreign people which the Aryans had to fight; they are barbarians, slaves......." On the Iranian *dahyu* he observes : "But in Iranian, dahyu is a part of the traditional and official vocabulary. Darius proclaims himself as 'king of countries' (dahyu). this is a reference to each of the'countries' Persia, Media, Armenia, Egypt etc., the union of which constitutes the Achaemenid empire." About the *dāsa-s* Benveniste says : "An eastern Iranian dialect, Khotanese possesses the word *daha* 'man'.... in the Iranian world there was a people, ... Dahae, as they are called by the Latin authors. This people, like many others, simply called themselves 'the men!' Later (p. 301) Benvenists observes:'...in India *ārya* serves as the antithetic form to *dāsa*—'stranger, slave, enemy'. R. S. Sharma (1977-78, p.1) links up Iranian dahyu and *dahae* with Indian *dasyu* and *dāsa* by saying that the *dasyu-s* were Indo-Iranian migrants in Indian soil. They, however, belonged to one of the earliest waves to cross the Hindukush. By the time the Vedic Aryans came they were fully'acculaturated' to the non-Aryan cultures which "accounts the condemnation of their way of life by the Ṛgvedic 'Aryans'. They on their part also resisted the new immigrants. According to Sharma the dāsa-s who corresponded to the Iranian Dahae, were also Indo-style and so did not become "prominent targets of the Aryan attacks as the dasyus do." The frequent occurrence of the word *dasyuhtya* in its different derivative forms like *dasyuhatyāya, dasyuhatye, dasyuhatyeṣu* and the total absence of *dāstahatya* go in favour of Sharma's view (see *ibid.*, p.1). But at the same time, as regards many other points in connection with the exploration of vedic society, we fail to produce any historical or archaeological data in support of the view on the chronology of the immigration of the *dāsa-s* and *dasyu-s*.[1]

The Paṇis were the other group of enemies of the Aryas. The word is connected with Greek *pernēmi* meaning something like niggard.[2] The Paṇis, as described by the Ṛgvedic poets, are rich, miserly and the main ground of their contention with the Aryans was, they were non-sacrificing and so non-givers of *dakṣiṇā.* The Paṇis are, however, not referred to in the *ṚV.* so frequently as the *dasyu-s* or the *dāsa-s.* the *ṚV.*, also except for the feeling of hatred, does not record direct clashes between the Aryans and the Paṇis. Gonda (1975, p. 97) observes : "The Paṇis are the mythical prototypes of the reprehensible and detestable wealthy niggards who do not give offering to the gods or *dakṣiṇā* to the priest."

The Dāsa-s and the Dasyu-s

On their onward march towards the new home the Aryans were quite naturally obstructed by the aborigines called *dāsa-s* and *dasyu-s* by the Aryans. Quite a few of these Aryan non-Aryan conflicts are recorded in the Ṛgvedic hymns. The theme of principal hymns dedicated to Indra, is naturally Indra's glorification through the narration of his heroic feats performed to give protection to his followers against the non-Aryan attacks. Basing our discussion on the Vedic texts we shall attempt to decipher history, as history lies at the base of mythology though in a very garbled or veiled manner.

Kutsa *vs* Śuṣṇa

Kutsa fought under Indra's leadership against Śuṣṇa and Kuyava, his dāsa-enemies. Indra fought directly against Śuṣṇa; he also applied magic power (māyā) against his enemy (I.11.7). Śuṣṇa's ramparts were devastated; Indra declared: "I am the killer of Śuṣṇa" (X. 49.3). Indra performed warlike feats for Kutsa's sake (VI. 26.3; VII. 19.20. Keith holds that Kutsa was a king.[3] Gonda (1975, p. 247) observes: "Thus there may possibly have existed more or less coherent story of Kutsa, the hero who is associated with Indra in the exploits of winning the.... demon Śuṣṇa.

Divodāsa Atithigva *vs* Sambara

In the list of Indra's protégés Atithigva come next to Kutsa in respect of the number of hymns referring to him. Dividāsa was the name and *atithigva* an epithet qualifying his hospitable nature (I.51.6). Divodāsa's greatest foe was the *dāsa* Sambara, a descendant of Kulitara (IV. 30.14). Sambara was the master of ninety (I. 130.7), ninety-nine (11.19.6) or a hundred (IV. 30.20) ramparts (*purah*).[4] Indra devastated those ramparts and killed Sambara (I.51.6). He also killed the non-Aryan enemies : Karañja and Parṇaya towards Atithigva's benefit (I. 53. 8).

Ṛjiśvan *vs* Pipru, Mṛgaya, Vaṅgṛda and Kṛṣṇa

Pipru was the strongest dasyu- enemy of Ṛjiśvan, whose cows had been śtolen by Pipru. They were recovered through Indra's grace (x. 99.11). Indra favoured Ṛjiśvan by destroying Pipru's numerous ramparts (I. 51. 5). Vaṅgṛda and Mṛgaya : Ṛjiśvan's two other enemies, Pipru and their 50,000[5] followers were killed by Indra (IV. 16. 13). Indra, assisted by Ṛjiśvan also killed the women of his very strong dāsa-enemy Kṛṣṇa :

Yaḥ Kṛṣṇagarbhā Nirahan Ṛjiśvanā : **(I. 101. 16)**

'who with Ṛjiśvan's assistance killed women of Kṛṣṇa (or black-breed ?).[6]

Purukutsa *vs* Śarat, the Dāsa

Purukutsa was imprisoned by his *dāsa* enemy Śarat. Through Indra's and Varuṇa's favour Purukutsānī, Purukutsa's wife, got a demi-god son who was named Trasadasyu. The name Trasadasyu suggests that he was 2 terror to his enemy. Through Indra's favour Śarat's seven ramparts were devastated and Purukutsa was blessed with prosperity (I. 63.7, 174.2. VI. 20. 10).

Babhru *vs* Namuci

The Vedic seer Babhru was Indra's ward. His cows were stolen by the dāsa Namuci. Namuci sent some women as weapons to Indra. Indra wondered, what harm could the women, do him. He, however, kept two of them and sent the others back.[7] He killed Namuci (v. 30.9-11). The *RV.* mentions only once (VIII. 14. 13) that Indra severed Namuci's head with foram, an event so frequently, mentioned in the alter Vedic literature (*Tai Br.* I. 7.1.6; *Vājas.* X. 14; *Sat Br.* V. 4.1.9. *et. al*).

No Ṛgvedic martial feat leading to the victory of the Vedic Aryaṇs is imaginable without Indra as their leader. He is represented in the relevant hymns as the performer of heroic feats more as a human chief, a war hero than as a god with an Olympian attitude[8]. This fact leads quite logically some scholars to look on Indra as a deified man : an euhemeristic deity.[9]

Very often the clue to the conflicts between the Aryan and the non-Aryan was cattle. V. 30. 10 narrates that the cows stolen by *dasyu-s* were recovered by Indra: these cows, separated from their calves, were moving helter skelter; altogether they, were four thousand in number (v. 30, 15).[10] One often comes across such cattle-lifting stories in the *Ṛgvedasamhitā*.

Aryans *vs* Aryans

Aryan immigration in Indian soil started long before the Vedic Aryans had arrived. They came in different waves. R. N. Dandekar (1985, p. 530 in the

Appendic of Umesh Sharma's *Dāṣarājña* states that there were two major waves of migration of Aryans into India. They were organised in tribal groups transformed into territorial states. Five of them became prominent; they were: Puru, Anu, Druhyu, Turvaṣa and Yadu; they are often referred to in the *ṚV.* as pañca janāḥ.[11] Side by side there were some non-Aryan settlements in and around the region also. Dandekar holds (*Ibid*, p. 54) that the Aryans arriving in the second wave were more homogenous. They constituted one single tribe, the tribe of the Bharatas. Sudās was their leader. We shall come to this point soon.

The Aryans not only fought with the non-Aryans, they also fought among themselves.[12] Dikshitar observes (1948, p. 42, Ist ed. 1944) : "War was inevitable in primitive communities as their was neither a social organisation nor a pronounced political status. In the earlier stages of civilization war was regarded as a normal feature of life. But with the growth of civilization, war comes to be looked upon as a serious business which should not be entered into recklessly and ruthlessly but should be governed by ethical and moral codes." Benveniste (1969, [Eng. tr. 1973, p. 299]) statues : "The relation between peace and war was once exactly the reverse of what it is today. For, peace is the normal condition, which is interrupted by a state of war; for the ancients, the normal state was war, to which peace puts an end."

We have already seen that Indra killed Śuṣṇa, Kuyava and Śambara for the sake of Kutsa and Atithugva. The young Suṣravas was probably a greater favourite of Indra. Suṣravas was attacked by twenty *janarāja-s*, i.e. tribal chiefs followed by their 60,099 people (I. 53.9); Indra fighting from his chariot vanquished them. Indra killed Kutsa, Atithigva and Āyu to favour Suṣravas (10). It becomes evident that either these three left Indra or Indra abandoned them. *ṚV.* VIII. 53.2 (Bālakhilya) also tells the same story.[13]

Dāsarājña

The best known story about enmity between the Aryans and the Aryans is the war between the ten (?) tribal chiefs on one side and the Bharatas and the Tṛtsus with Sudās as their leader on the other. This war is known as the Dāṣarājña, i.e. the battle of ten kings. Much work has already been done on this topic. With a view to giving the idea how the different Aryan groups fought among themselves. He attempt to give a gist of this story.[14] Bharatas, led by Sudās, belonged to the last wave of the Aryan immigration. There were already many Aryan tribes settled in different territories. Quite naturally, there were non-Aryan tribes too. Sudās ambitious idea led him to join the Tṛouses too. Sudās ambitious idea led him to join the Tṛtsus, another Aryan group; Sudās accepted their priest Vasiṣṭha as his priest also. According to ṚV. III. 33 earlier Visvāmitra was the priest of Sudās. Visvāmitra through his prayers made the rivers Śutudrī, Vipāṣ (1) etc. agree to bend their streams with Indra's co-operation (6) and thus made it possible for Sudās' troops along with their carts and chariots cross them smoothly in their downward march (9). Under Viṣvāmitra's priesthood Sudās was blessed with Indra's favour. The story, nevertheless, took a new turn in Book VII. This is an inference that Sudās considered Vasiṣṭha, the priest of the Tṛtsus, his allies, as more competent and accepted him as his priest. At this juncture, we believe, the seed of eternal rivalry between Visvāmitra and Vasiṣṭha was sown. Viśvāmitra reacted against Sydās behaviour. He joined Sudās opponents and organised them along with their non-Aryan allies against the Bharatas and the Tṛtsus. On the one side were the pre-Vedic Aryan tribes under the leadership of Puru, Yadu, Anu, Turvaṣa and Druhyu—the paṇca janāḥ with Viṣvāmitra as their priest and allied by non-Aryan peoples like Alinas, Pakthas, Bhalānases, Śivas, Viṣāṇins, and others. Number 'ten', however, is a round figure. On the other side were the Bharatas and Tṛtsus under the leadership of Sudās and Vasiṣṭha as the priest. Two principal battles were fought : one on the bank of the Yamunā against Ajas, Sigrus and Yakṣus under Bheda's leadership. According to VII. 18. 9. Indra plundered all the enemies of Sudās. The second and the greater battle was fought on the bank of the Paruṣṇī (modern Ravi) ending in a miserable defeat of the tribal chiefs, the non-believers in Indra (cf. *anindra* VII. 18.6).[15]

Dandekar observes (1985, p. 56) "I believe that the source of the name Bhāratavarṣa by which India came to be known is to be sought in this great historical event."

The above is a skeleton of the Dāṣarājña war.[16]

The Atharvaveda

"For all practical purposes. The *Ṛgveda* may be characterized as the Veda of the 'classes' and the *Atharvaveda* as the Veda of the 'masses'.[17] A people usually cannot live without some religious faith, preserved in the manifested forms of observance of rituals or worship which are conceptually endowed with the potency of magic power. It was beyond the means of the upholders of the Little Tradition to appoint priests who only had the right to perform the actual sacrifice and who had to be offered abundant dakṣiṇā at the end of the sacrifice, and also to fulfil other sacrifical prerequisites. The religious faith of the upholders of the AV. was popular in character which entails magic, incantations, imprecations, where the spirits govern the good and evil of life.

The Atharvanic way of fighting with the enemies was not in the battlefield as it was with the Ṛgvedic people and also not in the sacrificial ground as on, the brahmanical way.

Following the *AV.* a few instances of fighting with the enemies are mentioned below.

AV. I. 7. invokes Agni, the killer of dasyu and urges him to bring to the spot the sorcerer *(yātudhāna)*, the Kimidin (1). The idea of the seer of the hymn is : let them when brought to the sport be burnt by Agni (5). XIII.1 is dedicated to Rohita. It is a long hymn consisting of sixty verses. Verses 28, 29 and 31 pray to the god Agni to burn the enemies (ari) and slay them. The worshippers want to burn their enemies by the flesh-eating fire.[18]

Rivalry between two contending sacrificers is very vigorously expressed in VII. 70. 4. 5 :

api nahyāmi te bāhū api nahyāmy āsyam :

anger ghorasya manyunā tena te vadhiṣaṃ haviḥ : : VII. 70.5

I fasten back thine arms; I fasten up thy mouth: with the fury of terrible Agni-therewith have I smitten thy oblation.' (tr. Whitney, HOS VII, p. 435)

Intense feeling of enmity between individuals gets expression in the desire of stopping the progeny of the enemy by the application of cruel method as stated in VII. 35. 3 :

paraṃ yoner avaraṃ te kṛṇomi mā tvā prajābhi bhūn mota sūnuḥ

asvaṃ tvāprajasaṃ kṛṇomy aṣmānaṃ te apidhānaṃ kṛṇomi ::

The upper part of thy womb I make lower; let there not be progeny to thee, nor birth; I make thee barren *(asū)*, without progeny, I make a stone thy cover.' (tr. ibid, p. 411)

V. 20 and 21 are in praise of the war-drum. By means of the very loud sound of the wooden war-drum, as loud as the roarings of a lion, the enemy is to be driven away. The other purpose of beating the drum so loud is to collect the cattle together which have gone astray (20. 1; 2). By the loud sound the singer also intends to frighten the woman of the enemy, who out of fright would hold her son's hand for support (20.5). The enemy is designed to be thoroughly terrified by the terrific sound of the drum (20.11). All the gods invoked, may also by means of the sound of the drum, made of wood and hide, drive away the enemy (21.7). May Indra (21.8), may Āditya (21.10) co-operate with them by beating the drum.

The Atharvavedic singer desires ruin of his enemies :

men or women, in the following words :

yathā sūryo nakṣatrāṇām udyaṃs tejāṃsy ādade :

evā strīṇāṃ ca puṃsāṃ cā dviṣatāṃ varva ā dade :: VII. 13.1

'As the sun rising takes to itself the brilliancies (tejas) of the asterisms, so both women and men that hate me I take to myself the splendor. (tr. Whitney : HOS VII, p. 307)

An academic enemy is desired to be won over in a disputation by the use of a herb and the herb is addressed :

nec chatruḥ prāṣaṃ jayāti sahamānābhibhūr asi :

prāśaṃ pratiprāśo jahyarasān kṛṇvoṣadhe :: II. 27. 1

'May my foe by no means win (ji) the dispute, overpowering, overcoming art thou; smite the dispute of (my) counterdisputant; make them sapless, O herb.' (tr. Whitney, HOS VII, p. 67).

The Brāhmaṇas

Before we enter our discussion on the feeling of enmity as presented in the Brāhmaṇa literature we take it for granted that the words 'asura' and 'deva', so frequently used in this branch of Vedic literature, stand for 'non-Aryan' and 'Aryan'[19] respectively.

(a) Asuras, the original owners of this land

The asuras originally possessed this land, the devas lived as their subordinates. The gods, however, by dint of their intelligence and perseverance brought the asuras under their control. *Jaimi Br.* III. 117 states : *asurāṇāṃ ha vai agra ime lokā āsuḥ : upajīvina iva hi devā āsuḥ :* The same Brahmaṇa (III. 352) again states that the gods by their hard labour vanquished the asuras and the rakshas : *devā vai ṣrameṇa tapasā brahmacaryeṇāsurān rakṣāṃsy abhyabhavan.* Such statements definitely point to the historical backdrop of the Aryan settlement in India.

(b) Asura : South *(dakṣiṇa)*

In contrast to the Ṛgvedasaṃhitā which often mentions the names of enemies, their military strength etc. with regard to both, the Aryans and the non-Aryans the Brāhmaṇas refer to two classes of enemies, the 'asuras' and the 'rakṣases'; 'asuras' occurs more frequently than 'rakṣases'. The 'enemy' lost its individual identity. This probably indicates the loss of intensity of the feeling of enmity and so consequently diminution of actual fights. In fact, the devas[20] and the asuras did not have actual fights against each other; the devas drove away the asuras by observance of prescribed rituals. South *(dakṣiṇa)* became the home of the asuras and the rakṣases; the devas were scared of this direction and had always suffered from the feat that the enemies might at any time come from the South and spoil their sacrifice, *Śat Br.* IV. 2. 4. 19 : 6 Now, once on a time, the gods while performing sacrifice, were afraid of an attack from the asura-rakshas. The asura-rakshas assailed them from the South, and overturned those southern cups of Soma,—even that southern Soma-cart they overturned : ...' (tr. Eggeling, SBE 26. p. 303).[21]

This frequent mention of the association of the asuras and the rakṣases with the Southern direction takes us back to the early historical background. Being defeated by the powerful Aryans, the aboriginal people fled away towards south or sometimes, probably, they were driven away towards that direction by the victors. As the Vedic Aryans entered India from the north-west through the Hindukush so quite naturally southern part of the land gradually became the home of a group of defeated non-Aryans, beacause/they either refused to be the slaves of the victors, or they refused to accept their sacrifice-oriented religious faith or they were simply driven away. The author of the *Śat Br.* IV. 2.4.19 (already referred to) narrates what happened in the past as he starts his narration with "Once on a time' etc.

(c) 'Who hates us and whom we hate'

(yo 'Smān dveṣṭi yaṃ ca vayaṃ dviṣmaḥ)

All the branches of vedic literature have very frequently used the above expression yo 'smān dveṣṭi etc. except for the *Ṛgveda* and *Sāmaveda.* According to the *Vedic Concordance* (p. 814) this expression occurs around 140 times in the Vedic literature (from the Saṃhitās to the Sūtras). The frequent use of this expression reveals the sense of insecurity from which Vedic Aryans suffered, causing a feeling of enmity towards their enemies, the non-sacrificing aborigines. Sense of insecurity arouses suspicion in man which leads to the feeling of enmity.

Av.XVI. 7. 5 : *Yo smān dveṣṭi tam ātmā dveṣtu*
yaṃ vayam dvismaḥ sa ātmānaṃ dveṣtu:

'whoso hates us, him let [his] self (ātman) hate; whom so we hate, let him hate [his] self.[22] (tr. Whitney, HOS VIII, p. 800).

Tais. I. 2. 5.1 : yo *'smān dveṣṭi yañ ca vayaṃ diṣma idam asya grīvāpi Kṛtāmi*

'Thus I cut the neck of him who hates us and whom we hate.'

(tr. Keith, HOS XVIII, p. 25)

Śat Br. I. 8. 3. 1—4 drives away enemies by repetitious utterance of yo 'smān dveṣṭi etc. along with other words bearing similar sense of hatred and rivalry. Śat Br. VI. 6. 3. 11. comprises the extreme example of this feeling of hatred against the enemy. First the story of the gods is alluded to, they made food of them who hate them and whom they hate (*yaścainān dveṣṭi yañca dvisuh*) and gave them upto Agni, they then became Agni's food and Agni burnt up the evil of the gods. Following the gods' path the Vedic sacrificer also makes food of him whom he hates and who hates him and gives him to Agni. The victim becomes Agni's food and thus Agni burns up the sacrificer's evil.[23] This appears to be an instance of sacrificing human beings in fire in order to make the sacrificer free from evils.

Doubts arise in the mind, was it possible to live a perfectly mentally healthy life with so much feeling of hatred against those who did not belong to their tradition and religious discipline. Or, we could say, this was not a Vedic problem, rather this is a universal and eternal problem.

(d) Devāsura

The contests between *dāsa-dasyu-s* and the Aryans of the *ṚV.* now take up the name *devāsura*. The devas and the asuras were in conflict (*devāsurā saṃyattā agan*)—this sentence is repeated numerous times in the Tais, and in different Brāhmaṇas.[24] According to *Ṣaḍvi Br.* I. 2. 1. when the Subrahmaṇya priest invokes at that moment the asura-rakshas attack the sacrifice.

The devas suffered from a constant fear from the asuras. According to Tais, VI. 2.2.6 the devas out of fear entered Agni. *Ait Br.* II. 16 states that the gods apprehended that the asuras might take away their morning sacrifice as they were stronger.[25] The devas realised their deficiency; they did not have a chief, a king; hence they decided to have a king and unanimously agreed to make Indra their king. Indra was crowned with all grandeur. *Ait Br.* VIII. 14 states : 'Anoited with this great anointment Indra won all victories, found all the worlds, attained the superiority, pre-eminence and supremacy over all the gods....'[26] Dikshitar (1944, p. 3) rightly thinks that the non-Aryans had already kingship among them which the Aryans adopted from them: "if we are to identify the devas and the asuras with the Aryans and the Dravidians, the testimony of history supports the earlier advancement of political institutions among the Dravidians which served the Indo-Aryans a model.' This conjecture of Dikshitar tallies with *Jaimi Br.* III. 117 : *asurāṇāṃ ha : vā agra ime lokā āsuḥ* - already referred to.

(e) Devas and Asuras : Children of Prajāpati

It is very surprising to note that these two groups of deadly enemies were both Prajāpati's children.[27] *Śat Br.* v. 1. 1. 1. tells us that these two groups of Prajāpati's children contested against each other. The asuras were too arrogant. They therefore offered into their own mouths : "Unto whom, forsooth, should we make offering". This arrogance was the cause of their downfall.[28]

(f) Prajāpti : a Partial Father

It is all the more surprising to notice Prajāpati's step-fatherly behaviour towards asuras, the group of his elder sons (*BṛĀra* U. 1. 3. 1).

A few instances in this regard : According to the *Pañcavi Br.* VIII. 3. 1. the devas and the asuras contended for these worlds. The defeated devas resorted to Prajāpati who gave them the Kāleya Sāman by means of which the devas drove away the asuras. The same Brāhmaṇa XVIII. 1.2-4 tells us that Prajāpati who gave them the Kāleya Sāman by means of which the devas drove away the asuras. The same Brāhmaṇa XVIII. 1. 2. -4 tells us that Prajāpati secretly meditated and found the Upahavya sacrifice and gave it to the devas who consequently became prosperous by defeating the asuras. One may question, why did Prajāpati secretly meditate for the Upahavya? He did so because prosperous by defeating the asuras. One may question, why did Prajāpati secretly meditate for the Upahavya? He did so because otherwise the asuras might destroy it.

Ṣadviṃśa Brāhmaṇa V. 1. 1. gives a clear picture of Prajāpati as a partial father. He underwent penance with the desire to create devas. He created them during the day he also created the asuras at night. As they were created during the day (*divā*) so they were devas and as the asuras were created when there was no sun (*sūra*) so they are asuras.

Prajāpati who is mentioned only six times in the ṚV plays a very important role in the Brāhmanas.

(g) Battlefileld Turned into Sacrifical Ground

Numerous conflicts between the devas and the asuras are referred to in the Brāhmaṇa literature and also in the *Tais*. The difference between the Ṛgvedic and the Brāhmanial contests lies in the fact, that the venue of the latter's contests was shifted to the sacrificial ground from the actual battlefield. The battles which the devas fought against their enemies were not with *vajra* or riding on the horse-driven chariots, but by means of different ritualistic measures like building the altar, utterance of corresponding mantras, use of sacrificial laddles like *juhū* upabhṛi[29] and the like. The background is a mythological warfield but the actual venue is the sacrificial ground. Heesterman (1993, p. 48) very rightly observes : "While the rules deploy a comprehensive and exhaustive order regulating each move and each utterance with painful precision, the mythological explanations speak of an entirely different order. They continually refer to conflict, contest and battle. The devas and their adversaries, the asuras are for ever fighting each other."

Upasad is a ritual related to the Jyotiṣṭoma sacrifice. The word *upasad* literally means a 'siege'. We shall try to find out how these two unrelated phenomena, i.e. a military operation and a religious rite, bore identical name. According to the *Ait Br.* I. 23 the asuras who had constant fights with the gods (cf. *devāsurā vāeṣu lokeṣu samayatanta* etc.) transformed the three regions, i.e. the earth, the atmosphere and heaven into three citadels made of iron, and gold respectively in order to protect them from the attacks of the gods. The response from the gods' side, in this respect, however, was not belligerant. They innovated as a means for counterpoising the sadas, the Agnidh's altar and the two oblation-holders (havirathāne). Then the gods introduced three upasad-5 a kind of ritual. As in life, through the *upasad-s* (i.e. siege) one besiges the enemies' citadels so through the performance of the three *upasad-s* the gods repelled the three citadels, made of iron, silver and gold belonging to the *asuras*.

Likewise, life was made free from enemies (*asapatna*) by laying 'foeless' (asapatna) bricks while building the sacrificial altar (*Śat Br.* VIII. 5. 1. 4.)[30].

Indra's thunderbolt once devastated row of enemies. In the Brāhmaṇas it has been equated with the eight-cornered sacrificial post (*astāsri yūpa*), [31] with spade (*abhri*)[32] and with clarified butter (ājya)[33]. All these show that the ends which the Ṛgvedic Aryans achieved in the battlefield could now be achieved in the sacrificial ground. Jaimi Br. I. 105 tells us that the devas desired to conquer all the worlds in order to vanquish enemies. The ājya chants were revealed to them and they conquered all the worlds by chanting them. *BāĀrau.* I 3. 1-7 states that the gods and the asuras were the children of Prajāpati. The younger ones were the devas and the elders the asuras. The asuras had been overpowering the devas. The devas planned to kill them by chanting the Udgītha Sāman; after long endeavours the gods achieved their ends.

With the battle scenes pushed off the background, and with the emergence of importance of sacrifice in life, society became more or less stable. The Vedic Aryans needed not to fight with enemies any more for their survival. Society had started to flourish centering around sacrifice and community life had become primanity agrarian. Dandekar (1977, p. 324) holds : "The later Vedic literature shows a considerable advance in material culture... The society of the later Vedic period had become essentially agrarian with a more than subsistence economy."[34]

(h) Family Feuds

The *Jaiminīya Brāhmaṇa* provides us with glimpses into family feuds. In the story of *Śākamāṣva's* son *Vyaśva* and his uncle Gaya (III. 221) we find a jealous and revengeful uncle in Gaya. After knowing that his nephew who was going to be born soon, would be a seer *(ṛṣi)*, Gaya, the irate uncle, planned to kill the baby. He ordered his people to kill the baby as soon as it was born : "This is a baby who is to be killed at its birth". When the first attempts failed Gaya threw a musala (thunderbolt/Club/mace?) at the baby. Unfortunately for Gaya the musala hit back him and killed him through Vyasva's prayer. One observes a very selfish, cruel; and intolerant uncle in Gaya.

This story has been narrated in praise of Vaivṣva *Sāman : gātuṃ nāthaṃ vindevahi sam ayaṃ kumāro Jīvat* etc.... Vyaśva, the new born baby, saved its life against its uncle's rages by reciting this *Sāman.*

In the story (cf. *JaimiBr.* III. 72-74) of Kaṇva, the son of Nṛṣada, who married Khagāsura's daughter, one sees Aryan and non-Aryan conflict and also family feud. Khagāsura's daughter gave birth to two sons of Kaṇva : Trisoka and Nābhāka. Displeased with her husband Khagāsura's daughter returned to her relatives. Nonetheless, Kaṇva followed her. The asuras planned to kill Kaṇva by making him blind. He was saved through the Aśvins favour (see Ṛv. I. 47. 5; 117. 8; 118.7). The asuras made a second attempt on his life. His two sons from Khagāsura's daughter saved him this time.

This story has been narrated in praise of Nābhāka and Triśoka Sāmans.

This is also a story of intermarriage between Aryans and non-Aryans. Two people living side by side have to exchange each other's culture, customs, hearts knowingly or unknowingly. The extreme feeling of emity and hatred between these two peoples came down along different channels. Keith (1922, p. 86) infers such marriages even in the age of *ṚV.* : "We must therefore recognise that in the age of the Ṛgveda there was going on a steady process of amalgamation of the invaders and the aborigines, whether through the influence of intermarriage with slaves or through friendly and peaceful relations with powerful Dāsa tribes."

(i) Personal Rivalry

A few references related to the feeling of enmity, not classified are mentioned below :

AitBr. VIII. 28 states in clear language what should be the vow of a person in relation to his enemy : "His vow is 'One should not sit down before the foe; if he thinks him to be standing, he should stand also. Nor should he lie down before the foe; if he think him to be sitting he should sit also. Nor should he go to sleep before the foe; if he think him awake, he should keep awake also. Even if his enemy has a head of stone, swiftly he lays him low."[35] tr. Keith, HOS 25, p. 343).

The above, we believe, refers to individuals rivalry.

A rivalry between the two neighbouring sacrificers is observed in Saṃsava— a sin incurred by one of the two who has been initiated later for a soma sacrifice, intended to be performed at the same time. The gods will come to the sacrifice of the one who has been initiated earlier and not to his neighbour.[36]

ṢadviBr. I. 1. 25. tells us that the Aryans (Indra) applied the technique of espionage in their warcraft. The story in brief is : Gautama was roaming among the asuras and also simultaneously practising his penance. Indra requested him to act as a spy for them while roaming about among the asuras. On Gautama's refusal, Indra decided to assume the form of Gautama and work as a spy.

ŚRAUTASŪTRAS

The ṚV. acquinted us with enemies to be fought in battlefield entailing killings, loot (esp. cattle), women fighting (cf. Vispalā and the *dāsa* women of Namuci) so on and so forth. The Brāhmaṇas take us to the peaceful world of ritual through the veil of war scene (cf. *devāsurā saṃyattā āsan*). The Śrautasūtra lead us straight away to a fully settled society based on sacrifice and ritual. Almost all problems of life of this society are now solved by the observance of ritual. For each and every minute problem of life, especially, religious, the ritualists set down ritualistic remedy. Consequently, one could suppress one's enemy by adopting ritual-based measures. This trend of becoming the Vedic society fully ritual-oriented started with the *Iais*, and it is not extinct in the Hindu society even today.

We are referring here only to two such examples of overcoming rivals by performing ritual out of innumerable instances in the Śrauta literature. "One who desires to overcome his rivals (should offer the *upāṃśu* oblation) to Agni-Soma."[37] The next goes about Agnihotra offering. After offering the relevant offerings the sacrificer has some more rituals to observe : "If he views with person inferior to himself, he should (think of that person and) press his right heel upon the ground with *nimrado* "si..... If he vies with his equal, he should press his right foot upon the ground towards the south uttering *abhibhūr asi*..... If he vies with a person superior to himself, he should press front part of his right foot upon the ground uttering *paribhūr asi*..'[38]

A human being is a combination of good and bad elements; he cannot live in a blissful mental state with no malice to anybody. He loves some one and at the same time hates another. The latter could be subdued, as the ritualists belived, by following ritual-based measure. This state of total dependence on the potency of rituals shows that the Vedic society which had its inception in the Ṛgvedic period, and was nomadic in its initial stage, had now become pretty old in around thousand years. There was no more constant threat to life due to the resistance from the *dāsa-dasyu* enemies and the identity of the enemy had changed and consequently also the method of suppressing the enemy had undergone a change. Society had become by now fully settled presenting its good and evil facets more clearly.

Summing Up

The Vedic Aryan' identity of the enemy changed along with the varied situations they had undergone in course of their settling down in the new land. The conflicts and contests described in the RV., the earliest literature of the Vedic Aryans, may be classified under two categories : Aryans vs. non-Aryans and Aryans vs. Aryans. The Aryans called their enemies, the earlier inhabitants of the land of their migration *dāsa-s and dasyu-s*. The two words, i.e. *dāsa* and *dasyu* have link with the Iranian words *dahyu* and *daha*. The Aryans, the Indra-worshippers, had all along been the winners of the battles they fought against their enemies, Aryans or non-Aryans. They likked their non-Aryan enemies in large numbers, captured their cattle, destroyed their ramparts (*pur*) and the like. The second category of battles which the Aryans fought against their Aryan enemies comprises along with others the famous earliest recorded historical war, the *dāsarājñā* which literally means (war) against the ten kings. Indra's protege Sudās, the chief of the Bharata tribes, assisted by the tribe called the Tṛtsus, under the able guidance of the priest Vasiṣṭha, fought against the five Aryan tribes (*pañca janāḥ*) who were probably the earlier settlers and who on their part were joined by five non-Aryan tribes. Thus was formed the group of enemy comprising around ten kings (cf. *dāśarājña*). The *Atharvaveda* prescribes Atharvanic way, i.e. application of incantation, imprecation etc. to fight against the enemy : belligerent, social or academic.

The Brāhmaṇa literature introduces the term *devāsura* which never occurred in the earlier literature. The devas and the asuras stood for the Aryans and the non-Aryans respectively. All these lands originally belonged to the asuras *(jaimiBr.* III. 147); the gods overpowered the asuras by their endeavours, austerity and penance (*ibid* iii. 352)... such statements bear history. The repeated mention that the soutern direction (*dakṣiṇa*) was for the asuras; that the devas drove them towards the south, that the devas were always scared of associating themselves with the southern direction also hint at the historical backdrop : the Aryans entered India from the north-west through Hindukush and drove the defeated enemies to the south. Or, the devastated enemies saved themselves from, the rage of their enemies by fleeing to the south, the home of the Dravidians. The devas constantly suffered from the threat that they might be attacked by the enemy; the oft-quoted expression in the vedic literature : who hates us and whom we hate' *(yo' smān dveṣṭi yañ ca vayaṃ dviṣmaḥ)* speaks of this fear of the Aryans. They even thought of burning the enemies by offering them to the Fire-god (*Śat Br.* VI. 6. 3. 11). What, however, is suprising is that the two groups of enemies were children of Prajāpati. This might hint at the frequent intermarriage between the Aryans and the non-Aryans. The devas were Prajāpati's weaker children approached by his weaker group of sons Prajāpati suggested, innovated rituals, chants, hymns etc. for them by the application of which they defeated the asuras. Though the texts constantly speak about contests between devas and asuras but in fact the battles as fought between two groups of enemies according to the Ṛgvedic literature, were not fought any longer; the enemies were now put down by observance of rituals. Though a warlike screen we enter an atmosphere of peace. That the real battles yielded place to rituals tells us that the Vedic Aryans now attained stability. They had achieved this mainly through adoption of a regular agrarian system and intermarriage with the non-Aryans.

The Śrautasūtras speak of a society which took a definite shape standing on the structure of four castes (*caturvarṇa*). The ritualists were the real guardians of this society who formulated rules in details in codes, covering all aspects of life, especially religious. The atmosphere of war with the description of which we started this discussion disappeared in around a thousand years by the age of the Śrautasūtras.

References

1. Also see Nath, 1996, pp. 19; 48; 51.
2. See Keith, 1922, p. 86
3. See Keith : The *Religion and Philosophy of the Veda and Upaniṣads*, HOS 31, p. 130.

4. Wilhelm Rau (1976, p. 41) Summarises his research on pur, mainly based on the Vedic texts in the following words "

   "A *pur* consisted of one or several concentric ramparts on a round or oval ground-plan.... was built of mud or stone...'

   Was fortified with combustible defence, certainly prickly shrubs.....,

   was furnished with wooden sheds as quarters for human occupants.....'

   Was stocked with provisions, water and grass or fodder for cattle...'

   Was not permanently occupied but served mainly as a refuge in times of danger.....,

   was erected in war as a protection, a base of operations, or a beleaguering camp.....".

   Probably needed repairs after each rainy season...."

   Also see Zimmer, 1879, p. 148; Keith, 1922, p. 86; Chakravarty, 1997, p. 171 n. 111.

5. In several places of the ṚV. We come across statements consisting of huge number of enemy-people killed by Indra. IV. 30.21 states that Indra killed 30,000 enemies for the sake of his protege Dabhiti. Susravas was attacked by twenty chiefs who were escorted by 60,099 people (ṚV. I. 53. 9). More instances could be quoted. This is very true that the Ṛv. is not a history book but such statements bear elements of history. The number mentioned in the verse may not be exact yet such statements hint at the historical backdrop.

6. Also see Chakravarty, 1997, p. 172n. 114.

7. Jaiswal (1989-90. p. 140 in course of her discussion on the conflicts between the Aryans and *dāsa-dasyu-s* refers to ṚV V. 30. 9. The verse is quoted below :

   a. *striyo hi dāsa āyudhāni carkre*

   b. *kiṃ mā karann avalā asya senāḥ :*

   c. *Antar hy akhyad ubhe asya dhene*

   d. *Athopa praid yudhaye dasyum indraḥ ::*

   It talks about the Indra-Namuci Contest. Her point of discussion is, in contrast to Aryan tradition the non-Aryan women took part in warfare. She add : "They may have had certain matriarchal traits". In the Aryan tradition we get only one instane of queen Viśpalā (I. 116. 15) who lost her thigh (and not leg as mentioned by Jaiswal) which was replaced by metal (*āyasī*) thing by the Aśvins. Cf. ṚV. I. 116. 16 C : *sadyo jaṅghām āyasiṃ vispalāyai*

   What we are aiming at is the interpretation of the word *dhene* (c) which has been interpreted by Jaiswal as female breasts. This of course goes in accordance with Geldner (ee HOS 34, p. 28 "Frauenbrüste"). But neither Sāyaṇa, nor St. Petersburg dictionary, nor Grassmann (1936, p. 695), nor Griffith interprets dhenā as (in Acc. dual *dhene*) as 'female breasts'. According to them dhenā menas a milch cow. Women in the Ṛv are often compared with cow and men with bull for obsious reasons. We also would like to interpret dhene here (V. 30. 9 c) as 'women', sent by Namuci to Indra, and not 'female *breests*'. This intepretation which is lexically more authentic, does not bring any difference in the context and also avoids unnecessary and imposed cruelty and ugliness of thought.

8. A glimpse into a list of the Aryans' non-Aryan enemies is given below. This may, however, include some of their atmospheric enemies also :

   Ahīśuva, Anarṣani, Sṛbinda (VIII. 32.2.26; 77.1, 2, 3), Ahnavāyya (VIII. 45. 27), Aṃh (I. 63, 7), Araru (I. 129.3; X. 99.10), Arbuda (I. 51.6; II. 11.20; 14.4; VIII. 3. 19; 32.26), Arsasana (II. 20.6), Aṣna (II. 14.5) Daśoṇi, Ibha, Tugra, Tūtuji, Vetasu (VI. 20.8), Dṛbhīka (II. 14.3), Duhya (?), Śruta, Kavasa, Vrddha (VII. 18.12), Gandharva (VIII. 77.5)—(cf. Avestan Ganderwa), Karañja, Parṇaya (I. 53.8), Krivi (II. 17. 6; 22.2); Kuṇāru (III. 30.8); Kuyavāca (I. 174. 7); Mṛgaya (X. 49.5); Nārmara, Sahavasu (II. 13.8), Navavāstva, Bṛhadṛatha (x. 49.6), Ourṇavābha (VIII. 32.26), Rauhiṇa (I. 103.

2); II. 12.12), Ṣaṭgṛbhi (x. 49. 5), Sanaka-s (I. 33. 4; 5) Uraṇa (II. 14.4) Varcin (II. 14.6; IV. 30.15; VI. 47.21), Vesa (x.49.5), Vṛṣaśipra (VII. 99.4), Vyaṃsas . 103. 2; II. 14.5; IV. 18.9) etc.

9. See Chakravarty, 1997, pp. 156-158.
10. Also see *ṚV I.* 132. 4 ; V. 30.10; VI. 35.2 et. al.
11. For the early, settlement of the aryans in different tribes in the land of the five rivers See Keith, 1922, pp. 81-84, Pusalkar in the Vedic Age (4th ed. 1965, pp. 249-255 [Ist. ed. 1951).
12. Sharma, 1990, p. 58: "The Aryans were engaged in two types of conflicts ...... the first, they fought with pre-Aryans, and secondly, the fought amongst themslves."
13. Geldner, HOS 33, p. 294 n. 7 cd observes about Indra's becoming the enemy of his favourities Kutsa, Atithigva and Āyu : "Die gennnten sind sonst Schützlinge des Indra. In dioeser Sage aber steht er auf Seiten des Tūrvavāṇa" (Suśravas).
14. while summarizing the Dāśarājña story I drew mainly upon Keith (1922), Pusalkar (1965 [Ist ed. 1951]), Umesh Sharma and Dandekar (1985).

    ṚV. III 33; VII,. 18; 33 and 83 narrate the story of Sudās. The word *dāśarājña* occurs thrice in the *ṚV.* (VIII. 33. 3 83.8).
15. River banks seem to be the favourite spots of the Aryans. Zimmer (1879, p. 148) observes: "Sie mögen besonders häufig an den Ufern der Flüsse gewesen sein, da an diesen nach den Zeugnissen der vedischen Lieder sich die hartnäckigsten abspielten : Zehnkönigesschlacht an der Paruṣṇi (*ṚV* 7, 18), Kampf der Tṛtsu und des Bheda an der Yamunā (*ṚV* 7, 18, 19).......". Their special fascination was to be often on the river banks, as according to the Vedic poems the most difficult (events) took place on these; the place on these; the (dāṣarāña on the Paruṣṇi (*ṚV* 7, 18), the battle between Tṛtsus and Behda on the Yamunā (ṚV. 7, 18, 19).

    Keith (1922, p. 98) : "Naturally enough the banks of rivers seem to have been frequently the spots chosen for the conflict, as in the case of famous battles of the ten kings."
16. For detailed description of Dāsarājña consult Umesh Sharmā's Dāsarājña (1985).
17. Dandekar, 1997, p. 236.
18. *AV.* XIII. 1. 28, 29 :

    Samiddho' gnih samidhāno ghṛtavṛddho ghṛtāhūtaḥ :

    abhīṣāḍ viśvāṣāś agniḥ sapatnān hantu ye mama ::

    hantu enān pra dahatv arir yo naḥ pṛtanyati :

    kravyādāgninā vayaṃ sapatnan dahāmasi ::
19. Cf. Dikshitar, 1943, p. 3 : "If we are to identify the Devas and the Asuras with the Aryans and the Dravidians, the teximony of history supports the earlier advancement of political institutions among the Dravidians, which served the Indo-Aryans as a model to copy and follow."

    We are here concerned with the first part of dikshitar's statement.
20. In this discussion I shall not translate the word 'deva' into 'god' and shall keep it as it is and the same will be followed in case of 'asura' also.
21. *ŚatBr. iv 2.4.19 :*

    Devā ha vai yajñaṃ tanvānāḥ : te surarakṣasebhya

    āsaṅgād bibhyayāñcakrus tan daksinān surarakasānyāsejus leṣām etān dakṣṃān

    grahān ujjaghnur apy etad dakṣiṇaṃ havirdhānam ujjaghnur... :

    Also See VI. 3.1.29; VII. 4.1.37; VIII. 5.1.10; IX. 2.3.4-6 et al.
22. Also see *AV.* III. 27. 1-6; II. 11.3.

23. *ŚatBṛ VI.* 6. 3. 11 ;
etad vai devāḥ : Yaś caitān dveḍyaṃ cādviṣus tam asmā annaṃā kṛtvāpy adadhus tenainaṃ prīṇann annamahaita-syābhavad adahad u devānāṃ pāpānaṃ tathaivaited yajamāno yaś cainaṃ dveṣṭi yañ ca deveṣṭi tam asmā 'nnaṃ kṛtvā pidadadhāti tenainaṃ prīṇāty annaṃ ahaitasya bhavati dahaty u yajamānasya pāpmānaṃ.
24. See *Tais*, VI. 2. 2. 1.; 6; *TaiBr.* I. 1. 6. 1. ; *AitBr.* 1. 23. et. al.
25. Also See *AitBr.* II. 31; II. 36; *SatBr.* III. 3. 3. 16; 5. 3. 15.
26. See *AitBr.* VIII. 12-14 *Aindramahābhiṣeka.* See Ghoshal., 1959, pp. 28-29.
27. See *SatBr.* III. 4. 4. 3.
28. *ŚatBr.* V. 1. 1. 1 :
devśca va asurāśca : ubhaye prājāpatyāḥ paspṛdhire tato 'surā atimānenaiva kasmin nu khalu vayaṃ juhūyāmeti sveṣv āsyeṣu juhavataś cerus te 'timānenaiva parā babhuvus tasmān nātimanyeta parābhavasya haitan mukhaṃ yad atimānaḥ :
29. See Heesterman, 1993, pp. 49-50.
30. Also see *ŚatBr.* VII. 4. 1. 37.
31. See *Aitbr. II.* I.
32. See *ŚatBr.* III. 6.1. 5.
33. See *ibid.* VII. 4. 1. 37.
34. Also See Bhattacharji, 1986, p. 98.
35. *AitBr.* VIII. 28.
tasya vrataṃ na dviṣataḥ pūrvam upaviśed yadi tiṣṭhantaṃ manyeta tiṣṭhetaiva na dviṣataḥ pūrvaṃ saṃviśed yady āsīnaṃ manyetāsītaiva na dviṣataḥ pūrvaṃ prasvapyād yadi jāgrataṃ manyeta jāgriyād eva : api ha yady asyāśmamūrdhā dviṣan bhavati kṣipraṃ haviainaṃ stṛṇute stṛṇute :
36. See Heesterman, 1993, p. 49
37. See *Śrautakośa*, 1958, Vol. 1, Part I. p. 367.
38. Quoted from *ibid*, p. 128.

Abbreviations

AitBr.	*Aitareyabrāhmaṇa*
AV.	*Atharvavedasaṃhitā*
BṛĀraU.	*Bṛhadāprankropaniṣad*
JaimiBr.	*Jaimīyabrāhmaṇa*
ṚV.	*Ṛgvedasaṃhitā*
ṢadviBr.,	*Ṣadviṃśabrāhmaṇa*
ŚatBr.	*Śatapathabrāhmaṇa*
TaiBr.	*Taittirīyabrāhmaṇa*
TaiS.	*Taittirīyasaṃhitāp*

Select Bibliography

Aitareyabrāhmaṇa,		Anandashram Sanskrit Series 32 Pune : Anandashram Press.
____________,		tr. A. B. Keith, HOS 25.
Atharvaveda (śaunaka) Parts I, II, III, IV 1960, 1961, 1961, 1962		ed. Vishva Bandhu Hoshiarpur : Vishveshvarananda Vedic Reseach Institute.
Atharva-Veda		edo Sripad Damodar Satavalekar, Satara : Pardi, Savadhyaya Mandala.
Atharava-Veda-Saṃhitā		tr. W. D. Whitney, HOS 7, 8
Benveniste, Emil	1973	Miāmi linguistic Series No. 12
* Bhattachariji, Sukumari	1984	Literature in the Vedic Age Vols. I and II. Calcutta : K. P. Bagchi & Co.
Bloomfield, Maurice	1964	Vedic Concordance. Delhi : Motilal Banarsidass (Ist ed. 1906)
Böhtlingk, O and Rodolf Roth	1855 –1875	Sanskrit Wörterbuch 7 Vols., St. Petersburg.
Bṛhad-Āraṇyaka-Upaniṣad		Gorakhpur : Gita Press, (3rd ed.) 1958, (Ist ed. 1943). Sharma, 1985.
____________,	1958	Śrautakośa (English Section) Vol. I, Part I, Poona : Vaidika Saṃśodhana Maṇḍala.
____________,	1997	Indological Miscellanea, Pune : Bhandarkar Oriental Reserach Institute.

Dikshitar, V. R. Ramachandra	1944	War in Ancient India (Ist ed) London : Macmillan & Co. Limited.
Gonda, Jan	1975	Vedic Literature Wiesbaden : Otto Harrassowitz.
Grassmann, Harmann	1936	Wörterbuch Zum Rigveda Leipzing : Otto Herrassowitz.
Heesterman, J. C.	1993	The Broken World of Sacrifice, Chicago & London : The Chicago University Press.
Jaiminiya-Brāhmaṇa		ed. Prof. Raghu Vira and Dr. Lokesh Chandra, Nagpur : International Academy of Indian Culture, 1950.
Das Jaiminiya-Brāhmaṇa in Auswahl		tr. W. Caland, Amsterdam : Johannes Müller, 1919.
Jaiswal, Suvira	1990	"Stratification in Ṛgvedic Society : Evidence and Paradigm," In Indian Historical review, Vol. 16 (1-2), 1989-90, pp. 1-34.
Keith, A. B.	1922	"Ancient India", in Cambridge History of India, Vol. I, Cambridge : At the University Press.
________,	1925	The Religion and Philosophy of the Veda and Upanisads, HOs 31. 32.
Majumdar, R. C.	1965 (2nd ed)	ed. The Vedic Age, Bharatiya Vidya Bhavan, London : George Allen and Unwin, (Ist ed. 1951).
Nath, Jyotish	1996	The Dāsas,. dasyus and Rakṣases in the Ṛgvedic Literature, Calcutta : Sanksrit Pustak Bhandar.
Rau, Wilhelm	1975	The Meaning of 'pur', München : Wilhelm Fink Verlag.
Ṛgveda-Saṃhitā		Pune : Vaidika Saṃśodhana Maṇḍala (4th ed.) 1995. (1st ed. 1933).
		The Hymns of the Ṛgveda Tr. R. T. H. Griffith, Delhi : Motilal Banarsidass, (reprint) 1995, (1st ed. 1889).
Der Rigveda		German tr. K. F. Geldner, HOS 33-36,
Ṣadviṃśa-Brāhmana		ed. Bellikoth Ramachandra Sharma, Tirupati : Kendriya Sanskrit Vidyapeetha, 1967
______________,		tr. W.B. Bollee, Utrecht : Drukketij A Storm, 1956.
Ṣadviṃśa-Brāhmana Vol. I - III 1967, 1969, 1970		New Delhi : The Research Institute of Ancient Scientific Studies.
______________,		tr. Julius Eggeling, Sacred Books of the East, 12, 26, 41, 43, 44.

Sharma, R. S 1977-78 "Conflict, Distribution and Differentiation in Ṛgvedic Society, " in Indian Historical Review, Vol. IV (1—2) pp. 1-12.

__________, 1990 Ancient Indiam. New Delhi : National Council of Educational Research and Traininng.

Sharma, Umesh Ch. 1985 The Dāśarājña War, Aligarh : Viveka Publications.

Taittirīyabrāhmaṇam Anandashram Sanskrit Series No. 371-373. Pune : Anadashram Press.

Taittirīyasaṃhitā Anandashram Sanskrit Series 42/1-8. Pune : Anandashram Press,

Taittirīyopaniṣad Anandashram, Sanskrit Series 12 Pune : Anandashram Press,

Zimmer, Heinrich 1879 Altindisches Leben, Berlin : Weidmannsche Buchhandlung.

The Atharvan Roots of Āyurveda

16

Prof. K.V. Sarma

Introduction

Two of the earliest treatises which systematically deal with Āyurveda or 'Science of Life' in Indian medicine are admittedly the *Caraka Saṁhitā* and the *Suśruta* Saṁhitā, the basic texts of both of which have been dated well into the first millennium B.C. Well-set classification, codification and presentation as full-fledged text-books characterise both the texts. Both speak of a long tradition of *ācāryas-s* who had preserved and handed the discipline down the ages and had, obviously, made their own contribution to the further systematisation of the science. It should be instructive to investigate how far the presently perfected Āyurvedic systems are rooted in the *mantra-s* of the Vedic *saṁhitā-s* which date back, at least, to the third millennium B.C. This investigation would also give a clue to the systematisation during the later ages, not only in the basic concepts and theories, diagnosis of ailments and their cure but also of the drugs used and the practices adopted during Vedic times.

Reference to Medicine in Vedic Literature

In Vedic literature there occur a number of references to diseases and their cure. Several of the hymns of the *Rgveda* (*RV*) consist *mantra-s* which are to be recited during the application of medicines or are addressed to curative herbs or the deities who are supposed to cause or cure diseases. The *mantra-s* of this nature occur in a greater measure in the *Atharvaveda* (*AV*) for which reason Atharvan *mantrās* in general are called 'medicine', *bheṣajam vā atharvaṇāni* (*Tāṇḍya Mahābrāhmaṇa*, 12.9.10).

A point to note in this connection, is that the Vedas are not textbooks on medicine nor, for that matter, of any material discipline. Rather, they are compilations (*saṁhitā)* formed, at some period of time, by collecting together hymns from the large floating sage of hymns composed much earlier, on the basis of their importance. In text, in sacrifices and prayers, poetic quality, and utility in sacrifices and prayers, or other considerations, the compiled hymns have little mutual or topical connection whatsoever.[1]

Mention to medicine and cure in Vedic literature are quite substantial. However, for the reasons pointed out above, their treatment herein cannot be expected to be descriptive, systematic, sequential or full-fledged. Naturally enough, they can also be repetitive or cross-refer themselves. All the same, if the mentions occurring at all different places are collected, classified and put together in some sequential order, with duplications deleted and omissions supplied, the result would form at least a vague picture of the Āyurvedic system in its formative period. In other words, a correlative analysis of the diseases, drugs and methods of application as adumbrated in Vedic hymns with the parallel forms in the *Caraka* and *Suśruta Saṁnitā-s,* which is attempted herein below would show that the roots of later developments are well testified both in theory and practice in Vedic literature, especially in the *Atharvaveda.*

Tradition of Āyurveda

The *Caraka Saṁhita* which has come down to us in eight sections called *sthāna-s,* pertaining respectively to : (1) *Sūtra* on general principles and medical philosophy, (2) *Nidāna* on causes of diseases, (3) *Vimāna* on taste, nourishment and pathology, (4) *Śārīra* on anatomy and prognosis, (5) *Cikitsa* on treatment of diseases, (6) *Kalpa* on pharmacy and (7) *Siddhi* on cure of diseases (1.30.35). Under these broad divisions are dealt with numerous topics pertaining to the different branches of medicine such as *Kāyacikitsā* (the rapeutics) *Śapakya* (relating to the eye, ear, nose, mouth and throat), *Śalyāpahartṛka* (Surgery), *Viṣa* (toxicology), *Bhūtavidyā* (psychiatrics), *Kaumarabhṛtya* (pediatrics), *Rasāyana* (rejuvenation) and *Vājīkaraṇa* (Augmentation of Virility) (1.30.30). In about one hundred and fifty chapters comprised in the said eight sections innumerable topics pertaining to diseases drugs, application thereof and cures are specified.

The *Suśruta Saṁhita* presents the medical material in five sections called *sthāna-s,* respectively dealing with: (1) sūtra in 46 chapters, (2) *Nidāna* in 16 chapters, (3) *śārīra* in 10 chapters, (4) *Cikitśa* in 40 chapters and (5) *Kalpa* is 8 chapters. There is also a sixth section called *Uttaratantra.*

Landmark References of Medicine in the Vedas

Before taking up specific topics in medicine occurring in the Vedas and correlating them with the developed aspects thereof in later texts like those of *Caraka* and *Suśruta,* attention might be directed to certain authoritative statements on the subject. The *Suśruta saṁhita* calls Āyuveda as a 'Vedic subsidiary of the *Atharvaveda, iha khalu Āyurvedam nāma upāṅgam Atharvavedasya* (su. saṁ 1.5). The Kāśyapa *Saṁhita,* another early te:.t on *Ātharvaveda, Āyurvedah katham cotpanna iti........ tasmad Atharvavedam śrayati* (Edn. N.S. Press, Bombay, p. 42). The *Caraka Saṁhita* adduses several reasons as to why a physician should be affiliated to the

Atharvaveda, in exclusion to the other three vedas. Thus it states: *tatra bhiṣaja...caturṇām Ṛk-Sama-Yujur-Atharva-Vedānām ātmano Atharvavede bhaktir ādeeśyā* (*Caraka S.* 30.21-21)

Atharvan Sages of Āyurveda

Several sages have been mentioned in early Āyurvedic treatises as progenitors of Āyurveda. It is instructive to note that the names of some of these sages occur in the *mantra-s* of the *Atharvaveda* also in connection with medical herbs and cure, as would be clear from the undermentioned citations.

(i) *Kaṇva, identifier of a life-healing herb*

āyurdadam vipaścitam *śrutām Kaṇvasya*

vīrudham viśvabheṣajim asyādṛṣṭān ni śamayat" (*AV* 6.52.3)

'The life-giving, inspired, famous plant of *Kaṇva,* the all-healing one, have I brought. May it quench this man's unseen (maladies)'

(ii) *Atri, Kaṇva, Jamadagni* and *sgastya* destroyers of worms *Atrivad* vaḥ Krimeyo harnmi *Kaṇvavaj* Jamadagnivat *Agastyasya* brahmaṇā sam pinaṣmy ahm krimīn (*AV* 2.32.3)

'Like Atri I slay you, worm is, like Kaṇva, like Jamadagni with the incantation of Agastya I mash together the wormis.

(iii) *Atharvan, Agastya Kaṇva and Kaśyapa destroy diseases* tvayā pūrvam Atharvāṇo jaghnū rekṣāmsy oṣadhe tvayā jaghāna Kaśyapas tvayā Kaṇva Agastyaḥ (*AV* 4.37.1)

'O herb! Through you, the Attarvan slew the demons. Earlier. O herb! through you Kaśyapa slay. Through Kaṇva, Agastya (slay) (the disease).

(iv) *Jamadagni's recipe for growth or hair*

yām Jamadagnir aghanad duhitre keśavardhanīm ı

am Vītahavya ābharad asitasya gṛhebhyaḥ ıı (AV 6.137.1)

'(The herb) which Jamadagni dug out for his daughter for the growth of hair, that one *Vītahavya* has brought from *Asita's* house.

V. Sage *Mātali* who brings medicine.

Sage *Matali,* one of the progemitors of Āyuveda, is said to have brought the rejuvenating medicine by selling a chariot. The medicine was thrown into the waters by Indra, and the waters are prayed to give back the medicine.

yan Mātalī rathakrītam amṛitam veda bheṣajam ı

tad Indro apsu prāveśayat tad āpo datta Aheṣajam ıı (AV 11.6.23)

'The immortal remedy bought by the sale of a chariot, which Mātali knows, which Indra threw into the waters, that remedy, O waters! give ye back.'

The word Atharvan which originally referred to the sagefamily and the sagecomposer and also the sage-composer-physician came, in due course, to mean also the medicine.[2] The circle came to be completed when the word *bheṣaja* itself came to the sage[3] and the *Atharvaveda* began to be called *Bhaiṣagya-veda*.[4]

Āvurvedic Theories in Abharvaveda

Tridoṣa theory

The Humorial Theory which postulates that the three humors, *Vāta* (Nerve force), *Pitta* (Metabolism and bodily heat) and *Kapha* (combustion), pervade the entire Āyurvedic system *Caraka* (S., 1.27.3; *Suśruta S.*, 1.21.3). Suśtruta equates this theory in essence with the *Triguṇa theory* of the Sāṅkhya philosophy, of *sattva* or being, *rajas* or energy and *tamas* or inertia (*Suśtruta S.*, 2.1-18; 3.1.20). A reference to the three *guna-s* (Attributes) appears in the *Atharvaveda* :

puṇḍarīkam navadvāram tribhir guṇebhir āvṛtam ।

tasmin yad yakṣmin yad yakṣam śtmanvat tad vai brahmavido viduḥ ।।

(*AV* 10.8.43)

'The lotus flower of nine doors, (viz., the human body with its nine orfices) covered (imbued) with the three temperaments (*Sattva, rajas* and *tamas*) what soulful prodigy is within it, that only Brahman-knowers know.'

Trivṛtkaraṇa and Pañcīkaraṇa

The Āyurvedic theory of the composition of the world and the human body from three elements *(tri-dhātu-s)*, viz., *tejas* (Agni or fire or heat), *āpaḥ* (water), and *anna* (earth food), and that any imbalance thereof would cause diseases is obviously rooted on the theory underlaying statements in the *Atharvaveda* and other Vedic literature.

Cf. *tridhātu śarma vahatam śubhaspatī* (*Ṛgeda* 1.34.6)

'May the two lords of auspiciousness (the Aśvins) bring well-being to us through the three *dhātu-s*.'

The *Trivṛtkaraṇa* is obviously the basis of the later *Pañcīkarana* theory of Āyurveda.

Kālavāda of Āyurveda

Caraka saṁhita in its *Yajjaḥpuruṣīyapariṣad* chapter (I.25) speak of a Kālavāda, being the theory that *Kāla* or time is the cause of all things in the world, including human diseases.

Kālajas tv eva puruṣaḥ Kālajās tasya āmayāḥ ।

jagat kālavaśam sarvam kālaḥ sarvatra kāraṇam ।। (*Caraka S.* 1.25.24)

'Man is caused by Time. Time determines his diseases. The entire world depends on Time. Time is the cause for everything.'

Obviously, this *Kālavāda* is based on the *Kālavāda* elucidated in full in two hymns of the *Atharaveda*. To cite one *mantra* thereform.

Kālād āpaḥ samabhavan kālād brahma tapo diśaḥ ।

kālenodeti sūryaḥ kāle ni viśate punaḥ ।। (*AV* 19.54.1)

'From Time originated the waters, from Time Brahman, penance and the directions. The sun rises because of Time and sets too in Time.'

Origin of Diseases and Possession by Spirits

Āyurveda asserts in many a context that diseases are caused by the anger of gods. In order to assuage divine anger Āyurveda specifically prescribes in many cases fasts and worship of the gods, alongside prescriptions and remedies, the practice has come down from the Vedas, especially to *Atharvaveda* wherein certain disease like *takman* and *āsrāva* are considered to be due to the displeasure of specific deities, for which remedies have been suggested through prayers which form the individual hymns. To cite an example, the diseases *takman* and *kāsikā* are said to be brought about by Rudra's weapons :

yasya takmā kāsikā hetir ekam aśvasyeva vṛṣaṇah kranda eti ।

abhipūrvam nirṇayate name ast asamai ।। (*AV* 11.2.22)

'Of which (Rudra) the *takman* and *kāsikā* form the weapon like the noise of a stallion horse, to that Rudra, leading out in succession, our homage'.

For a parallel idea in Āyurveda, see :

jvaram ādau pravakṣyāmi sa rogānıkarāṭ smṛtaḥ ।

Rudra-kopāgnisambhūtaḥ sarvabhūtapratāpanaḥ ।। (*Suśruta S.* b.39.9)

'Dhanvantari said :) Is shall speak at the outset about *jvara* (Vedic *takman*), the foremost of the army of diseases. It is produced due to the wrath of Rudra and agonises all creatures'.

The *Atharvaveda* carries numerous instances of spirits affecting people in all sorts of ways. In Āyuvedic treatises the subject takes up one entire branch of the discipline, vi., *Bhūtavidyā* or Demonology. Such diseases as *unmada* and *apasmāra* are taken to have been caused by ghosts and goblins. In the section on *Kaumārabhṛtya* spirits which go by the names *skanda, graha, pūtama* and many others are supposed to affect children and due remedies are prescribed.

The importance given by later Āyurveda to his aspect of mediciation would be apparent when it is noted that Suśruta devotes fourteen chapters to diseases at tributed to evil spirits.

The treatment for these diseases includes the appeasement of the spirits by the recitation of sacred texts, offerings to gods and making gifts.

(*Suśruta S.* 6.27-37, 60-62)

Prāṇa and Vāyu

The prime function of *Vāyu* (air), according to Āyurveda, is *praspandana* (pulsation). It courses through the oral and noval cavities. Its functions are the sustainment of the body, transmission of food into the internal organs and the maintenance of the vital breath. Suśruta says :

tatra praspandana-udvahana-pūraṇa—viveka-dhāraṇa-lakṣaṇo vāyuh pañcadhā pravibhaktaḥ. (*Suśrutes,* 1.15.3)

The five types of *vāyu are parāṇa, udāna, samāna, vyāna* and *apāna*. See *Suśruta S.,* 2.1.121 :

prāṇodāna-samānaś ca vyānaś cāpāna eva ca ।

sthānasthā mārutā vañca yāpayanti śarīriṇam ।।

The above enunciation goes back to the *Atharvaveda* which recognises only four but obviously with similar functions :

Ko asmin prāṇam avayat ko apānam vyānam u ।

samānam asmin ko devo'dhi śiśrāya pūruṣe ।। (*AV* 10.2.13)

'Who wove in man breath? Who expiration and respiration? Which god attached conspiration (*samāna*) to man here?'

Worms and Germs

The *Atharvaveda* refers, in numerous mantrās, to worms and germs which manage to enter into the human body from without, thrive in the body and cause diseases of different sorts. Refer, for instance, to the hymn for the eradication of worms.'

Udyann ādityaḥ krimīn hantu nimrocan bantu raśmibhiḥ ।

ye antaḥ krimayo gavi ।।1।।

viśvarūpam caturakṣam krimim sarangam arjuna

śṛṇāmy asya pṛṣṭīr api vrścāmi yac chiraḥ ।।2।।

Atrivad vaḥ krimayo nmi kaṇvavad Jamadagnivat ।

Asgastyasya brahmaṇā sam pinaṣmy aham krimīm ।।3।।

hato rājā krimīṇām utaiṣām sthapatir hataḥ ।

hato hatamāhā krimir hatabhrātā hatasvaśa ।।5।।

★ ★ ★ ★

pra te sṛṇāni śṛṅge yābhyām vitudāyasi ।

bhinadmi te kuṣumbham yas te viṣadhānaḥ ।।6।। (*AV* 2.32.1-6)

'Let the rising sun smite the worms at him smite with his setting rays, the worms which are in the cow. (1)

'The worm of all forms, the four-eyed, the variegated, the whitish—I crush its ribs. I hew at what is its head. (2)

'Like Arti I slay you, O worms!, like Kaṇva, like Jamadagni. With the incentation of Agastva I mash together to worms.' (3)

'Slain is the king of the worms; also the chief of theirs is slain; slain is the worm with its mother slain, its brother slain, its sister slain. (4)

★ ★ ★ ★

'I crush the two horns with which you thrust. I split your receptacle which is your poison pouch.' (6)

The parts of the body which the worms attack are also mentioned in the *Atharvaveda* :

anvāntryam śirṣaṇyam athb pārṣṭeyam krimin ।

avaskvam vyadhvaram krimin vacasā jambhayāmasi ।। (*AV* 2.31.3)

'The one along the entrails, the one in the head, likewise the worm in the ribs, the *avaskava*, the *vyadhvara*—all these we grind with our *mantra*.'

Suśiruta saṁhitā elaborates upon the *Atharvaveda* statements and devotes a full chapter (6.54) to worms and germs with the indication of their places of origin in the human body, their propagation, the distress caused by them and the cures thereof (*Susruta S.* 6.54.1-18).

Seasonal Diseases

Caraka and Suśruta speak of diseases whose onslaught occurs only at specific periods in the year or which aggravate during certain seasons. In this wake Suśruta says :

yasmin yasmin rtau ye ye doṣāḥ kurvanti dehinām ।

teṣu teṣu pradātavyā rasās te te vijānatā ॥ (*Suśruta S.*, 64.5)

He then enumerates the diseases which are liable to occur or aggravate and indicates precautions or cures therefore. Caraka too treats the subject elaborately in ch. 3 of the *Cikitsāsthāna* of his *Saṁhita*.

Both these authors have taken the cue from the *Atharvaveda* which refers to this aspect in the case of *takman* (fever) which can occur at any time of the year and, so, is called *hāyana* (*AV* 19.39.10) but aggravates at certain seasons and is therefore called, respectively, *graiṣmika*, related to summer, *vārṣika*, related to the rains and *śārada* related to autumn (*AV* 5.22.13).

Hereditary Ailments

Diseases inherited from parents have been identified both by Caraka and Suśruta. Analysing the sources of diseases Suśruta :

tatra punaḥ saptavidhā vyādhayah tad yatha ādibalapravṛttāḥ, janmabala-pravṛttāḥ, dosabala-pravṛttah saṇghātabalapravṛttāḥ, kālabalaprvrttāḥ, devabalapravṛttāḥ, svabhāvabalapravṛttāḥ iti (*Suśruta S.* 1.24.4).

Here *ādibala-pravṛttāḥ* and *janmabala-pravṛttāḥ* are hereditary and congenial. About the first he says : *tatra ādibaha-pravṛttā* ye śukra-śoṇitadoṣānvayāḥ kuṣṭha-arśa-prabhṛtaya te'pi dvividhāḥ, mātṛjāḥ pitṛjās ca ('There, the disease termed *ādibala-pravṛttāḥ* has to be ascribed to any inherent defect in the semen or the ovum of one's parent which forms the original and primary factors of 'being' and includes leprosy and piles. This is of two sub-divisions, according as the disease is generated by the degranged paternal; or maternal factors at the time of incubation.'

Suśpruta continues : Janmabala-pravṛttā ye mātuḥ apacārāt paṅgu-jātyandha-badhira-mūka-minmina-vamana-prabhṛtayaḥ jā yante;

('The cogenital type or *janamabala-pravṛtta* occurs due to the improper conduct of the mother during the period of gestation and embraces maladies like lameness, blindness, deafness, dumbness, nasal voice, decreptitude and the like. (*Suśruta S.* 1.24.5).

For the elaboration as above by later authors of Āyurveda for these *kṣetriya* or hereditary diseases see the *Ātharvaveda mantra* when it speaks of the faults committed by one's parents devolving on one's children :

yad enaso mātṛkṛtāt śese pitṛkṛtāc ca yat (*AV* 5.30.4)

Human Anatomy

Detailed understanding and analytical depiction of human anatomy form some of the highlights of Āyurveda. Among these might be mentioned Osteology, Human organs, Blood circulatory system and Nervous system. An examination of the hymns of the *Atharvaveda* shows that a comparatively fair knowledge of these systems was existent even during Vedic times. Obviously, the systems had been developed further down the ageo by generations of physicians some of whose names have been mentioned both by Caraka and Suśruta in their works.

(i) Osteology

Caraka who is called 'Vedavādin' or 'Followers of the Vedic school' by Suśruta (3.5.18) names 360 bones in the human body while Suśruca 300. (3.16.28) with individual or group names. The 'Veda' referred to by Suśruta is obviously the

Atharvaveda whose enumeration of the human bones bones is instructive. The relevant *mantrās* might be extracted here.

Kena pārṇī ābhṛte puruṣasya
Kena māṁsam sambhṛtam kena gulphau ।
Kenāṅgulīḥ peśanīḥ kena khāni
kenocchlaṅghau madhyataḥ kaḥ pratiṣṭhām ॥ 1 ॥

Kasmān nu gulpñāv adharāv akṛṇavann ।
aṣṭhīvantāv uttarau pūruṣasya ।
jaṅghe nirṛtya nyadadhuḥ kva svij ।
jānunoḥ sandhī ka u bac ciketa ॥ 2 ॥

Catuṣṭayam yujyate saṁhitāntam
janubhyām ūrdhvam śithiram kabandham ।
śroṇī yad ūrūka u taj jajāna ।
kusincham sudṛḍham babhuva ॥ 3 ॥

Kati devāḥ katame ta āsan
ya uro grīvācikvuh purusasva
Kati stanau vyadadhuḥ kaḥ kaphoḍau
kati skandhān kati pṛṣṭīr acinvan ॥4 ॥

Ko asya bāhū samabharad iti
aṁsau ko asya tad devaḥ kusindhe adhyāk dadhau ॥ 5 ॥

Kaḥ sapta khāni vi tatarda śīrṣaṇi
karṇāv imau nāsike cakṣaṇī mukham
yeṣām purutrā vijayasya mahmani
catuṣpādo dvipado yanti yaāman ॥ 6 ॥

hanvor hi jihvām adadhāt purūcīm
adhā mahim adhi śiśrāya vācam
sa-a varīvarti bhuvaneṣvantar
apo vasānaḥ ka u tac ciketa ॥ 7 ॥

mastiṣkam asya yaamo lalāṭam
kakāṭikām prathamo yaḥ kapālam
citvā cityam hanvoḥ pūruṣasya
divam ruroha katamaḥ sa devaḥ ॥ 8 ॥ (*AV* 10.2.1-8)

The bones identified in the human skeleton in this long hymn of 33 *mantrās* the Vedic poet describes the various parts and aspects of the human being and wonders as to which god could have created such a perfect form. The bones named are :

Parṣṇi (heels) 2; *gulphau* (ankle) 2; *aṅguliḥ* (digits) 50; *ucchlaṅkha* (metacarpal bones) 2; *prtiṣṭhā* (base) 1; aṣṭhīvantau (knee-caps) 2; jaṅghe(Shanks) Janghe sandhī (knee-joints) 2; śroṇi (pelvieavity) 2; ūru (thigh bones) 2; urah (breast-bone) 1; grīvā (wind-pipe) 1: *stanau* (ribs) 24; Kaphoḍau (shoulder-blades) 2; *skandha* (shoulder bones) 15; *pṛṣṭiḥ* (backbone) 1; *aṁsau* (collar bones) 2; *lalatam* (forehead) 2; *Kakāṭikā* (central facial bone) 1; *kapāla* (cranium) 1; and *chityam hanvoḥ* (pile of the jaw) 1. Elsewhere in the *Atharvaveda* mention is also *kīkaṣaḥ* (spinal column) *kīkaṣaḥ* (spinal column) 1; and *chityam hanvoḥ* (spinal column) 1; and *anukyā* (thoracic portion of the spine) (*AV* 2.32.2).

(ii) The Organs

For puposes of identification and medical treatment or surgery every organ of the human body has been differentiated and named in the Āyurvedic treatises. (See *Caraka* 1.7.18; Suśruta S. 8.5.4). In this matter also *Atharvaveda* has formed the source of such identification and nomenclature. Thus *AV* 2.33 is a hymn in seven *mantra-s* with the recitation of which the Atharvam priest exercises the disease of *yakṣmā* or tuberculosis from every organ of the patient with the enumeration of the several limlis :

Akṣībhyām te nāsikābhyām karṇābhyām chubuukād adhi ।
yakṣmam śīrṣaṇyam mastiṣkāj jivāyā vi vṛhāmi te ॥1॥
grīvābhyas ta uṣṇihābhyaḥ kīkasābhyo anūkyāt ।
yakṣmam doṣanyam aṁsābhyām bāhubhyām vi vṛhāmi te ॥2॥
hṛdayāt te pari klomno halīkṣṇāt pārśvābhyām ।
yakṣmam matasnābhyām plīhvo yaknas te vṛhāmasi ॥3॥
āntrebhyas te gudābhyo vaniṣṭhor udarād adhi ।
yakṣmam kukṣibhyām plaāer nābhyā vi vṛhāmi te ॥4॥
ūrubhyām te asthīvadhyām pāṛṣṇibhyam prapadābhyām ।
yakṣmam bhasadyam śroṇibhyām bhāsadam bhaṁsaso vi vṛhāmi te ॥5॥
asthibyas te majjabhyaḥ snāvabhyo dhamanibhyaḥ ।

yakṣmam pāṇibhyām aṅgulibhyo nakhebhyo vi vṛhāmi te ı 6 ıı
aṅgeaṅge lomnilomni yas te parvaṇiparvaṇi ı
yakṣmam tvacasyam te vayam
Kaśyapasya vivarheṇa viṣvañcam vi vṛhāmasi ı 7 ıı (*AV* 2.33.1-7)

The organs specified are :

	Kukṣi (ride of abdomen)
akṣi (eye)	plāśi (colon)
nāsikā (nose)	nābhi (navel)
karṇa (ear)	ūru (thigh)
chubuka (chin)	aṣṭhivat (knee)
śīrṣa (head)	pārṣni (heal)
mastiṣka (head)	prapada (arch of foot)
jihvā (tongue)	bhāsadya (glans penis)
grīvā (neck)	śroṇi (waist)
uṣṇiha (nape of neck)	bhaṁsasa (vagina)
anūkyā (thoracis portion of spine)	asthi (bone)
doṣan (upper arm)	majjā (marrow)
aṁsa (shoulder)	snāvā (muscle)
hṛdaya (heart)	dhamani (artery)
kloma (stomach)	pāṇi (hand)
halīkṣṇa (gall bladder)	aṅgula (finger)
pārśva (side of chest)	nakha (nail)
matasnā (gall duct)	aṅga (limb)
plīha (spleen)	loma (hair)
yakna (liver)	parven (joint)
antra (small intestines)	tvak (skin)
guda (faecal passage)	vaniṣṭha (rectum)
uddra (abdomen)	Kukṣi (side of abdomen)

The organs of the human body have been mentioned in the *Atharvaveda* in other hymns as well, for instance in 4.12.3-5, 11.8.11015. AV 10.9.13-15 names the organs of the body of a cow.[5]

(iii) Conception, Pregnancy and Childbirth

A subject of the highest importance given by major Āyurvedic texts relates to Conception, Pregnancy and Childbirth. Caraka devotes three chapters, two, three and four of the Śārīrasthāna of his *Saṁhita*. Sukśruta deals with the subject more elaborately, again in three chapters, two, three and four, of the Śārīrasthāna of his

Saṁhita. Both these authors have actually based themselves on the *Atharvaveda* where there is detailed notice of these topics in several contexts. Indeed, the Atharvan physician has laid much stress not only on the physical aspects of these matters but also in the philosophical and spiritual aspects involved, a course which Āyurveda has also followed.

The bringing forth of a soul into the mortal world is a sacred act and several deities are prayed for towards safe guarding and nurturing the foetus :

yatheyam pṛthivī mahī bhūtānām garbham ādadhe /
eṣā dadhāmi te garbham tasmai tvam avase huve // 2 //
garbham dhehi Sinīvāli garbham dhehi Sarasvati /
garbham te Aśvinobhā dhattam puṣkarasrajā // 3 //
garbham te Mitrā-Varuṇau garbham devo Bṛhaspatiḥ /
garbham te Indraścāgniś ca garbham Dhātā dadhātu te // 4 //
Viṣṇur yonim kalpayatu Tvaṣṭā rūpāṇi piṁśatu /
ā siñcatu Prajāpatir dhātā garbham da dhātu te // 5 //
yad veda rājā Varuṇo yad vā devī Sarvasvatī /
yad Indro Vṛtrahā veda tad garbhakaraṇam piba // 6 // (*AV* 5.25.2-6)

'As the great earth receives the embryo of existence, so do I set thine embryo; I call thee to its aid. (2)

'Place the embryo, O Sinīvāli; place the embryo O Sarsvati let both the Aśvins, garlanded with blue lotus, set thine embryo. (3)

'Thine embryo let Mitra and Varuṇa, thine embryo let god Bṛhaspati, thine embryo let both Indra and Agi, thine embryo let Bhatar place. (4)

'Let Viṣṇu prepare the womb; let Tvaṣṭar adorn the forms; let Prajāpati pour on; let Dhātar place thine embryo. (5)

'What King Varuṇa, or what divine Sarasvatī know, what Indra the Vṛtra-slayer knows, that embryo-making portion do thou drink. (6)

Equally instructive are several other hymns occurring in the *Atharvaveda* on the subject, among which might be mentioned hymns 8.23 and 6.11 for the birth of a son, 6.17 for the protection of the embryo and 1.11 and 8.6 for a safe normal delivery. The Atharvavedic *Garbhopaniṣad* gives details about the month by month growth and changes in the embryo in the mother's womb.

Blood Circulatory System

The treatment of the Blood Circulatory System is rather brief in the *Caraka Saṁhita* (1.9.3-5), but Suśruta devotes two chapters on the subject (3.7 and 9), wherein the innumerable ducts or channels in the human body are dealt with and their functions specified. These be names as *sirā, srota* and *dhamanī* which are generally taken to stand for the veins, ducts and arteries, though there is some mix-up. The *Atharvaveda* also refers of the *dhamanī* and the *sirā (hirā)* in a hymn directed to be recited while the flow of blood from a cut is sought to be stopped (*AV* 1.17) :

amūr yā yanti yoṣito hirā lohitavāsasaḥ ।

abhrātara iva jāmayas tiṣṭhantu hatavarcasaḥ ।। 1 ।।

tiṣṭhavare tiṣṭha para uta tvam tiṣṭha madhyame ।

kaniṣṭhikā ca tiṣṭhati tiṣṭhādid dhamanir mahī ।। 2 ।

śatasya dhamanīnām sahasrasya hirāṇam ।

asthur inmadhyamā imāḥ sākamantā araṁsata ।। 3 ।।

'You maidens that flow, viz., the red-garmented veins like brotherless sisters, stop with your flow arrested (1)

'Stop, Lower one' Stop upper one! Do thou stop Midmost one! If the smallest stops, shall stop forsooth the arteries. (2)

'Of the hundred arteries, of the thousand veins, the Midmost ones have stopped. The cut-ends have come together. (3)

Ailments Sought to be Cured

The *Atharvaveda* seeks to cure a large number of ailments, physical, mental and spiritual, through the recitation of its hymns during the attendant medical practices. It might be noticed that considerable symbolism is also involved in these practices. The ailments identified in the *Atharvaveda* and treated witht the chanting of the hymns, as listed below, with the documentations of the hymns used would provide an idea of the extent of the Atharvam practices :

Apacit, AV 6.25; 6.83; 7.74; 7.76
Āsrāva, 1.2; 2.3; 2.3; 6.44
Asthibhaṅga, 4.12
Balāsa, 6.14; 6.127
Grāhī (Apasmāra), 6.112; 6.113
Harimā, 1.22
Jalodara, 1.10; 6.24; 6.127
Jāyānya, 7.76.3-5
Kāsa, 6.105; 6.107
Keśavṛddhi, 6.21; 6.136
Kilāsa, 1.23; 1.24
Kriminā́śana, 2.31; 2.32; 5.23
Kuṣṭha 5.4
Kṣetriya, 2.8; 2.10; 3.7
Mūtrakṛcchra, 1.3
Pakṣaghāta, 6.80
Palita, 1.23; 1.24
Rājayakṣmā 3.11; 7.76
Rudhirasrāva, 1.17
Sarpaviṣnāśana, 4.6; 4.12.10.10
Śula. 6.90
Ślesmapatana, 6.105; 6.107
Takman, 1.25; 5.4; 5.22;
6.20; 7.116; 19.39
Vājikaraṇa, 4.4; 6.72; 6.101; 7.90
Viṣakandha, 2.4'; 7.9
Vraṇa, 6.57; 6.109
Yakṣmā m2.33; 3; 31; 6.85; 9.8

Materia Medica

The *Atharvaveda* makes mention of more than a hundred plants whose roots, leaves, bark, splinters, flowers, fruits or juices have been made use in the medication concerned. Besides the vegetable kingdom, minerals and the animal kingdoms also contributed to the materia medica of Atharvam medicine. It is instructive to note that the materials used as above continued to be used in later Āyurveda, of course with additions without number.

Conclusion

It is only natural that later texts on Āyurveda make the maximum use of the medical material available in the Atharvaveda. Indeed, the tradition of Āyurveda has been developed on the basis of Atharvam medicine, towards which the information documented above should bear ample proof.

Bibliography

Atharvaveda Saṁhitā. Ed. Pt. Madhavacharya Shastri. Madhav Vidya Bhvan, Kamala Nagar, Delhi, n.d.

Atharvaveda Saṁhitā. Translated into English by William Dwight Whitney. Rep. Motilal Banarsidas, Delhi, 2 vols, 1984.

Caraka Saṁhitā with Commentary, Āyurvedadıpika of Cakrapaṇidatta. Ed. Vaidya Jadavaji Trikamji Acharya. 3rd edn., N.S. Press, Bombay, 1941.

Suśruta Saṁhitā with the Commentary of Dallaṇācārya. Ed. Jadavaji Trikamji Acharya. N.S. Press, Bombay, 3rd ed., 1988.

Karambelkar, V.W. *The Atharvavedic Civilization*. Nagpur, 1959.

Karambelkar, V.W. *The Atharvaveda and the Āyurveda*. Nagpur, 1961.

Bahulkar, S.S. *Medical Ritual in the Atharvaveda Tradition*. Poona, 1994.

References

1. That the Vedic saṁhitās like *Ṛgveda-saṁhita* and *Atharvaeda-saṁhitā* are but 'collections' or 'compilations' and not composed in the form in which they have come down, as is often supposed, would be clear when one looks at the 'logical' arrangement of the hymns contained therein. Thus, in the *Ṛgveda*, which is divided into ten sections called *maṇḍala-s*, which *maṇḍalas* 1 and 10 contain hymns of a miscellaneous nature numbering exaeshy 191 in each, all the hymns each of the sections 2 to 7 are hymns composed by members of individual families, *viz.*, Gṛtsamada, Viśvāmitra, Vāmadeva, Atri, Bharadvāja, Vasiṣṭha and Kaṇva-Aṅgiras, respectively, and the hymns themselves have been arranged according to their presiding deities and, that too, in the order Agni, Indra and the like. All the hymns orbieh have *Soma* as the deity have been collected together in section 9. Arrangement of the *mantra-s* under similar consideration can be seen in other Vedic texts also.
2. Cf. *ye Atharvāṇah tad bheṣajam*, (*Gopatha Brāhmana*, 1.3.4).
3. Cf. *bheṣajaṁ vai devānāṁ attarvaṇaḥ* (*Pañcaviṁśa Brahmaṇa*, 16.10.10).
4. Cf. *rcaḥ sāmāni bheṣajā yajūṁsi*, (AV 11.6.14). The four Vedas are *Ṛk*, *Sāma*, *'bhaiṣajya'* and *Yajus.'* See also *atharvadedo vedaḥ, soyam iti bheṣajam nigadet*ı (*Sāṅkhāyana Śrautasūtra*.
5. For a full-fledged documentation of *Atharvaveda* anatomy see V.W. Karambeklar, The *Atharvaveda and the Āyurveda*, pp. 294-98.

Vedic System of Education

17

Dr. V. Ramachandran Nair

Any educational system in a society seem to have been moulded according to the life style and is aimed to fulfill the various needs of that society. Therefore, before directly entering into the subject of Vedic System of education, a short description of vedic age, the people and their mode of life is worth mention.

After the rich Indus Valley Civilization, another civilization, flourished in India later on. The people who evolved this culture called themselves Aryas or Aryans.

Part–I
THE ARYANS

From their original home at 'Althai Mountain' (Ilavartha)[1] they moved in many directions. One such branch moved in the direction of Persia and India, and lived at some place for a sufficiently long time. To this branch the name of Arya is applied. This branch further developed a new religion; they created new gods, and a class of people, the priests, to act as intermediaries between themselves and their gods; they conceived of a moral order ruling the universe and evolved the institution of sacrifices in which the cult of fire predominated. At last, they divided into two branches one entering Persia and the other India.

There are evidences outside India to show that in Asia Minor and other countries in Western Asia there was some activity of the Aryans. Some inscriptions about the fourteenth century B.C. found at Boghaz Koi in Cilicia (Asia Minor), the capital of the ancient Hittites, mention some Aryan deities, such as, Indra, Varuna, Mitra and the Nasatyas (Asvins). The kings of the Mitanni in the upper Euphrates invoked Aryan deities to witness and safeguard a treaty made in 1400 B.C. The Kassite princes, who held Babylonia for about six centuries (circa 1000 to 1200 B.C.), used Aryan names. The relationship of the Aryans who entered the Punjab with the inhabitants of the Iranian plateau is shown by the close resemblance between their language and sacred books. Some scholars hold that these facts indicate that these regions were visited by the Aryans in the course of their ramblings before they entered India; others, however, hold the opinion that these Aryan influences were the result of contact, commercial or otherwise, with the Aryans of India.

In contrast to the then inhabitants of India, the Aryans appear to have been a comparatively fair folk with long heads straight noses, well-developed foreheads and a high facial angle. Their advent in India has been variously dated, from 5000 B.C. and even earlier to 1500 B.C.

The Aryan migration into India was gradual. They did not enter India in one stream. The immigration was a prolonged process distributed over a period of a few centuries. The Aryans came not as invaders but as peaceful emigrants with their flocks of cattle, their wives and families, their household goods and gods; successive waves of immigrants followed one another at considerable intervals. But their entry was not unopposed. As they advanced in easterly direction, they came into conflict with peoples living in fortified areas (puras and durgas), under their own kings and chiefs. They are contemptuously spoken of in the Vedas as Dasyus or slaves. The Rigveda itself describes a hundred pillared fort of the enemies that the Aryans had to contend with. The fact that many of the hymns of the Vedas are addressed to the gods for assistance in fighting their enemies reveal to us that the Aryans waged prolonged wars with the non-Aryans. The high god of the Vedas, Indra, who is described as Purandara (the shaker of cities), is stated to have destroyed many cities for the Aryans. There is also an interesting account of an attack on a hundred towns of an aboriginal king. The Vedic hymns constantly refer to the wars between Divodasa, the ruler of the tribe of the Bharatas, and he Dasyu prince Sambara. Gradually, however, the contest became less fierce. The pre-Aryan inhabitants were completely conquered by the Aryans who intermixed with the vanquished. As time went on, Indo-Aryans became absorbed in the population of the country, though they left behind them indelible traces of their culture.

Vedic Literature

The only source of information about the Aryans in India is the vast literature known as the Vedas. The word "Veda' comes from the root Vid, to know. It means knowledge in general. It is specially applied to a branch of literature which has been handed down from time immemorial by verbal transmission and is declared to be sacred knowledge or divine revelation (Sruti). The Vedas are four in number - Rigveda, Samaveda, Yajurveda, and Atharvaveda.

The parts which constitute the Vedas — (1) the Samhitas of the four Vedas; (2) the Brahmanas attached to each of the Samhitas; governing and controlling the Universe seems finally to have emerged and to have superseded the earlier conception of a number of deities co-ordinating in their work of controlling the great cosmic phenomena.

The Origin and Early Evolution of the Hindu Civilization bear traces of the pre-Aryan Culture. The battle of the Ten Kings also witnessed the end of the 'Pure Aryans'. The earlier settlements in the Punjab were predominantly Aryan. But the new state of Sudas to the east of the Jamuna was a composite kingdom where the Aryan population, though exercising dominant influence, was numerically smaller. The victory of Sudas was the triumph of a coalition of Aryans and the indigenous non-Aryan people. The Yakshas and other tribes, that were fighting on the side of Sudas under their own king Bheda, were non-Aryans. "This victory, therefore, established the political assimilation of Aryans and the non-aryans in the new Aryan colonies of the Gangetic plains."

The logical outcome of this political assimilation of the Aryans and the non-Aryans was the evolution of a civilization known as Aryan, but predominantly that of the conquered indigenous people. The synthesis of the Aryan and the pre-Aryan people resulted in the Hindu civilization bearing the traces of the rich pre-Aryan civilization and culture. The first clearest evidence of this is afforded by the Aryan attitude toward the Lingam and the God whom it symbolizes. In Rigveda, VII, 21, 5, a significant statement is recorded, "Let those, whose deity is Phallus, not penetrate our sanctuary." "This fear of the Phallic worshippers of the pre-Aryan civilization is replaced later on in the Vedas by its recognition in the official ritual, the Lingam finding its place even in the Aswamedha. Shiva Pashupati also assumes greater significance in the later Vedas, and from the period of the Yajurveda Shiva assumes the aspect of a greater deity.

The second clearest evidence is the gradual disappearance of the Aryan gods in the later Vedic civilization. Varuna, to whom a large number of hymns had been addressed, disappears altogether from the pantheon and becomes a mere Dikpāla. Vāyu is also reduced to the backward position, while Indra, the mighty destroyer of cities and the chief eater of sacrifices in the early Vedic period, is merely a super king of the lower heavens where he holds luxurious court and is depicted as a debonair debauchee. The Vedic gods died soon after the Aryans conquered the Dasyus or non-Aryans, and were reborn as minor sacrifices were performed later on to gods who had ceased to be potent; the same mantras were repeated and enchanted but to gods who were no longer worshipped. It is probable that the script which the Indo-Aryans evolved was also based on the script of the Indus Valley. Obviously, the pastoral Aryans who slowly conquered the local population assimilated their culture and civilization. Consequently, Hinduism, as it is today, was the outcome of this assimilation. Therefore, the theory of Aryan origin of Hindu civilization is to be greatly modified.

The third evidence to show the traces of the pre-Aryan culture is that the rishis of the Upanishads in the post-Vedic period were no longer concerned with the Vedic gods. In the later Vedic literature, allusions to the mother-goddess also occur indicating the influence of the non-Aryan religion. Many of the rishis are alluded to by their mother's name. As the Aryan society was patriarchal, this system of identification perhaps indicates the influence of a matriarchal system of the indigenous people. Thus, the system which has been evolved as a result of the contact between the Aryans and the non-Aryans was a synthesis in which, while the forms of Aryan conquerors predominated, the thought and tradition of the conquered non-Aryans found new expression.

Again, in the Rigveda the gradual transformation of the Aryans from a pastoral to an agricultural state of society brings the village into prominence. It is more probable that the self-contained village is merely a continuation of the organization of the earlier peoples, rather that the outcome of the Rigvedic Aryan system. Cities like Mohenjodaro could only have flourished on an elaborate system of agriculture and a rural economy based on villages. It is, therefore, more reasonable to assume that when the Aryans became an agricultural people they took over the village organization as they found it existing in the indigenous system. Even today the village continues to be the unchanging backbone of Indian economic and social life.

Aryan Doctrine of Racialism and Colour Distinction

Aryans introduced into India the ideas of racialism and colour bar. Their sense of being fair-complexioned in contrast to the indigenous or non-Aryan people who were dark-skinned, dominated their whole thought and all actions. To this was added their two strong convictions: (i) that God had revealed Himself to them through the Vedas, and (ii) that their power which enabled them to conquer and subdue the Dasyus was derived from their mystical rites and magical practices. They had to keep them inviolably secret. The sense of colour couped with their sacred knowledge led to the perpetuation of distinction between the Aryans and the non-Aryans, or between the twice-born and the once-born. The twice-born or the dvijas were the people who after performing certain mystical rituals were entitled to receive the sacred knowledge and participate in the Aryan worship and sacrifices. This was the starting-point of the caste system which was elaborated and developed later on in the form of chaturvarnya system by the Dharma Sastra writers.

But is should be noted that this colour and racial distinction theory of relegating the dark-skinned to an inferior position, was never wholly effective. There is ample evidence to show that the races mixed together and the Aryans accepted the dark-skinned even among their rishis. Badarayana Veda Vyas, who edited the Vedas and arranged them, was the dark-skinned son of a fisher woman-the illegitimate progeny of an Aryan saint, and was called as Badarayan the Black. The doctrine non-Aryans or the non-Dvijas were inferior affected in no way the position of the indigenous rulers whose support King Sudas had to seek. We have many references to the matrimonial alliances of kings and even priests with the indigenous population. This establishes the fact that before the caste system took shape, much intermixture of the Aryan and the non-Aryan blood had already taken place. "Though racialism remained in the form of the doctrine of the Aryans, the initiation into the secrets and mysteries of the Vedic Mantras, became the test of the dvija and the non-dvija and in course of time the conception of Aryanhood became one of status and culture rather than a varna or colour."

LATER VEDIC AGE

"The period following that of the Rigveda is known as the Later Vedic Age. It was in this age that the three later Veda-Samhitas, namely, the Samveda Samhita, the Yajurveda Samhita, the Atharvaveda Samhita as well as the Brahmanas and the Upanishads of all the four Vedas and later on the two great epics-the Ramayan and the Mahabharat-were composed. The composition of the Brahmanas of the Rigveda Samhita was about the same time as the Samhitas of the three other Vedas were composed. Not much time elapsed between the composition of the later Vedic Samhitas and their Brahmanas. This later Vedic literature together with the epics enables us to form some idea of the development that took place in that age.

Aryan Expansion.[2] In the Rigvedic Age, the Aryan tribes had spread over the regions from Kabul to the Upper Ganga and had built up small kingdoms mostly under hereditary kings. As a result of the internecine strife in which some of the weaker tribes were engaged in the Rigvedic times, a few of the weaker tribes were absorbed by their more powerful neighbours. Consequently, the wealth and the territory of the conquering tribes increased Stately, cities and extensive compact kingdoms came into existence. They are mentioned for the first time in the later Vedic texts.

With the growth of the extensive kingdoms and large cities, the political and cultural sway of the Aryans further extended towards the east and the south. By the end of the Vedic period the Aryans had thoroughly conquered and subdued the fertile plains of northern India watered by the Jamuna, the Upper Ganga and the Sadanira (the Rapti or the Gandak). Later on some adventurous enterprising groups of the Aryan people penetrated into the Vindhya forests and went into the Deccan. There they established powerful kingdoms.

Simultaneously, with the Aryan expansion and colonization, the west Punjab gradually got out of the Aryan ken, and centre of the Aryan world shifted from the Punjab to the land between the Saraswati and the Ganga. This region was know as the "First Middle Country" (Dhruva Madhyamandis). It was occupied by the Kurus, the Panchals and some adjoining tribes. It was from the region that Brahmanical civilization spread to east and south-east. It was extended to the land of the Kosalas and the Kasis, modern Oudh and eastern U.P. It was further carried to the swamps of east of the river Gandak and to the valley of the Wardha (western Bihar and Madhya Pradesh of the present time). Beyond these regions lived the non-Aryan tribes of mixed origin. They were the Angas of east Bihar, the Magadhas of south Bihar, in addition to the Dasyus or aboriginal people known as the Pundras of the north Bengal, the Pulindas and Savaras of the Vindhya forest and the Andhras of the Godavari valley.

Many of the famous tribes of the Rigvedic Age had passed into oblivion and new ones had taken their place. Thus, the Bharats, the Purus and the Tritsus were superseded by the Kurus, the Panchals and the Kasis. Though their names do not occur in the Rigvedic hymns, but in the later Vedic Age they played an important part in the political life of the country. It seems that the Purus and Bharats who were enemies at the time of the battle of the Ten Kings were now amalgamated under the new name Kurus. They occupies Kurukshetra as well as the districts of Delhi and Meerut. Their capital was Asandivat. They were considered the most cultured of the Aryans. They were the best masters of rituals and could perform sacrifices without fault. The later Vedic texts describe powerful Kuru Kings like Balhika-Pratipiya, Parikshit and Janamejaya. Closely allied to them was another distinguished tribe-the Panchals with Kampila as their capital. They occupied the northern portion of the Ganga-Jamuna Doab and held an equally important position in popular estimation. The Panchals also produced conquering kings. For a long time, they engaged in wars and alliances with Kurus. But they were famous chiefly because their land was the house of theologians and philosophers like King Pravahana and Jaivali, and the sages like Aruni and Svetaketu.

Later on, in the time of the Upanishads, the reputation of the land of the Panchals as a centre of Brahmanical learning dwindled. Soon it was eclipsed by the fair name and fame of the land of the Vedehas or modern north Bihar. Their king Janaka won the proud title of Samrat. He gathered the celebrities of the Kuru-Panchala lands in his court. To the west of the Vindhyas was the kingdom of the Kosalas in the country now called Oudh. Near modern Banaras, the Kasis established their power. Further east, that is beyond Bihar, as noted above, lived the Magadhas and the Angas who were yet outside the pale of the Aryan civilization. In two passages of the Aitareya Brāhmana, mention is made of Vidarbhas of Bihar. A few other tribes like the Matsyas, the Sur-Senas and the Gandharas were also existing having governments of their own. Thus, nearly the whole of Northern India, from the Himalayas to the Vindhyas and perhaps even beyond, had not come within the ken of the Aryans. However, in the Śatpatha Brāhmana frequent allusions to the aggressive and ambitious wars, waged between the neighbouring Aryan rulers as also between the Aryan and he non-Aryan States, explain the consequent rise and fall of these States.

Growth of the Royal Power

The early Rigvedic tribes and principalities were amalgamated into powerful political units. The amalgamation of the tribes, the acquisition of new territories and the subsequent swelling of the kingdom in size, and the successful leadership of the kings in war inevitably led to a growth in the royal power and prerogatives. "Without a king, the position of men would be like that of a herd of cattle without a herdman" was the principle accepted. Kings claimed absolute royal power over their subjects. Even the Brahmans were "liable to removal at will." Tributes, such as, bali, sulka and bhaga were paid to the king by common men. They could be "oppressed at will", while the members of the servile classes or lower groups were liable to be "expelled and slain at will". Elaborate consecration ceremony with sacrifices and prayers was performed to raise the king to a higher status than ordinary humanity. Though there was no divine right of kings, but divine virtues were attributed to him.

The theory of the divine origin of kingship was given expression in the later Vedic period. In the later Samhitas and the Brahmans the divinity of the king is put forth as a general doctrine. The king is declared to have gained identity with Prajapati by virtue of the Vajapeya and Rajasuya sacrifices.[3] The Śatpatha Brāhmana definitely declares, "He, the Rajanya, is the visible representative of Prajapati (the Lord or creatures); hence, while being one, he rules over many."[4]

The ideal of paramountey or universal sovereignty began to loom large on the political horizon. Successful and powerful kings began to claim the rank of universal king (raja visvajanina), lord of all the earth (sarvabhumi) or sole ruler (ekarat) of the land down to the seas. To symbolize their success over other rulers they celebrated sacrifices befitting their status like the Rājasuya (royal consecration), the Vajapeya (drink of strength), and Aśvamedha (horse-sacrifice). These sacrifices demonstrated the degree of power and prestige attained by the ambitious kings. Frequent references to such terms as Samrat, Bhoja, Virat, Adhiraja, Rajadhiraja, etc., for the title and designation of the king, point to the growth of imperialism and feudal ideas. They also denote various gradations of suzerains.

The kind had to perform mainly military and judicial functions. He was to protect his people, maintain the laws, and destroy the enemies of his subjects. He used to dispense with justice and punish the criminals. He wielded the rod of chastisement (danda). He was usually, though not invariably, a Kshatriya. Prevailing form of government was monarchy. It was even now hereditary. The coronation songs in the Atharvaveda prove that the people elected monarchs some time.[5]

Theoretically, the king was absolute, but in practice his absolute authority did not exist. His royal claim to absolutism did not pass unchallenged. At his coronation, he had to take an oath by which he promised to be loyal to religion, to protect the Brahmans and the laws of the realm. He said -

"If I play thee false, may I lose the merit of all my religious performances and gifts of my good deeds, my place, my life, and even my progeny!"

The king is thus addressed-

"To thee this state is given for agriculture, progress and for the commonweal."

This indicates that the kingdom was regarded as a trust and not a possession, and the condition of holding it was the promotion of the common welfare and prosperity.

Sabha and Samiti: The popular assemblies-the Sabha and the Samiti-of the Rigvedic period continued and it is stated in Atharvaveda[6] that concord between the king and the assembly was essential for the former's prosperity. The king sought their support, but the details are not clear. It appears that they deliberated upon matters of public importance, such as, war, peace, finance, and sometimes they decided lawsuits about land, debts, inheritance and criminal offences. Occasionally through Samiti popular wrath vented itself in the expulsion of absolute or tyrannical kings together with erring officials. There are references to Samiti sometimes electing or re-electing a king. In other words, the system of government and organization in the later Vedic period was perhaps more 'democratic' in the sense that the authority of the leaders of the Aryan tribes was still recognized by the king. In spite of the popular assemblies the king's power was on the increase due to the growth of large territorial states and the evolution of an official hierarchy in place of the old nobility by birth.

Elaboration of the Administrative Machinery

With the growth of the realm and the royal power came an elaboration of the machinery of the government. The king and his officials seem to have grown greatly in importance. The officers were collectively known as Viras or Ratnins. They included, according to Dr. R. C. Majumdar, "Samgrahitri (treasurer), the Bhagadagha (collector of taxes), the Suta (royal herald, bard or charioteer), the Kshattri (chamberlain), the Akshavapa (superintendent of gambling), the Govikartana (king's companion in the chase), the Palagala (courtier) in addition to the older ecclesiastical and military officials like the Purohita (chaplain), the Senani (general) and the Gramini (leader of the host or of the village)." Gramini in the Rigvedic period was chiefly a military officer, but in the later Vedic period he was both a military and civil official. He presided over the city or village where the court was held. The post of gramini was the summit of the ambition of the Vaisyas. In later years the gramini formed the channel through which the royal power was exercised in the village." (The Cambridge History of India, Vol. I, p. 131). Gramini and Suta were known as rajakartri or 'king-makers.' It reveals their importance in the politics of the day. We have references to the generic title Sachiva which was applied to ministers in later ages. People contributed to the state taxes known as bali and sulka, and they were collected by officers known as Bhagadugha and probably deposited with Samgrahitra (treasurer). This indicates significant development in the system of taxation and revenue administration.

The main burden of the taxation fell on the 'people' who pursued peaceful occupations, such as, agriculture, cattle-keeping, the arts, crafts, industries, and trade. The texts of ten describe the 'people' as forming the back bone of royal power.

Reference to the Sthapati and the Satapati point to a regular system of provincial government. The duty of the Sthapati was to administer outlying regions often inhabited by aboriginal tribes, while the Satapati probably "looked after a group of a hundred villages and was the precursor of the long chain of rural officials mentioned in the law-books." According to the Prasna Upanishad the lowest official was the Adhikrita, the village officer. He was appointed by the king himself. As regards the police arrangements we know very little. However, we have a reference to police officials in the Jivagribh of the Rigveda and the Ugras of the Upanishads. The King's share in the administration of justice was greater. He upheld the law, Dharma, and punished the wicked. But sometimes he delegated his powers to Adhayakshas or overseers. Occasionally certain cases were referred to the tribe for adjudication. A small body of Sabhasads or assessors used to conduct the judicial work of the tribal assembly, the Gramyavadin or village judge and his court (Sabha) used to decide petty cases in the village. Civil cases were sometimes decided by arbitration method. Private vengeance in the criminal cases was recognized. Punishments for crime were rather severe. If a thief was caught red-handed, death or cutting off the hands was the penalty; in milder cases, blinding to posts and the return of stolen goods sufficed as punishments. Miscreants were punished with fines and trial by ordeal was sometimes resorted to.

The property of the family was the property of the head of the house, usually the father.The sons, when grown-up, might claim the property and induce the father to divide it. As regards the divisions, preference was shown to the elder son if it took place after the death of the father; during his lifetime, the preference was usually shown to the elder son but not rarely to another. Women were excluded from inheritance or partition. Neither they nor the Sudras had any right to property.

Society

The later Vedic literatures reflect a complete change in the social life of the Aryans.

Dress, Diet and Amusements: Though little change can be traced in the mode of house-building and the style of dress, in dietary the eating of meat was disfavoured. Variety of eatables had increased. New forms of social entertainments had come into existence. Music, both vocal and instrumental, dancing, chariot-racing, horse-racing and gambling were the amusements of the Age. There are "reference to the Sailusha (actor), and gathas or Verses were sung by the lute-players (vinagathin) at great public festivals to the accompaniment of musical instruments which were sometime furnished with a hundred strings (satatantu). Such gathas foreshadow the 'songs of victory' which developed into the Great Epic."[7] There were many lute-planers, flute-players, conch-blowers and drummers.

The position of the woman had deteriorated. She could not inherit property and her earnings belonged either to the husband or the father. The birth of a daughter was regarded as a source of misery and a son was an object of desired. Women were not allowed to go to the tribal assembly (Sabha). They had no share in politics. Polygamy was practised and married women of the upper-classes had often to suffer the presence of rival wives. The lot of queens was specially unenviable in this respect. The Mahishi or the official chief queen and the vavata or the favourite one, were loved and respected, others like the parivrikti were neglected. Conjugal morality stood on a high level. The women continued to participate in religious rites. Some of them received education of high order. It enabled them to participate prominently in philosophical deliberations at royal courts. The rules of marriage underwent a change towards greater rigidity. A marriage was banned within the circle of agnates and cognates. There were instances of child marriage and Sati.

Social Doctrine of Varnashrama Dharma: It is social concept which prescribes suitable activities for different stages of life. According to it life is divided into four periods, namely, Brahmacharya (the period of celibate education), Grihastha (the period of domestic life), Vanaprastha (the life of retirement into the solitude of forest for meditation and introspection), and the Sannyas (the life of renunciation and the ascetic search for divine life). The later Vedic Age was gradually organizing this ideal for every householder to follow.

Chaturvarnya or Caste System: The caste system developed during this period in many directions. Hereditary occupations, workers' guilds, gotra-traditions, the race-feeling between the Arya Varna (Vedic Aryans) and Dasyu Varna (aborigines), and the mixed marriages were the factors in caste elaboration in this age. The functions and duties, the privileges and status of the four castes were differentiated minutely in the religious and social spheres.

In the early Vedic times there seems to have been a threefold division of the society into Brahmana (priest), Rajanya (nobility or the aristocratic section of the population), and Vis (the common folk). There are many references about hunters, fishermen, ploughmen, domestic servants, field servants, cooks, basket makers, rope-makers, fire-rangers, chariot-makers, bow-makers, carpenters, tanners, hide-dressers or furriers, washermen, dyers, weavers, barbers, potters, smiths, musicians, merchants, moneylenders and others.[8] Women mostly participated in industrial persuit as makers of embroidered garments, workers in thorns, dyers, make of baskets, etc. A class of hereditary merchants (Vanija) came in being. The use of silver was increased and various types of ornaments were made out of it.

There were inland trades with the Kiratas inhabiting the mountains. They exchanged the drugs, which they dug up on the high ridges, for clothes, mattresses and skins. People were well acquainted with the sea and the mention of the legend of the flood the Satapatha Brahmana is considered by some scholars as an indication of intercourse with Babylon. Regular coinage had not stated Dr. R.C. Majumdar holds the opinion that commerce was facilitated by the use of convenient units of value like the nishka, the sataman and the krishnala. But it is doubtful if these had acquired all the characteristics of a regular coinage. The nishka which was previously a necklet, was now probably a lump of gold possessing a definite weight which was equal to three hundred and twenty ratis, which also was the weight of a satamana. A krishnala weighed one that is 1.8 grains. Reference to ganas or corporation and sreshthins or eldermen indicate that merchants were probably organized into guilds.

House-building and Means of Transport: The house (harmy) was large enough the contain not only a large family, but also for cattle and sheep, and evidently had many rooms with a special place for the Grahapatha fire which was kept continuously burning. Houses apparently were generally built of wood as in the Rigveda period. The Dhan dhani (treasure-house) mentioned in the Taittiriya Aranyaka[9] was probably a special type of room or house. The Atharvaveda mentions Patninam Sadan or a part of the house known as women's apartments. A seat with a pillow or cushion or covering a bed, and a couch were among the articles of furniture mentioned.

As regards means of transport there were wagons (anas) draw by oxen, chariots (ratha) for war and sport, and a rough vehicle (vi-path)[10] used for bad tracks. Riding of horses and elephants was in use. Ships and boats were plying on rivers and seas. They were popular modes of transport.

Religious Development

Great significant changes took place in the religious life of people during the later Vedic period. During this Age we discover three distinct currents of religious thoughts-the ritualistic, the philosophic and the ascetic.

Gods. The old gods, Varuna, Indra, Agni, Surya, etc., were worshipped by the people with less zeal. The characters of these Rigveda gods had now become quite colourless. Their natural basis was utterly forgotten. They were now evoked as 'demon destroyers'. New gods Shiva, Rudra, Vishnu had arisen. Thus, the lustre of the older Rigvedic gods was gradually growing dim, though here and there, especially in the Atharvaveda, we find magnificient hymns celebrating the omniscience of Varuna or the beneficence of the Earth-goddess, Common people began to express their favour for certain deities already known to the Rigveda, but not so prominent as Indra or Varuna. One of them was Rudra, who already bore and epithet of Shiva (propitious). This Rudra is not merely a development of the Rigvedic Rudra, but an adaptation of him by amalgamation with a popular god, an aboriginal god of Vegetation closely connected with pastoral life. He soon came to be regarded as the Great God (Mahadeva) and the lord or animate beings (Pasupati). His popularity was probably due to his identification with the chief male deity of the prehistoric people of the Indus Valley Civilisation and culture.

Side by side with Rudra rose god Vishnu. He was a solar deity and was well-know in the Rigveda. "As the source of cosmic and moral order, the deliverer of mankind in distress and the saviour of the Gods, Vishnu soon occupied the place of Varuna as the most sublime among the celestials, and his highest step (parampadam) became the goal of sages and peers. Before the final close of the Vedic canon, he came to be identified with Vasudeva-a hero or demi-god known to epic tradition as Krishna-Devakiputra."

Gandharvas, Asparas, Nagas, etc., were raised to a semidivine rank. Snake-worship (borrowed probably from the aborigines) and the mechanical motif of the 'Devasura' battles made their appearance now. Monotheism was being advocated.[11]

Rituals and Sacrifices: Another change that took place during this period was the elaboration of the rites and ceremonies concerning the old vedic religion. In the Rigvedic days the ways of worship and the performance of yajnas were a simple affair which every householder could do. Even on the occasion of public sacrifices, a tribal chief himself used to act as the high priest. In the later age, however, sacrifice became the all-important thing in worship. The sacrifice dominated everything. Gods were subordinate to them. People believed that gods must submit to the sacrifice if properly performed. Hymns were considered as charms or spells to be used in sacrifices. They were no longer the outburst of a poetic wonder as some power of nature. Popular superstitious beliefs in spirits, imps, spells, charms, incantations, and witchcrafts found a place in the sacred canon. The ceremonial side became more elaborate, complicated and expensive. The minutest details of the rituals were worked out and countless varieties of rituals were planned out, each to ensure some success on other. A regular science of sacrifice had now evolved. The belief that gods were propitiated by yajnas led to an increase in the number, variety and splendour of sacrifices which were prescribed for every householder. There were daily and periodical sacrifices.

There are references to sacrifices lasting several years and requiring the services of as many as seventeen priests, each with a definite business at different stages. In fact, the life of an Aryan was a series of sacrifices performed under the supervision of the Brahmana priests. This firmly established the supremacy of the Brahmanas.

High Sense of Morality and Duty: That life is a duty and a responsibility was a great ethical code of this period. "Man is born with certain "rinas" or debts which he must discharge in his life. He has a debt to pay to his gods, to the rishis, to the manes, to men, and to the lower creatures. And he discharges these debts, if he worship the gods, studies the Vedas, performs funeral ceremonies, is hospitable to guests, and offers oblations to the 'bhutas'." All this indicate high moral sense and noble sentiments. Selflessness was to characterize all actions. Everything was to be sacrificed to attain the freedom of spirit. Prayers and good works constituted godliness, which was supposed to be the first requisite of a good life. Inner purity was insisted on as much as external purity. Truth, performance of 'dharma' (duty), respect for parents, love of fellow-beings, and abstaince from theft, adultery, and murder were the sine qua non of good life.[12]

The Doctrine of the Supreme Brahmana, Punarjanma, Karma and Moksha. While the right spirit of religion and simple worship of the Vedic Age had disappeared and the priests and the theologians were evolving sacrificial rites, there appeared another current intellectual thought. Philosophers threw doubts on the efficacy of ritual and speculated about the underlying unity of the universe. The inquisitive mind entered deep into the problems of creation, and death, and came to the conclusion that there is one unchange principle (Brahmana) beyond the universe-the creator and control of the whole order. A verse in the Atharvaveda suggests the idea of Brahmana as the First Cause of all Existence and of the oneness of man with the world-soul.[13] It is the universal Soul or the Absolute "that dwelleth in everything that guideth all beings within, the Inwane Guide, Immortal." After the death of a person his soul passes to another body and again into another and so on before it can be five another body and again into another and so on before it can be five from all its imperfections and mingle in the Universal Soul. This the doctribe of transmigration of souls. Allied with this was another doctribe of Karma. "It lays down that no act or deed is lost that all actions, good or bad, bear their proper fruits and help the authors up or down the scale of transmigration." Souls have to be born again and again and reap the fruits of the actions (Karma) of their previous lives.

Closely connected with the doctrines of Karma and transmigration of soul is the doctrine of Moksha. It is a state of "birth-lessness and deathlessness," a point of time in the journey of the soul when it is liberated from the cycle of births and deaths, and becomes merged into the infinite Universal Soul of which it is but a small particle. A man was required to keep before his mind this ideal of Moksha, and he was expected to strive for it throughout his life.

The idea of reward and punishment after death, in exact correspondence to the good and bad deeds of a person in this life had gained a firm hold in this period. The attainment of immortality and the company of gods in the heaven was the deeply cherished aim of and incentive to, the practice of piety and good works in this life. The theory that Penance and atonement could purify and absolve the soul from guilt and exhaust the period of suffering, was also believed in and followed.

These doctrines and the philosophical speculations about the abstruse problems of God, Nature, Matter, Soul, Creation, Death, etc., are embodied in the Upanishads which were composed in this age offering the greatest contribution of India to world philosophy. A more systematic and logical examination of these problems is again made in the words collectively known as the "six systems of philosophy"—the Sankhya, the Yoga, the Nyaya, the Vaisheshik, the Purva Mimansa and the Uttar Mimansa. Thus, religion became more philosophical. Serious-minded persons began to ponder over the purpose of creation and the relation of the Individual to Brahma or the Universal Soul.

Ascetism: Another current of the religious though before the final close of the Age was the ascetic ideal of life. Tapa (austerity) and Brahmacharya (celibacy) were emphasized much and asceticism was favoured considerably. An ascetic was a person who renounced worldly life and retired to the solitude of the forest to meditate on the spiritual side of life. Disregarding caste system he believed in the transmigration of souls and the law of Karma. He subjected his body to severe austerities. His outlook of life was asceticism which was marked by self-mortification and was believed to be the means of purifying the soul, acquiring supernatural power and merging himself into the Universal Soul.

THE GLORY OF GURUHOOD

A Guru is a man of renunciation. He is one who has banished himself and loves to live in utter loneliness outside the pale of society. Not to be dictated to by any society but to try and tell society something good for it, is the difficult role that Gurus are expected to play. Otherwise society will drift its own way without any standards or norms which might lead social units to become stagnant and steeped more and more in the bog of relativism. It is Guru's influence that can act as a leaven to raise the moral and spiritual standards in any society and mix in fresh water and clean out the stagnation that is otherwise to be expected.

A long line of Gurus has been known on the soil of India, from the most ancient times. They should not be mixed up with pontiffs or dignitaries of institutionalized religions but should be seen as free representatives of the Wisdom heritage of the common man. This Wisdom heritage tends to become out-moded time and again in the history of peoples. When such a deterioration of standards in life takes place, it is the Gurus who enter the scene and by a dialectical revaluation of the Wisdom situation, together with its language and idioms, bring fresh life for the thoughts to be retained once again for use and contained, as it were, like old wine in new bottles. Thus the role of Gurus is a delicate yet a significant and glorious one.

Model Gurus of Indian Tradition: From the time of Brihaspati and Dakshinamurti we have had ancient models of Guruhood in India. They were free individuals who lived sometimes in dry-leaf-huts in the forests or in out-of-the-way places, far from the madding influences of the crowd and its ignorable strivings. The Yogi meditating under a tree with wild and domesticated beasts standing around him, has been an ideogram known in the Mohenjo-Daro seals. The same picture is retained later in the famous hymn to Dakshinamurti written by Sankaracharya in which the ideogram is seen repeated after thousands of years. Translated it reads;[14]

A picture-marvel, under you banyan tree behold:

Old are the pupils and the teacher he is young withal:

In uttar silence the teaching goes on

And yet the pupils with full-banished doubt remain:

This picture has nothing in common with what a religious dignitary might represent. The tree under which the Guru chooses to live, is to ensure his utter independence and freedom from those obligatory aspect of religious life into whose harsh aspects a Guru would never wish to dip his hands to stain them with anything not perfectly just. The Inquisition and the bloodshed that has drenched the soil repeatedly in the history of religions is not a chapter that could be associated with Guruhood. The burning at the stake of a man of science or the sin of having an innocent maid consumed in fire lit in a market place or, enviously hacking to death a beautiful woman philosopher have fortunately never tainted the glory of Guruhood as it has been preserved in forest hermitages by men of utter renunciation.

The Gurus have always stood for kindness to all life, and it accrues to the credit of one disciple of a Guru at least, that an emperor once laid down his sword when engaged in actual warfare in the name of non-hurting of fellow man. Living on roots or fruits that involve no hurt even to vegetable life, wearing the barks of trees only, and observing the everlasting vow of not hurting even an ant, such is the dedicated model of Guruhood and its glory.

Godly Men and Fully Human Divinities: Further, a Guru's glory consists in that he is ever free from any relativistic affiliations or commitments, whether in the name of his own or other religions, races or nations. He speaks in the name of all of them and refuses to add to any of the flames of separation or fanaticism.

Exclusiveness is a word unknown to all model Gurus and, although orthodoxy can sometimes become so harsh as to connive at such ideas as cutting out the tongue or filling with molten lead the ears of a low-born in the name of so-called caste in India itself, references that blemish the pages of some of the most respected of canonical writings of even the most tolerant of peoples otherwise found within any religious groups, amends are soon made by the Gurus who come after them, in the same spiritual lineage, so as to raise their reputation above all taint of relativistic attitudes within the Wisdom they represent. Untainted by anything mundane or what sets one man against another, Gurus generally may be said to have remained above the dust clouds of relativistic dispute and to have represented God on earth. They could be called godly men or fully human Divinities. Whether put one way or the other, one and the same truth in respect of the normal and neutral Guruhood, is revealed by either statement.

PURPOSE OF THE STUDY OF VEDIC EDUCATIONAL SYSTEM

The edifice of modern Indian education has been built primarily upon the foundation of ancient educational ideals. The practices of modern education have been largely moulded though the process of past experiences. As we cannot cut off the root of a live tree from its trunk and branches and still make it grow, we cannot cut off the past practices from a growing educational system. Ancient thought is the root of our civilization. If we are earnest about studying our educational system, we cannot therefore neglect the sphere of ancient thought from which our civilization has developed to its present form.

It is true that the system of education as practised in modern India was organised during the period of British rule in India by western educationalists. Western education has nothing to do with our culture and ancient heritage. Therefore, it failed to shape the minds of its recepients in accordance with the age old tradition of India. If dissatisfaction with this educational system was in evidence it was but natural. Grave responsibilities rest upon those who have the control of Indian education to see that its development shall be on such liens as may be most suitable to our country. If a system is to be evolved for India which shall be truely Indian, it must, while assimilating much that is western, also gather up what is best and most useful from its own ancient system. In these circumstances it becomes the duty of educators in our land to study the educational practices of the ancient preceptors in its original from.

LITERATURE ON ANCIENT EDUCATION — A SURVEY

When we search for the books written by scholars on ancient education we become rather disappointed as we find that only a few books are produced on the subject. We have a vast literature signifying the cultural heritage of India composed in Sanskrit language by great sages. Upanishads, Puranas, Dharmasutras, Epics etc. are pregnant with ideas on education and social life to be studied by modern educationists. Some of the modern studies available in this field are given below according to the chronological order, with short description.

(1) 'The Educational system of ancient Hindus' written by Santhosh Kumar Das popularly known as Dr. S. K. Das, and published by Mitra Press, 31-1, Grey Street, Calcutta, in the year 1930 was the first and foremost work produced in this field. The author who was a professor of Trichandra College, Nepal has discussed every aspect of educational system of ancient Hindus. The book contains 15 chapters in 500 and odd pages.

(2) 'Ancient Indian Education' by Dr. A. S. Altekar was published from Benares in the year 1934. It is another well written treatise on ancient educational practices. This book contained 10 chapters in 400 pages. The subjects such as educational rituals, the teacher had the student, students life, curriculum, useful education, primary education, female education, aims and ideas of education etc. are discussed in this work. A sample of the convocation address of ancient preceptors translated from Taittireeya Upanishad is also reproduced in the appendix of the book.

(3) **'History of Indian Education' :** Ancient and in Later times' by F.E. Key is another work of outstanding merit. It was published in 1942 by the Oxford University Press. There are some glimpses of ancient educational ideals in the first half of the book.

(4) 'Ancient Indian Education' by Radha Kumuda Mukerji published by Macmillan and Co. Ltd. in 1947 is an elaborate study on ancient educational systems. According to the publishers, 'this work is intended to fill a gap in the literature on the history of Education which has not taken adequate account of the unique contributions made by Hindu thought to both educational theory and practice.' This book stresses the importance in Vedic and post Vedic practices of education. In it we get short studies about the works of Kautilya and Panini. But original references from their words are not given there. Bibliography is also not given at the end of the book. The author who died recently is acclaimed to be a profound scholar in the subject.

(5) 'Some Aspects of Education in Ancient India' is a good research work prepared by late Dr. C. Kunjan Raja and published from the Adyar Theosophical society Madras in 1950. An earnest attempt to study some important aspects of ancient education is seen in all of the eight chapters of the book.

(6) 'History of Indian Education' (Ancient to Modern) by P. L. Rawat, published from Agra is a recent work in the subject. It was first published in the year 1953 in Hindi. In 1956 it was translated into English. Only the first part is

devoted to ancient education which contains only some short accounts collected from previous works.

(7) A book on Indian Education by K.S. Vakil and another by Bokil also throw some light on this sphere.

(8) 'Ancient Indian culture at a glance' written by Swami Tatwananda is also worth mentioning, especially its fourth chapter. These are the important works available in current literature on ancient Indian Education.

VEDIC SYSTEM OF EDUCATION

Eligibility of the Student

In ancient times great case was taken to discover the aptitude and fitness of an individual to receive any particular kind of education. The teachers fully realised that disastrous results are sure to happen if knowledge were to be imparted without any consideration of what suited one's tastes and ways of doing things.

The Goddess of learning came to a brahmin and said 'Preserve me, I am thy highest treasure. Do not impart me to a malicious person, there by my potency will be kept unimpugned.'[15]

'To him whom thou shalt know to be pure, perfectly continent and free from the follies of the world, to that brahmin shalt thou impart me.'[16]

In another passage Manu advises that 'even in the absence of a means of livelihood, rather let a Vedic preceptor die with his knowledge than impart it to an unworthy recipient.'[17]

From these reference it is clear that all pupils were not given education by the ancient preceptors, but the selected ones who have shown an aptitude to study.

Selection and Admission of Students

'The teacher should select only ten classes of pupil for instruction-the son of one's teacher, one who did personal service, one who taught some other subject, a good man, a man pure in mind and heart, a reliable person, one capable of comprehending and applying the knowledge acquired, a patron a recluse and a relative.'[18] The Indian teacher was thus not a believer in making higher education open to all. He imparted instruction to a student only when he was duly qualified for it by his character and capacity and by his heredity and environment.

Rules of Studentship

The rules for studentship were rigorous. Studentship begins at the age of 8, 11 and 12 respectively for the three castes but at 5, 6 and 8 for precocious pupils

(Manu II, 36, 37). The course of discipline and ạusterities regarding food, dress, habits, control over the senses (II-93, 94) as prescribed by him are also very severe. The duties of the pupils are performance of Sandhya (prayer) and Agnihotra sacrifice (II, 101, 106) tending the sacrificial fire (II-187) Swadhyaya (study of the Vedas) attending to the lectures (Pravachana) of the teacher etc :

Tonsure Ceremony

The weaning of the child from the sweet and softening influences of family life was signalised by a great ceremony which took place probably at the age of five. Later Charaka insists on the postponement of the school-going age to the 5th year. According to Vishnupurana also the period from birth to the fifth year of the child was regarded as the time for play, after which the time for study commenced.'[19]

Tonsure ceremony was a bodily sacrament to be conducted before the time of first initiation. 'Even for all the twice born, the tonsure ceremony must be performed according to rules; it has to be done in the first year or in the third as has been advised in the vedas.'[20]

Time of Upanayana

'The Upanayana ceremony which marked the beginning of vedic study was fixed at the 8th the 11th and the 12th year in the case of a Brahmana, Kshatriya or a Vaisya boy respectively.'[21] But it might take place between 8 and 16 in the case of a brahmana, between 11 and 22 in the case of a Kshatriya and between 12 and 24 in the case of Vaisya.[22] According to some Guru it is better to perform the ceremony of initiation at the age of five, six and eight respectively for the three castes for the attainment of Brahman for Brahmins, strength for Kshtriyas and wealth for Vaisyas.[23] Perhaps the suggestion of different ages for initiation of different castes, was done because of the supposed difference in I. Q. of the three castes due to the hereditary and environmental reasons.

Upanayana: The Ceremony of Initiation

In Satapathabrahmana (XI 5, 4) we get a short account of Upanayana (initiation) ceremony of a brahmana student. He is made to say to the preceptor 'I have come for studentship let me be a brahmacharin.' Before receiving him the teacher makes enquiry into his name, is birth and family. In Chandogyopanishad also we see such a conversation between the preceptor Gautama and the pupil Satyakama.[24]

At the time of initiation the pupil was given a sacred thread to indicate the vow of celebacy. From that time onwards he becomes a true 'follower of that preceptor. Manu says: 'Having initiated a pupil, let the preceptor teach him the rules of purification and good conduct as well as the mode of doing burnt offerings and worshipping Sandhyas.[25] He further says: To a brahmana duly initiated with the thread, shall be given instructions, regarding the practice of vow gradually and in conformity with the regulation; he shall be Samit twigs, for seven days in succession he must do the penance of an Avakirni (of broken vow). Thus it is clear that 'a student who was initiated properly must perform,' the fire sacrifice etc., a daily duty, till the time of the ceremony of samavartana or sacred bath.[26] 'In a later passage Manu also insists that the students should perform fire sacrifice twice daily i.e. in the morning and evening.[27] For the above purpose the student is bound to do the duty of 'collecting sacred fuel from the forests.[28]

Begging Alms

Since the students are the assets of society, society must help them to perform their day to day duties. The pupils have no time or ability to earn their livelihood. So they ought to go outside to beg for alms. Hindu thinkers made it an incumbent duty on all house holders to offer cooked food to the begging student. He begs not only for himself, but also for his teacher. As a rule all brahmacharins must go outside for begging alms on all days.[29] Before going outside to beg for alms a brahmacharin should take his staff, worship the sun and go round the fire as per rules.[30]. But the students should not collect more food than they needed. 'The brahmacharin has to collect just the necessary amount of food, if he collected more or retained it he would be guilty of theft.[31] Begging alms for himself for the teacher was considered as an inevitable duty of each pupil in the period of studentship. 'If in health, a brahmacharin fails to beg alms for seven days in succession, he must do the penance of an Avakirni (of broken vow) Manu II-187).

There are many rules to be observed by the pupils in the time of begging alms. The rules are as follows:

"He shall beg alms first of his own mother or sister or mother's sister or of any other woman who might not insult him with a refusal.'[32]

'He should beg alms from those who are given to Vedic study, the celebration of sacrifices and are intent on the performance of the duties of their respective castes and orders.'[33]

'He shall not beg alms of his preceptor's family nor of his cognates and relations.'[34]

'All articles obtained by begging should be undeceitfully made over to the preceptor. After becoming clean the brahmacharin may receive a part of it and eat it facing an eastward direction.'[35]

Days of Non-study

In Vedic period some of the important days were observed as holiday. The academic year has several terms. Each term is inaugurated by a ceremony called

Upakarma and ends by the Utsarga ceremony. 'The Vedas should not be studied for three days in connection with these two ceremonies.'[36] 'The king would allow three days as holidays on the birth of his son.'[37] 'The Vedas should not be studied on the full moon day and on the days of Amavasi and Ctuardasi.'[38]

"The Vedas should not be studied for one whole day and night on an animal (cow, cat etc.) happening to pass between a student and his preceptor.'[39] 'The study of Vedas must be terminated for one whole day and night when a dog a jackal or an ass emits a noise and when camels scream.'[40]

The fundamental condition of inspiring thought is peace within oneself and harmony with nature's forces. 'Hence when one shall hear thunder or see lightning he should not study the Vedas.'[41]

'After the Vedic studies had formally terminated with Utsarjan in February, bright half of the remaining months of the year should be devoted to the cultivation of the Vedas and the dark half to that of the Vedangas.' He thinks that 'Vedangas and non-Vedic works would be studied on the official holidays.'[42]

'In the case of serious students apart from the four monthly holidays studies seem to have been suspended only when they themselves or the place they were studying was impure.[43]

Curriculum

The syllabus for the course of studies in this period is very elaborate. The subjects mentioned by Manu are as follows :

(1) Three Vedas (II-10, XI-264) with their different charanas (III-145)

(2) Vedic hymns and verses (XI-249, 260)

(3) Atharva Veda (XI-33)

(4) Brahmanas

(5) Aranyakas (IV-123)

(6) Upanishads (II-140)

(7) Vedangas which are six in number Siksha, Kalpa etc. (III-185)

(8) Dharmasutras (1-10, III-232)

(9) Puranas (III-232)

(10) Heretical Sastras (XI-65)

(11) Varta (Secular subjects) (IX-19) Anvskshaki (dialectics) and Dandaniti (Politics) VIII-43.

There were different schools of thought which imparted education according to their syllabi. The Srautasutra schools taught the details of ceremonials relating to Vedic sacrifices. Next came the Dharmasutra schools which taught the students the customs, manners and laws of the society. Then came the Grhyasutra schools which taught the rights and obligations of the son, husband, wife, father etc: The code of Manu grew up in one of the above Dharmasutra schools.

REGULATIONS GOVERNING STUDENT LIFE

Early Rising

Gurus were very particular as to the habit or early rising. Late rising was considered as punishable.[44] 'If the sun rises; seeing the pupil asleep out of wilful laziness, let him mutter the Gayatri manthra and fast for a whole day.' 'Indeed a sleeping brahmacharin roused from his sleep by the sun, if he fails to do this penance is associated with a great sin.'[45]

Prayer

Guru insists that the students should pray to the deities and pay homage to them regularly. He says:[46] 'Both in the morning and in the evening let the student, pure and self-controlled, mutter the Gayatri and pray, sitting in a holy place.' He further says: 'After his daily bath a student must give oblations to gods, to great sages and to his ancestors, and worship the deities and collect the sacred fuels, On all days.'[47]

Daily Bath

'The student should take his bath every day,' according to Vishnu Samhita (38-9) twice a day, while according to Vasishta Samhita thrice a day. All preceptors advocate regular bath for a student to obtain physical purity which leads to mental purity also.

Dress

The student of different castes did not enjoy equal status in the practice of wearing dresses. Different kinds of dresses were used by them according to the order of merit. The brahmacharins of the three social orders shall respectively wear hempen, silken, and woollen clothes.' There are some restrictions in the case of wearing upper garments also. 'They shall put on upper sheets made of the skins of the antilope, ruru (a species of deer) and goat respectively.' Then Manu describes about the types of sacred threads : 'The holy thread of a brahmana shall be made of three strings of cotton thread, that of a Kshatriya with three strings of hempen thread and that of a Vaisya with three strings of woollen thread, suspended from the upper part of the body.'[48]

Staff

The student was invested with a staff for the sake of a long life of holiness. It was particularly useful for the life in the forest. Different kinds of sticks versed by the pupils of different casters.[49] According to Manu 'the staff of a brahmana shall be made of a height so as to reach to the hair of his head, that of a Kshatriya shall be of a height so as to reach his forehead while that of a Vaisya shall be of a height so as to reach the tip of his nose.'[50] 'Besides this it should be beautiful to look at, not eaten into by worms and uncreative of terror to any person.'[51]

The things used by the brahmacharin should be pure and perfect. That is why Guru insists the pupils 'to throw into water the girdle, staff, holy thread or the Kamandaly (ewer) which is broken or spoiled by use. They should take new ones, consecrated with mantras.'[52]

According to Manavagrhya sutra[53] the staff given to the pupil was to indicate his spiritual journey. Vajasaneya grhyasutra[54] says that the staff was given to the scholar to remind him that he was to be hence forward a watchman, armed with a staff to guard the Vedas.

Food

The student should daily support himself with a portion of the food acquired by begging. 'He should daily adore his food and taken it without speaking ill of it on seeing it he should be delighted and should welcome it with salutation.'[55] For says Manu 'Food daily worshipped, gives strength and vitality. Unworshipped food destroys both the world of the partaker.'[56]

'The student should eat his meal sitting with his face towards the east to acquire longevity.'

Only two meals per day was permitted for a brahmacharin. He should not take a third meal during the interval of his morning and evening ones. Manu says 'Let him avoid over-eating.' For says he: [57] 'Over eating brings on ill health and shortens the duration of life.' According to Manu the brahmacharins should be strict vegetarians. The food should not be a matter of pleasure but only a bodily need. So he advises the pupils 'to keep away from honey, mutton and such other articles.[58]

Sleep

The student should lie on the bare ground. He should not go to bed before sunset. Manu[59] says: 'If the sun goes down without the knowledge of the brahmacharin finding him resting in bed, let him mutter the Gayatri mantra and fast for a whole day.' He further says: 'If a student, who sleeps after sunrise and before sunset does not mind to perform the prayaschitta, he would surely attain great sin.'[60]

Celebacy

The word brahmacharya itself was considered as a synonym of celebacy. In the period of studentship the pupils were strictly prohibited from mingling with other sexes. Manu[61] says: 'Let the student refrain from visiting women.' 'Let him renounce embracing and casting lustful eyes on females.[62] 'Let him sleep always alone, and let him not cast his seed by any unnatural means, because it kills one's vow.'[63] It is interesting to note that even the nocturnal emission was considered as a sin in the part of the students. A brahmana student who was unintentionally spent himself in sleep, shall bathe and worship the sun and thrice mutter the hymn running 'Punaram' etc.[64]

Guru also advises the students to take utmost care in keeping the vow of celebacy especially when they happen to meet the young wife of the preceptor. 'If a preceptor's wife happens to be young, a disciple should not touch her feet during an act of obeisance, but returning from a sojourn in a distant country, he may be allowed to catch hold of her feet on the first day. On all subsequent days, he shall simply accost her without clasping her feet.'[65]

Serving the Teacher

The pupils should serve the teacher by word, mind and deed. 'The brahmacharin shall fetch pitcherfuls of water, flowers, cow-dung and kusa grass as much as his preceptor might require every day.'[66] In general 'he should do what is conducive to the good of his preceptor till his final bath.'[67] Later Manu uses a beautiful simile to illustrate the idea of serving the preceptors: 'As by digging the earth with an instrument one gets water; so by faithfully serving him, a pupil acquires all the knowledge which is contained in the guru.'[68] Guru insists the pupils 'to do good to the preceptors at all times.'[69] 'The student who serves the teacher till the end of his life should enter the eternal home of God.'[70]

Some "Should Nots"

Gurukula imposed many restrictions upon the pupils to enable them to lead a disciplined life throughout the period of studentship. Some of them are mentioned below:[71] 'The pupil should not take honey and articles of sweet taste which acquire an acid flavour when stale. He should forswear the use of scents. He should not use garlands of flowers. He should keep away from women, peals and such other articles of worldly pleasures. He should not kill or cause injury to animals. He should not use toilets to beautify his body and should not anoint his eyes. He should not use shoes and umbrellas.

Mental and Moral Discipline

Gurukula[72] requires the brahmacharin to overcome the passions by controlling the senses. He should renounce lust, anger, greed, dancing, singing, gambling, idle gossips, scandal, falsehood etc., to make a clear atmosphere for learning. But it may be argued that the severe discipline practised in ancient India was injurious to the growing minds of young students.

Dr. S.K. Das, author of the book 'The Educational System of the Ancient Hindus' however justifies the severity of the discipline in the following manner:[73] "All these conditions of studentship and rules governing Vedic studies seem to be very severe to us now; they seem to have made the life of the student miserable, as he was denied all worldly pleasures and had to live a beggar's or a menial's life in the house of a stranger. Indeed such restrictions might kill cheerfulness but they materially helped in the attainment of the spiritual ideal of the then education. They made students highly moral in conduct and respectful in behaviour."

General Discipline

Well behaved teachers are the assets of society. True discipline begins from the teachers. Gurukula stresses the importance of mental discipline for teachers in the following passages.

"The good of creatures should be effected with kind sympathetic means; desiring virtue, one shall use sweet and gentle words under the circumstances.'[74]

"He whose speech and mind are always pure and fully restrained derives all the benefits enumerated in the Vedanta.'[75]

Persecuted or oppressed, one must not hurt the feelings of others. Let him wish or do no injury to anybody.'[76]

Gurus were in favour of punishment but of a mild type; says he: 'Let him not raise a club to anybody nor strike anybody with a club, except his son and disciple for the sake of disciple.'[77] "A wife, son, servant, brother or disciple found guilty of an offence should be punished with a chord or with a bamboo-stick.'[78] 'But they shall be beaten only on the lower parts of the body and never on the upper limbs. For having flogged them in any other fashion one shall be liable to punishment for theft.'[79]

A student ought to obey the teacher in all respects. Without obedience learning would not take place. The teacher is free to punish the pupil if he becomes indifferent to his studies, but it is to be adopted as a last resort.

Importance of Character

"Conduct is the highest virtue as inculcated by the sruti and the smrti.' "Devoid of conduct a brahmana does not obtain the merit of reading the Vedas. Possessed of good conduct he reaps the entire fruit of such study.'[80] "Having thus observed the origin of virtue from good conduct, the sages accepted conduct as the basis of all austerities.[81] "A brahmana who knows only Gayatri but who is thoroughly self-restrained is better than he who knows three Vedas but who is not self-restrained, who eats all sorts of food and sells everything i.e., prohibited things.'[82]

Respect of Teacher

In the Vedic time teachers were highly respected by the pupils by word mind and deed. A little act of disobedience was considered as a great sin by the society. "The student shall eat food and wear garments inferior to those of his preceptor." "By the side of his preceptor he shall always occupy a lower bed or seat.[83] "He shall lie down in a lower bed than that of his preceptor and sleep after he has slept, leaving his bed before he rises.'[84] "He should avoid siting on the same bed or seat with his preceptor or at a place where his preceptor sits.[85] "He should not serve the preceptor while he stands aloof nor when he is angry, nor when a woman is near; if he is seated in a carriage or on a raised seat he should get down and salute the preceptor.'[86] "A disciple should stand up at the sight of his preceptor.'[87] Likewise 'he should behave towards his preceptor's wife, sons, friends and relations.'[88] "He should not utter his preceptor's name even at his back. Let him not imitate his speech, gait and manner.[89] 'Let him not wilfully leap over the shadow of his preceptor.'[90] It is, however very unkind on the part of Manu that he wants the pupils to respect not only the teachers, but also their shadows. He imposes discipline by the method of repression. He lays down rules for every thing and demands strict adherence to them. He even frightens the pupils by prescribing supernatural punishments. He says :[91] 'A calmniator of his own guru shall be born as an ass; and a vilifier of his down guru shall be a dog in his next birth; for having wrongfully enjoyed the property of this own guru, he shall be born as a worm; one who is envious of his guru's excellence shall take his birth as an insect in his next incarnation.

"The students were not allowed to speak to their relatives, parents etc: without the permission of the preceptors.

Teacher-Pupil Relationship

Some of the rules of the teacher pupil relationship are mentioned below. "The pupil must not sit with his guru when the wind will be blowing from his directing to that of his guru or the contrary; while in his company he must not say anything which is inaudible to his guru.'[92] "He must not speak to his preceptor when he is himself sitting standing lying down, eating or averting his face.'[93] If his preceptor sits, let him speak to him, standing up; he walks advancing towards him; if he comes towards him, meeting him; if he runs, running after him; turning round so as to meet him, if his face is averted; approaching him if he is at a distance; learning to him, if he be in a reclining posture.'[94]

"The pupils should not sit in a careless manner, before the eyes of their teachers." "Let them not in any way hurt or injure an acharya."[95] "Let the pupils shut their ears with hands or leaves the place where the guru is calumnised or lightly spoken of."[96] Of the progenitor and the teacher of the Vedas, more honoured is the teacher of the Vedas in as much as the birth of a twice born one in the knowledge of Brahman is the only abiding existence both in this world and the next.'[97] 'One must perpetually serve his parents and teacher and do what is pleasant and beneficial to them.'[98]

'By means of devotion and service to the preceptor one attains the region of God.' "This preceptor though he is younger than the pupils would also be respected by them, because he is their spiritual father.'[99] Manu cites an example for this practice in the following stanza. The young Angiras taught his old pupils by addressing them as my boys.'[100] This shows the shows the fatherly affection of the preceptors towards their pupils.

Teaching: The Monopoly of Brahmins

According to[101] Gurukula custom 'the brahmanas alone shall teach the Vedas and non else.'[102] 'Teaching the Vedas etc., shall never revert to Kshatriya as against the Brahmana.' 'Manu's law-code also should be taught in its entirety by an erudite brahmana and not by a member of any other caste.'[103] But in times or distress a brahmana student may take lessons from a non-brahmana teacher and he shall serve his guru only so long as he shall actually study.'[104] Wishing the most exalted existence after death, let not a brahmana student live for good in the house of his non-brahmana preceptor or in the house of an unlearned brahmin.'[105] 'The king shall learn from the people the theory of the various trades and professions'[106] seems to imply that in secular subjects other may be called in to give instruction to the princes.

Method of Teaching

According to Gurukula Culture, [107] 'the study commenced in the lastwatch of the night after which the student was not to sleep again. For the purpose of studying the Vedas, the student self-controlled, clad in a light garment looking towards the north shall do the achamana and unites his palms in the manner of Brahmanjale, after which lessons should be given to him.'[108] Catching hold of the feet of the preceptor was considered as a custom of students. 'At the commencement and at the close of his Vedic study, a student shall catch hold of the feet of his preceptor.[109] 'The preceptor then free from idleness, shall address him as 'O! You read now'.[110] Then the pupil shall purify his body by three (pranayamas breathing exercises and utter the word 'Om'.[111]

The reading lesson was followed by instruction (vidhi) and explanation (arthavada). The method of teaching the Vedic hymns was purely oral. The pupils were asked to memories the lessons by the method of recitation. Learning committed to memory was of a greatest use in sacrifices and scholarly discourses.

On Commercial Education

Gurukula down an ambitious scheme of commercial education as part of the education of the Vaisyas. "The Vaisya must possess the knowledge of defects or excellerences of articles, the good or evil traits of countries, profits or losses in manufactured articles....He must know the wages of artisans and workmen and languages of different races of men, shall be able to forecast the increase or decrease in the prices, and amelioration and deterioration in the quality of an article at a particular place and time as well as the mode of selling and buying. 'Thus the curriculum of commercial education for the Vaisya includes rudiments of commercial geography, arithmetic and some languages as well as the practical details of trade.

Education of the Prince

In ancient India the princes received the best education available in the country. They were taught all arts and sciences by well known scholars. That the princes used to have their initiation which marked the beginning of their student-life. In this passage he uses the word 'brahma samskara' for initiation. 'After his initiation' let him learn from those well-versed in the three Vedas, the threefold sacred science. The eternal principle of punishment, the science of reasoning, the science of self-knowledge and from the people the principles of trade, agriculture and cattle-rearing and the science of wealth.[112] Here we find the fact that the practice of a craft was not considered derogatory to the dignity of a prince.

High Regards to Learned Men

The learned men in ancient India were highly respected and protected by the kings. 'The king shall always provide for a srotriya.' 'Informed of his Vedic knowledge and holy rituals the king', shall provide for his proper means of subsistence; and like a son of his own loins he shall protect him from thieves etc.'[113] Again, 'Let the king make gifts of all kinds of gems as well as of fees for religious sacrifices to these brahmins and to those who are well-versed in the Vedas.[114]

'The king, we are told, even at the point of death must not take any revenue from a learned Brahmana; nor must he suffer a srotriya, living in his territory to be oppressed with hunger. The kingdom of king, wherein a srotriya is oppressed with hunger, is soon consumed by that hunger.[115]

The society not only honoured its learned, but also granted them special privileges. 'In the absence of a samanodaka, his preceptor and in the absence of a preceptor his disciple shall inherit one's property. In the absence of all kinds of relations, brahmanas, well-versed in the three Vedas, pure with their senses fully controlled, shall take the estates whereby virtue will not be impaired.'[116]

The students also enjoyed certain privileges. Thus, 'they are exempted from paying ferry-tolls.'[117] Students are never affected by death or birth-uncleanliness inasmuch as they are the representatives of Brahma.'

Importance of Learning

The ancient educators laid great stress on the acquisition of all knowledge especially Vedic learning. 'Wealth, relations, age, work and erudition which forms the fifth, are the sources of honour each succeeding one being more honourable than the one preceding.' 'Neither by years (age) nor by grey hairs' neither by wealth nor by friends does one become great. The sages made a compact of yore that, 'he of us who studies the Vedas will be called great.' The brahmana, illumined with the light of knowledge, consumes all sins and becomes like the god.'[118] 'Non-study of the Vedas extinguishes the prestige of a good family,[119] and 'leads to the destruction of Brahmins.'[120] The study of the Vedas and teaching the Vedas to pupils, as among the six duties of every brahmana (house holder).[121] Learning could be acquired from all available sources. 'Women, gems, knowledge, virtue, purity, good words and the various kinds of art may be acquired from anywhere.'[122]

Low Status of Unlearned Brahmins

'He, the twice-born householder, shall peruse each day, sastras whose perusal serves to improve the intellect as well as those which treat of the art of money getting. Likewise he shall study the Nigamas which elucidate the true import of the Vedas.' 'Let him not omit performing rsi-yajna, for by such study one can repay his debt to the sages[123] who were the founders of his religion and culture.

Even brahmanas when they were unlearned were looked down upon by society. An elephant made of wood, an antelope made of leather and a brahmana indisposed to the study of the Vedas these have nothing but the name.' He again says.[124] 'As an eunuch is sexually fruitless in respect of a woman, as useless is the meeting of two cows, as fruitless is the gift to an ignorant, so fruitless is the life of a brahmana who has not studied the hymns.' 'A brahmana who has not studied the Vedas is like in to a rush fire that is soon extinguished. To him oblations must not be offered, as no one casts fire-offerings in the ashes.'[125] 'A virtuous man, therefore must not give even water to a brahmana who is not read the Vedas.'[126] 'Like a man attempting to cross a river with the aid of a stone-raft both the ignorant donor and accepter of a gift, are drowned.'[127]

Classes of Teachers

There were three classes of teachers the guru, the acarya and the Upadhyaya. Manu defines a guru as 'one who performs the various sacraments and provides boarding for his students.'[128] The twice-born after performing the upanayan of disciple imparts instruction to him in Veda, along with the kalpas (the laws relating to sacrifices, sacramants and customs) and the secret meaning, they call a teacher or Acarya.[129] He defines an Upadhyaya as 'a person who teaches a portion of the Veda or the Vedangas in return for a fee.'[130] According to Veda the Acarya or Guru is ten times more venerable than the Upadhyaya.[131]

Tuition Fee

In ancient India, the teachers who accept remuneration for teaching were designated as equal to Sudras. Such teachers were condemned by society. In this connection it is interesting to note the difference of meaning between the words Upadhyaya and Acarya. He who is consideration of fees, teaches portion of the Veda and any of the Vedangas is said to be Upadhyaya, while Acharya is a selfless worker who imparts education without counting its material benefit. It is a pity that Upadhyaya stands in a lower step than that of an Acharya because of his attachment with money. It is true that a teacher needs money like others to maintain his day to day life. But he should not go after worldly pleasures.

Teachers' Remuneration (*Guru Dakshina*)

According to Veda[132] 'a student should not pay anything to his teacher before he finishes his education.' Gurukula considers that it is the sacred duty of a teacher to impart education without demanding any fee.

But Society is not against to give something to the teacher according to the ability of the student at the end of his studentship i.e. in the time of the sacred bath (samavartans) ceremony. 'When the student is about to take a final bath, let him procure a present for the venerable man according to his ability viz. a field, gold coins, a cow, a horse, a parasol and shoes, a seat, grain even vegetables etc: and thus give pleasure to his teacher.[133]

Snatakas

The pupils who finished their studies by the ceremony of Samavartana (the final bath) were called a Snatakas. They were to be taken to the assembly of the learned in a chariot or on an elephant to participate in the scholarly discourse. 'The king should honour those who had finished their education.[134] "A snataka was to be offered madhuparka as often as he visited one's house hold.'[135] 'A snataka who suffers from want of food may seek the help of the king.'[136] Manu gives equal status to the king and to the Snataka. That is why he insists the people 'to give way' to the king as well as to the snataka.'[137] After the ceremony of the final bath the brahmacarin can marry a girl of his caste, with the consent of his preceptor.'[138] Thus he enters to the second stage and ceases to be a brahmacarin.

Female Education

In the period of Smrti we find that women were thought incompetent to perform sacrifices and to read the Vedas as they could not be initiated. Old scriptures says that initiation of women consisted in their marriage: 'The nuptial ceremony is stated to be the Vedic sacrament for women and to be equal to the initiation, serving the husband equivalent to residence in the house of the teacher, and the household duties the same as the worship of the sacred fires.' Maintaining the home is the main duty of woman. 'They should be employed in looking after the income the expenses in maintaining the cleanliness of the house, in performing the household duties, in cooking food and is looking after the furniture etc.'[139] In later period, Manu refers to 'nursing as contingent on the wife of a man.'[140]

Manu was definitely against permitting women to recite Vedic stanzas. 'A brahmana is advised to boycott a feast given in connection with a sacrifice performed by a woman.'[141] It is the irony of the situation that although women were authors of some of the Vedic hymns, they were later denied the right to study the Vedas.

Vedic Guru is seen to be a favour of doing 'the bodily sacraments for girls, provided no Vedic mantra are used for the occasion.[142] The authors of smrtis wanted women to obey and serve men in all respects. That is why they have denied educational facilities and freedom of movement. According to Vedic custom 'she should stay under the authority of her father, husband and son in the period of childhood, youth and old age respectively.'[143] 'The women need not perform sacrifices, vows etc., to attain heavenly bliss but to do service for their husbands for the attainment of that aim[144]. This clearly indicates the attitude of Vedic people towards the fair sexes.

SALIENT FEATURES OF THE ANCIENT EDUCATIONAL SYSTEM

Aim of Education

The aim of ancient Vedic education was an all sides development of man. Education is not only for the present life of the pupils, but also for the future existence. Our ancient preceptors attempted for a happy synthesis of both these purposes.

The object of education was made three-fold: the acquisition of knowledge, the inculcation of social duties and religious rites and above all the formation of character.

In ancient times the ultimate aims of education was self-realisation. The individual's supreme duty was thus to achieve his expansion into the absolute, his self-fulfilment, for he was considered as a potential God, a spark of the divine. Education must aid in this self-fulfilment, and not in the acquistion of mere objective knowledge. It is more concerned with the subject than the object, the inner than the outer world.

Importance of the Initial Ceremonies

All the preceptors have approved the importance of the primary ceremonies such as Caula, Upanayana etc. The attention to the child in the first four or five years must be of high educative value. Jung and Freud have proved by psycho-analysis that the habits formed in these years have great influence in later life. The ceremony of tonsure is at the age of three or five. He is to rise early and wash specially his teeth and eyes. His home education would begin from now. Comenius calls the first years 'the mothers school' and finds here the rudiments of all later education. Kautilya even advised pregnant women to lead a pious life and cultivate acquaintance with learned priests so that they can kindle the light of knowledge in the minds of their future children.

The Initiation Ceremony

Upanayana is considered as the most important ceremony in the life of a student. Most of the authorities prefer that the Upanayana of the Brahman, Ksatriya and Vaisya should be performed in the 8th, 11th and 12th years respectively.

The pupil at the time of Upanayana dwells with his preceptor for three days where after being imparted a spiritual birth by the guru emerges in the form of 'dvija' i.e. twice born. He cultivates inner discipline, through self possession, serving the guru and renunciation, and thus becomes a residential pupil.

Upanayana ceremony was naturally a simple one. 'The student had simply to approach the teacher with sacred fuel in hand to indicate his willingness to serve him.'[145] It is the ceremony of a student being initiated to the study under a teacher. On this occasion the young scholar was offered a piece of deer skin or a piece of cloth as an upper garment. Invested with girdle and clothed in 'Kaupina' the boy was taken to the sacred fire with sacred fuel in hands. He was asked to offer it to the fire with sacred fuel in hands. He was asked to offer it to the fire so that God fire may endow him with brilliance and intelligence. After taking formal charge of the pupil, the teacher used to teach him the famous 'Savitri mantra' more popularly knows as 'Gayatri' from its metre. 'We meditate upon the excellent brilliance of God sun, may he stimulate our intellect.'[146]

'The boy was then given a staff to indicate his spiritual journey, or to remind the scholar that he was to be henceforward a watchman, armed with a staff to guard the vedas. Then he was asked to go outside to beg for alms and to follow the routine of the life of a brahmacharin.

Rituals in Brahmacharya Period

There are different kinds of rituals to be performed by the pupils in the period of studentship. They are as follows: At the end of the ceremony of initiation the boy asked to stand on a stone and enjoined to be steadfast in the pursuit of his studies. This is called the rituals of Asmarohana (Manava Gr. S.I-22-10). Three days after Upanayana a ritual, medhajanana by name, was performed with a view of invoke divine help in the sharpening of the intellect, memory and grasping power of the young scholar. (Bharadvaja Gr. S.I-10) Upakarma was a ritual performed by teachers and students at the beginning of the College or school session. The full moon days of July to October are mentioned by different authorities as appropriate days for this ritual. The annual education session will be closed with the Utsarjana ceremony which marks the beginning of a long vacation. It was performed in the month of January of February. 'After performing this ritual the teacher should go outside the village along with the pupils.'[147] This clearly indicates the fact that the practice of excursion was prevalent in ancient days. Besides, these rituals, the brahmacharin used to perform the 'Godanavrata' on the occasion of the first shaving of the beard. He should also perform five sacrifices on almost all days. It was essential for a brahmacharin to keep the vow of celebacy, which was considered as the foundation of all virtues, throughout the period of studentship, in spite of all provocations.

Curriculum

The education of the ancient period was mainly based on the four Vedas. The word Veda really means knowledge (from the root 'vid' to know) and so was used to designate the sacred lore or collection of sacred literature. The Rigveda means the Veda of hymns. It is the earliest and most illuminating work of the Aryan religion in India. No wonder that the Rigveda has become the main part of the curriculum since it is the fountain head of civilization and culture of that age.

The compilation of all the hymns recited on the occasion of Soma sacrifice came to the known by the name Samaveda. The Yajurveda is the collection of mantras in prose, the majority of them being spurious ones adopted from the Rigveda. Atharvaveda is a book of magic and witch craft. It refers to a number medicinal herbs. One portion of it refers to astronomy and another part deals with many rituals pertaining to domestic life. This Veda is thoroughly secular in character containing a vivid description of various arts and sciences.

The great sages who sought to the questions on birth, death and life after death, had retired to the forests where they spent their time in deep meditation and philosophical discussion. Their experiences manifested themselves through the Brahmanas i.e. treatises that deal with Brahma, composed in prose. To each of these Brahmanas is also annexed an Aranyaka or 'forest portion' to be studied in the forest by vanaprastas. Upanisads are treatises wholly given upto philosophical speculation and represent the last stage of the Vedic literature and hence called by the name Vedanta.

Coming to Kautilya's curriculum we find that it included four sciences: Anviksiki (Philosophy, science of logic etc.), Trayi (the three Vedas), Varta, (Economics) and Dandaniti (Penal code). The school of Manu holds that there are only three sciences. According to him the science of Anviksiki is nothing but a special branch of the Vedas. Besides these he has to study history, puranas, stories bearing on moral value, six darsanas, six Vedangas etc. Panini is in total agreement with the principles of curriculum approved by the other two preceptors.

Position of the Teacher

All the preceptors stress the importance of moral and religious qualifications necessary for a teacher. His plain living, high thinking, disciplined routine, abstinence from pleasures, mental control and above all, his sincerity of purpose were the principal factors responsible for the success in his work. Persons possessing such qualities could never fail to command respect from any body; they were living models for the pupils to follow and imitate in all walks of life. Though the practice of self study was commonly prevalent, yet the need and importance of the teacher could by no means be ignored or dispensed with. He was regarded as the builder guide and leader of the society. The man who prossessed the qualities required for guiding the society, and profound scholarship was naturally respected by all.

Teacher-Pupil Relationship

The residence of the pupil at the house of the teacher in a spirit of devoted service had been a usual practice is ancient India. The home of the preceptor served as an institution where the pupil lived after the upanayana ceremony. The teacher would, in place of the father, discharge the duties of the guardian also. The story of Sandipani acting as the spiritual father of Srikrishna and Kuchela is famous in our country. One day he hurried into the forest in search of his pupils who went there to collect fuels. It was one of the sacred duties of the pupil to (serve his teacher such as to) collect fire wood, supply water, feeding the cattle, begging alms for the teacher and for himself, doing the household jobs etc. In this way not only would he gain knowledge related to family life, but also learn the concrete lesson of dignity of labour and service. The pupil through close contact with his teacher would naturally imbibe his qualities and develop into a full man in accordance with the wishes of the preceptor. The teacher would also impart without reserve, whatever knowledge he possessed, regarding the pupil as his own son.

Method of Teaching and Learning

In ancient days the method of teaching was oral. Only the knowledge which was received from the lips of the teacher was regarded as pure and fruitful. Special attention was paid to the correct pronunciation of words. The actual teaching was to proceed in the following manner. 'A brahmacarin having quitted his bed early in the morning and having bathed and performed the fire sacrifice should accost his preceptor. Then having been commanded by his preceptor and having cast a look at his face, he should commence the study of the Vedas. He should not have his mind strayed away to any other subject. At the beginning of each lecture the pupils embrace the feet of their teacher and say "Om' and then pronounce two words. Then the first pupil repeats the first word, and after it has been explained the teacher says 'Om'. In this manner they go on till they have finished a portion. At the end of the last verse, the pupils embrace the feet of the teacher.

'Tapas' was regarded as the chief means of acquiring spiritual knowledge. The seers would impart the mantras to their disciples through oral preaching. They fixed them in the mind through the method of learning by heart immediately. Indeed the need for introspection and contemplation is never overlooked as Manu has given proof in one of his stanzas. He says: 'The student learns only a fourth part from his teacher, a fourth part by self-study, a fourth from his fellow-students, and the last fourth by experience in after life.[148]

Discipline

The pupils in ancient India were liable to obey the rules and regulations relating to brahmacharya, study habits and social behaviour. High morality was to characterise their life; lying, gambling and slandering were out of question. Food was to be simple; sweets, spices etc., were not to be used normally. Severe discipline was enforced upon them by most of the preceptors. Kautilya and Manu have agreed in principle to the privilege of punishing the pupils in case of emergency. In Gautama's opinion a preceptor should admonish his pupil without beating him or inflicting any kind of corporal punishment on him' (Ch. II). Apastamba (Ch. 1-2) seems to be more harsh and lays down a list of punishments that could be used by the teacher-such as frightening, fasting, bathing in cold water, striking with a cane and banishment from school etc. Panini considered scolding the pupils as a device to keep discipline in class room situations. The pupils in those days was under a some-what rigorous discipline but there was nothing harsh or brutal about it and high ideal or moral life and character was held be for the pupil and the teacher.

Samavartana: The Ceremony of Full Bath

Samavartana-the ceremony of final bath or sacred bath was performed at the end of the brahmacharya period to mark the termination of the educational course. At the time of this ceremonial bath the pupil sacrifices in the water his sacred girdle, staff and sacred thread which he had been using all these years. Before performing the bath the brahmacarin should shut himself up in a room throughout the morning. He would come out of his room at midday, cleanse his mouth and shave his head and beard. At that time the teacher would himself give him a bath in fragrant water. The bath was followed by an offer of new clothes. After performing a homa the student would proceed to the assembly of the learned men of the locality in a chariot or on an elephant.

Gurudakshina

When the ceremony of sacred bath was over the snataka would bid farewell to his teacher after paying him such a gift as he could afford. According to Manu (II-245) a pupil should not pay anything to his preceptor before he completes his study, because to teach in consideration of fees was looked upon as a sin (Yajnavalkya IIII-236). A student can pay anything to his preceptor as Gurudaksina according to his ability viz. a field, a cow, a horse, a parasol and shoes, a seat, grain or even vegetables.

Education of Women

In the smrti period the status of women gradually declined as that of the Sudras. They were denied the privilege of getting higher education. They were naturally disqualified for the ceremony of initiation. According to Kautilya serving the husband and doing the household duties are equal to the service done by pupils in the preceptors houses. He also considered marriage ceremony for girls as equal to the ceremony of initiation. Kautilya also followed the rules formulated by Manu regarding the education of girls. As far as education facilities for woman are concerned Panini seems to be more lenient than the other two. Yet there were many educated women and some of them had taken to the teaching profession. Patanjali, the great commentator of Panini holds that the term Upadhyaya indicates a female teacher.

The cause of degradation of women seems to have been the practice of selecting non-Aryan wives by the three higher classes. The marriageable age of girls also was being lowered at this time rendering any education worth the name next to impossible. When the vast majority of women were unable to recite properly the Vedic hymns, it was but natural that they should be regarded as ineligible for Vedic studies. Anyhow from the Smrti period onwards the education of girls came to be entirely domestic and vocational, in the sense that they were being prepared for that which was considered a woman's principal work-household duties.

Similarities and Dissimilarities

Manu, Panini and Kautilya totally agree with the major issues in the realm of education in ancient India. They have similar ideas about the initial ceremonies, the vow of celebacy, the duties of studentship etc. They all uphold the monopoly of brahmins in teaching and performing sacrifices. The three preceptors were not against corporal punishment if it would be administered in a mild manner. They agree wholeheartedly the method of teaching and learning. Teachers though they were in different categories were highly respected by the pupils as well as by the public in the time of Manu, Panini and Kautilya. It is no wonder, that the people will be asked to show great respect to the learned. Kautilya says: 'Such persons as are noted for their learning, intelligence, bravery, high birth or magnificent deeds shall be honoured' (Arthasastra, R.S. Sastri's Eng. Trans., p. 252). Manu says: 'Those brahmins who are foremost in all the Vedas and the Vedangas and whose ten ancestors were well-conversant with the Vedas are called Pankti-pavanas.[149] According to Panini, teachers are like tirthas (sacred waters), by immersing in which the pupils can purify themselves. The three preceptors, agree in principle on the rules and regulations governing the educational facilities of women. Only the primary education was given to girls. In the time of Dharmasutras the right of initiation and the right to study the Vedas or sacred literature were generally denied to women.

Now let us enumerate the dissimilarities and disagreements with regard to the educational practices, found in the three great preceptors. Though they were popular educators of their times, they worked in different fields of activities. As example Manu was considered as the founder of Indian Penal code. He dedicated his life in compiling and reforming the laws and regulations of the country governing all walks of life. Panini was only a grammarian and did not directly mould was the educational ideals. But we can understand the educational activities prevailed in his time, through his aphorisms. As we have already seen from Arthasastra, Kautilya was mainly a Politician. But as against others he actually engaged in the work of imparting education to the princes. According to legends he had adorned the position of the honorary preceptor and chief adviser of emperor Chandraguptamaurya. There are only slight differences in the educational ideals of the three preceptors. As far as female education is concerned, Manu was more rigorous in neglecting educational rights to the fair sexes. In his period low castes were also prohibited strictly to enter into the field of educational activities. Kautilya and Panini showed leniency to a certain extent in this matter. Panini and Kautilya have supported wholeheartedly the scheme of extending the training in crafts and arts to women and the Sudras. In the case of discipline also Manu was more rigorous than the other two. In all other matters such as methods of teaching, Curriculum etc., the preceptors do not differ much.

Influence on Modern Education

We can see the influences of ancient education in all spheres of modern education. In ancient India everything related to education was religious in character. The sacrificial ritual itself gave birth to some of the sciences. The elaborate rules for the construction of altars led to the science of Geometry and Algebra being developed. The desire to find out propitious times and seasons for sacrifices and other purposes gave rise to Astrology, from which Astronomy developed. The care taken to preserve to sacred text from corruption led to the development of Grammar and Philology, while the deep questions with regard to the universe and man's place in it which were discussed in the Upanishads led to the formation of elaborate philosophical systems and the study of logic. In fact most of the sciences are the offshoots of ancient literatures.

The modern system of introducing schools in different parts of our country was actually originated from the Gurukula system of education of ancient India. No doubt, Santiniketan founded by Tagore is only a modernised form of the forest universities prevailed in ancient times.The idea of starting boarding schools in natural surroundings also copes with the principles of Rousseau, Pestalozzi etc: who were perhaps inspired by the teachings of the great Indian preceptors.

Ancient educators of Indian laid the greatest emphasis on the spiritual development and the formation of the character of the pupils. Thus seems to influence some of the western educators also. According to Froebel 'to give firmness to the will, to quicken it and to make it pure and strong and eduring is the chief concern in education.' The German educator Heabart was also a staunch supporter of the formation of character as the aim of education. This rightly resembles with Manu's (I-108) opinion that 'conduct is the highest virtue as inculcated by the Smrti and the Sruti.'

According to Sayana-the great commentator of Vedas, there were three categories of students: the Mahaprajna the Madhyamaprajna and Alpaprajna i.e. very intelligent, normally intelligent and subnormal respectively. According to Kautilya pupils are of three kinds: those of sharp intelligence, those of stagnant intelligence; and those of perverted mind. Knowledge was imparted by the preceptors according to the ability of each pupil. Modern theory of I.Q. differences aptly resemble with the aforesaid practices.

According to Vachaspatimisra, the adhyayana (the hearing of words) sabda (apprehension of meaning) uda (reasoning leading to generalisation) Suhrtprapti (confirmation by a friend or teacher) and dana (application) are the five steps for the realisation of the meaning of a religious truth. Curiously enough these steps correspond wholly with Herbartian steps and with those of Dewey.

According to modern educationists discipline practised in Vedic ancient India was very severe. Education would not take place in such situations. They advocate more freedom to modern scholars to develop natural resources. We can apply most of the ideals of ancient education in the present situations also. Now a days the relationship between the teachers and students are becoming worse. In ancient India the teachers had loved the students like their own children and helped them in all difficult situations, so as to enable them to develop gradually under the shelter of the teachers. The pupils were also very obedient and worked sincerely according to the wishes of the preceptors. If the modern students and teachers may apply these principles in classroom situations they can raise the standards and can live a happier life. The vow of celebacy practised by the pupils in ancient India is also very much helpful for modern pupils to create a suitable atmosphere to learn and assimilate the difficult subjects. It is a pity that some of the students in modern universities behave like film stars and come to colleges partly to engage in love making and such other vulgar practices They spend more time to get sensual pleasures and naturally neglect their studies. We can easily check this dangerous situation by applying the high principles of celebacy in the day to day activities of the pupils. It is advisable to all modern educators to study and assimilate the worthy ideals of ancient preceptors for the betterment of their educational activities.

References

1. Manaver Adi Janmabhoomi, p. 119, Vayupurana, ch. 38
2. The Aryanization of India by N. K. Dutt
3. Satpatha Brahman: V. 1,4,2; 2,1,11; 2,1,24; Taittiriya Samhita, 1,8,16.
4. Ibid. V. 3.3.12.
5. Atharvaveda, 1.9; III. 4; IV. 22.
6. Atharvaveda (VII.12) describes the Sabha and Samiti as the twin daughters of Prajapati.
7. An Advanced History of India by Majumdar, Ray Chaudhari and Dutta. p. 45.
8. See the list of Victims at the Purush-medha in The Vajasaneyi Sanij (XXX), and The Taittiriya Brahmana, (III, 4).
9. The Taittiriya Aranyaka. X. 67.
10. Atharvaveda, XV, 2-1.
11. The Vedic Age, p. 444.
12. The Vedic Age, p. 445.
13. Atharvaveda. X. 8
14. Chitram vatatarormule vriddha sishya gurur yuva gurostu mauram vyakhyanam sishyastu cchinnasamsayah.
15. Vidya brahmanametyaha sevadhistesmi raksa mam Asayakaya mam madastatha syam viryavattama.
16. Yameva tu sucim vidyanniyatabrahmacarinam Tasmai mam bruhi vipraya nidhipayapramadine. M. S. II-115

17. Vidyayaiva samam kamam martavyam brahmavadina Apadyapi hi ghorayam natvenamarine vapet. M. S. II-113
18. Acaryaputrah susrusuh jnanado dharmikah sucih Aptah sak torthadah sadhuh svodhyapya dasa dharmatah. M. S. II-109
19. Kalah kridanakam te tadantedhyayanasya ca —Vishnu puranam I-12-18
20. Cudakarma dvijatinam sarvesmeva dharmatah Pradhamebde trtiyeva kartavyam srticodanet. M. S. II-35
21. Garbhastamebde kurvita brahmanasyopanayanam Garbhadekadase rajno garbhattu dvadase visah. M. S. II-36
22. A sodasad brahmanasya savitri nativartate a dvavimsat ksatrabandhora caturvimsatervisah. M. S. II-38
23. Brahmavarcasakamasya karyam viprasys pancame Rajno balarthinan saste vaisyasyeharthinostame. M. S. II-37
24. Gautamametyovaca brahmacaryam bhagavativatsyamyupeyam bhagavantamiti tam hovaaca kim gotronu somyasiti. Cha U. IV 4 (3-4)
25. Upaniya guruh sisyam siksayt saucamaditah Acaramagnikaryam ca sandhyopaasanameya ca. M. S. II-69
26. Agindhanam bahiksacaryamadhah sayyam gurorhitam. Asamavartaakuryat krtopanayano dvijah. M. S. II-108
27. Sayam pratasca juhuvat tabhiragnimatandritah. M.S. II-186
28. Devatabhyarcanam caiva samidadhanameva ca. M.S. II-176
29. Aharedyavadarthani bhaiksam Ceharahascaret. M. S. II-182
30. Pratigrhyepsitam dandam upasatheya ca bheskaram. Pradaksinam parityagnim caret bhaiksam yadhavidhi. M. S. II
31. Aharadadhikam varm na kvacidbhaiksamacaret. Yujyate steyadosena kamatodhikamaharan. M. S.
32. Mataram va svasaram va maturva bhaginim nijam Bhikseta bhiksam prathamam ya cainam navamanayet. M. S. II-50
33. Vedayajnairahinanam prassastanam svakarmasu Brahmacaryahared bhaiksam grhebhyah prayatonvaham. M. S. II-183
34. Guroh kule na bhikseta na jnatikulabandhusu. M. S. II-184
35. Samahrtya tu tadbhaiksam yavadannamamayaya Nivedya guravesniyadacamya pranmukhah suc ih. M. S. II-51
36. Upakarmani cotsarge triratram ksepanam smrtam. M. S. IV-119
37. Tryaham na kirtayed brahma rajno rahosca sutake. M. S. IV-110
38. Amavasyacaturdasyoh paurnamasyastakasu ca. M.S.IV-113
39. Pasumandukamarjarasvasarpanakulakhubhih antaragamane vidyadanadhyayamaharnisam. M.S. IV-126
40. Pamsuvarse disam dahe gomayuvirute tatha Svakharostre ca ruvati panktau cana padeddvijah. M. S. IV-105
41. Vidyutstanitanisvane sajyothih syadanadh ya yah. M. S. IV-106
42. Vedopakarane caiva svadhyaye caiva naityake Nanurodhostyanadhyaye homamantresu caiva hi M. S. II-105
43. Dvaveva varjayennityamanadhyayau prayatnatah Svadhyayabhumim casuddhamatmana casucim dvijah. M. S. OV-127

44. Tam cedabhyubiyat suryah sayanam kamacaratah Nimlocedvapyavi jnana jjapannupavaseddinam. M. S. II-220
45. Suryena hyabhinirmuktah Sayanobhyuditasca yah. Prayascittamakurvano yuktah syanmahatainasa. M. S. II-221
46. Acamya prayato nityamubhe sandhye samahitah Suca udese japan japyamupasita yadhavidhi M. S. II-122
47. Nityam snatva sucih kuryadhevarsipitrtarpanam Devatabhyarcanam caiva samidadhanameva ca. M.S.II-176
48. Karpasamupavitam syadviprasyordhravitam trivrt Sanasutramayam rajno vaisyasyavikasautrikam. M. S. II-44
49. Brahmano bailvaputasau ksatriyo vatakhadirak Pailavaudumbarau vatsyo dandanarhanti dharmatah. M. S. II-45
50. Kesantiko brahmanasya dandah karyah pramanatah Lalatasammi to rajnah syattu nasantiko visah. M. S. II-46
51. Rjavaste tu sarve syuravranah saum yadarsaneh Anudoegakaranranam satvaconagnidusitah. M. S. II-47
52. Mekhalamajinam dandamupavitam kamandalum Apsu prapya vinastani grhinitanyani mantravat. M. S. II-64
53. Manavagrhyasutra. I-22-11
54. Vajasaneyagrhyasutra (IV)
55. Pujayedasanam nityamadyaccaitadakutsayan Drstva hrsyetprasidecca pratinandecca sarvasah. M. S. II-54
56. Pujitam hyasanam nityam balamurjjam ca yacchat Apujitam tu tad bhuk tamubhayam nasayedidam. M.S.II-55
57. Anarogyamanayusyam asvargyam catibhojanam. M.S.II-57
58. Varjayanmadhu mamsam ca gandham malyam csan striyah. M. S. II-177
59. See ref: No. 44
60. See ref: No. 45
61. See ref: No. 58
62. Strinam ca preksanalambham. M. S. II-179
63. Ekah sayita sarvatra na retah syandayet kvacit Kamaddhi skandayan reto hinasti vratamatmanah. M. S. II-180
64. Svapne siktva brahmacari dvijah sukramakumatah Snatvarkamarcayitva trih punarmamityrcam japet. M. S. II-181
65. Kamam tu gurupatninam yuvatinam yuva bhuvi Vidhiradvandanam kuryadasavahamiti bruvan. M.S.II-216

    Viprosya padagrahanam anvaham cabhivadanam. M. S. II-217
66. Udakumbham-sumanaso gosakrnmrttikakusan Aharedyavadarthani bhaiksam caharahascaret. M.S. II-182
67. Adhah Sayyam gurorhitam asamavartanat kuryat. M.S. II-108
68. Yadha khaan khananitrena naro varyadhigacehati Tatha gurugatham vidyam susrusuradhigacchai. M. S. II-218
69. ... Priyam kuryadacaryasya ca sarvada. M. S. II-228

70. Asamapteh sarirasya yastu susrusate gurum Sa gacchatyanjasa vipro brahmanah sadma sasvatam. M. S. II-244
71. Varjayenmadhtmamsam ca gandham malyam rasan striyah Suktani yani sarvani praninam caiva himsanam. M. S. II-177

    Abhyangaman janam caksnorupanacchatradharajam. M. S. II-178
72. Kamam krodham ca lobham ca nartanam gitavadanam Dyutam ca janavadam ca parivadam tathanrtam. M. S. II-178, 179
73. The Educational System of the Ancient Hindus, p. 100
74. Ahimsayiva bhutanam karyam sreyonusasanam Vak caiva madhura staksna prayojya dharmamicchata. M. S. II-159
75. Asya vanm anasi suddhe samyaggupte ca sarvada Sa vai sarvamavapnoti vedantopagatam phalam. M. S. II-160
76. Naruntudah syadartopi na paradrohakarmadhih Yayasyodvijate vaca nalokyam tamudirayet M. S. II-161
77. Parasya dandam nodyachet kruddho naiva nipatayet Anyatra putracchisyadva sistyar tham tadayettu tau. M. S. II-164
78. Bharya putrasca dasasca sisyobhrata ca sodarah Praptaparadhastadyah syu rajjva venudalena va. M.S.VII-299
79. Prstatastu sarirasya nottamange kathancana Atonyatha tu praharan praptah syaccaurakilbisam. M. S. VIII-300
80. Acaradvicyuto vipro na vedaphalamansute Acarena tu samyuktah sampurnaphalabhagbhavet. M. S. I-109
81. Evamacarato drstva dharmasya munayo gatim Sarvasya tapsso mulamacaram jagruh param. M. S. I-110
82. Savitrimatrasaropi varam viprah suyantritah Nayantritastrivedipi sarvasi sarvavikrayi. M. S. II-118
83. Nicam sayyasaram casya sarvada gurusannidham. M. S. II-198
84. Uttistet prathomam casya caramam caiva samviset. M. S. II-194
85. Sayyasanedhyacarite sreyasa na samaviset. M. S. II-119
86. Durasth narcayedenam na kruddho nantike striyah. Yanasanasthascaivainamavaruhyabhivadayet. M. S. II-202
87. Gurun asavahamiti bruyat pratyuddhaya yaviyasah. M. S. II-130
88. Guruvatpratipujyah syuh savarae guruyositah M. S. II-210

    Sreyahsu guruvadvrittim nityameva samacaret Guruputresu caryesu guroscaiva svabandhusu. M. S. II-207
89. Nodaharedasya nama paroksamapi kevalam Nacaivasvanukurvita gatibahsitacestitam. M. S. 00-199
90. Snatak a caryayostath anakrametmataschyam M. S. IV-130
91. Parivadut kharo bhaavti sva vai bhavati nindakah Par ibhokta krmirbhavati kito bhavati matsari. M. S. 201
92. Prativatenuvate ca nasita gurnna saha Asamsrave caiva gurorna kincidapikirtayet. M. S. II-20
93. Pratisravanasambhasesayano na samacaret Nasino naca bhun jano na tistan na paranmukhah. M. S. II-195

94. Asinasya sthitah kuryadabhigacchamstu tistatah. Pratyudgamny tvavrajatah pascaddhavamstu dhavatash. Parnmukhasyabhimukho durasthasyaitya cantikam. Pranam ya tu sayanasya nidese caiva tistatah. M. S. II-196-197

95. Acaryam ca pravaktaram pitaram mataram gurum-na himsyat. M. S. IV-162

96. Guruyatra parivado ninda vaai pravartae. Karnau tatra pidhatayau gantavyo va tatonyatah M. S. II-200

97. Udpedakabrahmadatrorgariyan brahmadah pita Brahmajanma hi viprasya pretya ceha ca sasvatam M. S. II-146

98. Tesveva nityam sustusam kuryat priyahite ratah. M. S. II-235

99. Brahmasya janmanah karta svadharmasya ca sasita. Balopi vipro vrddhasya pita bhawati dharmatah. M.S.II-150

100. Adhyapayamasa pitrun sisurangirasah kavih. Putrakaiti hovaea jnanena parigrhya tan. M. S. II-151

101. Adhiyaramstrayo varnah svakarmastha dvijatayah. Prabrayad brahmanastvesam netaraviti niscayah. M. S. X-1

102. Trayo dharma anivartante brahmanat ksatriyam prati Adhyapanam yajanam ca trtiyasca pratigrahah. M. S. X-77

103. Vidusa brahmanenedamadhyetavyam prayatnatah Sisyebhyasca pravaktavyam samyan nanyina kenacit. M. S. II-103

104. Ahrahmanadachyanam apatkale vidhiyatde. Anuvrajya ca susrusa yavadadhyayanam guroh. M. S. II-251

105. Nabrahmane gurau sisyo vasamatyamtikam vaset Brahmane cananucane kamksan gatimauttamam. M. S. II-251

106. Varttarambhamce tokatah. M. S. VII-43

107. Na nisan te parisrante brahmadhitya punah svapet. M. S. IV-99

108. Adhyesyamanastvacanto yadha sastramudanmukhah. Brahman Jalikrotodhyapyo laghuvasa jitendriyah. M.S.II-70

109. Brahmramabhevasane ca padaugrahau guroh sada. M.S.II-71

110. Adhyesyamanam tu gururnityakalamatandritah. Adhisva bho iti Pruyadviramostviti caramet. M. S. II-73

111. Pranayamaistribhih putastata omkaramarhati. M. S. II-75

112. Traividyebhyastrayin vidyam dandanitim ca sasvatim Anviksikim catmavidyam vartarambhamsca lokatah. M. S. VII-43

113. Srtavrtte viditvasya vrttim dharmyam prakalpayet Samraksetsarvatascainam pita putramivaurasam. M. S. VII-135

114. Sarvaratnani raja tu yadharham pratipadayet Brahmanan vedaviduso yajnartham caiva daksinam. M. S. XI-4

115. Mriyamanopyadadita na raja srotriyatkaram. Na ca ksudhasya samsidecchrotriyo visaye vasan yasya ramastu visaye srotriyah sidatiksudha. Tasyapi tat ksudharatsramaecirenaiva sidati. M. S. VII-133; 134

116. Anantarah sapindadyastasya tasya dhanam bhavet. Ata urdhvam sakulyah syadacaryah sisya eva va. Sarvesamapyabhava tu brahmana rikthagaminah Traividya sucayo dantastatha dharmo no hiyate. M. S. IX-187; 188

117. Brahmana linginascaiva na dasyastarikam tare. M.S. VIII-407

118. Jnanagnina papam sorvam dahati vedavit. M. S. XI-146

119. Vedanadhyayanena ca kulanyakualtam yanti. M. S. III-63
120. Anabhyasena vedanam .... mrtyurvipran jighamsati. M.S. V-3
121. Adhyapanamadhyayanam yajanam yajanam tatha Danam pratigr, ahascaiva sai karmayagrajanmanah. M. S. X-75
122. Striyo ratannyatho vidya dharmah saucam subhasitam Vividhani ca silpani samadeyani sarvatah. M. S. II-240
123. Rsiyajnam ..... na hapayet M. S. IV-21
Svadhyayenarcayetarsin. M. S. III-81
124. Yadha sandophalah strisu yadha gaurgavi caphala Yadha canjephalam danam tatha vipronrocophalah. M. S. II-158
125. Brahmanastvanadhiyanastranagniriva samyati Tasmai havyam na datavyam no hi bhasmani huyate. M. S. III-268
126. Na varyapi prayacchet .... vipre navedavidi dharmavit. M. S. IV-192
127. Yatha plavenaupalena nimajjatyudake taran Tatha nimajjatodhastadajnau datrpraticchakau. M. S. IV-194
128. Nisekadini karmani yah karoti yathavidhi Sambhavayati cannena sa viprogurucruyate. M. S. II-142
129. Upaniya tu yah sisyam vedamadhyapaveddvijah. Sakalpam sacahasyam ca tamacaryam pracaksate. M. S. II-140
130. Ekadesam tu vedasya vedanganapi va punah. Yodhyapayati vrtyarthamupadhyayah sa ucyate. M. S.II-141
131. Upadhyayat dasacaryah. M. S. II-145
132. Na purvam, gurave kincidupakurvita dharmavit. M.S.II-245
133. Snasyamstuguruna jnaptah saktya gurvarthamaharet; Ksetram hiranyam gamasvam chatropanahamasanam Dhanyam sakam ca vasamsi gurave pritimavahet. M.S.II-245; 246
134. Snatako nrpamanabhak. M. S. II-239
135. Avrttanam gurukuladvipranam pujako bhavet M. S. VII-92
Vedavidyavratasnatan srotriyangrhamedhinah Pujayeddravyakavyena .... M. S. N-31
136. Rajato dhanamanvicchet samsidan snatakah ksudha. M. S. IV-33
137. Snatakasya ca rajnasca pantha deyah .... M.S. IV-138
138. Gurunanumatah snatvaa samavrtto yathaavidhi Udvaheta dvijo bharyam savarnam laksananvitam. M. S. III-4
139. Arthasya samgrahe cainam vyaye caiva niyojayet Sauve dharmennapaktyam ca parinahysya ceksane. M. S. IX-11
140. Susrusaratiruttama. M. S. IX-28
141. Nasrotriyatate yajne gramayajikrte tatha Striya klibena ca hute bhunjita bramanah kvacit. M. S. IV-205
142. Amamtrika tu karyeyam strinam .... Nasti strinam kriya mamtrairiti dharme vyavasthitih M. S. IX-18
143. Balya piturvase tistet panigrahasya yauvane Putranam bhartari prete na bhajetstri svatantratam. M. S. V-148
Pita raksati kaumare bharta raksati yauvane Raksanti sthavire putrah na siri svatantryamarhati M. S. IX-3

144. Nasti strinam prthagyajno na vratam napyupositam Patim susrusate yena tena svarge mahiyate M. S. V-155

145. Tadvijnanarthi sa gurumevabhigacchet samitpanih srotriyam brahmanistam. Mundakopanisat I-2-19

146. Om tatsaviturvarenyam, Bhargo devasya dhimahi, Dhiyo yo nah pracodayat (Gayatri)

147. Sahantevasibhih gramadabhiniskramya ... udsarjanavidhih. Baudhayana grhya sutra III-1-3

148. Acaryatpadamadatte padam sisyahsvamedhaya Padam sabrahmacaribhyah padam kalakramena tu. (M. S. Interpolated)

149. Agryah sarvesuve sarvapravacanesu ca Srotriyanvayascaivn vijneyah pamktipavanah. M.S.III-184

Warfare of the Vedic Period

18

Prof. N. Gangadharan

Introduction

The Vedas traditionally held as not composed by human agency is the bed-rock of Indian culture. Though the entire Veda is stated mainly as the basis of piety, we find references to secular matters also in the Vedic literature. It is a well-known dictum that the Vedas have to be amplified with the help of the Purāṇas. Truly the Purāṇas contain lot of material on secular topics besides the topics coming under the Pañcalakṣaṇa. The branches of learning are reckoned as fourteen consisting of the four Vedas, the six auxiliary texts, Purāṇa, Nyāya, Mīmāṁsā and Dharma-śāstra to which four more such as the Āyurveda, Dhanurveda, Gāndharvaveda, and Arthaśāstra are added making them as eighteen. The latter four are referred to as the Upavedas. The materials described in these texts have their roots in the Vedas. It is proposed in this article to deal with the material on warfare found scattered in the Vedic literature.

Ethical Principles of War

Since the Vedas are mainly devoted to the glorification of the gods, one may be inclined to think that the Vedic lietrature may not contain any material relating to warfare. We may classify wars into two groups as the war carried on the principles of *dharma* (*dharmayuddha*) and the unrighteous war (*kūṭayuddha*). While the former was a just and righteous one, the latter was a crafty fight carried on secretly. There is no reason to believe that the Vedic literature was not aware of any clear distinction between the two types of war. We find the Vedas referring to wars being fought involving fraud. But there was no definite formulation of the rules of conduct which came into being in the post Vedic period only. In the Brāhmaṇa literature we find some stray references to deceitful ways for gaining success over the enemies. For example the *Kauṣītaki Brāhmaṇa* (x. 8. 6) states, "Kin or no kin, crush the foes, conquer the attacking, conquer by attacking". It indicates that there must have been some sort of inexplicit convention followed by the members of the society. When we examine the Vedic lietrature we find that the Asuras were proficient in the art of war, they had well-fortified castles as abodess and quite often they resorted to unscrupulous methods in order to overcome the enemy. They were proficient in the art of employing spells. It may lead us to conclude that the use of fraudulent means accepted by the Hindu law-makers had their origin in those early primitive institutions of the Asuras. The *Atharvaveda* is replete with passages refering to the use of charms and amulets for the overthrow of the rival. We may cite some examples for the use of charms. Indra is requested to confound the army of the enemies, with the blast of fire, of wind and make them disappear after scattering them (III, 3., 5). In another hymn Indra is requested to confound the army, the Marut to slay with force and Agni to take away its eyes and let it go back conquered (III. 3, 6). In another hymn Maruts are addressed to pierce with baffling darkness the adversaries coming with force so that one of them may not know another (III. 2, 6). Thus this type of war negates the accepted laws of war and permitted the use of deadly and poisoned weapons capable of slaying thousands of men (I. 20, 21 and VIII. 8, 4 -5) thereby satisfying birds and beasts of prey (XI. 9 and 10). Another reference in the Atharvaveda clearly indicates that poisoned arrows were largely used leading to frightful consequences. (IV) 6). the Atharvaveda refers to number of battle-charms making use of plants such as the aśvattha in order to overcome a foe.

Weapons of War

As already mentioned Dhanurveda is recognised as an Upaveda and it classifies the weapons into four kinds—thrown (*mukta*), not thrown (*amukta*), thrown and not thrown (*muktāmukta*) and discharged by means of mechanism (*yantramukta*). Some other later texts divide them into three omitting the third in the above and substituting the last one with those discharged by *mantras* (*mantramukta*). Bows and arrows constitute the chief weapons of the firts type. We find the terms *isukṛt* and *iṣukāra* used in the *Ṛgveda* indicating that there existed professionals making arrows. The smith of this age was not only a steel-worker but also an arrow-maker. He prepared the head of the arrow and the rest as finished by a guild of arrow-makers (I.184,3). There is an interesting reference to fashioning of arrows by gods in the *Aitareya Brāhmaṇa* (I. 25. IV. 8), the different gods constituting the different parts of the arrow. The *Kauṣītaki Brāhmaṇa* mentions a bow with three arrows as the payment of fees. The same text (IV. 2) states that a bow is infailing in giving us safe and sound journey. The *Śatapatha Brāhmaṇa* (I. 2, 4 and VI. 5.2, 10) describes how the arrow had the appellation śara. When Indra hurled his thunderbolt against Vṛtra it got separated into four parts—the wooden sword, the post (*yūpa*), the chariot and the last part which broke and fell on the ground as an arrow (*śara*). Because it got broken it was known as the *śara*. Moreover the same text (II. 3, 3) states that Agni has the same relation to the sacrifice as the arrow-head to the arrow. We notice in the Vedic literature that Agni has been glorified for the purpose of vanquishing an enemy. The *Atharvaveda* (I.16,4) indicates the use of fire-arms with lead shots. The *Aitareya Brāhmaṇa*

(I.4, 8) describe an arrow with fire at its top. From the above references we understand that the principal weapons of this period were bows and arrows.

Among the twenty kinds of not thrown (*amukta*) weapons, Vajra or the thunderbolt is the most important. We are familiar with the mythological story relating to the fashioning of the thunderbolt from the backbone of the sage Dadhīci in the *Mahaābhārata* (III. 99). The *Śatapatha Brāhmaṇa* (I. 2.4) describes the thunderbolt wielded by Indra against Vṛtra as having one thousand spikes and one hundred edges. The *Kauṣitaki Brāhmaṇa* compares the sacrificial post to a thunderbolt hundred miles long and fifty miles broad having sharp points and a good handle with four kinds of movements.

Armour

We know that during the days of the *Ṛgveda*, the soldier was endowed with coat of mail, helmet and even an arm-guard. Varuṇa is referred to as wearing a lustrous golden mail (*Ṛgveda* I. 25.13).

Army and Divisions of Army

The ancient Indian geographical conditions required the extensive use of mounted forces comprising the calvalry, chariots and elephants. We come across in the Purāṇas and the Classical Sanskrit literature references to the fourfold divisions of the forces (*caturaṅgabala*) most probably having the origin in the Indian game of chess, the Caturaṅga, referred to in the *Ṛgveda* and *Atharvaveda*, indicating its popularity in Ancient India. The game of chess had the chess board consisting of sixty-four squares (*aṣṭāpada*) in which the major pieces occupy the edges of the board and in front of them are placed the foot-soldiers, the corner squares being occupied by the chariots, the next squares by the horses (Knight), the two central squares are the King and the Councillor and the foot soldiers are arranged on the second and seventh rows. This game of chess was a clever invention of a Hindu who devised a game of war with the board as described above as his field of battle. In early chess the checkmate an the barring of the movements of the opponent's king are the two methods of winning. It may be noticed that there was an exact reproduction of these methods in ancient warfare with the main purpose of vanquishing the enemy forces, secured by the capture or death of the opponent or by the destruction of his army. It further indicates that the symmetrial arrangement of the different segments of the army and its advantages must have been drawn from chess.

Chariots

We find that chariots were used in warfare from many references in the Vedic literatue. A hymn in the Ṛgveda (VI. 47, 26) addresses the war chariot thus :

"Lord of the wood ! Be firm and strong in body. Be bearing as a brave victorious hero. Show forth thy strength, compact with straps of leather and let thy rider win all spoils of battle" The *Atharvaveda* (VI. 125) has a similar hymn "O Forest tree! Stout-limbed verily mayst thou become our companion, further, rich in heroics; thou art fastened together with kine; let him who mounts thee conquer things conquerable." "Forth from heaven, from earth (is its) force brought up : forth from forest trees (is its) power brought hither : to the force of the waters, brought forth hither by the kine, to Indra's thunderbolt, the chariot do thou sacrifice with oblations. "Indra's forces, the Marut' front, Mitra's embryo, Varuṇa's naval do thou, enjoying this obliation, giving of ours, O divine chariot, accept the oblations." It is known that the chariot was an indispensable instrument in the Vedic days. Indra is stated to be attacking the chariot of Keśin *Atharvaveda* VI. 75, (1-7).

In olden days the warrior was his own charioteer as known from the reference to Indra and Agni yoking and guiding their horse themselves when they were attacked by the Asuras. The two offices, seemed to have separated about the time of the *Aitareya Brāhmaṇa* (IV. 1; XX I). The chariot was an important instrument of war in those days is indicated by large number of references to chariots in the *Aitareya Brāhamaṇa* (II. 37; X.5; V.21; XXIV.3; VII. 19; XXXIV.1 etc). The reference to a class of people called *rathakāras* or chariot-makers in the *Taittirīa Brāhmaṇa* supports this contention (*Cambridge History of India* I. p. 125). It is quite reasonable to suppose that the art of war during these days would not have been a complex one and hence a single combat (*dvandvayuddha*) was the normal order of the day. It must have become obsolute in later times consequent on the growth of the art of war.

Elephants

The *Rgveda* (X. 106, 6) describes two elephants bending their heads and rushing together against the enemy indicating the use of elephant in warfare. While it is referred to as a wild animal with one hand in another place it is referred to as *hastin*. (*Cambridge History of India* I. p. 81). The art of training the elephant has become a common feature from the period of the *Yajurveda* onwards.

Cavalry

Cavalry, the third division of the four-fold division of an army both in the east and the west requires brief notice. Although we have references to horses and war chariots drawn by horses in the *Ṛgveda* (I. 22, 6.7-8; VI, 46, 13-14 and I. 3, 1 etc) we may trace reference to cavalry as an organised force during the post-Vedic period only. There is no indication in the *Ṛgveda* to conclude that cavalry was a disciplined force during that period. However we find reference to dust-raising horesemen in the *Atharvaveda* (IV. 21,4).

Strategies of War

We find references to three kinds of war—land warfare, naval warfare and aerial warfare. The Daśarājyayddha (battle involving ten kingdoms) described in the *Rgveda* is an example for the first kind. We find from the *Ṛgveda* that tribes were living in fortifications known as *'pur'*, consisting of earthwork strengthened by a palisade or by a stone wall. We find numerous references to such kinds of fortresses being besieged and destroyed by the invading hosts of hostile army. There are distinct references to the existence of forts in the late Brāhmaṇa lieterature also. The *Aitareya Brāhmaṇa* (II.ii) describes the three fires as forming three forts in order to prevent the Asuras from disturbing the annual sacrifice. The *Kauṣitaki Braāhmaṇa* (VIII, 8) describes the Upāsadas as the citadel of the Asuras taken as refuge against the gods. The Asuras made citadels of iron in this world, of silver in the atmospheric regions and of gold in the sky states the Ṛgveda (II, 20; III, 12). In the Purṇas we get detailed description of these fortified cities in which the Asuras moved around the universe. The *Atharvaveda* has many references to the use of charms and spells in fighting one's enemies mainly to confuse the enemy and gain a victory. Though we do not find reference to ships being used as such in warfare we get reference to the concept of a ship sailing heavenwards. The *Śatapatha Brahmaṇa* contains the metaphor which refers to the Agnihotra rite, the ship bound heavenwards, the Āhavanīya and Gāhapatya fires constituting its two sides, steered by the Agnihotrin offering milk to the three fires (II. 3, 3, 15). The *Ṛgveda* (I. 1´7, 14 and 15) describes Aśvins as rescuing and conveying Bhujya safely using winged ships.

Diplomacy

Though we do not find the well-defined four kinds of political expediencies which we notice in later literature, there are some references to espionage etc in the Vedic lietrature. The Fire-god is invoked in the *Rgveda* (IV. 15, 4) in order to render help in overcoming enemies in battles by being the deceiver of the enemies, since his foes are full of deceit. In achieving his goal he employs spies (IV. 4, 3). This enables us to infer that the system of espionage was prevalent in those days. The battle of the ten kings described in the *Ṛgveda* (VII. 18, 33) refers to the diplomacy of the rulers getting supplemented by its association with priestly diplomacy, which exercised a healthy influence of the constitutional evolution. It is to be noted that diplomacy gained more and more importance with the march of time. The *Atharvaveda* (III. IV, 1-6) recognize the monarch as the centre of Hindu diplomacy, occupying an absolute position subject to discipline by his Purohita and public opinion. The Ṛgveda (IV. 16, 4) refers to a number of spies of Varuṇa possessing thousand eyes moving hither and tither. This and other hymns read together conveying the prayer made for the victory of the king indicate the prevailing diplomatic practices. But in the *Atharvaveda* we find recourse to conquest of enemies more by artifice, strategem and spells. The growing popularity of the *Atharvaveda* (X. 5) seems to be responsible for accepting the *indrajāla* (speels and charms as an expedient to win over the enemy in later times.

Diplomatic Agents

Agni is well known as the messenger of the gods. It is noticed in the *Ṛgveda* (I. 12, 1) that there existed the two diplomatic agents *dūta* and *cāra*. The *Taittirīya Saṁhitā* (IV. 5, 7) mentions the terms *prahita* distinct from the above two meaning an envoy. Sāyaṇa explains the dūta as a person skilled in getting correct information regading the strength and position of the forces of the enemy and *prahita* as an envoy sent by his master. The latter in its usage seems to signify a spy. The *Atharvaveda* (IV. 16. 4) gives details about these officials engaged in secret services. of Varuṇa. They had thousand eyes indicating that they were vigilant. Looking down on the earth from the sky they inspected in all the directions. They moved here and there implying that they gathered facts to be reported to their master. It is known that all important had their spies. For example the *Atharvaveda* (VIII. 61, 3 and IX. 73,4) refers to the spies of Mitra and Soma.

Flags and War Music

Besides the word *dhvaja* denoting a flag occurring twice in the *Rgveda* (VIII. 85, 2; X. 103, 11), we find a good number of terms used for denoting a banner such as *akra* (I. 143, 7, III. 1, 12) *Kṛtadhvaja* (7. 8. 3. 2), *ketu* (I. 27, 12), *bṛhatketu* (V. 8, 2) and *sahasraketu* (I.119, 1). It seems that during the vedic period the wielder of the weapons aimed his arrows at the banners of the enemy. If the banner was struck or captured, it was held as success over the enemy in the battle. The names as above indicate a small or big flag and probably a mightly monarch holding sway over thousand persons. It seems there was no common flag as it is commonly known now as the national flag. Each and every hero had his own insignia to distinguish him from the others. This was quite prominently noticed in the later epic literature. Besides that the conch was also significantly distinct during the epic period. It is noticed that music was a feature of ancient Indian warfare. We may classify them as those used at the time of sacrifical and festive occasions, others used in both war and peace like the kettle drum(*dundubhi*) and still others used only at the time of wars. The last one was made by digging up a hole in the earth and covering it with a hide as noticed in the Ṛgveda (I. 28, 5) and the *Atharvaveda* (V. 20, 1) referred to as the *bhumi dundubhi* in the *Taittirīya Saṁhitā* (VII. 5. 9. 3) and *Pañcaviṁśa Brahmaṇa* (V. 5. 10)-Bakura seems to be another war instrument as known from the passage in the *Rgveda* (I. 117, 21) referring to its use against the Dasyus and blown by the Aśvins in order to help their army against their enemies. One has to conjecture from that context in which *Bakura* has been mentioned that it was employed at the time of war only.

The fore-going notice enables us to understand the details relating to war and accessories of war in the Vedic literature.

Vedic Mathematics

19

Dr. S. Biswal

Prolegomenon

Vedic Mathematics is one of the alarming and the most focussing subjects of the Vedas. The mathematical principles and logical insights projected in the Vedas simply arithmetic and algebraic operations which have increasingly found acceptance the world over. It is being taught in some of the most prestigious institutions in England and Australia. NASA scientists applied its principles in the area of artificial intelligence.[1] But, in our country people have forgotten this mathematical science which had its origin here in India.

Vedic Mathematics is an ancient technique which simplifies mutiplication, divisibility, complex numbers, squaring, cubing, square and cube roots. Even recurring decimals and auxiliary fractions can be handled by Vedic mathematics. Experts opine that it could be a handy tool for those who need to solve mathematical problems faster by the day, especially in a system where the emphasis is an examinations. Jagadguru Swami Bharathikrishna Tirthaji of Puridhama, Orissa has meticulously revived the subject with much stress and strain. He researched the subject for years and left the result to be recorded by his disciples during his last days. Without the sincere efforts of some of his disciples, the outcome, of his long research would not have arrived at us in the form of the book *"Vedic Mathematics"* which came to light during 1960s. According to N. G. Dongre, "In ancient India where *Darśanas* were being developed, all the necessary tools of mathematics were available, but it seems that no philosopher made any effort to express the thoughts about the material world in algebraical terms. Had this mathematical method been brought into practice earlier, the knowledge earned by the westerners in the last three centuries would have been gifted to mankind one and a half millenia earlier".[2]

Among the six aṅgas or adjuncts of the Vedas, importance was given to mathematics and geo-astronomy in preference to all other disciplines. The Vedic sages discovered the early foundations of mathematics in order to study the earth and the universe and the mathematical foundations was laid in order to properly base their astornmical studies.[3] The reason is that mathematics is essential for the study of astronomy.[4] Both the subjects are interlinked. One can not be separated from the other. Above all, various branches of science, arts, philosophy, et seq. those are needed for the upliftment of human life, are based on mathematics. There is not a single part of human life which is not linked with mathematics. We derive all the informations about the creation of the universe from the knowledge of mathematics. Ostensibly, our all kinds of progress totally depend upon the subject of mathematics into which the Vedic seers had a deep insight.

Genesis and Growth of Ancient Indian Mathematics Astronomy

In ancient India, no science ever attained an independent existence. All sciences were developed with the primary objective of helping the Vedic rituals. In the earlier part of the Vedic age, science grew as a support to religion. Mathematics emerged as a help to it and was kept subsidiary[5]. But, in the later part of the vedic age, all the science outgrew with their individual identity and were cultivated for their own sake. Evidently, the significance of mathematics was realized during the later part of the Vedic age[6].

Life in ancient India was dominated by religion. Mathematics was created for designing *Yajñakuṇḍas* and Vedis (altars) for various types of *havanas*[7]. Gradually, astronomy was developed to regulate religious rituals. For understanding astronomy clearly, mathematics was used as a strong tool and more and more mathematical principles and sūtras were created to meet the needs of the astronomy.

Each Veda has its *Vedāṅga Jyotiṣa* which is a text containing the rules for calculating astronomical results. The Vedāṅga Jyotiṣa was probably written by Leghadha during 13th century B. C. Vedāṅga Jyotiṣa dealt only with rough calculations of solar and lunar elements. There were no calculations for planets. After the period of Vedāṅga Jotiṣa, the Siddhānta Jyotiṣa appeared in the field of Indian astronomy. Siddhānta Jyotiṣa means a system which gives rules for calculating time, motions of planets etc. from the beginning of the universe to the end. Another text depicting the rules for calculating astronomical events from a fixed epoch other than the beginning of *Yuga* of *Kalpa* is known as *Karana*. The time of composition of such astronomical texts is called the Siddhānta Jyotiṣa period. Five well-known Siddhāntas are available. They are

(i) Brahma Siddhānta
(ii) Vaśiṣṭha Siddhānta
(iii) Romaka Siddhānta
(iv) Paulisa Siddhānta
(v) Sūrya Siddhānta

Out of these, the Sūrya Siddhānta is the most honoured and scientific one. Its calculations are based in recorded co-ordinates of *Nakṣatras*. This book was possibly written in about 280 A. D.

Later, many other treatises on astronomy were written by some famous mathematicians and astronomers. These include Āryabhaṭṭiya by Āryabhaṭṭa, Brahma sphuṭa Siddhānta by Brahmagupta, Baswati Kran by Satānanda, Siddhārti Śiromaṇi by Bhāskarācārya, Grahalagyam by Ganesh and Siddhānta by Tattva Viveka by Kākalaka Bhaṭṭa. The texts written in Kerala are Deva Keralam, Śūkra Keralam, Sarkarānārāyaneeyam, Venwaroham, Karan Paddhaṭi, Saḍratnamāla, Tantra Saṁgraham and Yukti Bhāṣa by Brahmadatta. The last five books are in verse form and give infinite series expressions for sin x, Cos x and tan x about two and half centuries earlier than in Europe. The series known as Gregory's series for $tan^{-1}x$ was also known in India more than two centuries earlier than in Europe.[8]

Bhāskarācārya considered Brahmagupta as *Gaṇita Cakra* Curāmaṇi, first gem among the circle of mathematicians. The Siddhānta Śirimaṇi of Bhāskarācārya contains four parts, namely *Lilāvati, Bijagaṇita, Goladhāya* and *Grahagaṇita.*

Ancient Indian astronomors were aware of the practical aspect of astronomy. They designed suitable instruments for astronomical measurements. Therefore, every astronomical text included a chapter on the construction and use of such instruments. The earliest instrument available in Vedic times was *Turya,* which consists of a quadrant circle with a movable tube through the centre and resting on the arc of the quadrant that is graduated in degrees and minutes. An astronomer was observing the heavenly bodies through the tube, and the angle made by the tube with the vertical gave the zenith distance called *Natanṣk* and its complement *unantaś* or altitude[9]. Use of water clock was also prevalent during the time of *Vedāṅga Jyotiṣa.*[10] Many other instruments like *Śankuyantra* or *gnomon, Cakrayantra, Kapala Yantra, Dhanus Yantra, Nāryantra, Mayura Yantra, Vanaryantra,* et. seq. were in use during post-vedic period. Brahmagupta mentions seventeen instruments in his *Brahma Sphuta Siddhānta*".[11] Bhaskācārya introduced another instrument called phalak yantra. In the 14th century A. D., Padmanabhan designed another instrument called *Dhruvmrey youtra*[12]. Moreover Chakardan wrote a book on instruments under the caption *Yantra Cintāmaṇi.*[13]

Further, observatories or Māna Mandiras were erected with the patronage of kings and emperors. It appears that an observatory was constructed at Ujjain or Avanti. Another observatory was constructed at Varanasi by Raja Mansingh. Raja Jai Singh built one observatory at Jaipur and another at Delhi.[14]

Mohenjodero excavations of about 5000 years ago show highly developed mathematics. The *Sulvasūtras* belong to the period between 800-500 B. C., Jaina mathematics to about 500-100 B. C., and then emerged the mathematical persuits of Āryabhaṭṭa, Bṛahmagupta, Mahavirācārya and Bhāshkara from the 5th to the 12th Centuries A. D.[15] the *Bakṣali* manuscript found at the village Bakṣali near Peshwar in 1081 A. D. is supposed to belong to the 4th century A. D.[16] It contains problems on fractions, arithmetic and geometric progressions, solution of indeterminate equation, approximation of surds, solution of quadratic equations and simultaneous linear equations.

The Sulva Sūtras are seven in number, namely Bodhāyana, Āpasthamba, Kātyāyanam, Mānava, Maitrāyana, Varāha and Vidhuta. They explain a large number of simple geometrical constructions imparting knowledge of some geometric theorems including that of Pythagoras. Irrational numbers were first used here and the approximation to $\sqrt{2}$ as $1+\frac{1}{3}+\frac{1}{3.4}+\frac{1}{3.4\ 34}$ was given. Problems in the construction of altars were solved and illustrated. Such solutions were based on the solution of simultaneous linear equations in integers.

Jaina mathematics contains elementary formulae for mensuration, approximate values of square roots, (e.g. $\sqrt{10}$ correct to 13 places of decimals), approximation of π by $\sqrt{10}$, some concepts of infinity, laws of indices and the formula for permutations and combinations.

The algorithm for finding cube roots, sums of squares of cubes of first numbers, approximation of π by 3.1416, mensuration formulae and tables for sinQ were the contributions of Āryabhaṭṭa to Indian mathematics.

The indeterminate equation $Nx^2 + 1 = y^2$ in integers was solved by Brahmagupta, who also gave the sum of gemoetrical progression, determined the right angled triangles and cycle quadrilaterals with rational sides, designed interpolation formulae and the formula for the area of a cycle quadrilateral.

Gaṇita Sāra Saṇgraha, famous work of Mahaviracārya, was written in 850 A. D. This treatise contains problems on arithmetic, on quadratic equations, on the general formula for cube roots, on unit fractions, on construction of cycle quadrilaterals of any given area and results for the ellipse.

Bhaskarācārya in his Siddhānta Śiromaṇi gave the systematic treatment of mathematics known to his time. This work includes formula for surface area of a sphere and its volume, volume of frustums of a pyramid, problems on permutations and combinations problems on quadratic equations and indeterminate equations. Bhaskara's discourses and results in mathematics exhibit the discovery of calculus by him.

After the period of Bhaskara, mathematics was somewhat developed in Kerala only. Narayan Paṇḍita's *Gaṇita Kaumudi* was written in the 14th century A. D. This book and the work of Madhava are the two significant contributions to mathemtics of that time. Other works which followed these two works include *Tantra Sangraha* and *Āryabhaṭṭiyam* of Sakara Varman, *Karana Paddhati, Driggaṇita* and *Kāriya Kranakara.* The series expansions of sin x, cos x and $\tan^{-1x}$ etc. are given in these works at least two hundred years before they were found in Europe. The result

$$\lim_{n \to \infty} \frac{1^P + 2^P + \ldots + (n-1)^P}{n^{P+1}} = \frac{1}{P+1}$$

is also given. *Karana Paddhati* gives the values of π correct to 10 places of decimals whereas Saḍratnamālā gives the same value correct to 17 places. According to Nīlakaṇṭha of about 15th century A. D., the ratio of the cirumference to the diameter can never be expressed as the ratio of two integers.[17]

In spite of the influence of the Greeks and the Chinese on the Indian mathematicians of ancient time, still they had their original contributions for the research and development of mathematics in India. Out of the bifacets of the nature of mathematics, one is unveiled when it deals with quantitative relationship among material objects, and hence, resulting in its use in the field of business, economics, sciences, et. seq. The other aspect of mathematics is observed while it postulates and applies its theorems to arrive at their logical conclusions, without any use in practice. Such an aspect of the subject considers mathematics as philosophy.

Invention of Numerals

In the ancient time, counting, weighing and measuring were the pre-occupations of primitive trade. Evidently, the mathematical notion had its first inception in the trade and commerce. This seems to have embraced the invention of the numerals that developed in the Hindu-Arabic system, and the zero, which made the place value idea possible. In the beginning, no body felt the significance of these numerals and the zero symbol. There were other system of numerals prevalent at that time, and these were apparently quite as significant as those from which our familiar symbols were derived.

The Greek system of numerals, i.e, I, II, X, C, etc. made the progress in arithmetic difficult. Gradually, people understood this and invented the numerals alongwith their place values. According to Laplace, "the idea of expressing all quantities by nine figures (or digits), where by is imparted to them both an absolute value and one by position, is so simple that this very simplicity is the reason for our not being sufficiently aware how much admiration it deserves.[18]

The discovery of numbers and the origin of early, mathematics in the Vedas has been discussed by Satyaprakash.[19] Vedic scholars did not use figures for big numbers in their numerical notation. Instead, they preferred to use the Sanskrit alphabets, with each alphabet constituting a number. Vedic mantras have been codified with numbers. Famous *Gāyatrī mantra* has been decoded with 108. The bases of Vedic mathematics are the 16 *sūtras* which attribute a set of qualities to a number or a group of numbers.

There was a highly developed numerical system from the early Vedic period.[20] *'Daśan'* or ten forms the basis of the numerical system, as in the case of other

Aryan people in general. But, Macdonld and Keith opine that the numerical system was emerged unprecedently at a very early date.[21] It seems likely that the Vedic Indian had the knowledge of signs of numeral.[22]

Invention of Zero

When and how the symbol Zero came to existence is still in dark. The mathematician who devised the symbol for zero did a great service to our civilization, but there is no meticulous record for his identity. This is because of the fact that the history of mathematics in India reached the stage of preserving the names of important contributors, much later. Professor G. B. Holstead in his article in the American Mathematical Monthly views that the zero existed in India at the, time of Piṇgala's work *'Chandras-Sūtra'*, a work on prosody before 200 B.C.[23] He holds that the importance of the creation of the zero mark can never be exaggerated. This symbol became the helpful power in the characteristics of Hindu race when it sprang. Actually, the zero symbol was employed in metric by Piṇgala in his *'Chandas-sūtra'*.

Use of Decimal System

The invention of the decimal system is the most significant and fundamental contributions of our ancient mathematicians. The characteristic feature of the system is the usage of nine digits and a symbol for zero to denote all integral numbers by assigning place value to the digits. This was known as the decimal system of numeration. According to the famous archeologist Dr. S. R. Rao, the Harappans first gave to the world the decimal system of measurement and made use of gold as a medium of exchange.[24] The Harappans achieved great accuracy in the measurement of fundamental units of length, mass and time. The smallest unit of length was 1.7 mm and that of mass was 50 mg. However, the scales discovered at Harappa, Mohenjodaro and Lothal were all differently marked, but were inter-related.

Use of Fractions in the Veda

Vedic people were acquainted with fractional measurements. We notice the use of some fraction like *ardha, pāda, śapha, and kalā,* denoting $\frac{1}{2}, \frac{1}{4}, \frac{1}{8}$ and $\frac{1}{16}$ respectively, in the Vedic period[25]. The fraction *'tripād'* denoting $\frac{3}{4}$ also occurs in Ṛgveda.[26] Dimensional measurements of different parts of the chariots and carts were required by the specialized Crafts-men of Vedic time.

Vedic Units of Value and Weight

Vedic people used some units of value and weight. Ṛgveda[27] mentions that the cow was used as a unit of value in the barter system where the exchange of commodities took place. The 'niṣka', originally a gold ornament[28], at a later time[29] became a unit of value.

In the period of the later saṁhitās, the *'māna'* became a measure, of weight equivalent to the *'Kriṣṇala'* (the Berry), which was a unit of weight. The weight of one hundred *'Kriṣṇalas'* was equivalent to the weight of a piece of gold called *'satamāna'*, which has been evolved into a currency in due course[30]. According to Apte[31] and Keith[32], the *'niṣka'* and the 'cow' were also prevalent as units of value and which continued for a longer time.

Conclusion

Vedic people were not only familiar with mathematical formulations and astronomical laws, but also felt the intimate relationship between magic and science. This is quite evident from the significance of magical rites of the Vedic religion. Magic and science played important role in the evolution of human logic is quest of causality in nature and the universal order (Ṛta) to control over it. Ostensibly, this led to solve vital problems that came along the way of life. Therefore, Satron says, "science began whenever and wherever man tried to solve the innumerable problems of life"[33]. As a matter of fact, various branches of science emerged in the way human experience and practice in the Vedic age.

According to A. D. Alexandrov, what could not be attained by the Greek, scholars, that was done at the first stage in India. For example, the Greeks genius failed to give the most convenient notation of numbers, to extend the system of numbers, and to abstract irrational numbers from their geometric base. All such achievements could be possible in India and which reached Europe through middle Asia and Arabic countries.[34] India was thus a cradle of one of the most fundamental concepts of mathematics.

References

1. Chandhari, S., *The Times of India*, Bennett, Coleman & Co. Ltd., New Delhi, April 16, Friday, 1999, Front page.
2. Dongre, N. G., *Physics in Ancient India*, New Age International Publishers Limited, New Delhi, 1994, PP. 6-7.
3. Murthy, S. R. N., *Vedic View of the Earth*, D. K. Printworld (P) Ltd., New Delhi, 1997, pp. 37, 229.
4. Baldawa, B., *Theory of Orient*, Latur, Maharashtra, 1997, p.471.
5. Hooda, D. S. and Kapur, J. N., *Āryabhata : Life and Contributions*, New Age, International (P) Limited, Publishers, New Delhi, 1996, p. 2.
6. *Ibid.*
7. *Ibid.*, p. 3.

8. *Ibid.*, p. 9.
9. *Ibid.*, p. 10
10. *Ibid.*
11. *Ibid.*, p. 10
12. *Ibid.*
13. *Ibid.*
14. *Ibid.*
15. *Ibid.*, p. 19.
16. *Ibid.*, p. 13.
17. *Ibid.*, pp. 14-15.
18. *Ibid.*, p. 17.
19. Satyaprakash, Saraswati Swami, *Founders of Sciences in Ancient India*, 2 vols.
20. *Ṛgveda*, III, 6. 15; IV, 32.18; VIII, 1.5; 2.41; 21.18;
    Atharvaveda, VII, 2.22; 8.7; X, 8.24
21. Macdonell, A.A. and Keith, A. B., *Vedic Index of Names and Subjects*, Vols. I MLBD, Delhi, 1958, pp. 342-344.
22. *Ṛgveda*, X, 62.7.
23. Hooda, D. S. and Kapur, J. N., *op. cit.*, p. 17.
24. Hooda, D. S. and Kapur, J.N., *op. cit.*, p. 16.
25. Macdonell, A. A. and Keith, A. B., *Vedic Index of Names and Subjects*, Vol. I, MLBD, 1958, pp. 342-344.
26. *Ṛgveda*, X, 90.4.
27. *Ibid.*, IV, 24.10.
28. *Ibid.*, V, 19.3.
29. *Ibid.*, I, 126.2.
30. Gupta, U., *Materialism in the Vedas*, Classical Publishing Company, New Delhi, 1987, p. 136.
31. Apte, V. N., '*Religion and Philosophy*', *The Vedic Age*, (ed.) Majumdar, R. C. and Pusalkar, A. D., London, 1952, pp. 360-383 and 438-448.
32. Keith, A. B., *Ancient India*, Cambridge History of India, Vol. I, India, 1955, p. 124.
33. Gupta, U., *op. cit.* p. 130.
34. Hooda, D. S. and Kapur, J. N., *op. cit.*, p. 24.

Medicinal Herbs in the Atharvaveda with special reference to Āyurveda

20

Dr. Gauri Mahulikar

Introduction

The history of medicine and surgery dates back perhaps to the origin of mankind, but the records of prehistoric events are not available to us. The earliest textual evidence of Indian medicine is primarily the *Atharvaveda* and to some extent the *Ṛgveda*. *Caraka*, *Suśruta*, *Vāgbhaṭa* etc. physicians and medico-men, later on developed, systematised and gave an everlasting concrete form to the Indian medicine, in the form of *Ayurveda*—'the knowledge of life.'

Concept of Diseases

All illness and bad health for the Vedic seers, was part of an interlocking whole, comprised of body, mind and soul. Physical ailment was regarded as the reflection of psychological and spiritual imbalance. To reinstate the lost equilibrium, the harmony, was the chief objective of the ancient seers.

Medicine of the Vedic Indians was inextricably connected with their religion. It never stood in isolation from it. Wrath of the deity, deviation from the rules of the community, disrespect for the established norms and violation of values, invariably resulted into physical disease, according to the primeval man wherever he lived. Indian was no exception. Thus the Indian medicine was essentially characterised as a magico-religious system.

Types of Diseases and Physical Disorders

The AV refers to various body-aches, physical disorders and sickening ailments.[1] It mentions headache, earache, anaemia (*vilohita*), that could be expelled out of the body of the patient by incantations. The blindness and deafness of the patient is equally driven out. The word *pramota* meaning dumb, is obscure. It could be *pramohitam*, according to Whitney; but not supported by *Anukramaṇī*.[2] Limb-splitting, *takman* (fever) making one tremble, the *yakṣman*, creeping along the things and going to the groins, the *balāsa* (consumption?), yellowness of limbs (jaundice), sickening urine, rumbling in the bowels, poison in belly, lung, navel, heart, the stretch along the vertebrae, intestinal disorders, pain in joints, pangs in feet, knees, hips, buttocks, spine etc. are referred to in the AV.

Primary Source of Medicine

Ancient Indian was a worshipper of nature in all her aspects. He knew that the roots of human culture are deeply rooted and intertwined with plants. Plants affected his life in various ways. His basic needs were taken care of by the plants around him. He, therefore, had profound respect for the plant-life. In fact, it formed an integral part of the Vedic Indian's medical tradition and gave rise to an elaborate pharmacopoeia, which is evident in all phases of Indian medical history. Plants, thus, became the curative and preventive medicine for man. Plant-life became inseparable from human life. Ancient man praised plants, glorified them; so much so that, they got defied. Along with the medicinal use of plants, propitiation of plant-deities became obligatory. Healing, thus, became a ritual, which always require the recitation of incantations of charms.

Use of plants : Medicinal plants were used normally in two ways; internally as well as externally. Internal use could be the juice of the leaves, fruits and flowers or a decoction prepared from the roots the branches, or simply chewing of the leaves roots etc. External use can be further divided as;—a) application of the paste of some part of the plant to the body, b) having bath with water mixed with medicinal herbs, and c) tying amulets, talismans etc. to ward off the disease. The first two of these are mainly curative; whereas the *maṇidhāraṇa* is preventive in nature.

Medicinal Plants

"The Indian Materia Medica, including the common household remedies, at present includes about 2000 different drugs. Of this number, approximately 200 are of mineral origin and the remainder are of vegetable origin."[3] This observation reveals that 80 per cent of the common drugs are from plant life. A distinctive part of *Vedic* medicine is its rich description of the local flora. This botanical wisdom occurs largely in the hymns of the AV. Some of these plants are mentioned in the *Āyurveda* as well. Few such plants having significant use both in the AV and *Āyurveda*, are mentioned below. There are a great number of books on Indian medicinal plants, which give the botanical name of the plants, their uses, their names in other Indian languages etc.; but there is hardly a book that would give the *Vedic* references too along with the modern *Ayurvedic* uses. I have tried to maintain a comparative approach throughout, in the list of the plants, prepared according to the Sanskrit alphabetical order.[4]

Apāmārga

This is a common weed found all over India. It is a road-side plant (*apa-āmārga*). A. S. describes this as digestive (*pācana*), diuretic (*mūtrala*), and stimulant (*uṣṇa* or *dīpana*). As such it is taken before meals.

This is also known as *Sahadevī* and *Jīvalā*. Seer *Śukra* praises this herb in three hymns in the 4th *kāṇḍa*, as the mistress of remedies, curse-repelling, the sole controller (*vaśin*), the destroyer of witchcraft etc.[5] It is specially used for Ksetriya, a class of skin-disease or of syphilitic order. It is used against warts on the penis and other parts of the body, as a laxative and a promoter of secretions.[6]

AV VI. 59 describes *Atirundhatī*, which is identified with *Sahadevī*, as useful for the cattle. *Arundhatī* is also identified with *Lākśā* (AV V. 5). It is difficult to ascertain which herb it is. May be Arundhatī is a common epithet of many herbs that cure the wounds. (*aruṁ* wound; *dhatī* cure) KDN gives the varieties of *Apāmārga* as *raktāpāmārga* and *jalāpāmārga* and gives different uses thereof. The powder or decoction of leaves and seeds is emetic. Paste of the roots is applied for snake-bites.[7] It is also used in dog bites, rat bites and scorpion bites.[8]

Externally the roots tied to the waist, assure easy delivery of the child. Small pieces of roots are worn as garland in mums also.[9] A. S. gives nine herbs in this category of *Apāmārga-Varga*, almost all of which are used for pacifying body-heat.[10]

[2] *Arundhatī*—It is used to cure any wound caused by fire or stick or arrow. This is also known as *Lākṣā*, *Silāci* or *Rohiṇī*. [11] *Rohiṇī*, because it is a climber. For the prevention of flow of blood caused by a blow from a sword or the like; boiled *lākṣā* water is to be poured on the wound.[12] As *Ṛbhu* joins parts of the chariot, in the same way, *Rohiṇī* joins bone with bone, hair with hair, skin with skin and marrow with marrow.[13]

KDN describes this as lac, a red resinous exudation of twigs of some tropical trees, caused by lacinsect. It is astringent, cool, & prevents the flow of blood and febrifuge (*jvaraghna*). It should always be the clean resin, devoid of soil.[14]

Red lac (*alaktaka*) is used by Indian ladies to beautify their hands and feet, besides using it for rendering coolness. In this context, it is noteworthy that *Lākṣā* is called sister of waters.[15] *Arundhatī*, makes the cow-stall rick in milk and the men free from diseases. (AV. VI. 59.2).

[3] *Karīra*—This is used against worms (*Kṛminā́śana*). (AV. V. 23.), especially the worms that creep about the eyes, the nostrils and in the midst of the teeth. The incantations of sage *Arti*, *Kaṇva*, *Jamadagni* and *Agastya*, seem to be very powerful in smiting the worms.[16] The *Atharvanic* medicine was not just the medicinal use of the herbs, but is was accompanied by the recitation of the mantra-s, the magic charms.

According to the *Āyurveda, Karıra*, is a dense thorny bush, bearing bitter, astringent and pungent fruit. The raw fruits are used to make pickles and the ripe fruits are eaten. This removes tooth ache.[17] Curiously the small twigs of *Babool*, which too is a thorny bush, are used as tooth-brush and are supposed to be effective gum-massager and teeth-whitener.

[4] *Kuṣṭha*[18]—This is described as born on the mountains, effaeer of *takman*, fever. This is the flower of immortality, reliever of head-ache, eye-disease and having divine virility (*vṛṣṇya*). It is regarded as the highest of herbs, as the tiger of beasts of prey. It is all-healing (*viśvabheṣaja*) and stands along with Soma (AV. XIX. 39.5.8). It is generally identified with the aromatic Costus root, native of Kashmir and known to have been an important export from India in the spice trade. Kenneth Zysk observes,[19] that the hymns of the RV reveal less of a familiarity with indigenous plant life, and what is found there relates principally to a tradition of a male plant divinity. In the AV, are found myths of both healing plant of *Kuṣṭha* and plant goddess *Arunadhatı*. The mythology of *Kuṣṭha* links it closely both with the *Ṛgvedic* plant Soma, important to the sacrificial cults and the *Atharvavedic Arundhatı*, significant to the medical cults. He is called Soma's brother and like Soma, is known to have grown high in the *Himavant* mountains, the birthplace of eagles, the third heaven from earth and the seat of gods. Like *Arundahtı, Kuṣṭha* is perennial, life-giving and harmless.

KDN, describes this as a tall stout stomachic, (*pācaka*) stimulant, used in cough, *asthamā* and rheumatism. Only its root is used as medicine. The editor of KDN, adds that genuine *Kuṣṭha* is exported to China. It is also used in *Unānı* medicine.[20]

According to A.S.[21] it is used in skin-diseases. *Kuṣṭhalepa*, improves blood circulation, restores body-lustre and retain black colour and softness of hair. Massaging gums with the powder, relieves one of tooth-ache, bad odour etc. AV. too, refers to the *lepa* (VI. 95) AV. VI. 102, prescribes the ointment of *Kuṣṭha*, along with *Añjana, Madhūka, Nalada (Uśira)* to the limbs of a woman for winning her. AV. XIX. 39, speaks of *Kuṣṭha*, being burnt as incense. The aromatic smoke is believed to drive away all evils. According to *Āyurveda* also, it is burnt, specially in the lying-in chamber of a new mother.

Kuṣṭha is used to cure leprosy (*kuṣṭha*) as well. This can be called a homeopathic treatment.

[5] *Guggulu*— According to *Paippalada*, it is used in the ceremony of a king's entrance into his sleeping chamber, to the accompaniment of incense of *kustha* and *guggulu*.[22] It is said to be born from the river or ocean. One who attains the odour of this, him, *yakṣma*-s obstruct not; in fact they scatter away, like antelopes from a wild beast. (AV. XIX. 38.1,2.)

KDN describes this as a dwarfed hilly tree, tonic (*rasāyana*), stimulant (*uṣṇa*), antirheumatic (*āmavātaghna*) and nerving tonic (*medhya*).[23] It is a product of deserts.

This fragrant resin, burning in fire and melting in sun, is used for religious purposes.

It is used in the treatment of arthritis. A medicine prepared from this, called *Yogarājaguggula* is available in the market. It is also used in neurological disorders and for reducing obesity.[24] Powdered *guggulu*, mixed with *ghṛta*, is used for all sorts of skin-diseases, injuries etc. It is also used in poultice on boils, in the application of piles of piles and also for mouth sores, specially Delhi-sores.[25]

[6] *Nili* — This is a dark-coloured herb, used in a remedial rite against white leprosy (*śvetakuṣṭha*). As it is dark, it is asked to remove the white leprous spot and colour it dark.[26] Here an ointment prepared from turmeric and indigo is applied to the body of the patient of leprosy. *Nili* is a thin hairy shrub, stimulant, purgative and used in poisons and abdominal disorders.[27] The leaves, roots and the blue (indigo) colour extracted from the leaves, are used as medicine. It is cool, healing and therefore, in burns sores, skin diseases, the ointment is applied to the affected part of the body.[28] Even today, especially in summer, the white clothes are dipped in indigo colour to render coolness to the body. According to Some, this is the same as *Kṛṣṇabuija*, i.e. *Pharbitis* seeds used in *Unani* medicine.[29]

[7] *Pāṭhā* —This is used in prolonging one's life. Seer Brahman invokes herbs like, *Jīvalā, Naghāriṣā* and *Jīvantī*.[30] According to *Sāyaṇa*, these indicate *Pāṭhā*. Some read the word *nagharṣam* or *nagharuṣam*, which can be explained etymologically; as, *na*= negative particle, *gha* representing (*han* to harm and *ṛṣa* = anger. The meaning, thus would be, one whose wrath/anger also is not harmful. (*yasya kopo'pi na ghātakaḥ*.)

In AV II.27, it is used for victory in disputation. For overcoming an adversary in public dispute, one is to come to the assembly from the north-eastern direction, (because that is *Apartājitā* - unconquered) chewing the root of the plant, or binding an amulet of it, or wearing a wreath of seven of its leaves.[31] The refrain used is, "smite the dispute of my counter-disputants; make them sapless, O herb."

Pāṭhā is a slender twiner, bitter, stomachic, astringent and febrifuge. The synonyms given for *Pāṭhā* include *Vṛkki* i.e. kidney-shaped.[32] This seems quite significant, as the herb, according to modern *Āyurveda*, is used for kidney disorders and urinary infections. It is anti-inflammatory and pain-killer. It is used along with *gudūci* and *yaṣṭimadhu*.[33] It is popular known as *pahāḍmūla*.

[8] *Pippali* - Gods created this as a remedy for all diseases. Citrav gives the specification as *'dhanurvātādi roganivāraṇā'*, curer of titanus.[34] It is surprising to note that this is a single reference to *Pippalī*, which attained tremendous importance in later period.

KDN describes that as carminative, stomachic, expectorant and laxative.[35] It is also called *Māgadhī*, as it is grown in *Magdha* (modern Bihar) in abundance. When mixed with dried ginger (*śunṭhi*), and black pepper (*marica*), it is known as *trikaṭu*.

[9] *Pṛṣniparnī* — AV II.25 is recited while smearing this to the body of a lepor. Whitney remarks, "Weber and Grill regard this hymn as directed against abortion; but no sufficient indications of such value are found in its language, though some of the native authorities intimate their discovey of such. According to K. S., it is employed along with AV II.7 and VI.85, in a remedial ceremony, against various evils."[36]

The word means a plant with spotted leaf, *citraparṇi.* According to Some, it is the same as *Lakṣmaṇā,* a plant having upon its leaves red spots, *lakṣma*. This is also known as *putradā, putrajananī* and is believed to have the power to cure barrenness of women. The powder of its bulb or juice of the leaves, when given to women after after their menstruation, surely yields son.[37]

[10] *Bhṛṅgarāja* — The herb mentioned in AV VI.136, as *nitatnī* is probably *bhṛṅgarāja,* as it is used for the growth of the hair. *Nitatnī,* down-stretcher, is apparently not the name, but an epithet. (e.f. commentary-*nyak prasaraṇaṣīlā*). This is used in hair-loss, to fasten, strengthen and increase the hair. This herb is supposed to be dug by *Jamadagni,* for his daughter and brought from *Asita's* house (*asita*=black.[38] According to K.S. (31.28.), one desirous of gaining luxurious hair, should take bath with water mixed with the herb on *amavasya*, should wear black clothes and eat things that are black. Dange, S.A. says, use of black things is for sympathetic magic in view of the black hair.[39]

KDN describes this as a slender marshy weed which is hair-blackener (*keśaranjaka*). It is also known as *mārkava,* from which the Marathi word *mākā* is derived. Hair-oils containing this, are available in market.[40]

It is stimulant, diuretic also, therefore, is used in liver tonics, to regularise the functions of liver, bile and intestines. The conventional saying that by eating this herb, an old man becomes young, is not just a hyperbolic expression; but is a fact. In medical terms, this contain the properties of Taraxacum.[41] It also has pain-killing property; as such, the root powder mixed in oil, is rubbed on forehead for headaches. The poultice of its leaves is used for scorpion stings as well.[42]

[11] *Madhūka* — Like *patha,* this sweet herb is used according to K. S. in a ceremony for superiority in disputation. The ambitious disputant is to come into the assembly from the north-east, chewing the sweet plant. It is used twice in nuptial ceremonies; once while tying an amulet of *madhūka* on the finger and once on crushing the amulet at the consummation of marriage. Whitney, however feels that all these applications are evidently imposed upon the hymn, not contained in it.[43] *Madhūka* is also used in a remedial rite against venomous bites of snakes, scorpions, insects etc.[44]

KDN describes this as large evergreen tree which is nutritive, cooling and tonic (*rasāyana*) and is used for skin-diseases. Being astringent, it is used against irritations. The juice of the flowers helps to stop hiccups; but when fermented, with the addition of jaggery, it turns into strong wine (*madhūkāsava*).[45] Jain adds that the paste of leaves mixed with ghee or butter is applied to the parts affected by scabies. The seed-oil is used in skin-diseases. Curiously enough, though this is a sweet herb, the decoction of the bark is useful in diabetes.[46] In small quantities, the flowers of *madhuka* are tonic. These trees are found all over Indian forests; therefore the foresters use flowers and oil profusely in their diet. Oil is also used in making soaps and candles. A. S. gives a long list of the properties of the medicinal wine prepared from *madhūka*. Especially the patients of anaemia, chronic fever, gastric trouble, insomnia, cough, heart-disease, etc, find it helpful.[47]

[12] *Śaṅkhapuāpi* AV. VI. 129, is used with VI. 139 and VII.38, in a rite relating to women. One binds *saurvacalā*, i.e. the root or flower of *Śaṅkhapuṣpi* on the head (as an amulet?) and enters the village. The refrain, *'tena mā bhaginaṁ kṛṇu'* may indicate fortune; but the association of this hymn with VI.139, implies something more specific and that is luck in love for a man, and it is evident from the epithets used for the herb, viz. The conciliator, love-awakener, rejoinder of the hearts etc. Here it is *strīvaśikaraṇa;* whereas in VII.38, it is *pativaṣṭkaraṇa*. Citrav states that a woman feeds her man with the root/flower of the plant,[48] whereas Whitney records a rite of fastening the plant on the arm of her man to ensure his return to her.[49] Tying a herb as an amulet is commonly found in *Atharvanic* rites.

KDN describes this as a trailing herb, that is laxative (*recaka*), *rasāyana* and a nervine tonic (*medhya*). Because of the bell-shaped or funnel-shaped white flowers, it is called *Śaṅkhapuṣpi*. A. S. states that this bitter plant is stimulant as well.[50] Perhaps due to this very property, it is used in *vaṣikaraṇa*.

[13] *Sarṣapa* AV. VIII.6. is employed in the *simanta* rite in the 8th month of a woman's pregnancy with binding an amulet of white and yellow mustard. Mustard is invoked to destroy the disease causing infant-deaths and to make the passage of child-birth, smooth and flawless. AV, however, does not specify any particular quality of mustard; but *Vāgbhata* records that mustard, being pungent, kills insects germs and soothes the irritation.[51] Mustard oil, boiled with some other herbs, is applied to the vaginal canal of the concerned woman.[52] Mustard is *garbha-rakṣaka*, protector of foetus. AV, being the Veda of witchery too, it does not stop merely by giving the medicinal property of mustard, but addressing it as *piṅga*, (reddish-brown in colour) asks it to transfer the problems of infertility and still-born babies to the enemies.[53] According to KDN, mustard plaster or poultice is especially beneficial in the inflammation of chest, joints and uterus.[54] Mustard-oil, used as killer of bacteria causing skin-disease, is recorded by a glossary of Indian medicinal words as well.[55] Use of mustard oil for the removal of scurvy, a disease caused by the deficiency of vitamin 'C', is recorded by the Encyclopaedia Britannica also.[56]

Conclusion

Åyurveda, Homeopathy and other spiritual healing sciences have now emerged as alternative medicine. A close and detailed study of the medicinal plants in the AV, however, would reveal that all these healing methods have assimilated and integrated in the AV.

Many of the AV herbs are still in use in *Åyurveda;* yet surprisingly, some of the most important *Åyurvedic* medicines are not mentioned in the AV. *Åmalakī* or *Dhātrī* (myrobalon), the richest source of vitamin 'C', used in health and strength tonics, and *Haritaki,* which again, is a vitamin rich combination, used in all basic tonics of *Åyurveda,* are conspicuous by their absence in the AV. All the books on *Åyurveda* eulogise these two along with *Vibhitaka.* These three are collectively known as *Triphalā.*

AV gives various types of amulets of herbs, grass, grain etc.[57] In fact the Vedic seer's knowledge of the local flora and his use of magical rituals, amulets, incantations etc. reflect fundamental folk beliefs. Gradually, the belief in a multitude of benevolent and malevolent deities or spirits and their impact, good or bad, on human beings, started declining. The reverence to plant-life, however, continued to be an integral part of the later physicians also. That is why, we have ample books on the analysis and description of various medicinal plants; but very less instances in the later *Åyurveda,* which would rely on the spiritual power and mystic charm of the incantations.

Abbreviations

(1) A.S - Aushadhi Saṅgraha
(2) AV - Atharvaveda
(3) KDN - Kaiya Dev Nighaṇṭu
(4) K.S - Kauṣika Sūtra
(5) RV - Ṛgveda

References

1. AV IX.8. 1-21.
2. Whitney, W. D, Atharvaveda Samhita, Delhi, 1993 (Reprint), vol. II, p. 580.
3. Indian Council of Medical Research, series 30, Delhi, 1955, p. 1.
4. Number of books were referred to before preparing this list. Some of the books are,
   (i) Indian Medicinal Plants, vol. I-IV, K.R. Kirtikar & B.D. Basu, Allahabad, 1935, revised by Blatter, Cains and Mhaskar in 8 volumes. It is the most authentic, comprehensive and valuable work on the medicinal plants of India and the adjacent countries like Ceylon, Nepal, Burma, Pakistan, Bhutan etc. The book gives botanical names, family names of the plants, but no Sanskrit names.

(ii) Medicinal Plants, Robert Bentley & Henry Trimen, vol. I-IV, London, 1980. The book gives 306 plants (not all Indian), a systematic account of the properties and uses of their parts and products of medicinal value.

(iii) Health Plants of the World, Fracesco Bianchini & Francesco Corbetta (Italian) English adaptation by M.A. Dejay, New York, 1977. The contents are divided according to various body functions, e.g. digestive system, nervous system, cardio-vascular system etc. the book has beautiful coloured illustrations.

(iv) Medicinal Plants, S. K. Jain, Delhi 1968. This gives family names, Indian regional names, short description, drug properties and other uses of 80 plants.

(v) Kaiya Dev Nighantu (KDN) Part I, (Hindi), ed. Surendra Mohan, Lahore, 1928. the book gives botanical names of the herbs, their synonyms, properties, doses, classification and groups, e.g. carminatives, purgatives, diuretic etc.

(vi) Audhisamgraha (A. S.) (Marathi), V. G. Desai, Mumbai, 1975. The book, 'Vegetable Materia Medica', gives the Latin names, the chemistry pharmacology and therapeutics as well.

5. AV IV. 17-19
6. 7. ysk, Kenneth, Medicine in the Veda, Delhi, 1996, p. 21, note 10; also A. S. 1. 137.
7. KDN. P. 334, 335
8. A. S. II. 137.
9. KDN. 334.
10. A. S. II. 134.
11. AV V.5 (Lākṣāsūkta)
12. Kauśika Sūtra. 28.5.
13. AV. IV. 12.
14. KDN. 274.

    लाक्षा च नूतना ग्राह्या मृत्तिकादिविवर्जिता।
15. Av. V.5.7
16. AV. II.32.3; V.23.10.
17. KDN. 76, also A.S.1.89.
18. AV. V.4.]
19. Zysk, op.cit. p. xii.
20. KDN. 248, 249.
21. A. S. 1.333
22. Whitney , op. Cit. II.958
23. KDN 269 ff.
24. Patnaik, Naveen, The Garden of Life. (An Introduction to the healing plants of India), New York, 1993, herb 29. (The book discusses 70 plants with illustrations)
25. A. S. I. 159.
26. AV. 1.23.
27. KDN. 176.]
28. A. S. 1.204, 205.
29. Jain, S. K. and Pandit Ganga Vishnu, the commentator of Bhāvaprakāśa Nighaṇṭu, feel that Nili is nothing but Pharbitis seeds that used in Unāni medicine. Surendra Mohan ed. KDN, however, refutes this view, for which see, KDN, 177.

30. AV. VIII. 2.6.
31. Kauṣika Sūtra. 38. 18-21.
    AV. II. 27. 1-6. The refrain is,
    पाशं. प्रतिपाशो जत्यरसान्कृण्वौषधे ।
32. KDN. 144.
33. A. S. I. 60.
34. Atharvavedāce Marathi Bhāshāntara, (Marathi), Citravshastri, Pune, 1972, p. 177.
35. KDN. 370-372.
36. Whitney, op. cit. I. 64
37. KDN. 402. However, Pṛṣniparṇı, a part of Daśamūla, is enlisted separately in this book, without even hinting at its identification with Laksmana A. S., too, lists these two herbs separately; the former in the Apāmārga-Varga, whereas, the later in Dhattūra-Varga.
    AV. II. 25. 3. Describes Pṛṣniparṇı as dispeller of embryo-eating dosa, and that strengthens its similarity with Lakṣmaṇā.
38. AV. VI, 137. I
39. Dange, S. A. Divine Hymns and Ancient Thought, vol. II, Delhi, 1995, p. 65.
40. KDN. 395.
41. A. S. 1.327
42. Patnaik, op. cit. Herb 25.
43. Whitney, op. cit. Vol. I. P.
44. AV. VII. 56.
45. KDN. 94.
46. Jain, op. cit. P. 90, 91.
47. A. S. II. 55.
48. Citrav, op. cit. P. 207.
49. Whitney, op. cit. Vol. 1.413.
50. A. S. II. 55.
51. Aṣṭāṇgahrdaya, ed. Kunte, Naravane, Mumbai, 1939, p. 79.
52. *Ibid.* p. 376.
53. AV. VIII. 6. 26.
54. KDN. 135, 136.
55. Vaidyakasabdasindhu (Marathi), compiled by Gupta, U.C. p. 1108.
    For details, see, "AV and the medicinal use of Mustard", by Gauri Mahulikar, published in the Vishveshvarananda Indological Journal, vols. xxxi-xxxii, Pts. i-iv, June 1993-94, pp. 75-80.
56. Encyclopaedia Britannica, vol. 2, p. 239.
57. For details, see, Mahulikar, Gauri, "Maṇidhāraṇa in the AV, A comparative study." Vishveshvarananda Indological Journal, op. cit. p. 37-46.

Contributors

1. Dr. (Mrs.) Bidyut Lata Ray, Reader and Head, Department of Sanskrit, R. M. Mahavidyalaya, Kantabad, Dist. Khurda, Orissa.
2. Dr. Ganesh Umakant Thite, Department of Sanskrit, University of Poona, Pune-7, Maharashtra.
3. Dr. Didhiti Biswas, Department of Sanskrit, Calcutta University, Calcutta-73, West Bengal.
4. Veda Vāridhi P. Rāmānujan, Co-ordinator, Indian Heritage Group, C-DAC, 2/1, Brunton Road, Bangalore-25, Karnatak.
5. Dr. Shrimanta Chattopadhyaya, Senior Lecturer in Sanskrit, Burdwan Raj College, Burdwan- 713104, West Bengal.
6. Sri Dukhishyam Das, Reader in English, Nayagarh College, Nayagarh-752069, Orissa.
7. Dr. Brajakishore Swain, P. G. Department of Dharmaśāstra, Sri Jagannath Sanskrit University, Sri Vihar, Puri, Orissa.
8. Dr. Padmakar Vishnu Vartak, 521, Shaniwar Peth, Pune-411030, Maharashtra.
9. Dr. Pradyot Kumar Datta, Reader in Sanskrit, Jadavpur University, Calcutta-32, West Bengal.
10. Dr. Sadasiva Biswal, Reader in Physics, Nayagarh College, Nayagarh-752069, Dist. Nayagarh, Orissa.
11. Dr. (Mrs) Vaijayanti Shete, Faculty of Fine Arts, Department of Art, History and Aesthetics, M. S. University, Baroda, 39002, Gujarat.
12. Dr. Kahnu Charan Mahalik, Teacher, Govt. High School, Sudrukumpa, Phulbani-762001, Orissa.
13. Dr. R. K. Panda, Senior Lecturer, Department of Sanskrit, Pali & Prakrit, Faculty of Arts, M. S. University, Baroda-390002-Gujarat.
14. Dr. Uma Chakravarty, C/o Mrs. Mrinalinin Chakravarty, H. C. Road, Guwahati-781001, Assam.
15. Prof. K. V. Sarma, Director, S. S. E. S. Research Centre, 623-B, III Main Road, Gandhinagar, Adyar, Madras-20, Tamil Nadu.
16. Sri V. Ramachandran Nair, (Ex. Dy. Controller of Legal Metrology, Govt. of Kerala) Kannuvilakom, Manakkara, P. O. Sasthamcotta, Dist. Kollam, Kerala.
17. Prof. N. Gangadharan, Joint Director, Sree Sarada Education Society Research Centre, 63-B, III Main Road, Gandhinagar, Adyar, Chennai- 600020, Tamil Nadu.
18. Dr. (Mrs) Gauri Mahulikar, 202 Snehal, Kasturba Road No. 5, Borivli (E), Bombay-400066, Maharashtra.

Index